Beginning Teaching, Beginning Learning

IN EARLY YEARS AND PRIMARY EDUCATION

Beginning Teaching, Beginning Learning

IN EARLY YEARS AND PRIMARY EDUCATION

Edited by Janet Moyles, Jan Georgeson and Jane Payler

Open University Press

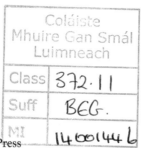
Open University Press
McGraw-Hill Education
McGraw-Hill House
Shoppenhangers Road
Maidenhead
Berkshire
England
SL6 2QL

email: enquiries@openup.co.uk
world wide web: www.openup.co.uk

and Two Penn Plaza, New York, NY 10121-2289, USA

First published 2007, this edition published 2011

A catalogue record of this book is available from the British Library

ISBN-13: 978-0-33-524412-6 (pb) 978-0-33-522131-8 (hb)
e-ISBN: 978-0-33-524413-3

Library of Congress Cataloging-in-Publication Data
CIP data applied for

Typeset by RefineCatch Ltd, Bungay, Suffolk
Printed and bound by CPI Group (UK) Ltd, Croydon, CR0 4YY

Fictitious names of companies, products, people, characters and/or data that may be
used herein (in case studies or in examples) are not intended to represent any real
individual, company, product or event.

The McGraw·Hill Companies

Contents

PART 5

Working together

Acknowledgements

We should like to thank all those who supported this 4th edition of *Beginning Teaching: Beginning Learning* in many different ways. To the students, teachers, practitioners and academic colleagues who provided insights into their everyday practices; to the children whose education and care experiences we have reflected in the numerous cameos and to the schools and settings whose work we have discussed in the various chapters. Open University Press staff have been as supportive as ever in helping us to shape the book in its final form as well as to publish it. We are also grateful to John Wiley and Sons Inc. for its permission to reproduce the extracts from Usha Goswami's 2008 article which constitutes Chapter 2 of this book.

List of figures

List of tables

Notes on the editors and contributors

Deborah Albon has worked in a variety of early childhood settings as both a nursery nurse and later a teacher. She now works across a range of early childhood programmes at London Metropolitan University as Senior Lecturer in Early Childhood Studies. Deborah's recent PhD research looked at 'food events' in four early childhood settings and she has published a number of articles in this area as well as the book *Food and Health in Early Childhood* (Sage 2008) co-written with Penny Mukherji.

Ann Burnett taught in primary schools before moving into Support for Learning. During this time she developed an interest in the educational needs of children absent from school due to ill-health and has since been on a national working party contributing guidelines on their education. She is now Deputy Head of the Hospital and Teaching Service working with children whose education is interrupted by ill-health (mental or physical), pregnancy, exclusion from school, being 'looked after' and children who are gypsies or travellers. Her MSc dissertation explored the issues surrounding the education of children and young people with CFS (ME).

Carrie Cable is Senior Lecturer in Education and Director of the Masters in Education at the Open University and was Director of a major DCSF-funded longitudinal research project examining the learning and teaching of languages in primary schools from 2007 to 10. Carrie has been involved in teaching and research relating to primary and early years education for many years. Other research interests include English as an Additional Language and bilingualism. She co-edited *Professionalism in the Early Years* (Hodder 2008) and *Professionalization, Leadership and Management in the Early Years* (Sage 2011) with Linda Miller.

Liz Chamberlain is a Senior Lecturer on the English team and is also Route Manager for the part-time PGCE programme at the University of Winchester. She has worked as a primary teacher for over 20 years and regularly spends time in school, teaching and supporting children. Her research interests are in the field of English, in particular the writing process. She was Strategic Consultant for the Everybody Writes project and continues to use this work to reflect on effective literacy practices. She is working on her PhD exploring shared understandings of writing between practitioners and children.

Helen Clarke is a Senior Lecturer in Education at the University of Winchester. She teaches across a range of courses for undergraduates and postgraduates. She has particular expertise in learning and teaching science in both the early years and primary phase and her doctoral research explored young children's ideas about materials. She was co-researcher for the AstraZeneca Science Teaching Trust project *Young Children and their Teachers Exploring their Worlds Together*. Committed to celebrating the energy and enthusiasm that children, students and teachers bring to their learning, her current research interests include children's early exploration and enquiry and teacher development.

Alison Closs taught in and managed educational provision for many years in special and mainstream primary and secondary schools and in the FE sector. She also worked as a development officer and researcher for her local authority before being appointed as a lecturer in special and inclusive education at Edinburgh University. She has researched the education of refugee children and also of children with medical conditions. Alison edited and part-wrote *The Education of Children with Medical Conditions* (runner-up; 2000 NASEN/TES Special Educational Needs Academic Book Award). Now semi-retired, she works as a Member of the Additional Support Needs Tribunals of Scotland and undertakes consultancy on inclusive education.

Penny Coltman is coordinator of the East Anglian regional Cambridge Primary Review Network. She had wide experience throughout the range of early years education as a teacher and freelance consultant before engaging in initial teacher training. She has written widely for a number of educational publishers, notably BBC Worldwide, including a range of science and mathematics DVD resources for use on Interactive Whiteboards. Penny is particularly interested in young children's development of mathematical metalanguage, scientific concepts and self-regulation. Penny has been involved in a number of research projects and has extensive publications in journals and books.

Jean Conteh has been a Senior Lecturer in the School of Education at the University of Leeds since 2007, teaching on the PGCE primary course. She has worked as a primary teacher and teacher educator in many different countries. Although she has published many books, chapters and articles, she is still proudest of her first book, *Succeeding in Diversity: Culture, Language and Learning in Primary Classrooms* (Trentham 2003). Her interest in issues of equity and social justice in multilingual primary classrooms has led her to keep researching the processes of teaching and learning from the points of view of the participants and the ways these contribute to children's success.

Aline-Wendy Dunlop is currently Emeritus Professor, having previously been Chair of Childhood and Primary Studies in the School of Education at the University of Strathclyde. She previously worked at Edinburgh University and as a teacher in a variety of nursery, primary, further education and additional support for learning roles. Her current research includes educational transitions, curriculum and work with very young children and their families. She has recently focused on a new postgraduate early years teacher specialism, a policy-based functional analysis of the Children's Workforce for the Scottish Government and an Early Years Framework Impact Scoping Study for Scotland's Commissioner for Children and Young People.

Jan Georgeson is Research Fellow in Early Education Development at the University of Plymouth. She has a background in psychology and researched into reading and visual perception before becoming a teacher, working mainly with children with special educational needs in a range of secondary, primary and preschool settings. In 2006, she completed an EdD in Educational Disadvantage and Special Educational Needs at the University of Birmingham, and worked on research projects concerned with disability and disadvantage. More recently she has taught candidates working towards Early Years Professional Status and evaluated projects remodelling social work.

Usha Goswami is Professor of Education at the University of Cambridge and a Fellow of St John's College, Cambridge. As Director of the Centre for Neuroscience in Education, she carries out research into the brain basis of literacy, numeracy, dyslexia and dyscalculia. Her current research examines relations between phonology and reading, with special reference to the neural underpinnings of rhyme and rhythm in children's reading. She has received a number of career awards, including the British Psychology Society Spearman Medal, the Norman Geschwind-Rodin Prize for Dyslexia Research, and Fellowships from the National Academy of Education (USA), the Alexander von Humboldt Foundation (Germany) and the Leverhulme Trust.

Jacqueline Harrett is Senior Lecturer in Education at the University of Glamorgan where she lectures on the Early Years Development and Education degree. She has experience of teaching from nursery to post-graduate masters' level, with interests in all aspects of literacy development. Her doctoral research focused on language and imagination in the oral stories of young children. Jacqueline has been consultant on Oxford Reading Tree's Assess and Progress, has published a series of stories commissioned for the Foundation Phase in Wales and a teachers' resource book for Sage, *Exciting Writing*.

Rita Headington is a lecturer in primary education at the University of Greenwich where she is also a member of the University's Educational Development Team. She is an experienced teacher and advisory teacher, specializing in primary mathematics and assessment and has taught in schools and local education authorities in the UK and with the British Forces in Germany. Rita's work has centred on the use of assessment in schools and universities as a tool for 'measuring' and enhancing learning. She authored *Monitoring, Assessment, Recording, Reporting and Accountability: Meeting the Standards* (David Fulton 2003), a book written for students and newly qualified teachers.

Mary Kellett is Professor and Director of Childhood and Youth at the Open University, UK, where she is also Founding Director of the Children's Research Centre. She has worked with children and young people for over 30 years, starting out as a children's social worker and then a primary teacher before moving into academia. She has an international reputation as a leading pioneer in the empowerment of children and young people as researchers and has published widely in this and associated fields. She sits on a number of advisory panels and her work is the focus of many international initiatives.

Rachael Levy is a Lecturer in Early Childhood Studies at the University of Sheffield. She is responsible for the teaching and supervision of Masters, EdD and PhD students studying various aspects of early childhood education. Having completed her own ESRC-funded doctorate at the University of Cambridge, Rachael went on to receive the UKLA Postgraduate Research Award for her dissertation, 'Becoming a reader in a digital age'. She has published a range of papers in peer-reviewed academic journals and has contributed chapters concerned with literacy and digital text use.

Elizabeth Marsden trained as a PE teacher at Bedford College of Physical Education and has worked in England, Canada, the USA, Africa, India and Scotland. She presently works in the University of the West of Scotland where she has taught PE to early years and primary student teachers, with her research interests mainly in creative movement with children in the early years; physical education with children who have additional support needs and both children and adults who have health-related issues (especially diabetes mellitus). Elizabeth has written a variety of journal articles and book chapters, recently co-editing a book of international research into the effects of the Sherborne Movement with many different types of populations.

Trisha Maynard is Professor and Director of the Research Centre for Children, Families and Communities at Canterbury Christ Church University, UK. Trisha moved into academia in 1991: she was appointed as Professor of Early Childhood Studies at Swansea University in 2007. Trisha's research interests include student teachers' school-based learning, the role of the mentor and young children and gender. Her most recent research has focused on the Foundation Phase for Wales, outdoor play and child-led learning. Her publications include *Boys and Literacy: Exploring the Issues* (RoutledgeFalmer 2002); *An Introduction to Early Childhood Studies* (edited with Thomas; 2009) and *Siyabonana: Building Better Childhoods in South Africa* (with Penn; 2010, Children in Scotland). She is the current Chair of TACTYC (www.tactyc.org.uk).

Karen McInnes is currently a senior lecturer in Play and Human Development at the University of Glamorgan. She has worked as a paediatric speech and language therapist with young children, having been an early years teacher and Foundation Stage Manager in schools in London and Bristol. She lectured in early years education at Bath Spa and was also a senior researcher for Barnardo's National Policy and Research Unit. She has recently completed her PhD on playful practice and learning in the early years. Karen has written a number of publications, including (with Wiliams) *Planning and Using Time in the Foundation Stage* (Fulton 2005).

Janet Moyles is Professor Emeritus, Anglia Ruskin University, and a play/early years consultant. She has worked as an early years teacher and head and has written and edited widely, including *Just Playing?* (OUP 1989), *The Excellence of Play* (OUP 2009) and *Effective Leadership and Management in the Early Years* (OUP 2007). She has directed several research projects including *Jills of All Trades?* (ATL 1996), *Too Busy to Play?* (Esmee Fairbairn Trust/University of Leicester 1997–2000), *SPEEL* (*Study of Pedagogical Effectiveness in Early Learning*) (DfES 2002) and *Recreating the Reception Year* (ATL 2003). Her PhD was in the area of play, learning and practitioner roles.

Theodora Papatheodorou is Professor of Early Childhood and Director of Research at Anglia Ruskin University, where she convenes the Early Childhood Research Unit. Her teaching and research interests are in the area of early childhood pedagogy and curriculum, children's behaviour, social inclusion, multicultural education and bilingualism. She has worked on major research and evaluation projects, including Preschool Multicultural Education in England, Germany and Greece and The Evaluation of the On-Track and Violence against Women programmes. She is the author of *Behaviour Problems in the Early Years,* and editor (with Janet Moyles) of *Learning Together: Exploring Relational Pedagogy*, both published by Routledge.

Pia Parry's career with children and their families began in the mid-1970s in a large day nursery in South Wales. After more than 20 years' experience as a practitioner and manager, she moved into higher education where she now leads the Department for Childhood and Youth Studies at the University of Chichester. Her qualifications include an MA in Therapeutic Child Care, a Diploma in Management and she is a qualified social worker, practice teacher and nursery nurse (NNEB). Her interest in supporting practitioners who work with young children comes from her own experience and her belief that this is where the greatest difference can be made.

Jane Payler is Senior Lecturer in Early Years Education at the University of Winchester. Most recently, she has been researching reactions to the introduction of the Early Years Professional Status. While at the University of Southampton, she researched inter-professional education for professionals in Children's Services and the experiences of young children with special educational needs. Her PhD and MPhil research, both funded by the ESRC, studied aspects of learning processes in 4-year-old children at pre-school and in a reception class. Jane was previously a health education officer in inner city Birmingham, a supervisor of a crèche and chair of a pre-school.

Karen Phethean is a Senior Lecturer in Initial Teacher Education at the University of Winchester. She teaches on the BA Primary Education programme for both Core Science and Professional Studies and on the PGCE programme for Primary Science. Prior to joining the university, Karen was a class teacher, science co-ordinator and Leading Science Teacher. While in school she became involved in a research/CPD project at the University of Winchester funded by the AstraZeneca Science Teaching Trust, *Teachers and Young Children Exploring Their Worlds Together.* She is currently undertaking a PhD into the relationships between play, anxiety and learning within the context of primary science.

Sue Robson is a Principal Lecturer in Education at Roehampton University, and Subject Coordinator for Early Childhood Studies. Sue is a National Teaching Fellow, a Roehampton University Teaching Fellow and a Trustee of the National Froebel Foundation. She is currently the Chair of Hounslow Early Years Development and Childcare Partnership. Sue's research interests include parent/professional relationships, environments for young children, and children's thinking, self-regulation and metacognition. She is currently conducting research funded by the Froebel Research Committee, on *The Voice of the Child: Ownership and Autonomy in Early Learning* (http://www.froebel.org.uk/frc_fellowship.pdf).

Mary Scanlan is an experienced infant, nursery and primary school teacher, and has taught in a variety of settings. She was a teacher-researcher at the University of Bristol on *The Home–School Knowledge Exchange Project*, funded by the ESRC, and completed a doctorate which explored how home and school can work together to support children's literacy learning. Since 2005, Mary has worked as a Senior Lecturer in Education at the University of Winchester, teaching early years and literacy.

Gary Walker is a Principal Lecturer in Childhood and Early Years at Leeds Metropolitan University. He has worked in a variety of social care settings for over 20 years, including as child protection education co-ordinator and children in care education co-ordinator for a large education authority. He has extensive experience of teaching and training adults in social care issues, with special interest in child development, child protection and social work, children in care and multi-agency working. His publications include a sole-authored book *Working Together for Children: A Critical Introduction to Multi-Agency Working*, and an edited volume (with Jones) *Children's Rights in Practice*.

Jane Waters has been Lecturer in Early Childhood Studies at Swansea University since 2007. She was previously a professional tutor on the ECS programme and the primary PGCE course. Her doctoral research focused on the interaction taking place between children aged 3 to 7 and teachers in their indoor and outdoor spaces. She is deeply interested in the agency of the child within educational interaction and her research interests include children's access to, and action within, outdoor spaces and the impact of social and cultural norms on this behaviour.

Carrie Weston taught in London as SENCo and deputy head, then led a team of peripatetic teachers in Kent, before working for educational psychology and inspection and advisory services. She gained a PhD studentship in Scotland then returned to the University of East London in 2007 as Programme Leader for Special Needs and Inclusive Education. Carrie is particularly interested in young children as physical learners and how good practice in special education informs mainstream provision, thus identifying inclusion. Carrie writes children's books and her book *Oh, Boris* (OUP 2008 – now a trilogy) was chosen to launch a state-wide literacy programme in the USA.

David Whitebread taught as a primary school teacher for 12 years and is now a Senior Lecturer in Psychology and Education at the University of Cambridge. He is a developmental psychologist and early years specialist and is currently involved in research projects concerned with metacognition and self-regulation in young children's learning. His other interests include children learning through play and the application of cognitive neuroscience to early years education. He is also a governor of his local Children's Centre. His publications include *The Psychology of Teaching and Learning in the Primary School* (2000) and *Teaching and Learning in the Early Years* (2008), both published by RoutledgeFalmer.

Maulfry Worthington is engaged in doctoral research into the emergence of children's mathematical graphics in play at the Free University, Amsterdam. Maulfry taught children for many years in the 3–8 year range, was a National Numeracy Consultant and has lectured on primary and early years mathematics and early years pedagogy. Maulfry's publications include *Understanding Children's Mathematical Graphics* (OUP 2011), co-authored with Elizabeth Carruthers. Their work is featured in the *Williams Maths Review* (DCSF 2008) and they were commissioned to write *Children Thinking Mathematically* (DCSF 2009). They are co-founders of the international Children's Mathematics Network (http://www.childrens-mathematics.net/).

JANET MOYLES, JAN GEORGESON AND JANE PAYLER

Introduction

Cameo 1

On her first teaching practice, Jan had settled for a not very adventurous topic – My Senses – which she hoped would work as a framework to pick up on the interests of the group of children she was still getting to know. After a solid but not very inspiring week on Seeing, she turned to Hearing in week 2, and invited a friend who played double bass to join the group. The children were at first overcome by the size of the instrument – 'It's big! It's a guitar!' – and listened in awe to the deep loud tones it made. Then the musician encouraged the children to place their hands on the body of the instrument as he played. The children were amazed; they could feel the sound as well as hear it! He continued to play louder and louder and the sound filled the room; one child called out in delight, 'I can feel it in my tummy!' After that the topic really took off; children found lots of other ways of feeling sound, and some made drawings as they listened to music, saying they could see sounds too.

Cameo 2

Later that week, Jan planned a movement session in the hall. She had observed the teacher working with the children the previous week, encouraging them to think about different ways of moving. Jan wrote up her lesson plan carefully, including some of the musical instruments that had aroused the children's interests earlier in the week. She booked the hall and included in her plan time for children to get changed. It was all going well; children had placed their clothes in neatish piles along the side of the room and gathered in a circle. Jan played the tambourine slowly and softly at first and the children started to move around

> the room slowly. Then as the tambourine speeded up they were soon racing round the room with glee. They didn't hear the tambourine slowing down; they just kept on racing round until Crash! Two children collided and one landed heavily on her ankle and yelled out in pain. As she sobbed loudly, the teacher came in and took over. She called an ambulance and accompanied the injured child to hospital with a suspected broken ankle. All Jan's confidence built up in the first half of the week vanished.

In the beginning . . .

Beginning teaching, as we remember well, brings a heady mix of excitement and apprehension. Stepping over the line from observing and helping in a classroom to being the one 'in charge' brings responsibility as well as autonomy, accountability as well as the freedom to make decisions. This calls for a wide range of skills and attributes, knowledge and understanding, many of which can be acquired through the processes of initial teacher education courses. But with so many demands on course timetables, time for thinking more widely about the professional aspects of teaching as well as curriculum content has become somewhat limited.

The ways in which you might begin teaching have gradually changed over the past decade. The number of teachers training as undergraduates has declined, falling from 9,770 in 1998–99 to 7,650 in 2010–11, with a further overall decrease just announced for 2011–12 (although the good news is that primary school places have been increased to meet anticipated demographic needs). At the same time, the number of postgraduate teacher trainees has remained constant at around 25,000, with these programmes accounting for nearly 60 per cent of trainees (DCSF 2010). There are an increasing number of different routes into teaching, as well as an increasing number of other practitioners becoming involved in the education of children. The Children's Workforce Development Council (CWDC 2010) has successfully introduced Early Years Professional Status, a graduate-level professional status, to lead practice in early years settings outside the maintained sector in day nurseries and voluntary pre-school groups. Over 4,000 EYPs have now achieved the Status with over 4,000 more currently in training (CWDC 2010). For this reason, we have extended the intended readership of the book to include other professionals who are key in children's education from birth to 11 years. Where we use the term 'teacher', we are also referring to early years professionals. Beginning teaching means different things to different people; some follow a direct path from pupil to student to teacher, other newly qualified teachers might have a long history of involvement with schools behind them, while others might be 'career changers' immersing themselves in the life of early years settings and primary schools for the first time after a previous career in quite a different environment.

We have opened this chapter with two cameos again – the dream start and the nightmare scenario – because they capture the reality of good days and bad days for a beginning teacher. The recollection of hospitalizing a child on the first solo attempt at a PE lesson as a student teacher lingers long in the memory, only just offset by recalling the wonder on children's faces when they experienced the sound of a double bass by touch as well as hearing. While the first cameo captures how rewarding it is when it all comes together, the second cameo serves to emphasize that children and teaching can be unpredictable. What this situation highlights is that it is not sufficient merely to emulate the actions and behaviour of another in order to learn to teach. While observing (and being observed) can provide useful insights into what teaching can look like, it is being equipped with the tools and concepts for reflection and review which is the key to professional development. Michael Gove, Secretary of State for Education at the time of writing, has stated that 'Teaching is a craft and it is best learnt as an apprentice observing a master craftsman or woman' (Gove 2010) and, indeed, there are aspects of teaching which can be picked up through watching a talented experienced teacher at work. But what we notice from any situation depends on our pre-existing cognitive framework; if we have already studied classroom interaction, we will be much more likely to notice the subtle interplay between question and response which characterizes the best kind of pedagogic exchange (Mercer and Littleton 2007). To be an effective observer, you have to know what to look for, and that only comes with study, reflection and, of course, focused discussion with others.

Whereas we all might wish that someone could wave a magic wand and save us from the events which unfolded in cameo 2, these experiences are all part of learning to be a teacher. Beginning teaching is also about beginning learning, hence the title of this book. Learning to teach develops our professional personalities in harmony with our individual personalities. Every teacher is a mix of the personal and the professional and, whereas the professional may take a few knocks in the beginning stages, keeping the personal esteem intact is vital.

In any profession, the learning curve between a state of being a 'novice' and that of being an 'expert' (McNally and Blake 2010) is inevitably steep because there are always so many new issues to deal with simultaneously. Because early years and primary education concern birth to 11-year-old children – and often fairly large numbers of them at once – challenges are nearly always immediate and unrelenting: the children just do not go away while we get our acts together! And the drive to raise the level of education expected of new professionals is evident: for teachers and early years professionals, master's level education is being strongly encouraged: 'As well as giving teachers more control over their classrooms I want to give them more control over their careers, developing a culture of professional development which sees more teachers acquiring postgraduate qualifications like masters and doctorates' (Gove 2010).

The ways in which the careers of teachers and Early Years Professionals might propel them towards leadership and management roles have been investigated in some detail in recent times (Moyles 2006; see also Chapter 22). Even when a certain level of expertise has been gained, new initiatives often challenge existing securities. Whatever demanding roles people have had in previous experiences, new teachers may suddenly find themselves confronted with an overload of challenges. What needs to be acknowledged is that, with support and encouragement from others, the vast majority of people succeed as effective teachers and thoroughly enjoy their vocation. Any teacher education course, of whatever duration or type, is only the start of a professional career; the beginning of learning about teaching – and about ourselves!

Aims of this book

The fourth edition of this book addresses all those just entering teaching either as students or as newly qualified teachers, as well as early years professionals leading practice in early years settings. It will also be of interest to those whose job it is to help these individuals learn about pedagogy. The original book grew out of increasing concern on the part of course tutors that there is too little time (especially on PGCE courses) to cover all the underlying issues that make the early and primary years of education different and special. Students also report that there are many crucial aspects, such as child development and achievement and social class, which were not covered in sufficient detail on their initial training courses (Revell 2005: 52). This still obtains, and even more so given the breadth of the teacher's role following the embedding of collaborative multi-agency working, which we have addressed in this new edition.

By undertaking this fourth edition at a time when the nature of teaching and the role of the teacher are again being questioned and redefined (DfE 2010a), we continue to argue for not just trained teacher-apprentices but an educated and reflective workforce. As government rhetoric promises an increased respect for the knowledge and competence of professionals, then the need for those professionals to have broad and confident knowledge and competence is emphasized: 'It [reform] can only come from giving much more autonomy to professionals – headteachers, teachers, support staff and governors – so that they have the freedom to transform our education system' (DfE 2010b).

Like its predecessors, this book does not aim to do everything. We have used the expertise of individual contributors to raise issues which they think are important for new teachers and early years professionals. Further reading is signalled by **bold typeface** at the end of chapters so that readers have easy access to other informative sources.

The context of early years and primary education

In the face of a global economic recession and government policy to reduce the UK's deficit, attention has turned once more to finding ways to achieve a soundly educated population efficiently and effectively. Reports influencing government thinking (Field 2010; Allen 2011) rightly encourage a renewed and more vigorous emphasis on the importance of early intervention. Seeing education as a continuum from birth has never been more important. As McInnes discusses in Chapter 1, we are (again) in a time of review of curriculum and teacher education for children from birth to 11 years. The promise of greater professional flexibility is exciting – but may be daunting.

The curricula for early years and primary children have undergone a series of revisions since their introduction. Subject dominance, particularly of national literacy and numeracy strategies, has impacted heavily on teacher education. However, although a subject-dominated curriculum takes *knowledge*, and the handing *down* of that knowledge, as its basis, it is widely acknowledged that, for all children up to 11 years of age, the *processes* of their learning are far more important (Claxton 2008). So while a major part of course time is spent on subject curricula, students are also assessed on professional standards, all of which must be met for Qualified Teacher Status (QTS) to be awarded, and further standards are incorporated into the induction year processes for newly qualified teachers (NQTs) (see www.tda.gov.uk). There are also specific standards for early years professionals which must be met before the status is awarded (www.CWDCouncil.org.uk). Both sets of standards have been based on a common core describing the skills and knowledge requirements for everyone working with children, young people and families. These are grouped into six areas:

- effective communication and engagement with children and families;
- child development;
- safeguarding and promoting the welfare of the child;
- supporting transitions;
- multi-agency working;
- sharing information (CWDC 2010).

Clearly these are extensive areas to be covered. Hence the need for a book of this type, which explores some of these vitally important areas and related issues that we feel are important for beginning teaching and learning about teaching.

The structure and content of the book

This fourth edition of this book has grown to five parts to address the issues identified above. Each chapter for the most part encompasses the full age range reflected in the cameos, enabling readers to understand the context and concepts about which the various contributors are writing.

Part 1 (Chapters 1–4) explores the context of education from birth to 11 years and includes issues about policy, brain research, attachments and relationships and safeguarding children. Part 2 (Chapters 5–9) examines organizational issues, touching on planning for learning, the links between assessment and accountability, the environment indoors and out, promoting positive behaviour and successful transitions.

Part 3 (Chapters 10–15) deals with different ways of learning and supporting children aged birth–11 years, encompassing the development of self-regulated learners, supporting symbolic meaning-making, encouraging investigative skills, learning with new technologies, the role of physical development in learning and putting story at the heart of the curriculum. In Part 4 (Chapters 16–19) we review the various influences on children's learning, exploring social class as an inclusion issue, empowering through language diversity, accessing children's voices and promoting the role of health in children's learning.

In the final section, Part 5 (Chapters 20–23), we look at how teachers and early years professionals work with other people in support of children, their learning and development, offering a new conceptualization of parent partnership, support for children with long-term health issues, and an exploration of leadership and teamwork, both within the school and with other children's services. The conclusion offers a brief preview of where we might be going in relation to the issues raised in the book, and a few words of wisdom are offered to support new starters in the early days of teaching and learning. The final chapter presents the Afterword by the editors.

Each chapter is written in a straightforward style and includes a summary and cameos of classroom life as experienced by beginner teachers, early years professionals and children so as to offer an immediate point of reference with everyday encounters. Each chapter concludes with its own thought-provoking questions and suggested further reading (the **emboldened** references).

As will be obvious by now, the scope of the book is very broad-based but by keeping the focus on the learning partnership between the beginner teacher, early years professional and children, it is hoped that the book will be manageable and useful, as its predecessors were. Whatever the intensity and rigours of the Foundation Stage and the primary curriculum, the children and their teachers both need to gain enjoyment and satisfaction from the educational process and a real desire to continue learning: school and learning should be fun for everyone. Beginner teachers and early years professionals are usually welcomed by the children because they bring new ideas and different ways of doing things. As one 8-year-old child wrote in a letter to a student – 'We are very greatful that you came to help us in your spare time and we're sorry that your liveing'!! [*sic*]. Here's hoping that you will always be able to see the humorous side of school.

References and suggested further reading

Allen, G. (2011) *Early Intervention: The Next Steps. An Independent Report to Her Majesty's Government.* London: The Cabinet Office. Available online at: http://www.dwp.gov.uk/docs/early-intervention-nextsteps.pdf (accessed 25 April 2011).

Claxton, G. (2008) Cultivating positive learning dispositions, in H. Daniels, H. Lauder and J. Porter (eds) *Routledge Companion to Education.* London: Routledge.

CWDC (Children's Workforce Development Council) (2010) *The Common Core of Skills and Knowledge.* Available online at: http://www.cwdcouncil.org.uk/common-core (accessed 4 February 2011).

DCSF (Department for Children, Schools and Families) (2010) *School Workforce in England (Including Local Authority Level Figures) (Revised).* Available online at: http://www.education.gov.uk/rsgateway/DB/SFR/s000927/index.shtml (accessed 4 February 2011).

DfE (Department for Education) (2010a) *The Importance of Teaching: Schools White Paper.* Available online at: http://www.education.gov.uk/b0068570/the-importance-of-teaching (accessed 4 February 2011).

DfE (2010b) *DfE Response to Public Comments on the Coalition Agreement on Schools.* Available online at: http://dfe.gov.uk/inthenews/inthenews/a0063460/dfe-response-to-public-comments-on-the-coalition-agreement-on-school (accessed 3 February 2011).

Field, F. (2010) *The Foundation Years: Preventing Poor Children Becoming Poor Adults: The Report of the Independent Review on Poverty and Life Chances.* London: The Cabinet Office. Available online at: http://webarchive.nationalarchives.gov.uk/20110120090128/http://povertyreview.independent.gov.uk (accessed 25 April 2011).

Gove, M. (2010) Speech to National College Annual Conference, 17 June. Available online at http://www.michaelgove.com/print/1575 (accessed 4 February 2011).

McNally, J. and Blake, A. (2010) *Improving Learning in a Professional Context: A Research Perspective on the New Teacher in School.* Abingdon: Routledge.

Mercer, N. and Littleton, K. (2007) *Dialogue and the Development of Children's Thinking: A Sociocultural Approach*. Abingdon: Routledge.

Moyles, J. (2006) *Effective Leadership and Management in the Early Years (ELMS)*. Maidenhead: Open University Press.

Pollard, A. (2008) *Reflective Teaching: Evidence-informed Professional Practice*, 3rd edn. London: Continuum.

Revell, P. (2005) *The Professionals: Better Teachers, Better Schools*. Stoke-on-Trent: Trentham Books.

PART 1

The context of education birth–11

1

KAREN McINNES
Policy context and current issues

Summary

This chapter provides an overview of policy and curriculum initiatives implemented between 1997 and 2006, when the previous edition of this book was written. An in-depth discussion of policy and curriculum changes since 2006 is also provided, focusing on: children, education and curriculum. How these changes relate to the standards for trainee and newly qualified teachers and practitioners gaining Early Years Professional status is discussed. Further discussion is centred on continuing professional development for all those practitioners across the Foundation and primary age phases. This chapter is underpinned, and informed, by the voices of those working with children drawing on their experiences as trainee and newly qualified practitioners.

Cameo 1

Lisa is a newly qualified teacher in a junior school. She has just started her second year of teaching in a mixed Year 3/4 class. She completed a BEd in primary education. She enjoys teaching and being with her class and, since qualifying, has had a lot of opportunities for further training and development.

Cameo 2

Jen is a newly qualified teacher in an infant school. She has also just started her second year of teaching and is currently teaching in a reception class two days a week and a Year 1 class three days a week. During her first year she taught in the reception class for two days a week and the rest of the week she taught nursery and Year 1 and 2 classes. She completed a BEd in primary education but received little training in the English Foundation Stage.

> **Cameo 3**
>
> Sarah is a mentor to newly qualified teachers in an infant school. She is also the deputy headteacher, Foundation Stage teacher and provides educational leadership to the on-site Children's Centre. She provides mentoring sessions on a regular basis and ensures there are opportunities for continuing professional development for newly qualified teachers.

Introduction

At first sight, understanding, and working with, policy may seem somewhat esoteric to trainee practitioners and those in their first year of teaching. However, educational and social policies affect all those working with children and they cannot be ignored. A policy may be defined as: 'an attempt by those working inside an organisation to think in a coherent way about what it is trying to achieve (either in general or in relation to a specific issue) and what it needs to achieve it' (Baldock et al. 2009: 3).

Policies may arise from different levels of organization, from government to classroom, and they require practitioners to think about what, why and how they are doing something. Thinking through this process enables practitioners to implement policies effectively and may also enable them to influence policy.

There are also standards to achieve in relation to policy for teaching and Early Years Professional Status (EYPS). Standard 3a of the initial teacher training standards for trainee teachers in England states that they need to be aware of their professional duties and the statutory framework within which they work (Teacher Development Agency (TDA) 2008). One of the resources to which they are referred for this standard is the *Every Child Matters* framework (DfES 2003). Standard 3b is even more explicit about policy and practice, stating that trainee teachers need to be aware of policies and practices of the workplace. It also requires them to work as a team to implement policy (TDA 2008).

There are two standards in relation to policy to achieve EYP status and they are just as explicit. Standard S4 requires practitioners to understand the national and local statutory and non-statutory frameworks within which children's services operate. Standard S5 refers directly to policy and requires practitioners to have reference to national policies and guidance on health and safety and safeguarding and promoting the well-being of children (Children's Workforce Development Council (CWDC) 2010). As well as having to achieve these standards to work with children, there is also another reason why trainee practitioners and all those working with children need to understand and work with policies, as Baldock et al. state, 'children need more than our enthusiasm. They need us to think about what we are doing' (2009: 11). Ultimately this provides the overarching definition of what policy means in a practice context.

Historical overview of policy and curriculum initiatives, 1997–2006

This section will identify key policy and curriculum initiatives under New Labour from 1997 to 2006. During this time legislation was concerned with raising standards in education while erasing disadvantage in society through improved schooling (Ward and Eden 2009). In 1997, the White Paper *Excellence in Schools* was published by the Department for Education and Employment (DfEE 1997). This contained the main policy initiatives of this time, paving the way for the introduction of the National Literacy Strategy in 1998 and the National Numeracy Strategy in 1999 (DfEE 1998b, 1999). Both these strategies prescribed the content of what had to be taught as well as specific teaching methodology. This year also brought the National Childcare Strategy (DfEE 1998a); this sought to coordinate provision for young children across education, health and social services through the development of Early Excellence Centres. These centres were designed to provide care and education for children from a few months old to 5 years of age. Additionally, in 1998, Sure Start was launched with the aim of tackling social exclusion at community level. Both of these initiatives demonstrated New Labour's belief and commitment to early years education as a way of raising standards and eradicating poverty.

In 1998, as well as introducing the National Numeracy Strategy, the Early Learning Goals were published. These were intended to guide early years practitioners as well as to raise standards at the earliest opportunity. In 2000, the National Curriculum was slimmed down although the format was unchanged and the Foundation Stage was introduced alongside the *Curriculum Guidance for the Foundation Stage* (QCA/DfEE 2000) which organized the curriculum for under-5s around six areas of learning: personal, social and emotional development, communication, language and literacy, mathematical development, knowledge and understanding of the world, physical development and creative development. The Education Act (2002) made the Foundation Stage a part of the National Curriculum and introduced a national assessment scheme for this age phase: the Foundation Stage Profile.

In 2003, Lord Laming's Report was produced following the death of Victoria Climbié (the young child who died through abuse and neglect at the hands of relatives). The report highlighted the lack of coordination between different children's services as well as deficiencies in responsibility and overall leadership. This heightened the depth of change in the early years agenda and services resulting in the *Every Child Matters* Green Paper in 2003 which became law with *The Children Act* 2004. These specified broad outcomes for all ages of children across five domains: be healthy, be safe, enjoy and achieve, make a positive contribution, and achieve economic well-being. It also laid the foundations for future initiatives and policies. Following this, Sure Start was extended and, building on early excellence centres, Children's Centres were introduced. A curriculum framework for under-3s was also established with the publication of *Birth-to-3 Matters* which mapped on to the *Curriculum Guidance for the Foundation Stage*. Although the main focus at this time appeared to be on the early years, the primary curriculum was not ignored. The *Every Child Matters* Green Paper also required Local Authorities to provide 'joined-up' education and care through multi-agency working and extended schools. This meant that schools should be involved in providing wrap-around care for children up to the age of 14 from 8.00 a.m. to 6.00 p.m. In addition, in 2003 the new primary strategy paper, *Excellence and Enjoyment,* was launched. Despite the focus being on creativity and fun, this paper primarily consolidated the literacy and numeracy strategies.

Finally, in 2006, there was the review of the teaching of early reading. This was designed to clarify the position on the place of phonics in the teaching of reading. At the same time a review of primary education in England was initiated, the *Cambridge Primary Review.* This review was an independent look at the state of primary education, aiming to make far-reaching recommendations for the future. The next section will explore policy and curriculum initiatives in primary education since 2006 in more depth.

Recent policy initiatives in relation to children

There have been a number of recent policy initiatives which, although not necessarily directed at schools and the curriculum, have had an impact on schools and how they work with children and families. In 2006, *The Good Childhood Inquiry* was commissioned by The Children's Society. This was led by Professor Judy Dunn and the aim of the inquiry was to review society's understanding of modern childhood and to inform, improve and inspire relationships with children. Evidence was given by over 30,000 children, adults and professionals and, as would be expected, there was considerable focus on school and education. Children stated their need for good human interactions and that schools were instrumental in this. They thought that schools and parents need to work together to influence values in relation to human interaction and that a common vocabulary needs to be based on respect, trust and generosity. In addition, school and education themselves were seen as important elements of a good life. Children want a good education and like teachers who are supportive, helpful and understanding. However, they also feel a lot of school-related pressure and stress (Layard and Dunn 2009).

In 2007, there was a plethora of initiatives aimed at improving the lives of children and young people. *The Children's Plan* (Department for Children, Schools and Families (DCSF) 2007b) was a White Paper that announced a 10-year strategy to make England the best place for children and young people to grow up. In addition, *Every Parent Matters* (Department for Education and Skills (DfES 2007) was published. This report set out the rights and responsibilities of parents, especially in relation to schools. Home–school agreements were strengthened and communication between parents and schools was to be strengthened so that parents could have more involvement in their children's learning and more involvement in running schools. It was also stated that by 2010 all schools would have access to extended services. To assist in this, *Extended Schools: Building on Experiences* (DCSF 2007c) was published. This gave guidance for schools on providing extended services for children and families.

Finally, in 2007, a two-year research project was set up, funded by the DCSF, called *Narrowing the Gap.* This project was set up to significantly narrow the gap in outcomes between vulnerable and excluded children and the rest of the child population. This was to be achieved while improving outcomes for all children with the focus on children aged 3–13. The first report from this was published in 2008 (LGA 2008, cited in Pugh 2010) recommending a number of strategies to help improve outcomes for children and young people. Also in 2008, the *2020 Children's and Young People's*

Workforce Strategy was published (DCSF 2008a). This strategy aims to raise the quality and capacity of all those working with children and young people to enable them to achieve the outcomes specified by *Every Child Matters*. An interesting discussion of achieving these outcomes is provided by Butcher and Andrews in *Whose Childhood Is It?* (Eke et al. 2009).

Recent policy initiatives in relation to the curriculum

This section discusses policy and curriculum initiatives directly aimed at education and schools. As previously stated, the Children's Plan was launched in 2007. While the overarching aim was to make England a better place for children and young people, this White Paper also included higher targets for 11-year-olds for literacy and numeracy, although less stringent on testing. It also announced that there would be an in-depth review of the primary curriculum led by Sir Jim Rose but under the control of the DCSF. Finally, in relation to teachers, there was a stated aim to make teaching a master's degree profession.

In addition, in 2007, the Early Years Foundation Stage (EYFS) was introduced (DCSF 2007a). This brought previous curriculum guidance for birth-to-3-year-olds and 3- to 5-year-olds together, as well as standards for daycare, with an aim to make a coherent framework of care and education for all children aged from birth to 5 years. In 2008, the final report of the *Williams Review of Maths Teaching* was published (DCSF 2008b) which recommended a specialist in every primary school within ten years. Also in 2008, the interim report from the Rose Review of the primary curriculum was published with a recommendation to combine the National Curriculum subjects into six broad areas of learning.

In 2009, the final report of the Rose Review was published (Rose 2009). This recommended that a National Curriculum should be retained but framed around six areas of learning which would map on to the EYFS. It also stated that priority should be given to literacy and numeracy, as well as ICT, and that a modern foreign language should be taught in primary schools. Its recommendations were accepted and a new Primary Curriculum was to be introduced in 2011. Many interim reports were issued from the *Cambridge Primary Review* initially launched in 2006. However, the final report was published in 2010 (Alexander 2010). Included in the 75 recommendations was that there should be a new set of 12 aims appropriate for schools in this new century. There was also a call to strengthen and extend early years education and to replace Key Stages 1 and 2 with a single primary phase. In addition, a new curriculum was advised with eight domains of knowledge, building on the 12 aims for education.

Where are we now?

In May 2010, a new Coalition Government came to power and the Department for Education (DfE) was formed on 12 May 2010. One of the new government's first acts was to disregard the Rose Review and to keep the present National Curriculum. In November 2010, an Education White Paper was published: *The Importance of Teaching: The Schools White Paper* (DfE 2010). In this document, the Government announced that there would be a review of the National Curriculum for 5–16 year-olds starting in December 2010 with the aim of introducing a revised curriculum in

September 2013. This new curriculum is likely to be slimmed down so that it reflects the body of essential knowledge which the government feel all children should learn. Outside of that, it is thought that schools and teachers will have greater freedom to construct their own programmes of study in subjects outside of this new curriculum. In the interim, schools are in an exciting position whereby, although they have to adhere to the National Curriculum, they have increasing flexibility in how they implement this with pupils.

In relation to the early years curriculum, there has been an independent review of the Early Years Foundation Stage led by Dame Clare Tickell (2011). This review has recommended changes to the six areas of learning with three prime areas of learning which are seen as essential for learning, health and life: personal, social and emotional development, communication and language development and physical development. These three areas are then complemented by four specific areas of learning which are: literacy, mathematics, understanding of the world and expressive arts and design. Changes have also been recommended to the Early Learning Goals which specify where children should be developmentally by the end of the EYFS. Currently, there are 69 goals which should be reduced and simplified to 17. Alongside this, it is recommended that there is a three-part scale which identifies what working towards, achieving and exceeding looks like for each of the 17 goals. This should then overlap with expectations for the National Curriculum at Key Stage 1. In terms of formal assessment, it is recommended that the EYFS profile is kept but, again, is reduced from 117 pieces of information to 20. Overall, this new streamlined and slimmed down EYFS and associated assessment should be more manageable and user-friendly for both practitioners and parents.

Policy initiatives, trainee and newly qualified teachers

Both Lisa and Jen, the newly qualified teachers introduced in the cameos at the beginning, agree that, as trainee teachers, they collected school policies while on teaching practice. However, they both thought that it was harder to have due regard for national policies although these would have been covered in formal lectures during training. Lisa stated, 'I needed to collect school policies and to know them so that I could work within the school's framework. National policies were not a priority.' They both agreed that generally they were 'curriculum-focused rather than policy-focused'. Jen felt that she had learnt a lot more about policies since she had qualified and was working in school. She said that discussing different policies was often the focus of sessions with her mentor so that she could 'understand the way her school worked'.

Sarah, the mentor introduced in cameo 3, felt that properly understanding policies, especially national policies, could only be achieved once trainees were working in school. She stated that some policies were critical, for example, safeguarding (see Chapter 4), as 'A school could fail an OfSTED inspection if staff did not have due regard for, and understand, safeguarding.' She also emphasized the importance of understanding school policies within the context of the school: 'We have a whole school approach to policy dissemination and newly qualified teachers need to understand the rationale behind our policies, to understand why we work the way we do; otherwise it's meaningless.' She also felt that understanding policy, both local and national, was an ongoing process for all teachers: a point that Lisa and Jen both appreciated.

Continuous professional development

According to the *Cambridge Primary Review* (Alexander 2010) a clear finding from the submissions was that teachers need to be qualified, knowledgeable and caring. In order for them to be qualified and knowledgeable, in 2007, the Teacher Development Agency published the professional standards encompassing not only the induction year but also four further stages of a teacher's career up to Advanced Skills Teacher. The standards for the induction year are framed around five themes:

- developing professional and constructive relationships;
- working with the law and frameworks;
- professional knowledge and understanding;
- professional skills;
- developing practice.

Under these themes there are standards directly related to policy such as: Standard C3, contributing to the development, implementation and evaluation of the policies and practice in the workplace and Standard C22, understanding national policies and guidance concerned with safeguarding and well-being. There is also a standard about teachers' continuing professional development: Standard C7 states that teachers need to be committed to improving practice through appropriate professional development (TDA 2007).

Continuing Professional Development (CPD) is aimed at supporting individual needs and improving professional practice. There are three ways to achieve this:

- by attending external courses;
- by undertaking cross-school activities;
- by networking and attending in-school activities such as mentoring, lesson observation and feedback and whole school development sessions.

A recently commissioned report from the Training and Development Agency for Schools by Pedder et al. (2008) examined the state of CPD for teachers. This report focused on three core themes: the benefits, status and effectiveness of CPD, the planning and organization of CPD and teachers' access to CPD. There are many findings from the report but in relation to the benefits of CPD they found that teachers' main reasons for engaging in CPD were:

- to work with other colleagues;
- to impact on pupil learning;
- to improve professional abilities;
- to address classroom needs and gain a better understanding of the National Curriculum.

However, there were differences between teachers of different age phases, with primary teachers seeing a wider range of benefits and head teachers valuing school-based CPD activities. They also found that new teachers favoured accreditation as a tool for career development which was perhaps a reflection on their recent engagement with training and achieving qualified teacher status.

The main impacts of CPD were judged to be, first, the development of individual professional skills and knowledge and, second, increased awareness of teaching and learning issues. However, the impact of attending CPD was limited as much of the training was neither informed by research, nor contextualized by classroom practice. It was also found that, in relation to planning, there was often no strategic approach to CPD, although this did vary between schools. In terms of access to CPD, this also varied by school. However, most teachers reported that CPD was delivered in-school and that there were few opportunities for external CPD. In primary schools, most external CPD was delivered by local authorities.

The *Cambridge Primary Review* (Alexander 2010) also addressed CPD, and overall submissions to that Review reflected a view that CPD was too closely related to national initiatives and consequently lacked challenge and did not address individual needs and circumstances. This may change with the new Master's in Teaching and Learning, a result of the aim within *The Children's Plan* (DCSF 2007b) to make teaching a master's profession. This new qualification is a practice-based master's programme aimed primarily at NQTs. The emphasis of the qualification is on classroom-based practice and learning with a focus on children and young people. It has four core content areas: teaching and learning, subject knowledge, knowledge of how children and young people develop and leadership and management. The uptake of this new qualification and its impact on the profession, however, will be limited as funding has been currently halted. However, this does not imply a move away from master's level qualifications for teachers but to increase the range of master's qualifications that teachers may pursue. To this end, the White Paper (DfE 2010) announced the introduction in 2011 of a comprehensive scholarship scheme to support professional development for teachers.

CPD for newly qualified teachers

The opportunities for CPD experienced by Lisa and Jen were varied, as found by Pedder et al. (2008). Lisa stated that 'Opportunities for CPD varied between schools and between local authorities.' Lisa's reasons for engaging with CPD were to increase her understanding of the curriculum and teaching and to make her a better classroom practitioner. She had plenty of opportunities for CPD both within school, from a literacy consultant, and externally from the local authority, through attending courses on reading, mathematics and modern foreign languages. Her CPD opportunities were designed to fit in with the strategic objectives of the school and will allow her to lead on aspects of the curriculum in the future.

Jen had mainly received CPD from her mentor which she felt was more appropriate as she had personal development needs focused on the Foundation Stage (FS) as she was not trained to work with this age group. Her training had focused on policy and practice in relation to the FS. The training was both theoretical and practical with opportunities to observe more experienced members of the Foundation Stage team in the school.

Both trainees were unsure about the master's degree in teaching and learning. Neither of them had had an opportunity to pursue this qualification yet. However, neither of them thought it was appropriate at the present time. They both considered that they were not ready to embark on the training and were unsure of the benefits of obtaining it. As Lisa stated, 'I want to be a good classroom teacher and I'm not sure if it will lead to that.'

Conclusion

From the cameos of the newly qualified teachers and mentor it is clear that, while in training, understanding of policy is focused on collecting and working with school policies during teaching practice, with theoretical understanding of national policy being provided during lectures. This changes once appointed as a newly qualified teacher, when understanding of school-based, local and national policies and the rationale behind these policies is needed within the context of the school and daily interaction with children and families.

In relation to the curriculum, current practice is located within the National Curriculum and the EYFS. However, both are subject to current reviews with the potential for change. Despite this, it would appear that, while acknowledging the current curriculum frameworks, teachers are excited by the opportunity for flexibility and creativity within that.

If the teachers in the cameos are typical, there appear to be many opportunities for CPD for newly qualified teachers, although this is dependent on the school and the local authority in which they are working. CPD would appear to be based not only on personal need but also on the strategic development needs of the school which has implications for career development. The value of the Master's in Teaching and Learning will be limited: however, the new national scholarship scheme to support professional development should enable opportunities for CPD to be grasped so that, in the words of Lisa, all newly qualified teachers can aspire as Lisa does, to be 'the best classroom teacher I can be'.

Questions to Promote Thinking

1 What is the rationale underpinning the policies used in your school?
2 How do national policies influence work with children and families in your class?
3 How does CPD relate to the school development plan within your school?
4 How can you feed back your learning from CPD to all the staff in your school?

Acknowledgements

Special thanks to Tom Hutchings, Louisa Omato (both Broomhill Junior School) and Jan Palmer (Broomhill Infants School).

References and suggested further reading

Alexander, R. (ed.) (2010) *Children, their World, their Education.* Abingdon: Routledge.

Baldock, P., Fitzgerald, D. and Kay, J. (2009) *Understanding Early Years Policy*, 2nd edn. London: Sage Publications.

CWDC (Children's Workforce Development Council) (2010) *On the Right Track: Guidance to the Standards for the Award of Early Years Professional Status.* Leeds: CWDC.

DCSF (Department for Children, Schools and Families) (2007a) *Early Years Foundation Stage.* London: DfES.

DCSF (2007b) *The Children's Plan: Building Brighter Futures.* London: DCSF.

DCSF (2007c) *Extended Schools: Building on Experiences.* Nottingham: DfES Publications.

DCSF (2008a) *2020 Children's and Young People's Workforce Strategy.* Nottingham: DCSF.

DCSF (2008b) *Independent Review of Mathematics Teaching in Early Years Settings and Primary Schools (The Williams Review).* London: DSCF.

DfE (Department for Education) (2010) *The Importance of Teaching: The Schools White Paper.* London: DfE.

DfEE (Department for Education and Employment) (1997) *Excellence in Schools.* London: HMSO.

DfEE (1998a) *Meeting the Childcare Challenge.* London: DfEE.

DfEE (1998b) *The National Literacy Strategy: Framework for Teaching.* London: DfEE.

DfEE (1999) *The National Numeracy Strategy: Framework for Teaching Mathematics from Reception to Year 6.* London: DfEE.

DfES (Department for Education and Skills) (2003) *Every Child Matters*, Green Paper. Nottingham: DfES.

DfES (2007) *Every Parent Matters.* Nottingham: DfES.

Eke, R., Butcher, H. and Lee, M. (2009) *Whose Childhood Is It? The Role of Children, Adults and Policy Makers*. London: Continuum.

Layard, R. and Dunn, J. (2009) *A Good Childhood.* London: Penguin Books.

Pedder, D., Storey, A. and Opfer, V.D. (2008) *Schools and Continuing Professional Development (CPD) in England: State of the Nation Research Project.* Available online at: http://www.tda.gov.uk/upload/resources/pdf/c/cpd_stateofthenation_report.pdf (accessed 4 August 2010).

Pugh, G. (2010) Improving outcomes for young children: can we narrow the gap? *Early Years*, 30(1): 5–14.

QCA/DfEE (Qualifications and Curriculum Authority/Department for Education and Employment) (2000) *Curriculum Guidance for the Foundation Stage.* London: QCA/DfEE.

Rose, J. (2009) *Independent Review of the Primary Curriculum: Final Report.* Available online at: http://publications.education.gov.uk/default.aspx?PageFunction=productdetails&PageMode=publications&ProductId=DCSF-00499-2009 (accessed 7 November 2010).

TDA (Teacher Development Agency) (2007) *Core Standards for the Induction Year.* Available online at: http://www.tda.gov.uk/teachers/induction/corestandardsandassessment/corestandards.aspx (accessed 24 September 2010).

TDA (2008) *ITT Standards Guidance.* Available online at: http://www.tda.gov.uk/partners/ittstandards/guidance_08 (accessed 3 August 2010).

Tickell, C. (2011) *The Early Years: Foundations for Life, Health and Learning.* Available online at: http://media.education.gov.uk/assets/files/pdf/F/The%20Early%20Years%20Foundations%20for%20life%20health%20and%20learning.pdf (accessed 1 April 2011).

Ward, S.L. and Eden, C. (2009) *Key Issues in Education Policy.* London: Sage.

2

USHA GOSWAMI

What cognitive neuroscience really tells educators about learning and development[1]

Summary

This chapter outlines the ways in which cognitive neuroscience seeks to improve our understanding of aspects of human learning and performance by combining data acquired with new brain imaging technologies with data acquired in cognitive psychology paradigms. The relevance of 'brain science' for the classroom has proved controversial, perhaps because of distrust of the applicability of so-called 'medical models' to education, perhaps because of the lure of neuromyths. Nevertheless, the brain is the main organ of learning, and so a deeper understanding of the brain would appear highly relevant to education. Improved knowledge about how the brain learns should assist educators in creating optimal learning environments and provide new methodologies to test the effects of educational interventions.

Introduction

Neuroscience is a large field and all aspects of neuroscience have some relevance to education. For example, some neuroscientists study how cells grow in the foetal brain and some study the chemical 'neurotransmitters' that cells use to transmit information to each other. Neither area of study appears *a priori* relevant to education and yet better knowledge of foetal brain development offers important insights into why children born to alcohol-addicted mothers have particular learning difficulties, for example, in numeracy (Kopera-Frye et al. 1996).

Cognitive neuroscience is one sub-field within neuroscience. Cognitive neuroscience takes psychological theories about the mind (for example, that short-term and long-term memory are distinct systems) or symbolic descriptions of mental processes (for example, that we can think using images versus 'inner speech') and explores them by measuring electro-chemical activity in the brain. Cognitive neuroscience involves both the direct measurement of electro-chemical activity and connectionist modelling. Direct measurement of the brain shows the patterns of activity across large networks of neurons (called cell assemblies) that correspond to mental states such as remembering a telephone number. Although this is essentially correlational information,[2] brain imaging also reveals the time course of the activity (e.g. which neural structures are activated, in which order) and interactions and feedback processes within these large networks. Modelling enables 'in principle' understanding of how synchronized neuronal activity within cell assemblies results in learning and development. I will argue that all of these kinds of information are useful for education, even though the field of cognitive neuroscience is still in its early stages.

At birth, considerable brain development has already taken place. Most of the neurons (brain cells) that will comprise the mature brain are already present and have migrated to the appropriate neural areas. Neural structures such as the temporal cortex (audition) and the occipital cortex (vision) have formed but will become progressively specialized as the infant and young child experiences environmental stimulation. Neural specialization depends on the growth of fibre connections between brain cells both within and between different neural structures (called 'synaptogenesis'). Some fibre connections reflect 'experience-expectant' processes. These connections are usually in the sensory system and reflect abundant early growth in response to classes of environmental stimulation (such as visual field information) that the brain 'expects' (via evolution) to receive. Connections that are not used frequently are then aggressively pruned. Experience-expectant plasticity is biologically pre-programmed. Other fibre connections are 'experience-dependent'. Here the brain is growing connections in order to encode unique information that is experienced by the individual. Every person has a distinctive environment, even children growing up within the same family, and so experience-dependent connections are the ones that make each brain subtly different. Experience-dependent connections include the connections formed by education. Experience-dependent synaptogenesis enables life-long plasticity with respect to new learning. The specialization of neural structures occurs within developmental trajectories that are constrained by both biology and environment.

Avoiding the seeding of 'neuromyths'

When evaluating neuroscience research, it is important to be vigilant: correlations are still correlations, even when they involve physiological measures. Yet many correlational findings that reach the popular media are given causal interpretations. A good example comes from data sets that have been interpreted to show that fatty acids such as fish oils play a potentially causal role in learning. Unsaturated fatty acids are important in brain development and in neural signal transduction, which has led to the belief that omega-3 and omega-6 highly unsaturated fatty acids may be good for the brain. For example, in a recent paper, Cyhlarova et al. claimed that 'the omega-3/omega-6 balance is particularly relevant to dyslexia' (2007: 116). This claim was based on a study measuring the lipid fatty acid composition of red blood cell membranes in 52 participants, 32 dyslexic adults and 20 control adults. No differences between dyslexics and controls were found in any of the 21 different measures of membrane fatty acid levels taken by the researchers. However, a *correlation* was found between a total measure of omega-3 concentration and overall reading in the whole sample. This correlation by itself does not show that fatty acids have anything to do with dyslexia. The correlation depends on the whole group; potentially relevant variables such as IQ have not been controlled, and there is no intervention to test whether the association is a causal one. No plausible mechanism was proposed by the experimenters to explain why omega-3 concentration should have specific effects on reading, rather than general effects on any culturally acquired skill (for example, arithmetic).

Nevertheless, when physiological variables such as changes in brain activation are involved, it is easy to suspend one's critical faculties. This has been demonstrated empirically by Weisberg and her colleagues (Weisberg et al. 2008). These researchers gave adults bad explanations of psychological phenomena, either with or without accompanying neuroscientific information. The neuroscientific details were completely irrelevant to the explanations given and yet the adults rated the explanations as far more satisfying when such details were present. The researchers concluded that the neuroscience details were very seductive. These details suggested to the participants that the explanations given were part of a larger explanatory system based on physiology that interfered with participants' ability to judge the quality of the explanations that they were being given. Weisberg et al. point out that this propensity to accept explanations that allude to neuroscience makes it all the more important for neuroscientists to think carefully about how neuroscience information is viewed and used outside the laboratory.

Principles of learning from cognitive neuroscience

Although the field of educational neuroscience is still relatively new, there are a number of principles of learning demonstrated by empirical studies that can safely be incorporated into education and teaching. Some of these are now discussed.

Learning is incremental and experience-based

Although this may seem almost too trivial to note, the fact that the brain develops fibre connections to encode each experience that we have into our nervous systems is fundamental when considering education. The growth of interconnected networks of simple cells distributed across the entire brain eventually results in complex cognitive structures such as 'language' or 'causal knowledge'. The complexity that can be achieved by simple incremental learning has been demonstrated by connectionist modelling, which has shown a number of important 'in principle' effects. For example, complex 'rules' or principles such as the syntactic 'rules' of language can be learned incrementally. There is no need for a specialized 'language acquisition device' (see Chomsky 1957) that pre-encodes 'innate' knowledge about the general rules that all languages obey, along with innate knowledge of permitted variations. Simple incremental learning also yields 'critical period' effects, originally argued to show that some kinds of learning are particularly effective during a given time window. Connectionist modelling shows that these critical time windows are a natural part of the learning trajectory when learning is incremental. Similarly, incremental learning processes can explain apparent 'gaps' in learning exhibited by children. Learning is distributed across large networks of neurons and so factors like the number of relevant neurons firing, their firing rates, the coherence of the firing patterns and how 'clean' they are for signalling the appropriate information, will all vary depending on how the current environmental input activates the existing network. As the fibre connections growing in response to received inputs are strengthened over time, it can also become difficult to reorganize the system when a new learning environment is experienced.

These demonstrations of the importance of incremental environmental input show that the learning environments created in schools by teachers and other professionals will have important cumulative effects. Clearly, it is important to avoid creating learning environments that support the acquisition of maladaptive connections, for example, environments that feel unsafe or stressful. Further, deep understanding of a given educational domain is required in order to present the cumulative information in the optimal sequence for the novice learner (this reflects classic educational concerns for consolidation of learning coupled with progression in curricula). The growth of new fibre connections in the brain always occurs in response to new inputs and so claims that brain-based learning packages enable 'neuroplasticity' are a redescription of what always occurs for any new learning experience.

Perhaps, most challengingly, the biological necessity for learning to be incremental questions the notion that we can ever engender 'conceptual change'. Any neural network develops over time and cannot suddenly be 'restructured' by one learning experience. On the other hand, certain experiences may result in previously distinct parts of the network becoming connected, or in inefficient connections that were impeding understanding being pruned away. Eventually, connectionist models may be able to show how and when this is achieved in a given learning trajectory.

Learning is multi-sensory

Different neural structures are specialized to encode different kinds of information, with sensory information being the most obvious example (for example, both visual and auditory information are encoded primarily by fibre growth in the visual and auditory cortex). However, most environmental experiences are multi-sensory and, therefore, fibre connections between modalities are ubiquitous. Furthermore, because learning is encoded cumulatively by large networks of neurons, cell assemblies that have been connected because of prior experiences will continue to be activated even when a *particular* aspect of sensory information in a *particular* experience is *absent*. This ability of the brain to respond to *abstracted dependencies* of particular sensory constellations of stimuli enables, for example, a missed word to be filled in when someone coughs across another speaker. Even though our brain received the sensory information about the cough rather than the phonemes in the missed word, prior learning enables the brain to 'fill in' the missing information.

This principle implies that, if children are taught new information using a variety of their senses, learning will be stronger (that is, learning will be represented across a greater network of neurons connecting a greater number of different neural structures and accessible via a greater number of modalities). A nice example comes from a study by James (2007) who tracked the neural networks that developed as pre-school children learned to recognize letters. Before taking part in the learning activities, the children's brains were imaged as they looked at letters and other familiar visual stimuli (such as cartoon hearts). As might be expected, significant activation of visual neural structures was found. As part of their initial reading activities, the children were then taught to recognize and write the letters. For example, visual letter knowledge was increased by helping children to recognize the target letters in story books and to pick out target letters from four alternative possibilities (including reversed letters). The children were also taught to form and write the letters, thereby using another modality (kinaesthetic) in conjunction with the visual and auditory modalities (recognizing and naming the letters). Following the writing training, the children's brains were again imaged while they looked at letters and other familiar visual stimuli. This time, significant activation in motor areas was found for the letters, even though the children were *looking* at the letters and were not making any writing movements. Because their multi-sensory learning experiences had led fibre connections to develop both within the visual system and between the visual system and the motor system, the motor parts of the network were activated even though the current environmental experience was purely visual. Whether this multi-sensory representation can actually be interpreted as showing stronger learning requires further empirical work. Nevertheless, it is clear that information stored in multiple modalities is being activated despite the fact that sensory stimulation is only occurring in one modality (here, vision). This kind of empirical paradigm offers a way of investigating whether children really can be said to have different learning 'styles', for example being 'visual' or 'kinaesthetic' learners. Given the principles of how the brain learns, this seems *a priori* unlikely.

Brain mechanisms of learning extract structure from input

As the brain experiences particular sensory constellations of stimuli over multiple times, what is common across all these experiences will naturally be represented more strongly than what is different. This is because the fibre connections that encode what is common will become stronger than the fibre connections that encode the novel details. This mechanism effectively yields our 'basic level concepts', such as 'cat', 'dog', 'tree' and 'car' (Rosch 1978). After 100 'cat' experiences, the strongest fibre connections will represent what has been common across all experienced instances, such as 'four legs', 'whiskers', 'tail', and so on. Therefore, the brain will have developed a generic 'prototype' representation of a cat. Sensory constellations of stimuli are also dynamic in space and time and so simply by processing features of the input and correlations and dependencies between these features, the brain will be learning about dynamic spatio-temporal structure and, therefore, about causal relations (Goswami 2008a). This means that the child's brain can in principle construct detailed conceptual frameworks from watching and listening to the world. As we learn language and attach labels to concepts, the neural networks become more complex, and as we learn new information via language, fibre connections will form in response that encode more abstract information and therefore more abstract concepts.

I discuss many examples of this in my book (Goswami 2008b) but to take an example pertinent to primary education, these learning mechanisms mean that the brain will extract and represent structure that is present in the input *even when it is not taught directly*. An example is the higher-order consistencies in the spelling system of English that I have previously described as 'rhyme analogies' (Goswami 1986). Spelling-to-sound relations in English can often be more reliable at the larger 'grain size' of the rhyme than at the smaller 'grain size' of the phoneme (Treiman et al. 1995). For example, the pronunciation of a single letter like 'a' differs in words like 'walk' and 'car' from its pronunciation in words like 'cat'. The pronunciation in 'walk' or 'car' can be described as irregular but it is quite consistent across other rhyming words (like 'talk' and 'star'). One way of exploring whether the brain is sensitive to these higher-level consistencies in letter patterns is to see how children read aloud novel 'nonsense' words that they have not encountered before. For example, children can be asked to read nonsense words matched for pronunciation like *daik, dake, loffi* and *loffee*. Only the rhyme spelling patterns in items like *dake* and *loffee* will have been learned from prior experiences with analogous real words (like 'cake' and 'toffee'). Hence only these 'chunks' of print and their connections with sound should be stored in the neural Visual Word Form Area (VWFA). There are no real English words with letter chunks like '*aik*'. English children indeed show a reliable advantage for reading aloud such analogous nonsense words, despite the fact that the individual letter-sound correspondences in the non-analogous items (e.g. '*d*', '*ai*', '*k*' in *daik*) were matched for orthographic familiarity to those in the analogous items (like *dake*, see Goswami et al. 2003). Such data suggest that orthographic learning reflects these higher-level consistencies, even though 'rhyme analogy' reading strategies have not been taught directly to these children.

Whether learning would be even stronger if such strategies *were* taught directly to children remains an open question. In fact, this is an important general question for education. Although it is often noted that learning is 'embedded' in the experiences of the individual, one goal of education is to help all individuals to extract the higher-order structure that underpins a given body of knowledge. It is generally felt that a combination of 'discovery-led' and directly transmitted knowledge provides the best way of doing this but there are many disagreements over the optimal balance between such teaching methods in different domains and in different views of pedagogy. A deeper understanding of how the brain uses incremental experience to extract underlying structure may help to inform such debates.

Learning is social

We have social brains. Many studies of infant and animal cognition are showing more and more clearly that the complex mammalian brain evolved to flourish in complex social environments. For example, there appear to be specialized neural structures in the human brain for encoding information about agents and their goal-directed actions (the so-called mirror neuron system). Neurons in this system will respond to a biological agent performing a certain action (for example, a person lifting a cup) but not to a robot performing an identical action (Tai et al. 2004). In infancy, the attribution of intentionality to the goal-directed actions of others occurs surprisingly early in development. For example, Meltzoff has shown that 14-month-old infants will imitate actions that they have never witnessed but which they infer to have been intended through watching a particular goal-directed action by a biological agent. If a baby watches an adult carrying a string of beads towards a cylinder, missing the opening and dropping the beads, the watching baby inserts the beads straight into the cylinder (see Meltzoff 1995). Babies who watch a robot hand modelling an action, even a completed action, do not imitate. Gergely et al. (2002) demonstrated that infants of the same age make very sophisticated inferences about intentional states. They used a different imitation paradigm devised by Meltzoff, in which an experimenter activates a light panel by leaning forwards and pressing it with her forehead. Some 69 per cent of babies who watched this event also switched on the light panel by using their foreheads. However, in another version of the event, the experimenter said that she felt cold, and she held a blanket around her shoulders with her hands while she illuminated the light panel with her head. Now 79 per cent of watching 14-month-olds used their hand to illuminate the light panel. They appeared to infer that in this latter scenario the experimenter used her forehead because her hands were constrained. She was not using her forehead intentionally because it was necessary to achieve her goal. Hence they no longer copied the 'forehead' action. As Carpenter et al. (1998) have pointed out, infants who selectively imitate only the intentional acts of others will thereby acquire many significant cultural skills.

The social nature of human learning means that learning with others is usually more effective than learning alone, and that language and communication are central to this social process. A long time ago Vygotsky (1978) argued that cognitive development did not just happen in the brain of the individual child. It also depended on interactions between the child and the cultural tools available for mediating knowledge. A primary cultural tool was language. As well as providing a symbolic system for communication with others, language enabled children to reflect upon and change their own cognitive functioning (in the terminology of modern psychology, by developing 'metacognitive' and 'executive function' skills).

Furthermore, Vygotsky proposed the notion of the 'zone of proximal development' (ZPD). In contrast to independent problem solving, the ZPD was the larger area of potential development that was created when learning was supported by others. Most ZPDs are created by the social and cultural contexts created by parents and teachers (although Vygotsky argued that play with other children also creates important ZPDs). This theoretical perspective is reflected in education in sociocultural theory. Csibra and Gergely (2006) revisited these theoretical ideas, recasting them in the language of brain science. They proposed that human brains have adapted to transfer relevant cultural knowledge to conspecifics[3] and to *fast-learn* the contents of such teaching via a species-specific social learning system. They called this learning system 'pedagogy'. On my reading, their definition of pedagogy is essentially cultural knowledge transfer via collaborative learning in the zone of proximal development.

Cortical learning can be modulated by phylogenetically older systems

Traditionally, cognitive psychology has separated the study of cognition (thinking and reasoning) from the emotions. Neuroscience has shown that cognitive and emotional processes are integrated in the brain at multiple levels. For example, cortical structures such as orbito-frontal cortex integrate cognitive and emotional information during learning via interactions with phylogenetically older structures that are primarily involved in emotional processing, such as the amygdala. The amygdala controls our response to threat (as in the 'fight–flight' response). A particularly active area of neuroscience with respect to the emotional modulation of cognition is decision-making ('neuroeconomics', Coricelli et al. 2007). Economics as a discipline has learned that human behaviour cannot be explained solely in rational cognitive terms. Learning based on cumulative emotional experience plays an important role in anticipating the possible future consequences of economic choices, and economic models incorporating emotional measures such as regret appear to be more efficient at modelling human behaviour. Cumulative emotional experience must also play a role in the efficiency of learning. This suggests that models of classroom learning must incorporate the emotions in order to better understand the behaviour of learners. There is certainly some relevant data from both human and animal cognitive neuroscience. Emotional information is prioritized by the brain, and receives privileged access to attention. When experiences are aversive, emotional responding blocks learning. The prioritizing of emotional information was presumably evolutionarily adaptive, as emotional stimuli lead to enhanced sensory processing by the brain, enabling better behavioural responding. Such studies may provide a neural framework for explaining why children who are anxious do not learn efficiently.

Finally, I consider another aspect of cognitive neuroscience research that is relevant to education.

Maximizing the learning efficiency of the brain

The brain is an organ of the body and, in terms of efficiency of function, it is not distinct from other organs such as the heart with respect to some of the basic factors that affect its ability to work effectively. Nutrition and diet are important for effective function, as are sleep and exercise. The obvious roles of nutrition and exercise have led to various 'brain-based learning' claims about particular types of nutrition (for example, fish oils, water) and particular types of exercise (e.g. Brain Gym®, see Howard-Jones 2007, for a useful discussion) and their particular effectiveness for learning by children. When evaluating such claims, it is of course critical to check the quality of the science cited in their support, and to distinguish correlational data from causal data.

In terms of underlying physiological mechanisms, there have been some pharmacological insights with respect to sleep, which appear to have an interesting role in consolidating learning. During sleep, there is behavioural inactivity accompanied by distinct electrophysiological changes in brain activity. These changes seem to affect memory, which appears to be consolidated during slow-wave and rapid-eye-movement sleep via the actions of certain neurotransmitters. Newly encoded memories are stabilized, and are integrated with pre-existing (long-term) memories via the action of neurotransmitters like acetylcholine. Low cholinergic activity is associated with slow-wave sleep and when cholinergic activity is blocked in the brain, there is enhanced consolidation of memory (see Marshall and Born 2007 for a summary).

One possibility is that we lose consciousness during sleep because the brain needs to use the same neural networks that support conscious activity for the processing and long-term storage of recently acquired information. Indeed, empirical studies of learning finger tapping sequences show that there is improvement in the learned skill after sleep, with performance levels after sleep which are significantly higher than performance levels at the end of initial training, before sleep occurred (see, for example, Fischer et al. 2002). However, sleep has to occur within a certain time window after training in order for benefits to accrue – the time window is approximately within 16 hours of the learning period. Conversely, severe insomnia is associated with decrements in learning. The growing evidence base with respect to sleep shows the importance of these basic aspects of human behaviour to education.

Conclusion

Cognitive neuroscience is important for education because it enables a principled understanding of the mechanisms of learning and of the basic components of human performance. It also enables componential understanding of the complex cognitive skills taught by education. Many of the principles of learning uncovered by cognitive neuroscience might appear to support what teachers knew already. For example, aspects of pedagogy such as the value of multi-sensory teaching approaches or of creating safe and secure environments for learning are highly familiar. Nevertheless, cognitive neuroscience offers an empirical foundation for supporting certain insights already present in pedagogy and disputing others. The evidence from neuroscience is not just interesting scientifically. It enables an evidence base for education in which mechanisms of learning can be precisely understood.

Nevertheless, the evidence base that it offers is a challenging one. An interesting analogy is provided by Clark (2006), who was discussing language but whose analogy also works for the entire cognitive system. Clark's argument is that we can conceptualize the brain as a 'loose-knit, distributed representational economy' (2006: 373). Some elements in the economy might conflict with other elements in the economy but this is inevitable as there is no 'homunculus', or single central overseer, who determines learning. Rather, there are many interacting parts of the overall reasoning machinery that the brain is maintaining at the same time. The activity of all of these parts is what the child brings to the classroom, and different parts are more or less affected by different cognitive or emotional experiences. The child brings a 'vast parallel coalition of more-or-less influential forces whose . . . unfolding makes each of us the thinking beings that we are' (Clark 2006: 373). To borrow from another insightful commentator on the potential of cognitive neuroscience for cognitive development (Diamond 2007), the truly ambitious goal for education is to cross and integrate the disciplinary boundaries of biology, culture, cognition, emotion, perception and action. Biological, sensory and neurological influences on learning must become equal partners with social, emotional and cultural influences if we are to have a truly effective discipline of education.

Questions to Promote Thinking

1 Incremental environmental input has enormous effects on learning. What might this imply for the effects of home environment on children's performance in school?
2 Learning is multi-sensory, so a task in one sensory modality (e.g. visual) might actually activate a different part of the brain (e.g. kinaesthetic). How can we then test claims that there are different learning 'styles': visual, auditory or kinaesthetic?
3 The brain automatically extracts underlying structure from different inputs. How can this principle be used to teach via play?
4 Emotional information is prioritized by the brain. How might this principle be applied to facilitate learning?

Notes

1 This is an edited extract from Goswami, U. (2008c).
2 Information that is correlated is reliably associated, so that as one type of information varies, the other type varies too, in systematic and predictable ways. However, the occurrence of this systematic and reliable relationship does not in itself imply a causal connection between the two kinds of information.
3 Of or belonging to the same species.

References and suggested further reading

Carpenter, M., Akhtar, N. and Tomasello, M. (1998) Fourteen- through 18-month-old infants differentially imitate intentional and accidental actions, *Infant Behavior and Development*, 21: 315–30.

Chomsky, N. (1957) *Syntactic Structures*. The Hague: Mouton.

Clark, A. (2006) Language, embodiment, and the cognitive niche, *Trends in Cognitive Sciences*, 10(8): 370–4.

Coricelli, G., Dolan, R.J. and Sirigu, A. (2007) Brain, emotion and decision making: the paradigmatic example of regret, *Trends in Cognitive Sciences*, 11(6): 258–65.

Csibra, G. and Gergely, G. (2006) Social learning and social cognition: the case for pedagogy, in Y. Munakata and M.H. Johnson (eds) *Processes of Change in Brain and Cognitive Development: Attention and Performance XXI*. Oxford: Oxford University Press.

Cyhlarova, E., Bell, J.G., Dick, J.R., MacKinlay, E.E., Stein, J.F. and Richardson, A.J. (2007) Membrane fatty acids, reading and spelling in dyslexic and non-dyslexic adults, *European Neuropsychopharmacology*, 17: 116–21.

Diamond, A. (2007) Interrelated and interdependent, *Developmental Science*, 10(1): 152–8.

Fischer, S., Hallschmid, M., Elsner, A.L. and Born, J. (2002) Sleep forms memory for finger skills, *Proceedings of the National Academy of Sciences*, 99: 11987–91.

Gergely, G., Bekkering, H. and Király, I. (2002) Rational imitation in preverbal infants, *Nature*, 415: 755.

Goswami, U. (1986) Children's use of analogy in learning to read: a developmental study, *Journal of Experimental Child Psychology*, 42: 73–83.

Goswami, U. (2008a) Analogy and the brain: a new perspective on relational primacy, *Behavioural and Brain Sciences*, 31(4): 387–8.

Goswami, U. (2008b) *Cognitive Development: The Learning Brain.* **New York: Taylor and Francis.**

Goswami, U. (2008c) Principles of learning, implications for teaching: a cognitive neuroscience perspective, *Journal of Philosophy of Education*, 42(3–4): 381–99.

Goswami, U., Ziegler, J., Dalton, L. and Schneider, W. (2003) Non-word reading across orthographies: how flexible is the choice of reading units? *Applied Psycholinguistics*, 24: 235–47.

Howard-Jones, P. (2007) *Neuroscience and Education: Issues and Opportunities. Commentary by the Teaching and Learning Research Programme.* **London: TLRP. Available online at: http://www.tlrp.org/pub/commentaries.html (accessed 20 October 2010).**

James, K.H. (2007) Perceptual-motor interactions in letter recognition: fMRI evidence, paper presented at the Biennial Meeting of the Society for Research in Child Development, Boston, MA, 29 March–1 April.

Kopera-Frye, K., Dehaene, S. and Streissguth, A.P. (1996) Impairments of number processing induced by prenatal alcohol exposure, *Neuropsychologia*, 34: 1187–96.

Marshall, L. and Born, J. (2007) The contribution of sleep to hippocampus-dependent memory consolidation, *Trends in Cognitive Science*, 11: 442–50.

Meltzoff, A.N. (1995) Understanding the intentions of others: re-enactment of intended acts by 18-month-old children, *Developmental Psychology*, 31: 838–50.

Rosch, E. (1978) Principles of categorisation, in E. Rosch and B.B. Lloyd (eds) *Cognition and Categorisation*. Hillsdale, NJ: Erlbaum.

Szücs, D. and Goswami, U. (2007) Educational neuroscience: defining a new discipline for the study of mental representations, *Mind, Brain and Education,* **1(3): 114–27.**

Tai, Y.F., Scherfler, C., Brooks, D.J., Sawamoto, N. and Castiello, U. (2004) The human premotor cortex is 'mirror' only for biological actions, *Current Biology*, 14: 117–20.

Treiman, R., Mullennix, J., Bijeljac-Babic, R. and Richmond-Welty, E.D. (1995) The special role of rimes in the description, use and acquisition of English orthography, *Journal of Experimental Psychology: General*, 124: 107–36.

Vygotsky, L. (1978) *Mind in Society*. Cambridge, MA: Harvard University Press.

Weisberg, D.S., Keil, F.C., Goodstein, E.R. and Gray, J.R. (2008) The seductive allure of neuroscience explanations, *Journal of Cognitive Neuroscience*, 20(3): 470–7.

3

SUE ROBSON
Attachment and relationships

Summary

This chapter argues for a deeper consideration of issues relating to attachment and children's relationships with parents and carers, friends and teachers. The author argues that learning is socially situated and that relationships have a central role in schools and nurseries. Children's relationships are significant for their development of social understanding and their socio-emotional well-being which is also so important to school success.

Cameo 1

Kate (4.5) is at the playdough table with three children and the teacher. Emma (3.3), new to the nursery, approaches and points to the nearby easel.

Emma: Me want do painting.

Teacher: You would like to paint? Well, there's space at the easel, so that's fine. Remember that you'll need to wear an apron.

Emma walks past Kate, takes an apron down and attempts to put it on, with difficulty. Kate gets out of her seat and walks towards Emma.

Kate: Do you want me to help you?

Emma holds out the apron and Kate takes it and holds it in a position that allows Emma to step into it.

Kate: Now this bit goes over your head. I know how to do it because I'm 4. Do you know where to get the paper?

Emma: Over there (pointing to store).

Kate: That's right. If you can't peg it up, I can help you.

> **Cameo 2**
>
> ## Relationships in the classroom
>
> Children were asked to define 'a good teacher'. Charlotte (age 10) said, 'A good teacher makes you work hard, but you have fun along the way. When they tell you off it gets into your head but it doesn't put you off coming to school.'

Introduction

This chapter focuses on attachment and children's relationships with parents and carers, friends and teachers. It starts from a perspective that learning is socially situated and, thus, that relationships play a central role in schools and nurseries. Children's relationships with family, friends and other people that matter to them, such as teachers, are significant for their development of social understanding, and their socio-emotional well-being, so important to school success (Carpendale and Lewis 2006). Neurobiological evidence points to the importance of emotion for vital aspects of school life such as learning, attention, memory and decision making (Immordino-Yang and Damasio 2007: Chapter 2). Noddings (1992) argues that the first task of school is to care for children. An understanding of these areas can be crucial in supporting teachers' effectiveness in fulfilling that task.

What is attachment and how does it develop?

Attachment is 'the lasting psychological connectedness between human beings' (Bowlby 1969: 194), characterized by a nurturing, affectionate bond between carers and children formed early in life. Five phases have been identified in its development. Initially, very young babies do not discriminate between the people who comfort them but, generally within the first six months, a preference to known carers begins to be expressed. In the third stage they start to actively seek contact with particular caregivers and may experience separation anxiety and fear of strangers. The period of about 18 months onwards shows growing reciprocity and understanding on the child's part of adults' feelings and intentions. There may also be a lessening of distress on separation. In the fifth stage (generally school age onwards), relationships are characterized by more abstract considerations such as affection and trust.

For the majority of children, the usual outcome of this process is secure attachment, a lasting emotional tie to their carer, which gives children the confidence to go out and explore their world. In many instances, this is the mother but it does not need to be and fathers, grandparents and siblings can all take this role. What seems to matter is the responsiveness and engagement of the person involved and the accuracy of their interpretations of the baby's signals. Meins (1999) suggests that mothers who are 'mind-minded' with their children, focusing on their children's thoughts and feelings in their interactions with them, may be scaffolding the children's understanding of their own behaviour. Over time, these interactions support the child in seeing the attachment figure as responsive, reliable and trustworthy. This helps the child to develop an internal working model of relationships, which Bowlby (1969) believes conditions a child's expectations about relationships throughout life, influencing their social understanding, sense of self and development of self-esteem (Siegler et al. 2006).

The importance of culture

Attachment behaviours vary across and within cultures reflecting different values and practices. For example, the anxious/resistant pattern (Ainsworth et al. 1978) has been more common in studies of Japanese children and may reflect childrearing practices whereby children are relatively unfamiliar with being left with strangers (Siegler et al. 2006). By contrast, Meadows (2010) cites research showing German mothers particularly valuing emotional self-sufficiency in their children and the children showing levels of independence which might count as denoting insecure attachment. Awareness of such cultural variation can contribute to evidence for QTS Q18 ('Understand how children and young people develop and that the progress and well-being of learners are affected by a range of developmental, social, religious, ethnic, cultural and linguistic processes') and EYPS S29 ('Recognise and respect the influential and enduring contribution that families and parents/carers can make to children's development, well-being and learning') and highlights the importance of not making assumptions about the experiences of children and families. Educational practice may also impact here: in Reggio Emilia, the focus on mutually influencing networks of relationships may emphasize interdependence and group relationships rather than a relationship between child and carer (Degotardi and Pearson 2009).

Attachment as a lifelong process

Originally focusing on relationships between parents/carers and children in the first years of life, ideas on attachment have now begun to be extended to older children. A toddler's attachment may be obvious when they protest loudly at separation. In older children, the need for security is no less powerful but may be expressed in different ways. Miller and Commons (2007) outline processes and behaviours that occur over a lifetime, not just infancy. In older children, these would include an increasing ability to report one's own perspective and to see things from another's perspective and increased attachment to peers.

Alongside this, attachment theory has begun to have more influence in education and care practice (see, for example, Elfer et al. 2003; Bergin and Bergin 2009). This is reflected in the EYFS in the significance attached to the role of the key person: 'The named member of staff with whom a child has more contact than other adults. This adult shows a special interest in the child through close personal interaction day-to-day. The key person can help the young child to deal with separation anxiety' (DfES 2007: 19).

Why does attachment matter?

In the context of education, attachment matters because security of attachment is linked to academic achievement and school success (Bergin and Bergin 2009). Secure attachment has been associated with curiosity and problem-solving skills at age 2 and with empathy and independence at age 5 (Smith et al. 2003) and possibly with higher grades and more attention and involvement throughout the school years (Siegler et al. 2006). Socially, there is evidence to suggest that early attachment relationships between children and carers are predictive of later peer relationships (Meadows 2010). Children with a secure attachment have been found to be more popular with peers, more empathetic, more competent in conflict resolution (Cortazar and Herreros 2010) and, as older children, to be less likely to either be bullied or to be bullies themselves (Walden and Beran 2010). The positive internal working models they have developed may help them to develop what is often referred to as 'emotional literacy', being able to regulate their emotions and 'read' the emotional expressions of others, alongside seeing themselves as worthy of friendship and affection and attaching importance to emotional communication with others. By contrast, children with insecure attachment histories may be less motivated to complete challenges (Cortazar and Herreros 2010) and be less self-confident and socially competent (Bergin and Bergin 2009). These effects seem to persist throughout (and beyond) the primary years, and will impact on children's success at school.

Friendship and peer relationships in school

> The best thing adults could do to make school a better place would be to 'make sure everyone's got a friend'.
>
> (Anna, aged 8 years, in Peters 2003: 51)

After family, friends are the most important relationships for the majority of children. Friendship is emotionally important for children and a source of support, particularly at times of potential stress, along with other advantages such as higher levels of self-concept (Smith et al. 2003). For children whose earlier experiences of relationships have been problematic, positive experiences with peers can help them to develop greater resilience.

The development of peer relationships and attachment

Over the primary period, children's relationships change in a number of ways. In the early years, attachment may be more towards significant adults such as a key person. In the later primary years, attachment is often more to the peer group, particularly for boys, where other 'high status' boys may serve as the most important role models (Ashley 2003).

Children's growing social, emotional and intellectual skills have an impact on their peer relationships. For example, children's developing oral competence and increased ability to take on the perspectives of others mean that negotiation and compromise are more evident in the primary years than in nursery age children

(Dunn 2004). Physical aggression and recourse to physical acts such as snatching a toy decline over time but may be replaced by more verbally skilled, longer-term hostility (Meadows 2010). Intimacy between friends also changes. In the early years, the context may be sharing feelings of fear and excitement in pretend play. By the age of about 5–7 years, children's growing ability to understand what friends are thinking helps more explicit sharing. By the later primary years, confiding in friends, especially for girls, may be a key marker of intimacy (Dunn 2004).

Friendship and school success

Dunn (2004) suggests three ways in which young children's friendships may be significant, all of which are important for success in nursery and school life. First, children make particular efforts to negotiate and make compromises in friendships because they want to maintain the relationship. Second, the talk about thoughts, feelings and inner states that takes place in the sharing of imagined worlds and which may be particularly significant for later socio-cognitive outcomes is especially likely to happen between friends. Third, she suggests that friendship 'is a context in which moral understanding is demonstrated very early' (Dunn 2004: 157).

Supporting social networks

This suggests an important role for teachers in supporting children's relationships and social networks. This may be particularly valuable for children at times of potential stress, such as transition, as in cameo 1. Even the presence of a friend at such times can be beneficial, and Margetts (2004) suggests that early years teachers focus on the development of social skills such as cooperation, assertion and self-control, to support young children in the move from nursery to school, advice which is valuable throughout the primary phase (see also Chapter 9). Older children can also often have an important role at such times, acting as buddies and guides for younger children, for example, developing books about the realities of school life: 'When there's something to eat that you don't like . . . you should tell the teacher. Don't throw it under the table!' (Reggio Children 2002).

What about teacher–child relationships?

Teachers may be the most significant adult relationships in many children's lives outside the family. Thinking about how those relationships can be most supportive is valuable for all adults and children but may be particularly beneficial for specific groups of children, for example, those who may be less verbally competent, lower achieving or vulnerable (Bergin and Bergin 2009). Positive relationships with significant adults may even support 'repair [of] unhelpful working models' (Meadows 2010: 125) for children with insecure attachment, as their expectations of unresponsive or even hostile relationships are challenged.

Elfer et al. (2003: 12) highlight the importance of 'trust, reliability, familiarity and respect' in their discussion of the relationship between very young children and their key person. Such a relationship may be 'attachment-like' (Bergin and Bergin 2009), with similar qualities, and a range of potential benefits. For example, in the early years, the impact may be on children's empathy, independence, achievement orientation and engagement in more complex and cooperative play (Degotardi and Pearson 2009). In primary children, the impact of warm, supportive relationships with teachers has been linked to academic achievement, positive relationships with peers, more positive attitudes to school and lower rates of negative behaviour (Bergin and Bergin 2009).

What can teachers do?

Talking openly about thoughts and feelings and developing a listening culture in which children's views and ideas are respected and acted upon (National Children's Bureau Young Children's Voices Network 2009) are positive strategies which support standards such as QTS Q1 ('Have high expectations of children and young people including a commitment to ensuring that they can achieve their full educational potential and to establishing fair, respectful, trusting, supportive and constructive relationships with them') and EYPS S25 ('Establish fair, respectful, trusting, supportive and constructive relationships with children').

One key role for teachers is acting as a model of positive relationships in their own interactions, as emphasized in QTS Q2 ('Demonstrate the positive values, attitudes and behaviour they expect from children and young people') and the similar EYPS standard S28. Practitioners in Reggio Emilia, for example, model intellectual conflict and its resolution in their discussions with one another, believing that, in so doing, they are helping children to develop skills of negotiation and cooperation, empathy and an ability to understand and respect the views of others (Edwards et al. 1998). This approach also acknowledges that conflict is part of life, which can be reassuring for children trying to deal with difficult feelings, and a sense that everyone should 'get along'.

Bergin and Bergin make six recommendations for teachers:

1   Increase sensitivity and warm, positive interactions with children.
2   Be well prepared for teaching and hold high expectations for children.
3   Be responsive to children's agendas by providing choice where possible.
4   Use non-coercive discipline, explaining reasons for rules and consequences of breaking them, avoiding threats and abuse of teacher power.
5   Help children to be kind, helpful and accepting of one another.
6   Implement interventions for specific, difficult relationships (adapted from Bergin and Bergin 2009: 158–9).

This is not without its challenges. In the early years, for example, balancing the personal closeness described in the EYFS definition of the key person with appropriate professional distance can be emotionally demanding (Elfer et al. 2003). For teachers of school-age children, the issues are not fundamentally different: the closeness which develops between a class teacher and children over the year is often a key source of job satisfaction while simultaneously being emotionally challenging. It will be important for beginning teachers, in particular, to talk about these issues with colleagues and mentors, as well as for them to be discussed at whole school level.

Relationships with parents and carers

The other important relationship for all teachers is that which they develop with a child's parents or carers (see Chapter 23). In the domain of children's relationships, parents remain better attuned to their children's emotional states than do teachers, who may be better placed to support cognitive development and behaviour regulation (Ahnert and Lamb 2003). So the extent to which parents and teachers can work together may have a real impact on children's emotional well-being. QTS Q5 ('Recognise and respect the contribution that colleagues, parents and carers can make to the development and well-being of children and young people and to raising their levels of attainment') and EYPS S31 ('Work in partnership with families and parents/ carers, at home and in the setting, to nurture children, to help them develop and to improve outcomes for them') acknowledge the vital importance of strong relationships between homes and settings for children's well-being.

Thinking about implications for practice

Two underpinning aspects to thinking about classroom practice are important: first, how can teachers promote the positive behaviour and relationships associated with secure attachment and, second, how can they act to support those children whose relationships are more problematic (see Chapters 8, 17 and 21)? In practice, both of these may be addressed often in similar ways but, for those children who find it harder to develop relationships with peers and adults, particular attention to aspects such as support for their self-esteem, social skills, resilience, emotional intelligence and empathy will be valuable. The National Children's Bureau (2006) highlights some of the ways that more vulnerable children, including those who have experienced loss or trauma, such as looked-after children and children with refugee status, may be affected physiologically, physically, emotionally and socially. For example, a child who often seems to be in trouble at playtimes and during moves between classrooms may seem to be behaving poorly. However, her life experiences may have led her to feel more secure in small groups with people she knows, and panicky in crowds.

Belonging

The starting point should be a consideration of children's attachment to their nursery or school as a place: their sense of belonging. As with attachment to a special person, attachment to school can help children feel secure and valued and able to go out and meet challenges in their learning and relationships. Clearly, relationships between children and teachers are important in this process but there are also ways in which the environment can help children to feel that they belong. An on-going task for teachers should be a realistic appraisal of the environments they create, asking themselves: 'If I were a (girl/boy/child with special educational needs/child with English as a second language/refugee, etc.) – how would this classroom help me to feel that I belong here?' (see Chapters 16 and 17). This sense of belonging to school impacts upon children's participation in school life and on their achievement and may be particularly important in supporting more vulnerable children (Bergin and Bergin 2009).

It is recognized in QTS Q19, which requires trainees to 'take practical account of diversity and promote equality and inclusion in their teaching', and EYPS S18 ('Promote children's rights, equality, inclusion and anti-discriminatory practice'). The use of persona dolls (Persona Doll Training and EYE: www.persona-doll-training.org) can be valuable in supporting a sense of belonging and inclusion through talk and role play about equality issues, which may develop children's ability to empathize as well as empowering them to stand up for themselves and others when they experience unfairness and exclusion.

In the early years, a 'home-like' environment, with its sense of familiarity and intimacy, is often suggested as helping young children to feel they belong. However, focusing too strongly on this home-like metaphor may result in teachers overlooking the rich potential that nurseries (and classrooms) have for developing group relationships (Dahlberg et al. 2007). The development of a shared classroom culture, based upon group relationships and the creation of shared experiences among the group, may be a means of engendering feelings of belonging for everyone (see Chapter 16).

The remainder of this chapter looks briefly at some aspects of practice which may be especially supportive of the development of positive relationships in the classroom.

The physical environment

The organization of the environment has an important part in supporting or constraining relationships. Traditional seating arrangements, particularly for older primary children, of tables in rows facing the teacher, convey powerful messages to children about learning, including the idea that it is an independent process, in which children's peer relationships play little part. While this may be appropriate for some activities and contexts, furniture can be easily (and speedily) rearranged by the children themselves in order to create spaces that favour interaction and collaboration. Teachers' active promotion of collaboration and shared working is also needed. This can be done in many ways. With younger children, for example, provision of resources which oblige children to collaborate is valuable: pulleys and levers in the sand tray can only be used successfully if children cooperate. Broadhead (2004), looking at role play areas, found that collaborative play among 4- and 5-year-old children increased when the resources were non-representational materials such as pieces of fabric and boxes. This may be because such resources stimulate social interaction, as the children negotiate with others about what the play areas and resources will become. With older children, it may be valuable to think of structuring tasks so that each member of the group has a specific part to play. For example, in a problem-solving task, one member might chair the discussion, another might be responsible for note taking, a third might be responsible for gathering resources, and so on.

Sustained shared thinking

Sustained shared thinking (SST), a process defined by Siraj-Blatchford et al. (2002: 8) as 'An episode in which two or more individuals "work together" in an intellectual way to solve a problem, clarify a concept, evaluate activities, extend a narrative, etc.', supports the development of deeper relationships between teachers and children by focusing on the co-creation of shared meanings. Its value is recognized in EYPS S16 ('Engage in sustained, shared thinking with children'). Siraj-Blatchford et al. (2002) identify the types of interaction which may support SST, including:

- *scaffolding* to extend children's knowledge and understanding through the use of strategies such as open-ended questioning;
- *extending* by making a suggestion that helps a child to see other possibilities;
- *discussing* which supports the interchange of information or ideas;
- *modelling* which includes the demonstration of activities and verbal commentary from the adult;
- *playing* when the adult uses humour or plays with a child.

This research showed that episodes of SST were more likely to happen when teachers were working with smaller groups and individual children. While this is, of course, not easy to achieve in large classes, it points to the value of trying to provide opportunities for it: teachers and classroom assistants, for example, can work together to provide time for teachers to focus on individuals and groups.

Project work

Group and class projects, particularly those that arise out of the children's own interests and concerns, can provide rich contexts for discussion and negotiation, with shared experience of events that can be thought about, supporting the creation of a collective classroom culture.

Narrative and story

Narrative, in the form of children's own stories as well as published fiction, is intimately bound up with our cultural and communal histories and fundamental to how children make sense of the world (Robson 2006: Chapter 17). It provides rich opportunities for children to make sense of their own thoughts and feelings, as well as gaining experience of how others might think, act and feel. The Story Links Project (Story Links Training: http://storylinkstraining.co.uk) exploits these opportunities, using therapeutic storywriting to support the emotional well-being and reading skills of primary children at risk of exclusion. Teachers, children and parents/carers work together with the aim of co-creating stories that may become a positive attachment object for a child.

Socio-dramatic and pretend play

As an activity that often has considerable emotional and social significance for young children, socio-dramatic and pretend play may be particularly valuable contexts for the development of children's social understanding and social self-regulation. In pretend play, children step in and out of role, represent situations, talk about mental states and have to negotiate meanings and actions with others. This act of sharing an imagined world with peers involves empathy, recognition of others' intentions and sharing perspectives, often termed intersubjectivity.

Pretend play is often seen as the province of young children. However, in older children, while the kinds of imagined worlds characteristic of younger children's play may die out or become increasingly private (Dunn 2004), opportunities to engage in dramatic play and enactments of story scenarios have affective benefits for children throughout the primary years.

Circle time

Circle time is a familiar routine in many classrooms, with children and teachers engaged together in Circle Meetings which address issues of group interest, aimed at enhancing self-esteem and self-confidence and supporting better relationships and positive behaviour (Jenny Mosley and Positive Press Quality Circle Time: http://www. circle-time.co.uk). However, as Lang (1998) suggests, teachers need to be clear about what they are trying to achieve in employing circle time as a strategy. Johnson (2010) identifies some fundamental aspects if it is to be most effective, including mutual respect between children and adults and genuine commitment from everyone. Teachers will need to plan for it carefully and be skilled at active listening and time management. Crucially, as she identifies, teachers need to be skilled in emotional containment, managing feelings when emotions, positive and negative, run high.

Extra-curricular activities

Extra-curricular activities provide opportunities for establishing relationships with other children and adults and children's participation in them may engender a greater sense of involvement and connectedness to school. This may be particularly so for lower achieving children and highlights the need for activities like this to be freely available for all and not just be targeted at children in sports teams, or those who play a musical instrument, for example (Bergin and Bergin 2009).

Questions to Promote Thinking

1 Looking back at cameo 2, what would you want the children to say about you?
2 What can you do to develop an atmosphere of mutual trust and respect?
3 How can you support each child's positive self-identity and sense of belonging?
4 Why is the development of positive peer relationships for the children in your class important?
5 What do you think it would be helpful to know about the children's family relationships?

References and suggested further reading

Ahnert, L. and Lamb, M.E. (2003) Shared care: establishing a balance between home and child care settings, *Child Development*, 74(4): 1044–9.

Ainsworth, M.D.S., Blehar, M.C., Waters, E. and Wall, S. (1978) *Patterns of Attachment*. Hillsdale, NJ: Erlbaum.

Ashley, M. (2003) Primary school boys' identity formation and the male role model: an exploration of sexual identity and gender identity in the UK through attachment theory, *Sex Education*, 3(3): 257–70.

Bergin, C. and Bergin, D. (2009) Attachment in the classroom, *Educational Psychology Review*, 21: 141–70.

Bowlby, J. (1969) *Attachment and Loss*. Harmondsworth: Penguin.

Broadhead, P. (2004) *Early Years Play and Learning: Developing Social Skills and Cooperation*. London: RoutledgeFalmer.

Carpendale, J. and Lewis, C. (2006) *How Children Develop Social Understanding*. Oxford: Blackwell.

Cortazar, A. and Herreros, F. (2010) Early attachment relationships and the early childhood curriculum, *Contemporary Issues in Early Childhood*, 11(2): 192–202.

Dahlberg, G., Moss, P. and Pence, A. (2007) *Beyond Quality in Early Childhood Education and Care*, 2nd edn. Abingdon: Routledge.

Degotardi, S. and Pearson, E. (2009) Relationship theory in the nursery: attachment and beyond, *Contemporary Issues in Early Childhood*, 10(2): 144–55.

DfES (Department for Education and Skills) (2007) *Practice Guidance for the Early Years Foundation Stage*. Nottingham: DfES.

Dunn, J. (2004) *Children's Friendships: The Beginnings of Intimacy*. Oxford: Blackwell.

Edwards, C., Gandini, L. and Forman, G. (eds) (1998) *The Hundred Languages of Children*, 2nd edn. Westport, CT: Ablex.

Elfer, P., Goldschmied, E. and Selleck, D. (2003) *Key Persons in the Nursery: Building Relationships for Quality Provision*. London: David Fulton.

Immordino-Yang, M.H. and Damasio, A. (2007) We feel, therefore we learn: the relevance of affective and social neuroscience to education, *Mind, Brain and Education*, 1(1): 3–10.

Jenny Mosley and Positive Press Quality Circle Time. Available online at: http://www.circle-time.co.uk (accessed 1 October 2010).

Johnson, J. (2010) *Positive and Trusting Relationships with Children in Early Years Settings*. Exeter: Learning Matters.

Lang, P. (1998) Getting round to clarity: what do we mean by circle time? *Pastoral Care in Education*, 16(3): 3–10.

Margetts, K. (2004) Identifying and supporting behaviours associated with co-operation, assertion and self-control in young children starting school, *Journal of European Early Childhood Education Research*, 12(2): 75–85.

Meadows, S. (2010) *The Child as Social Person*. London: Routledge.

Meins, E. (1999) Sensitivity, security and internal working models: bridging the transmission gap, *Attachment and Human Development*, 1: 325–42.

Miller, P.M. and Commons, M.L. (2007) How are the processes by which people become attached influenced by stage of development? *Behavioral Development Bulletin*, 13: 24–9.

National Children's Bureau (2006) *Understanding Why*. London: National Children's Bureau.

National Children's Bureau Young Children's Voices Network (2009) *Listening as a Way of Life*. London: NCB. Available online at: http://www.ncb.org.uk/dotpdf/open_access_2/YCVN_leaflet.pdf (accessed 12 June 2010).

Noddings, N. (1992) *The Challenge to Care in Schools: An alternative approach to education*. New York: Teachers College Press.

Papatheodorou, T. and Moyles, J. (eds) (2009) *Learning Together in the Early Years: Exploring Relational Pedagogy.* London: Routledge.

Persona Doll Training and EYE (undated) *Celebrating Diversity: Inclusion in Practice* (Video and Support Book). Available online at: http://www.persona-doll-training.org (accessed 26 May 2010).

Peters, S. (2003) 'I didn't expect that I would get tons of friends . . . more each day': children's experiences of friendship during the transition to school, *Early Years*, 23(1): 45–53.

Reggio Children (2002) *Advisories.* Available online at: http://www.sightlines-initiative.com (accessed 26 May 2010).

Robson, S. (2006) *Developing Thinking and Understanding in Young Children.* London: Routledge.

Siegler, R., DeLoache, J. and Eisenberg, N. (2006) *How Children Develop*, 2nd edn. New York: Worth.

Siraj-Blatchford, I., Sylva, K., Muttock, S., Gilden, R. and Bell, D. (2002) *Researching Effective Pedagogy in the Early Years.* London: Department for Education and Skills.

Smith, P.K., Cowie, H. and Blades, M. (2003) *Understanding Children's Development*, 4th edn. Oxford: Blackwell.

Story Links Training. Available online at: http://storylinkstraining.co.uk (accessed 26 May 2010).

Walden, L.M. and Beran, T.N. (2010) Attachment quality and bullying behavior in school-aged youth, *Canadian Journal of School Psychology*, 25(1): 5–18.

4

PIA PARRY
Learning about the teacher's role in safeguarding

Summary

This chapter offers a guide through the changing landscape of legislation, statutory guidance, policy and rhetoric about 'safeguarding' and the principles of partnership and information sharing. Case studies illustrate the importance of a clear understanding of procedures in typical and more challenging situations. The reader is encouraged to consider the emotional aspects of working with children in difficult circumstances from varied backgrounds, as well as the opportunities offered to make a difference in their educational communities.

Cameo 1

Paul arrives in reception class each day with his mother and two younger siblings in tow. He usually runs ahead of the family group and dashes into the classroom making loud noises, ignoring warnings from both teacher and mother in this reckless ritual. Other children seem to move out of his way and some complain he is smelly when he sits near them. David, his class teacher, could smell stale urine on his clothes and has noticed difficulties with his social interactions.

Cameo 2

Seven-year-old Justine and her 4-year-old sister, Clare, live with their mother and stepfather. Both children were being monitored by the Local Authority Children's Social Care Department following concerns over domestic violence in the home. They have a named social worker who checks on the children's progress and contacts the school regularly to hear how they are getting on. The designated teacher with responsibility for safeguarding, or the headteacher, usually talks to the social worker. Their class teacher, Sue, has observed that Justine has been more withdrawn and had said that she doesn't like her stepfather, but she refused to expand on this. Sue made a note of this and passed it on to the designated teacher in line with school procedures and it was subsequently shared with the social worker.

Introduction

Safeguarding is the term used to describe the supportive network of services and legislation to promote the welfare of children and young people from pre-birth to 19 years of age. Child protection forms part of safeguarding and promoting welfare, referring to action taken to protect specific children suffering (or likely to suffer) significant harm. Safeguarding encompasses those activities which were formerly the responsibility of Child Protection and Family Welfare Services who mainly responded to abuse and neglect after the event had occurred. It is now used to describe preventative as well as protective services and also includes the positive promotion of well-being as well as remedial steps taken to respond to those children who have been harmed or are at risk of further harm.

In the 2001 census, it was reported that, of the 14,769,137 children between the ages of birth and 18 years in England, about a third (4.9 million) were recognized as being 'in need' of additional services and support (NSPCC 2007). This included children with disabilities or other additional needs, and there may have been others who were not known to local authorities. In 2009, a new revised census of children in need was carried out using different methodology which altered the way in which children are identified as being 'in need' of additional services. It showed that:

- There were 304,400 children in need in England at 31 March 2009, a reduction of 4.5 million since the earlier census in 2001. This equates to 276 children per 10,000 aged under 18 years.
- For all children in need, 41 per cent (123,800) were in need as a result of, or were at risk of, abuse or neglect: 15 per cent (46,100) were in need due to family dysfunction and 13 per cent (39,800) were in need due to disability, illness or intrinsic condition (DCSF 2010).

This reduction in the numbers of children seen as being 'in need' by 2009 has led to a huge reduction in services, including preventative services, intervention and support to children and their families. In the 2009/2010 census, however, there was an 11 per cent increase in referrals to children's social care and a 25 per cent increase in the number of children in need (DfE 2010). This follows the death of baby Peter Connelly in Tottenham, North London, in 2007 and subsequent investigations into the circumstances surrounding his death. For teachers, the reduction in services and increased levels of concern mean they have had to take on additional roles in the classroom and in supporting vulnerable children and families outside the classroom too.

Preventative services in the UK traditionally begin pre-birth with support and advice for pregnant women. The idea of prevention can be interpreted by as 'protectionist'; Parton (2006) argues that increased concern with prevention inevitably leads to greater monitoring and surveillance. It is, therefore, important to be clear about the aims of any protection or prevention; the Children Act 1989 identifies the 'welfare of the child' as paramount (Section 1:1) and requires that the threshold for intervention into family life should be that the child has suffered or is at risk of significant harm (Section 31:2).

Recognizing and responding to children's needs

Although safeguarding children is the responsibility of all adults connected with the child, some adults, such as teachers, have a greater role by merit of their professional status, and it is a statutory duty for all educational staff to safeguard the children in their care (under the Education Act 2002). In cameo 1, the teacher, David, felt that Paul needed to have some help with his behaviour to protect him and others from harm: the 'reckless ritual' when he arrived at school was placing him and others in immediate danger. David could also see indicators that Paul's needs were not being fully met and was concerned that he might be experiencing neglect. Paul clearly needed some help with his behaviour and personal hygiene and, while his family were best placed to respond to these needs, David could see this was not happening. However, although David thought that Paul might not be receiving the sort of care and parenting he needed, this situation might not have met the criteria for 'significant harm' within the Children's Social Care Services (The Children Act 1989, Section 47), although 'significant harm' is ill-defined. This is because each local authority has 'thresholds' for intervention into family life and more information about Paul and his family would be needed before the Children's Social Care (CSC) team would become involved.

In the meantime, David could try to work in partnership with Paul's parents to discuss his needs and ways to support him. However, if there was no real progress with Paul's behaviour or his personal hygiene, David would need to think further about how to intervene and who else might help. Completing an assessment of Paul's needs using the Common Assessment Framework (CAF) (CWDC 2010) would offer the opportunity to look at all aspects of Paul's life; his development, his family's capacity to meet his needs and other situational and environmental factors. Although Gilligan with Manby (2008) have highlighted concerns among teachers about the effectiveness of the CAF, more recent statistics suggest teachers report evidence of improvements in outcomes for children, with the CAF providing a common framework for inter-agency work (NFER 2010; see also Chapter 23). Teachers and teaching assistants can use the CAF to carry out an assessment to help them identify and plan for children's needs. Assessment is, however, a voluntary undertaking and families may refuse to participate in the process. It is not necessary to complete such a detailed assessment on every child, but it can be helpful in identifying where there are unmet needs and in attracting services for the child. Detailed narrative observations in particular can help teachers to understand the situation from the child's perspective (Fawcett 2009), and Paul's assessment would be best supported by observations in school to provide insight into his day-to-day social interactions.

The assessment process itself and subsequent forward planning can alert the family to the need for change in established patterns of behaviour and communication. Ecological systems theory (Bronfenbrenner 1979) encourages us to think about families as systems of interconnected and interdependent individuals, none of whom can be understood in isolation. For example, offering to have a member of the teaching staff meet Paul at the gate and walk with the family to the classroom instead of running, might impact on individual members of Paul's family in a number of ways. Paul's mother may feel supported and valued in the task of parenting and develop a more authoritative approach. Paul may feel reassured that his behaviour and anxiety can be managed safely and he can learn a more appropriate way of separating from his family and managing the transition from home to the classroom (see Chapter 9). The other siblings in the family may experience this change positively as they witness their mother coping well with Paul's challenging behaviours. Other children in the playground may feel reassured that such behaviour can be managed and contained.

However, it is possible that David would feel anxious about taking on a role traditionally held by others and, if this level of intervention and family support are not sufficient to help resolve the presenting problem, this could lead to David's further involvement with issues about Paul's life outside the school, for example, the parents' own needs, while trying to remain child-focused. If this is the case, he should not hesitate to seek support and assistance from colleagues, for example with planning, to ensure the needs of other children in the class are not overlooked while Paul and his family are the focus of attention.

Cameo 2 identifies a more problematic situation where significant harm is alleged and the children have been removed from their family and local area. Local Authorities' Children's Social Care departments have a duty, under Section 47 of The Children Act 1989, to investigate where there is reasonable cause to suspect that a child is suffering, or is likely to suffer, significant harm. This does not automatically lead to a child being removed from home but often triggers action for services to support families or individual children. Where there are serious concerns about a child which meet or cross the 'threshold' for action, the local authority may decide to intervene in a more authoritative way. They currently conduct an initial assessment within ten days (DCSF 2010: 145) or sooner if there is a likelihood of further significant harm and hold a strategy meeting to discuss the situation and make decisions. The social worker needs to take into account the individual circumstances and needs of each child, including language, disability, age and the likely impact of any changes to their situation and attachments, before recommending any changes.

If the outcome of the initial assessment suggests that a more detailed understanding of the child and the family would enable better planning, then the social worker would be asked by the initial child protection conference to complete a more detailed assessment of the child or children and the family. This is known as a 'core assessment' (DCSF 2010: 173) and would normally be completed within 35 working days. This provides a more comprehensive view of the child in context for the purpose of identifying outcomes to protect and promote the child's welfare. This may include recommendations for legal action to secure a permanent arrangement for the upbringing of the child. In her independent report commissioned by the Department of Education, which proposes ways of simplifying child protection inspection procedures following the death of baby Peter Connelly, Munro suggests these timeframes should be linked to the situation rather than the statutory framework (DfE 2011: 63).

In Justine's case, the social worker had serious concerns for the safety of the two girls if they remained in the family home. Justine had told her teacher, Sue, she didn't like her stepfather. Although it was helpful for Justine to talk to the teacher whom she trusted, Sue needed to be careful about how she responded. It is important not to ask questions such as 'Did he hurt you?', since this sort of leading question could cause problems later if Justine is required to give evidence for any prosecution. Sue could help Justine talk about what happened by listening reflectively. For example, she could give Justine the space away from other children to talk with her, allowing Justine time to talk and mirror her words back to her. If Justine said 'He hit me', the teacher could say 'Hit you?' in a slightly questioning tone or 'He?' This careful mirroring of the child's words may help her tell her story without introducing any new ideas. The teacher should avoid questioning the child but allow her to talk if she wants to.

In this particular case, when the social worker visited the girls, they were hiding in their bedroom. Justine was very guarded and reluctant to expand on what she had said earlier to Sue but did mention that 'fighting' between her parents was increasing again. The mother was found to have visible bruises and was not willing to offer reasonable explanations for them. She refused to talk with the police or the social worker and would not agree to see a medical professional. The atmosphere in the home was tense and, although the stepfather was not present, it was understood he would be returning later. The girls were moved with their mother's reluctant consent to foster carers and a child protection strategy meeting was called. The foster carers lived at some distance from the school and this meant the sisters now had a long journey to school each day. Sue was informed that if either parent turned up at the school to collect one or both of the children, they should be asked to talk with the named social worker first but that the school had no legal right to prevent the parent from leaving with the child. The school would need to inform the social worker immediately and steps would then be taken by the social work team to recover the children, using the authority of the court and the police if necessary. Sue did notice the mother and stepfather near the school at lunch times and after school and on one occasion they called out to Justine and told her to keep her mouth shut. Sue passed this information on and was told that it would be discussed at the child protection conference with the parents present. This conference followed the initial investigation and strategy meeting (DCSF 2010: 187).

Although Sue, in passing on Justine's comments, was certainly not responsible for the break-up of the family nor the removal of the children, situations like this can often leave the professionals feeling blamed. Sue might also have strong feelings about the girls being moved to foster carers, away from their family and school. It is important for teachers to have support at times like this from a more experienced colleague in the school, as well as guidance from the school management team about the need to keep detailed records of any observations, conversations or incidents involving the children or the parents.

Child protection meetings

Teachers are often invited to attend a child protection conference along with other agencies and members of the family. The aim is to decide whether a child needs a child protection plan and to identify or review services to support or protect the child. These meetings can be stressful experiences for both professionals and family members. Good preparation can help to alleviate some stress and teachers should have training and guidance before being asked to attend. If children are of sufficient age and level of understanding, they might also be invited to attend. This should be discussed beforehand by the social worker or independent chair, along with ways to support children throughout the process.

There should be clear outcomes from this meeting leading to a child protection plan. The plan may include moving the child or children to a safer place. Most children under the age of 10 are placed with a member of their own extended family or family friend who is able to keep the child safe if they can no longer remain in their family of origin. If this is not possible, then the child may be placed in foster care. A small number of children may need to live in a residential care home for a period of time if this is seen as the most appropriate plan. Some children develop difficult behaviours as a result of their abusive experiences and may not be able to live in a family for a while. This small group of children may need psychological help or other services in a group care residential home before joining a substitute family. Moving from home is a worrying experience for any child and the teacher will be very aware of this and of the effects this may have on other children in the class. Information about Justine and her sister will need to be handled sensitively and Sue will need guidance on what can be shared with other children in the class. Other parents should not be included in any discussions about any child in the class but may ask about Justine: Sue will need to be ready to respond to enquiries or concerns.

There should be agreement about who will talk with the child about the outcomes if they were not present at the meeting. The outcomes should include not only recommendations for changes in the child's circumstances (where they live and with whom) but also whether further assessments are necessary and what services will be needed to support the individuals in the family or the family as a whole. The meeting will also consider the nature and extent of risk for each child in the family and whether legal action is needed to protect the child from further harm. In this example, it may be that Justine and Clare's social worker is given responsibility for making an application for a Care Order in respect of both children to the Family Court (Magistrates). A report would then be prepared for the court identifying where significant harm or risk of significant harm has occurred.

Teachers are asked to share information from their records at the meeting and are included in making decisions and recommendations. The teacher would need to prepare a report which will be shared with the parents and other professionals and may later be used in court. The parents may have legal representatives at the meeting and a copy of the teacher's report and any other reports will also be shared with them. The teacher's report should be a factual account of any incidents, conversations or observations about the child. Information sharing is an important part of protecting children and the school should provide training and procedures for its entire staff on good practice (DCSF 2008).

If the child has a child protection plan, there will be further regular meetings of the planning network, known as the 'core' group, to monitor the plan to which the teacher would be asked to contribute. These may be called Team Around the Child (TAC) meetings or child protection planning review meetings. The idea of creating a team or network around the child is not new and has often been used as an effective model in medical teams. For the newly qualified teacher, scenarios like this may initially seem daunting, but teams can offer support to individuals within the team and create a community of learning.

Training for safeguarding

Teachers are expected to have some understanding about the different types of harm that may affect children and how these might be recognized. Training and induction for teaching staff and the wider children's workforce should include recognition of signs that may indicate the child has experienced harm or is at risk of harm. Possible signs of abuse may indicate other non-abusive difficulties for the child but these too need to be explored and understood using tools such as the CAF. For further definitions and suggested signs of abuse, see Munro (2007); Smith (2008); Hughes and Owen (2009), the NSPCC website (www.nspcc.org.uk) or the government's own guidance, *Working Together to Safeguard Children* (DCSF 2010).

Training should also include guidance on record keeping. Good record keeping is an integral part of every teacher's role; as well as providing a contemporaneous account of each child's progress to share with colleagues and parents, records should reflect how and when child protection issues are discussed with the child or parents. Some records may be identified as confidential but each school will have procedures for staff to follow, in line with guidance from the Data Protection Act 1998.

Safeguarding communities

Schools have become central in developing stronger, safer communities and recent changes in government guidance (DCSF 2009, 2010) have emphasized the role schools can play. In the case of Victoria Climbié (1991–2000), the school and local neighbourhood knew little about her and failed to recognize her need for help. Jack and Gill (2010) present a strong argument for developing communities and support for families at a local level where schools are well placed to play an active role. However, teachers need to be aware that, for some parents, confiding in the school or the teacher would be counter-cultural and perhaps anxiety-raising for parent and teacher.

Communities are not static and some schools and communities experience more changes than others. Children move between families as complex arrangements sometimes exist between parents and new partners. Keeping records up-to-date can help the school and the wider network to ensure children do not disappear or go missing without being noticed. Schools have a duty under the Education and Inspections Act 2006 and subsequent revised guidance (DCSF 2009) to identify children missing education and teachers can consult the designated teacher about any child who causes concern.

Abuse in school

Teachers and other staff may feel reluctant to voice their concerns if they suspect abuse by a colleague, as found in the Plymouth nursery case (Plymouth City Council 2009). Whistle blowing may be seen by some as a bad career move and teachers might fear they will be blamed for accusing others wrongly, so it is important for teachers to know who they can turn to if they have concerns. There are opportunities for teachers to discuss their concerns through OfSTED, the police or the local authority. Schools have had access to a Local Authority Designated Officer (LADO) since the Bichard Report (Home Office 2004). The LADO is responsible for the monitoring and oversight of allegations about any person working with or having access to children. The police have responsibility for investigating any offence or allegation of an offence and work with the LADO where necessary. Schools need to provide the LADO with written records of any incidents involving staff including concerns or allegations about a member of staff to the LADO.

Children can abuse each other. There can be incidents of bullying, cyber bullying, sexual abuse, physical or emotional abuse which occur between children of all ages. Each school provides procedures for teachers to follow in the event of an allegation or suspicion of abuse to protect the victim and prevent further incidents of abuse. The teacher will be given help from the social work team in devising a plan for any child with a history of abusing others and information about risk should be shared with those staff who need to know. This may include ancillary staff and those who work part-time. The teacher will ensure that information is shared with other schools at the point of transition through agreed protocols. The government guidance for schools on safeguarding children and safer recruitment in education (DfES 2006) offers useful frameworks for anyone working in an educational setting who needs to respond to concerns or worries about an abusing child.

Managing with your own emotional needs

Every school has explicit guidance so that all staff know the appropriate action to take, with clear processes and procedures to follow if teachers have concerns about a child being abused. However, there is rarely any mention of the need for support for staff in dealing with the sometimes deep emotions aroused in this field of work. There is statutory guidance for all staff working in schools that have concerns for a child (DCSF 2010) but nothing for staff working in complex family situations. Teachers, unlike social workers, are not immersed as part of their daily work in contact with families where abuse and significant harm have taken place and so need more support when faced with these complex processes, highly charged situations and vulnerable people. It is important that inexperienced teachers feel able to approach more experienced colleagues for support and guidance.

Fear of being wrong can sometimes prevent professionals from speaking out about their concerns or worries, but other barriers may include uncertainty about cultural differences, perceived threats of violence, communication difficulties or anxiety about the possible outcomes for the child or the workers involved. Howe (2010) emphasized the need to support professionals in the tasks of processing and managing difficult feelings but anxieties can also arise over the need to keep up-to-date with policy, legislation and new initiatives. Action for Children (2008) identified over 400 different initiatives, funding streams, new legislation and changes in structures relating to children and families since 1987. The current guidance document, *Working Together* (DCSF 2010) has over 370 pages (Stafford et al. 2010) and it is difficult to imagine how much time it would take to memorize all this. As a new teacher it is important to prioritize becoming familiar with policy, legislation and initiatives relating to your particular school (see Chapter 1). Knowing where to access this information and who to talk to is useful so you can find help if you need it.

Conclusion

Safeguarding children can be a stressful, complex area of work and one where teachers are increasingly involved. It can raise questions about the teacher's own judgements as well as how well they can work with whole families and networks. Although statistics show a marked decline in the numbers of children identified as being in need, in reality, it is the methodology for counting these children that has changed. Thresholds for intervention by children's social care workers have been raised so that only the most serious cases are getting through. This trend is likely to continue with reduced resources available to local authorities. Teachers and other professionals will increasingly find themselves dealing with matters which they might previously have referred to other agencies, but now they are expected to work together with these agencies in unfamiliar processes. Keeping abreast of changes in legislation, policy and practice across their own and several other different agencies will continue to be challenging. Teachers, therefore, need training not only about how to respond to concerns or worries about a child within a multi-agency context, but also about how to develop coping strategies for the emotional impact of this kind of work with children and their families or carers. The impact can be personal as well as professional, with teachers questioning whether they were right to share their concerns and facing up to the consequences of sharing information with other agencies. Senior staff in the school need time and the emotional capacity to manage and contain the feelings of less experienced colleagues; fear has been identified as one of the most significant barriers in child protection work and teachers need somewhere safe to express their fears and anxieties, and receive the necessary support and guidance so that they can carry on working effectively.

Questions to Promote Thinking

1   What are the situations that may be frightening or stressful for you?
    Discuss strategies for dealing with difficult people or situations with a
    more experienced colleague.
2   Do you need any further training?
3   What could be in a curriculum that supports children in keeping
    themselves safe?
4   Do children discuss safe choices in the class?

References and suggested further reading

Action for Children (2008) *As Long as it Takes: A New Politics for Children*. Available online at: http://www.actionforchildren.org.uk/content/372/As-long-as-it-takes (accessed 1 February 2011).
Bronfenbrenner, U. (1979) *The Ecology of Human Development*. Cambridge, MA: Harvard University Press.
CWDC (Children's Workforce Development Council) (2010) *Early Identification, Assessment of Needs and Intervention: The Common Assessment Framework for Children and Young People: A Guide for Practitioners*. Leeds: CWDC.
DCSF (Department for Children, Schools and Families) (2008) *Information Sharing; Guidance for Practitioners and Managers*. Available online at: http://www.teachernet.gov.uk/_doc/13023/isgpm.pdf (accessed 1 February 2011).
DCSF (2009) *Statutory Guidance on Children Who Run Away and Go Missing from Home or Care*. Available online at: http://www.education.gov.uk/consultations/downloadableDocs/Runaway%20and%20Missing%20from%20Home%20and%20Care%20Guidance.pdf (accessed 1 February 2011).
DCSF (2010) *Working Together to Safeguard Children: A Guide to Inter-Agency Working to Safeguard and Promote the Welfare of Children*. Available online at: http://education.gov.uk/publications/standard/publicationDetail/Page1/DCSF-00305-2010 (accessed 1 February 2011).
DfE (Department for Education) (2010) *Referrals, Assessments and Children Who Were the Subject of a Child Protection Plan (2009–10 Children in Need Census, Provisional)*. Available online at: www.dcsf.gov.uk/rsgateway/DB/STR/d000959/index.shtml (accessed 6 February 2011).
DfE (2011) *The Munro Review of Child Protection: Interim Report, The Child's Journey*. Available online at: http://www.education.gov.uk/munroreview/downloads/Munrointerimreport.pdf (accessed 6 February 2011).
DfES (2006) *Safeguarding Children and Safer Recruitment in Education*. London: DfES.
Fawcett, M. (2009) *Learning Through Child Observation*, 2nd edn. London: Jessica Kingsley.
Gilligan, P. with Manby, M. (2008) The Common Assessment Framework: does the reality match the rhetoric? *Child and Family Social Work*, 13: 177–87.
Home Office (2004) *The Bichard Inquiry Report*. Available online at: www.bichardinquiry.org.uk/10663/report.pdf (accessed 1 February 2011).
Howe, D. (2010) The safety of children and the parent-worker relationship in cases of child abuse and neglect, *Child Abuse Review*, 19: 330–41.

Hughes, L. and Owen, H. (2009) *Good Practice in Safeguarding Children.* London: Jessica Kingsley.

Jack, G. and Gill, O. (2010) The role of communities in safeguarding children and young people, *Child Abuse Review*, 19: 82–96.

Munro, E. (2007) *Child Protection.* London: Sage.

NFER (National Foundation for Educational Research) (2010) *Teachers Have Their Say on How Well the Common Assessment Framework Works in Their School.* Slough: NFER.

NSPCC (National Society for the Prevention of Cruelty to Children) (2007) *Children in Need: Key Child Protection Statistics.* Available online at: www.nspcc.org.uk/Inform/research/statistics/children_in_need_statistics_wda48735.html (accessed 1 February 2011).

Parton, N. (2006) *Safeguarding Childhood: Early Intervention and Surveillance in a Late Modern Society.* Basingstoke: Palgrave Macmillan.

Plymouth City Council, Safeguarding Children Board (2009). Available online at: www.plymouth.gov.uk/localsafeguardingchildrenboard/littletednurseryreview (accessed 20 November 2010).

Smith, G. (2008) *The Protectors' Handbook. Reducing the Risk of Child Sexual Abuse and Helping Children Recover.* London: British Association for Adopting and Fostering.

Stafford, A., Vincent, S. and Parton, N. (2010) *Child Protection Reform across in UK: Protecting Children and Young People.* Edinburgh: Dunedin Academic Press.

PART 2

Getting organized

5

JANET MOYLES
Planning for learning – children and teachers

Summary

The curriculum is an overview of what a government decides should be taught during a term or year and is open to continuous change. It is the teacher's job to translate the designated curriculum into learning activities for the children and this is where planning comes in: it is a tool for implementing a curriculum appropriate to all the children in a class in line with the school's requirements and policies. Planning should be flexible so as to account for all styles of learning and the interests of children and teacher. Although time-consuming, written planning is eminently worthwhile: it requires reflection on what is needed and achieved and the development of a suitable pedagogy to put plans into actions.

Cameo 1

(Response from a newly qualified teacher when asked by students what had been her most successful strategy for dealing with Key Stage 2 children's learning.)

Planning lessons thoroughly in writing over the day, week and half-term. This gave me the confidence to know where I was heading. It also meant I could let the children in on what they're supposed to learn and that made it all much easier. I could give the children some information to start with and then add details later in the lesson – otherwise they would have got swamped and switched off.

> **Cameo 2**
>
> Deena, a student teacher working with a class of 5-year-olds, is dreading today's feedback session. Yesterday, the children all shouted out at once and the whole thing ended in disarray. Worse still, the teacher had tried to be nice to her and tell her that everyone has 'failures' and it was 'not too bad'. The trouble is that she can't think of any other way to plan the end of lesson feedback. To save a bit of time, Deena uses history as the focus of the literacy work and has been relieved to see that this appears to have worked well and the children have enjoyed describing, drawing and labelling the artefacts. Now comes the plenary and three pairs of children are given the opportunity to explain what they did. Deena notices that the second of the pairs treats the descriptive task rather like a quiz and the children give the rest of the class clues like 'I'm thinking of a word that begins with B' and 'The word sounds like red and you go to sleep in it'. All the children are entranced by this presentation and the feedback session goes smoothly. Deena uses this in her plans in future but keeps an eye open for other useful feedback strategies.

Introduction

It may seem that the legislated curricula – the National Curriculum and the Early Years Foundation Stage – determine all early years and primary children's learning and our teaching in the Foundation and Key Stages. In reality, the curriculum is really an overview of what the government decides should be taught in general during a term or year and is open to continuous change, as at present. It is the teacher's job to translate the designated curriculum into learning activities for any particular children in a class, bearing in mind what they already know and can do. We need also to bear in mind the *Every Child Matters* agenda (DfES 2003), given that this covers the overall principles underlying early years and primary education.

Medium- to short-term written plans which break down what it is possible to cover in a week or two and then daily (Woodward 2001) are the key to successful planning. These are the nuts and bolts of teaching and learning and hold together the relationship between what is taught, what is learned and the designated curriculum. They build on what has gone before and allow teachers and other practitioners to link the assessment of aspects of learning with the next set of teaching and learning experiences.

Primary and early years teachers spend a great deal of time on planning so it's worthwhile getting it 'right': that means ensuring that learning for children is 'authentic' (Burke 2009). Although time-consuming, written planning is eminently worthwhile for the teacher and children (see cameo 1): it means that we think through clearly what is needed and correlate our own and the children's interests and dispositions to the overall curriculum. As we saw in cameo 2, all planning should be flexible so that new ideas can be absorbed and used when something triggers a useful change –

often something contributed by the children themselves. But as Woodward (2001: 1) suggests, '[P]lans are just plans. They're not legally binding. We don't have to stick to them come hell or high water. They are there to help us shape the space, time and learning.' Such plans should also enable us to consider children's emotional and social development, now known to be vital to children's learning (Goleman 2006).

Primary teachers usually plan the programme of learning experiences (or lessons) with three specific things in mind:

- children's existing (individual and collective) knowledge, children's understanding of their own learning (metacognition), children's interests (often specific to the age group), and children's emotional responses to learning;
- curriculum intentions (the legislated curriculum, EYFS, schools' guidelines and things that have meaning for children);
- the teacher's own interests, strengths, motivations and professional responsibilities.

Each operates to both support and yet equally constrain the others. For example, whatever the teacher's curriculum intentions, the children often have their own agenda (as cameo 2 shows) and making as good a match as possible between them is a crucial yet challenging planning feat. It involves teachers in the following:

- having a good knowledge of a particular class of children as well as an understanding of children's development (including cognitive/metacognitive learning as discussed in Chapter 2 in this volume, and Dean 2005);
- detailed and thoughtful planning and implementation of children's learning experiences based on knowledge of individuals and curriculum (Kerry 2010);
- undertaking interpretation and analysis of children's experiences and responses and evaluating success criteria, often occurring through observation and discussion with children (see Chapter 6).

These three areas are the focus of this chapter and they are approached from the practical angle of offering a range of different kinds of thinking about curriculum and cross-curricular planning. First, we need to clarify what is meant by 'curriculum'.

What is the curriculum?

Very broadly, it could be said that the curriculum is everything the child experiences in the context of schooling which is intended to foster learning. But 'everything' is a very tall order and clearly there is a wealth of knowledge in the world which it would be impossible to transmit to every child everywhere. The school curriculum tends to operate first on thinking about subjects, such as English, science, geography, technology, art and the rest, and then within these certain concepts are apparent, e.g. form and structure, grammar, change, and so on. The 'subject' curriculum, therefore, is only a part of a broader overall integrated curriculum intended to ensure that children are required to think about and understand some of the major influences we experience and have experienced in the everyday world and have the skills to achieve.

Schools also have a 'hidden' curriculum, which centres around those aspects which children and teachers cultivate within their more informal relationships (see Chapter 3) but which contribute to the general ethos of the school and through which incidental learning often occurs, for example, children learning games from each other in the playground (Bishop and Curtis 2001) and learning in the socio-cultural context (Brooker 2002).

Curriculum processes should involve the children in many learning experiences of which knowing, thinking, doing, communicating and remembering are some main features. We know that any curriculum 'works' when, as Bennett et al. (1984) suggest, children can give evidence that they are:

- acquiring new knowledge and skills;
- using their existing knowledge and skills in different contexts;
- recognizing and solving problems;
- practising what they know;
- revising and replaying what they know in order to remember it.

What we attempt to do as teachers is to ensure, through our planning, that all of these processes are engaged in by children during most of the school day *in balanced proportions*. This will be achieved through planning experiences to develop particular skills, e.g. around individual subjects such as science, around pre-determined structures like those within the National Strategies or around 'themes', that is topics which are likely to interest the children, epitomized for under-7s by the Reggio Emilia system (see Rinaldi 2006). The balance comes through ensuring, for example, that children do not spend all day practising something they can already do, which is often the case with activities like worksheets – investigating a problem will be a better way of exploring a concept. Bennett et al.'s 5-point list is a very useful checklist for examining a day's or week's plans in relation to the quality of children's learning experiences. To this must be added our knowledge of each child's emotional learning – how they feel about themselves as learners in the context of this class (see Chapter 8).

Planning for learning

In some schools, planning is undertaken strictly in relation to the subject being taught, something which tends to happen most in the final two years of KS2. In other settings, particularly Foundation Stage settings, a number of subjects or areas of learning can be incorporated into 'themes', such as 'Weather', 'Travel Agents' or 'Light'. With activities planned in this way, close attention needs to be paid to ensuring that children understand fully the key concepts involved and can apply their understanding to new situations. Weather, for example, offers a range of options for very practical experiences, such as going out in cold, windy or wet weather, measuring wind speed/ direction, plotting graphs of weather over a period of time. But, remember, you are accountable for what they have *learned*, not just what they have experienced!

Of course, there is the danger that ten or so curriculum subjects, and general curriculum aspects such as citizenship, personal/social education and assessment procedures, will mean that the children's understanding will be shallow and superficial as we rush them and ourselves into the next focus (Laurie 2010). This only empha-sizes the need for medium- and short-term planning to be clear and realistic with consideration of the key concepts which need to be taught and learned (Kenyon 2004).

There are a few 'golden rules' for planning medium- and short-term curriculum experiences whatever the basis of the planning:

1   Start with something from which children can have an immediate experience – something to DO. (Torches and a darkened area of the room, or a 'Colour Walk'[1] around the local area could lead into much useful science teaching with older children and coverage of knowledge and understanding of the world with younger children.)

2   Children must be given opportunities to offer their suggestions to the planning and success criteria – it gives them some responsibility and ownership from the outset and the teacher has the security of knowing that learning experiences will be within the children's interests and current capabilities. For example, knowing that your quiz approach to the feedback session has been taken up by the teacher (cameo 2) will both motivate the children and enhance their self-esteem. It makes teaching and learning a suitably two-way process.

3   Relate the activities to children's lives and prior experiences. It is well known that children learn from a basis of things which have meaning to them and make 'human sense' (Donaldson 1992): we might call this 'authentic' teaching and learning. Teaching about the Aztecs or Ancient Egypt will require a great deal of work *from the teacher*, yet who is it who is supposed to be learning? At the very least, children need to access relevant sites on the internet, see plenty of pictures or DVDs of people and places, handle artefacts and have drama/role play oppor-tunities (Kitson 2010). These are not frills but key ingredients to deeper learning.

4   Include within your curriculum plans:
    (a)   content – subject/themes and wider curriculum, including reference to attainment and success criteria;
    (b)   skills and processes children should use and develop (and cross-curricular links);
    (c)   the main concepts to be covered;
    (d)   timings, what will happen when;
    (e)   responsibilities: who is responsible for what/when, including the children;
    (f)   resources, practical and human;
    (g)   points at which assessment will be undertaken and how, e.g. observation;
    (h)   assessment procedures/practices;
    (i)   health and safety considerations;
    (j)   analysis and evaluation
    (see also Butt 2003: 6/7, for other detailed ideas).

There are many examples online of different kinds of planning and planning sheets – see web-based sources and resources detailed at the end of the chapter.

Planning may be undertaken comprehensively on one large sheet (as in the Leeds University exemplar – see web sources), or different smaller plans showing how subjects or concepts integrate with each other. One example of this would be something like 'time' which is integral to history, mathematics, geography and the science curriculum.

5   Pin weekly and daily plans on the wall – this constant reminder to children and others who enter the classroom, often prompts the appearance of relevant books, websites, pictures, objects, and so on. It allows children the opportunity for prediction and gives an indication of what they are intended to learn and how success will be evaluated.

6   Try to introduce the focus of any forthcoming plans at the end of a week, then spend time talking over the potential learning with the children. Children may well use the weekend to seek out useful books or internet resources or talk it over with adults and older siblings. It is also your starting point for what children already know and can save a lot of unnecessary time and planning in teaching aspects which are already within the children's existing understanding but which need expansion and extension.

7   Involve the children in constantly *reviewing* and evaluating progress: what they have learned and what more there is to do and understand in the time available. This not only ensures everyone remains focused but means that planning each day's activities is done on the basis of what children already know. (But do make sure they don't end up feeling that they've 'done' the Aztecs or the Victorians – as one child said to me at the end of a topic – and that there is nothing more to learn!)

8   Ensure that plenty of opportunity is given for feedback (see Smidt 2005): by this is meant the chance for children to feed back to the teacher and other children what they have learned (as in a plenary session) but also for the teacher to feed back his/her impressions of the children's learning and approaches to learning. Feedback should also refer back to the objectives and learning intentions of the session.

9   Allow children with specific interests to follow these within the planned work and mark these on your overall plan. This is particularly important where some children's interest may be waning and personal motivation is required. Remember, too, that children are often 'experts' just as much as the teacher and other adults (especially about technologies!): they, too, should be allowed to 'shine'.

Support staff and specialist teaching

Needless to say, it is important to use the human resources available to support your teaching. Teaching Assistants (TAs), some with specialized knowledge, have burgeoned in our primary schools in the past few years (see Blatchford et al. 2009; Foulkes and Wallis 2010) and are a most valuable contribution to classroom life. They should be involved closely in planning so that they can make a 'seamless' contribution.

Some schools are now operating specialist teaching time, when the school's subject specialists work with different classes or groups of children. Many primary schools operate practices such as 'setting' for maths, English or science, which is a way of ensuring that children of different abilities receive teaching focused on their specific needs. However, many primary schools still operate a one-teacher/one-class system with teachers being required to teach all subjects to all abilities. Many TAs have complementary skills which can be well utilized in this context.

Detailed planning and implementation

The emphasis on children 'doing' and playing, is particularly vital with birth–7-year olds and for older children should only gradually be replaced by more 'formal' learning approaches (see Moyles 2010a).

Primary children who occupy too much time being 'instructed' or working at pencil and paper activities will soon get bored and may, at best, simply not learn and, at worst, may generate discipline problems, especially boys (Boys' Development Agency 2010). All children presented with too much too soon may be so busy exploring new materials that the planned learning intentions are lost and the children's dispositions to learning and self-confidence are affected adversely. Worksheet activities and continual exposition rarely enable children to be engaged actively in their own learning processes.

Long-term plans offer information about subjects or themes and include the concepts, processes and skills we are aiming for eventually, but the heart of day-to-day teaching is to undertake some quite detailed (yet flexible) planning of each particular learning experience involving the children. The chart shown in Figure 5.1 is one found helpful by beginner teachers to structure their activities, giving, as it does, opportunity to comment on both the children's activities and also on what the teacher or other adults will be doing. Students often need to recognize that children *can* learn without a continual adult presence but that if you do want to work with individuals or groups this must be incorporated into the planning. As indicated in the Bennett et al. model earlier, experiences will need different levels of teacher attention:

- teacher-intensive – when children are undertaking new learning or the teacher is assessing existing learning;
- teacher/adult in attendance – when children are engaged in applying knowledge and may need occasional teacher support;
- teacher/adult monitoring – when children are practising skills and knowledge in relatively familiar situations requiring little teacher involvement;
- teacher/adult available – when children are engaged in absorbing their own mastery and may need the teacher to tell or show an outcome at some stage.

The planning chart also ensures that each activity will need a specific introduction, something which develops it further, and a conclusion. The evaluation gives the basis for making decisions as to who has learned what and what is needed for progression to the next stage.

Session	Date	Time	Curriculum/EYFS area
Plan	*Comment*		
Aim(s)			
Objectives			
Curriculum links			
Resources			

Learning Experience Structure	Timing	Adult activity	Children's activity
Introduction			
Development			
Conclusion			
Feedback			

(Continue evaluation overleaf)

Figure 5.1 Structuring children's learning experiences

Remember with such planning charts that your AIMS are related to things you wish to achieve in the *slightly longer term*, for example, 'Children should enjoy science and learn a number of key concepts.' In contrast, OBJECTIVES are *short-term* related to what the children should have learned and done by the end of that experience or series of experiences – 'Children should be able to use their knowledge of light in order to explain how the beam falls on an object.'

Ready to teach?

The final level of planning is how you and the children are actually going to work together in the learning context. There are several phases in this interaction, summed up under the following headings and questions:

1   ENTERING STRATEGY
    What will be your starting point(s)? Introduction?

2   EXPLORATION MODE
    What exploration will the children undertake? What materials/resources will be available? How/by whom will they be set up?

3   CONTENT
    This will be as in your planning, but how will the children know what they are intended to learn as well as to do?

4   OWNERSHIP AND RESPONSIBILITY
    What level of ownership will the children have? What responsibilities? How will the children be expected to evaluate their own learning? How will these aspects be conveyed?

5   TEACHING STRATEGIES
    What will your role be? What will the role of TAs be? How will you and your TA interact/intervene in the activities and sustain/extend them? Will there be any peer-tutoring – child/child(ren)?

6   EVALUATION AND ANALYSIS
    How/when/who will you observe to see what children were learning in relation to concepts covered and the objectives set? Will other adults be involved in observation and recording? Who? When during the activities?

7   REFLECTION/REVIEW/FEEDBACK MODE
    What opportunities will you provide for children to reflect on their learning and be part of its feedback/evaluation/analysis?

8   JUSTIFICATION
    What quality and standard of outcomes will you expect? What success criteria are you using? How will the value of these be communicated to others (e.g. through display, website, records)?

It is necessary to consider different kinds of organizational strategies, for example, whether you introduce something to the whole class, give tasks to groups or pairs, or allow children free choice to explore materials for themselves. You and the children need also to reflect continually and effectively on what you did and the success or otherwise of the outcomes (see Moyles 2010b).

Interpreting, analysing and evaluating children's experiences

What we are essentially assessing is to what extent the children (and we as teachers) have been able to do the following:

- reach the objectives set in planning;
- develop appropriate learning dispositions, attitudes and opinions;
- reach high standards and offer quality outcomes;
- deal with the different styles and rates at which children learn;
- find out about children's dispositions, emotional responses, strengths and weaknesses;
- understand what learning should take place next for children to progress;
- know what experiences should now be provided or repeated and what differentiated learning activities are needed for individuals or groups of children.

These are then evaluated against longer-term aims to see what adjustments are required in planning. This process involves much interpretation of evidence and collection of data for written evaluations and records. Be careful that interpretations are as value-free and objective as possible and involve the children and, sometimes, their parents/carers.

Finding out about children's learning

Another main strategy for finding out about children's learning has to be through talking to them or getting them to write down what they did and what they think they learned. However, in analysing, interpreting and evaluating learning capabilities in this way, we need to remember that children's ability to understand is not always matched in their written or oral performance. Children who can *give* an extensive oral explanation of an exciting science experiment often then write 'I put it in the cup and it disappeared. the end' [*sic*]. This happens right across the primary school particularly where fine motor development is slow and a child actually finds writing difficult if not actually physically painful. Just those very processes of *active learning* discussed above, are nearly always more important to primary children than writing about tasks. After all, would you always want to write about what you had done, or would you rather move on to the next exciting learning journey?

Finding other ways of analysing and evaluating what children know is vital, not least through planning classroom activities in such a way that you have time to *observe and record* (see Edgington 2004). It is in active situations that children frequently illustrate advanced knowledge. For example, I well remember a boy who stood on the edge of a group of children attempting in a design technology lesson to make a pulley out of various items of 'found' materials. He chose to watch, and flatly refused to explain his reticence to become involved. After half-an-hour the group had still not managed to produce a pulley. Almost at the end of the session, the boy walked up to the table, picked up three or four items and rapidly and ingeniously made a working pulley. It would have been easy to have thought of him as dull, lazy, insecure, sullen or downright obstinate. This is just one example of how we must be sensitive to the different ways in which pupils learn and perform (Hayes 2004).

Other ways in which children can demonstrate learning

As well as oral and written language outcomes, children could be expected to show different aspects of their learning in several other ways, for example:

- drawings;
- poems (and other different forms of writing, e.g. acrostics);
- diagrams and charts;
- mind maps (see Buzan 2009);
- composing lists;
- digital photographs, with or without children's captions;
- making booklets about different activities – 'This is what we learned when we worked with the sand . . .'; 'This is what we found out about Ancient Egyptians';
- explaining to other children what to do (peer learning and teaching);
- web-based communications, e.g. blogs;
- digital camera/video/audio recordings of activities;
- undertaking drama/role play;
- doing demonstrations for others.

However assessment is undertaken, you need to ensure that children are given opportunities to do the following:

- make their own ideas explicit: starting from what children know is vital in on-going planning (see Fisher 2007);
- produce an end result in different ways and with several alternative solutions. Investigations and problem-solving activities allow children to show physically what they 'know'.
- explore ideas with peers – it is much easier to argue your points with peers than with adults particularly as children get older;
- actively question their own thinking and undertake explorations in order to learn about their own misconceptions;
- challenge their own outcomes through open-ended questioning 'What would happen if . . .?'
- be part of situations in which they need to generalize in order to use and develop concepts;

- observe rather than simply look at objects and artefacts and raise questions. Help children to detect relevant similarities as well as differences.

- achieve by setting goals with and for children which are attainable with just the right amount of effort – this means knowing individual children's capabilities well – and sharing them what they are intended to learn;

- explore materials before expecting them to do something specific with them (Drake 2005);

- apply their knowledge in a situation where they can succeed;

- learn and use the appropriate vocabulary for each topic so that they have the means to explain their activities to you;

- gather all the information they need in order to fulfil the demands of the activity. We don't have to wait for children to re-invent the wheel every time but, having been told, children *must* be allowed to 'prove' whatever the concept is for themselves);

- be part of the planning process;

- be praised genuinely for achieving real learning and being able to reflect on their successes and challenges.

The teacher's role

Teachers should give themselves plenty of opportunity for interpreting, analysing and assessing what their role has been in the children's learning and reflecting on it (Moyles 2010b). The following questions will act as a conclusion to this chapter and also serve as a reminder of the importance of planning for children's learning on a daily, weekly and termly basis.

Questions to Promote Thinking

1 How positive or otherwise do you feel about the curriculum activities you provide for children's learning?

2 In what ways do your teaching and learning appear successful/challenging to you?

3 What do you learn – about planning, curriculum, children, developing a quality learning environment?

4 How would you describe the atmosphere you generate in the classroom – pleasant, adventurous, task-oriented, positive ...?

5 Are you more involved with the children in relation to supervision of *activities* or the enriching/sustaining their *learning* as individuals, in groups, as a class?

6 Are your teaching strategies congruent with the objectives you set? Do you offer a structured sequence of experiences?

7 Do you offer a good balance between teacher-oriented and child-initiated learning experiences?

8 Are your interactions with children 'professional' and do you give and receive appropriate feedback?

9 How well do you communicate with children? Do you pace your talk appropriately and are your instructions (verbal and non-verbal) clear?

10 How well are you able to integrate children with specific learning or physical needs within your overall planning and the learning environment you create (see Chapter 8)?

11 Do you use a variety of teaching styles and strategies – exposition, different groupings, discussion, play and active learning, practice tasks, problem-solving, investigations . . .?

12 Have you marked, analysed and diagnosed children's learning errors and noted those who need support?

13 Have you made appropriate observations and evaluations of children's learning?

14 Would you have enjoyed the activities if you had been one of the children?

15 Have you discussed your progress with a mentor and noted points for professional development?

16 Have you enjoyed the experience of teaching – and learning?

17 What are you going to share with the parents/carers/other staff in your records?

18 What have *you* learned – about planning for children's learning?

Note

1 A 'Colour Walk' is very useful for all ages of children in helping support their observational and discernment skills. Use paint colour strips or pieces of different colour wools, stick them on cards and let children find a matching colour on their walk. For Foundation Stage children, the colours should be easily findable – for KS2 children, the colours can be more subtle and difficult to find.

Useful websites

Learning and Teaching Toolkit Personal Learning Planning, The Highland Council. Available online at: http://www.highland.gov.uk/learninghere/supportforschoolstaff/ltt/issuepapers/personallearningplanning.htm (accessed 24 October 2010).

Leeds University planning and questioning document. Available online at: www.education.leeds.ac.uk/current_students/files/408.doc (accessed 25 October 2010).

National Strategies: *Designing Opportunities for Learning (Planning)*. Available online at: http://nationalstrategies.standards.dcsf.gov.uk/node/18024 (accessed 25 October 2010).

School Zone: educational intelligence. Available online at: http://www.schoolzone.co.uk/webguide/index.asp?searchit=yes&engine=0&search=lesson+planning&subject=0&levelid=1&num=20 (accessed 25 October 2010).

Teachers TV: *Professional Skills – Planning with Pupils*. Available online at: www.teachers.tv/video/5441 (accessed 24 October 2010).

Teaching Ideas – *Planning and Assessment*. Available online at: http://www.teachingideas.co.uk/more/management/contents01planningassessment.htm (accessed 24 October 2010).

References and suggested further reading

Bennett, N., Desforge, G., Cockburn, A. and Wilkinson, B. (1984) *The Quality of Pupil Learning Experiences*. London: Lawrence Erlbaum.

Bishop, J. and Curtis, M. (2001) *Play Today in the Primary School Playground: Life, Learning and Creativity*. Buckingham: Open University Press.

Blatchford, P., Bassett, P., Brown, P., Martin, C., Russell, A. and Webster, R. (2009) *Deployment and Impact of Support Staff in Schools (DISS) Project*. Available online at: http://www.ioe.ac.uk/study/departments/phd/5619.html (accessed 24 October 2010).

Boys' Development Agency (2010) *Boys Going to School (A Brief Guide)*. Available online at: www.boysdevelopmentproject.org.uk (accessed 24 October 2010).

Brooker, L. (2002) *Starting School: Young Children Learning Cultures*. Buckingham: Open University Press.

Burke, K. (2009) *How to Assess Authentic Learning*. Thousand Oaks, CA: Sage.

Butt, G. (2003) *Lesson Planning*. London: Continuum.

Buzan, T. (2009) *The Mind Map Book: Unlock Your Creativity, Boost Your Memory, Change Your Life*. London: BBC Active.

Dean, J. (2005) *The Effective Primary School Classroom*. London: RoutledgeFalmer.

DfES (Department for Education and Skills) (2003) *Every Child Matters*, Green Paper. Nottingham: DfES.

Donaldson, M. (1992) *Human Minds: An Exploration*. Glasgow: Penguin.

Drake, J. (2005) *Planning Children's Play and Learning in the Foundation Stage*. London: David Fulton.

Edgington, M. (2004) *The Foundation Stage Teacher in Action: Teaching 3, 4 and 5 Year Olds*, 3rd edn. London: Sage.

Fisher, J. (2007) *Starting from the Child: Teaching and Learning from 3 to 8*, 3rd edn. Maidenhead: Open University Press.

Foulkes, P. and Wallis, J. (2010) Managing the contribution of support staff to cross-curricular learning, in T. Kerry (ed.) *Cross-Curricular Teaching in the Primary School: Planning and Facilitating Imaginative Lessons*. London: Routledge.

Goleman, D. (2006) *Emotional Intelligence*, 2nd edn. New York: Bantam Books.

Hayes, D. (2004) *Planning, Teaching and Class Management in Primary Schools*. London: David Fulton.

Kenyon, P. (2004) *Planning, Assessing and Record-Keeping*. Leamington Spa: Scholastic.

Kerry, T. (ed.) (2010) *Cross-Curricular Teaching in the Primary School: Planning and Facilitating Imaginative Lessons*. London: Routledge.

Kitson, N. (2010) Children's fantasy role play – why adults should join in, in J. Moyles (ed.) *The Excellence of Play*, 3rd edn. Maidenhead: Open University Press.

Laurie, J. (2010) Curriculum planning and preparation for cross-curricular teaching, in T. Kerry (ed.) *Cross-Curricular Teaching in the Primary School: Planning and Facilitating Imaginative Lessons*. London: Routledge.

Moyles, J. (ed.) (2010a) *The Excellence of Play*, 3rd edn. Maidenhead: Open University Press.

Moyles, J. (ed.) (2010b) *Thinking about Play: Developing a Reflective Approach*. Maidenhead: Open University Press.

Rinaldi, C. (2006) *In Dialogue with Reggio Emilia: Listening, Researching and Learning*, London: Routledge.

Smidt, S. (2005) *Observing, Assessing and Planning for Children in the Early Years*. London: Routledge.

Woodward, T. (2001) *Planning Lessons and Courses: Designing Sequences of Work for the Language Classroom*. Cambridge: Cambridge University Press.

6

RITA HEADINGTON
Assessment and accountability

Summary

This chapter is based on my experience of schools in England and the use of performance data/OfSTED for accountability. I explore reasons for the current assessment
practices in schools by looking at the development of National Curriculum assessment,
then consider the intrinsic links between assessment and accountability in relation to
taxpayers, education professionals, parents and children. We see that assessment *of*
learning has the potential to provide more information and greater transparency, while
assessment *for* learning centres on the quality of teaching and learning and the relationships between teachers and children. The challenge for teachers is to use assessment effectively and demonstrate accountability to a range of audiences.

Cameo 1

When she was at university Sarah had assessed children's work in the core
and some of the foundation subjects. During her final school experience, she'd
tracked the learning of the children in her class and developed case studies on a
few individuals. Assessment seemed to be quite straightforward.

But in her newly qualified teacher year, assessment felt different to Sarah.
It was real; she was making decisions based on her assessment judgements
that impacted directly on children's learning. Sarah felt apprehensive about
assessment until she realized that talking to other teachers about children's
learning at the half-termly 'levelling meetings' helped her to feel more confident
about the judgements she was making in the classroom.

She was amazed how much teachers knew about each of the children
and that the head and deputy seemed to know everything about every child in
the school! The children's records dated back to before their arrival at school,
with notes on home–school visits, and included details of sub-levelled teacher
assessments, interventions, outcomes and targets as well as annual progress
reports and 'official' communications between home and school. A few records
included Statements of Special Educational Need and Individual Education Plans,

and some had letters from health and social care and learning support services. She'd looked through the records when she started her job and was surprised to discover how many professionals had already been involved in some of the children's lives.

At the 'pupil progress meeting' teachers and teaching assistants shared their knowledge of the children; not just what they had learnt and the progress they'd made but how they learned best, any difficulties they had encountered and what their next targets should be. Sarah felt equally involved. She realized she had an important contribution to make, having observed the children in the classroom, marked their work and talked regularly to parents before and after school and at the mid-year consultation event. Sarah knew the children as real people and this made it much easier than she'd expected to get to grips with the school's assessment records that she'd originally seen as daunting colour-coded charts and graphs.

Cameo 2

It was touch and go for Ash at the end of June. Would the Key Stage 2 test results be returned to the school in time for the parents' consultation event next week? He knew they'd arrive too late in the term to make any difference to the children's learning, but the parents and children were itching to know what National Curriculum levels had been given.

Of course, as the Year 6 teacher, Ash would need to go through the papers to make sure all the questions had been marked accurately. He hadn't found any problems yet but felt it was important to check. Year 6 was always a huge investment of time and effort for everyone; with its half-termly mock-tests from September, the weekly 'SATs club' for the Level 3–4 and 4–5 borderlines from January, alongside the regular and detailed marking and moderation between teachers and target-setting activities with children. And now children, parents and teachers all waited anxiously for the results of May's National Curriculum tests to arrive through the post.

Cameo 3

The Woods Primary School staff breathed a collective sigh of relief as the last OfSTED inspector left the building. They knew the inspection would come out well but hints of the word 'outstanding' made all their efforts seem worthwhile.

The teaching observations had gone well. All the information requested had been in place. There were records of pupils' progress and evidence of consistency of judgement between teachers. The school staff knew where they were going and how they were going to get there. The children had proved to be the greatest of advocates for the teaching and learning that were taking place. They were involved in lessons, knew what they were learning and regularly worked with peers and teachers to identify their next steps.

The school's next step was to celebrate their achievement with the children, their parents and all the staff. 'Outstanding' would be finding its way into all their materials from now on!

Introduction

Assessment and accountability are intrinsically linked. Assessment is about measuring, or judging, what someone knows, understands and can do. Accountability is about being answerable to others and taking responsibility for one's actions. In its simplest terms, the information from assessment provides evidence for accountability.

Assessment is recognized as having four main purposes – diagnostic, formative, summative and evaluative (DES 1988). Each of these plays a part in accountability to different audiences. Children, parents (including guardians and carers) and professionals are concerned with the day-to-day aspects of learning identified through diagnostic and formative assessment. This includes making judgements about how well individual children are learning, the difficulties they may have, the next steps they should take and the support they will need. The government, taxpayers and the wider public are more concerned with the year-on-year aspects of learning identified through summative and evaluative assessment. Their interests focus on measurements through end of Key Stage test and school inspection results, and using these to determine value for money and the effective use of public funds in education.

Accountability is not new. Parents and education professionals inevitably show concern for the learning of individual children. Concern for the effective use of public funds stretches back to the origins of state-funded education and the Revised Code of 1862 (Lawson and Silver 1973). More than a hundred years later the Education Reform Act 1988 (ERA) led to the birth of the National Curriculum (NC) with its regular, systematic assessment of the core subjects at the end of the Key Stages. The 1988 ERA brought NC assessment to England and Wales; Scotland and Northern Ireland were not included in this (Maclure 1992). With devolution, Wales later brought in what Daugherty (2009) calls 'adaptations and divergence'. Shortly after this the Education (Schools) Act 1992 launched the Office for Standards in Education (OfSTED) which has the remit to 'regulate and inspect . . . education and skills for learners of all ages' (OfSTED 2010a). The outcomes of assessments and inspections have since provided the data by which teachers, schools, local authorities and the government can be held to account for the quality of teaching and learning in the state education sector.

The three cameos demonstrate different aspects of assessment and accountability which will be discussed within this chapter. In the first cameo, Sarah contributed to and used information about children's progress from a range of sources. The school's structure of record keeping and meetings enabled information about attainment and other aspects of children's learning to be shared and built upon to inform future teaching and learning.

In the second cameo, Ash's school acknowledged the pressure to meet end of Key Stage targets for the individual children and their parents and for the school and local authority as a whole. The additional support provided by Ash and his colleagues mirrored a widespread response to 'high stakes' testing and the publicly accessible Achievement and Attainment Tables (DfE 2010a).

In the third cameo, OfSTED inspectors witnessed the cohesion of Woods Primary School as it enabled individual children's learning. It was evident to them that progress was monitored closely by staff who worked together with the children towards common goals.

Assessment, accountability and the taxpayer

The UK Coalition government, in its 2010 White Paper on education, stated: 'It is vital that schools should be accountable to parents for how well pupils do, and how taxpayers' money is spent' (DfE 2010b: 12). The publication of assessment and inspection data has, for some time, been seen as a means of achieving public accountability; encouraging members of the general public to become involved with the educational provision to which their taxes contribute.

A wealth of performance data has been building since the early 1990s (for example, DfE 2010a; OfSTED 2010b). The data have been analysed to identify issues, explore trends and provide evidence for increasing provision in some areas and the reduction of funds in others. They have led to comparisons of children's attainment between schools, local authorities, national regions and across countries. They have provided governments with the mandate to make large-scale changes to education, whether or not this agrees with the recommendations of educational research.

As this powerful set of data is based on the summative, end of Key Stage tests undertaken by children at the ages of 7 and 11, in English, mathematics and, for a number of years in science, it is vital that the tests are both valid and reliable. In other words, the tests should measure what they are meant to measure – children's attainment across the subjects – and should be administered fairly and marked consistently.

When National Curriculum testing was introduced in England and Wales, there was much questioning of its validity. How could a test that sampled the subject on one day truly demonstrate children's abilities when the more frequent assessments made by teachers enabled a range of learning opportunities to be taken into account and provided coverage of the whole curriculum? But was the objectivity and rigour of tests more appropriate a basis for national and comparative statistics than the potentially subjective judgements made by teachers? The tug-of-war that developed between the validity of tests and teacher assessments was eventually resolved by recognizing the status of both, as different assessment instruments: one offered measurement, the other professional judgement. This anomaly needed to be explained to parents, particularly when there appeared to be a disparity between the two on a child's annual report.

Key Stage 1 tests provided some flexibility of approach, with the opportunity to spread formal testing across a month and mark papers within schools. Key Stage 2, on the other hand, operated a formal test system at set dates and times and with external marking of papers. Coupled with spot-checks by outside agencies to moderate the operation, the approach appeared to provide fair testing, enable consistency and deter cheating. But were the test outcomes completely reliable?

The very nature of formal written tests for young children is seen as unauthentic and stressful, with the potential to demotivate learners (Harlen 2006). To counter these inherent difficulties, a variety of pre-test practices developed across schools, according to their differing ideologies and available resources. This was most evident in Key Stage 2 where the test results were subject to publication. As the second cameo shows, Ash's school wanted to support its children by allowing them to rehearse test situations. Additional support was given to those whose work suggested they were close to the 'borderline' of the next level with the development of 'booster classes'. Mock tests were used in this and many other schools, actively encouraged by the Qualifications and Curriculum Authority (QCA), which provided optional test papers for all Key Stage 2 age groups. The QCA materials were used to familiarize children with tests and give teachers an indication of progress within the Key Stage to support their own judgements.

The 'high stakes' nature of the assessments at the end of Key Stage 2 had a narrowing effect and led to curriculum washback; in other words the tested subjects took precedence in the classroom. Researchers soon reported a bleak picture with transmission teaching (Harlen 2006: 16), superficial, rote learning (Black and Wiliam 1998) and an adverse affect on the quality of teacher–pupil interaction (Wyse et al. 2008: 2). As had happened with the Revised Code, teachers were found to be 'teaching to the test' (TES 2008), as not doing so would be detrimental to the school. This was identified by researchers and recognized by government (Wyse et al. 2008; DfE 2010b) and served to undermine the validity and reliability of the data produced.

Assessment, accountability and education professionals

The arrival of National Curriculum testing in the 1990s suggested a lack of trust in education professionals' judgements of children's learning, particularly for the short period of time when tests results over-ruled teacher assessment in reports to parents, rather than being reported in parallel. There was suspicion that teachers would give the benefit of the doubt when marking the work of children they knew, increasing test scores and being subjective in their judgements. It was considered that more objectivity would prevail when tests were marked externally, as the children would be unknown to the markers of their work and extensive cross-moderation could be employed (Kingdon 1995).

Teachers needed to build trust and make themselves professionally accountable by demonstrating their abilities to make objective, criteria-based judgements in relation to the curriculum. This could only come about through teachers' participation in moderation exercises within and across schools. Local authorities and schools launched staff development meetings to discuss examples of children's work and create portfolios of 'levelled' work in the core subjects, drawing upon materials developed nationally to exemplify standards (QCDA 2010a). Through these discussions teachers became more conversant with the curriculum and more adept at making objective judgements. The meetings supported new teachers such as Sarah from the first cameo and those of greater experience. They rebuilt teachers' reputations for making accurate judgements of children's levels of attainment and enhanced their professional confidence.

Increased reliability of teacher judgements benefitted the quality of data in schools' assessment records and enabled more purposeful tracking of individual children and groups of learners. Information technology made the detailed interrogation of data more achievable. When used alongside comparative statistics from the national assessments (see DfE 2010a, for examples of available comparative data), school senior management teams were able to interrogate data at macro and micro levels to determine the needs of cohorts, specific groups and individual children and use this to determine the effective deployment of staff and resources.

Professional accountability was strengthened by increased confidence in teacher judgements that built a community of trust and teamwork between schools. It was vital that receiving schools were able to build upon the work already done 'to promote continuity and coherence', one of the four main purposes of the National Curriculum (QCDA 2010b). Indeed, data transfer at pupils' transition to different schools demanded reliable information and professional trust.

Similarly, professional accountability between schools and other agencies has developed through education professionals' involvement in multi-agency teamwork to improve children's well-being (see also Chapter 23). This took on a legal dimension in the wake of the Victoria Climbié case, where a lack of communication led to devastating consequences. Schools were identified as key strategic partners within the multi-agency context (DfES 2003) and teachers' legal responsibility was to work with other professionals, to share knowledge and responsibility and to integrate services to enable the safeguarding of children. Shared knowledge benefits children's well-being and is an important aspect of life in school where, as Sarah in the first cameo found, pupil progress meetings have the potential to go beyond consideration of the curriculum attainment of individuals defined by *Assessing Pupils' Progress* (DfE 2010c), to the regular review of every child's progress and welfare.

OfSTED inspections provided a further level of professional accountability through an overview of policy and practice. The *Framework for the Inspection of Schools* stated that:

> Under Section 5 of *The Education Act* 2005, schools are required to be inspected at prescribed intervals and inspectors must report on:
>
> - the quality of the education provided in the school
> - how far the education meets the needs of the range of pupils at the school
> - the educational standards achieved in the school
> - the quality of the leadership in and management of the school, including whether the financial resources made available to the school are managed effectively
> - the spiritual, moral, social and cultural development of the pupils at the school
> - the contribution made by the school to the well-being of those pupils
> - the contribution made by the school to community cohesion.
>
> (OfSTED 2010c: 7)

The Section 5 short inspections used Self-Evaluation Forms (SEFs) and drew on the data from national tests, to keep teachers 'on their toes' (Drake 2008: 18). All OfSTED reports on schools are published, giving interested parties the opportunity to learn about the quality of provision identified by the team of inspectors at a given point. There has been much criticism of the OfSTED approach (de Waal 2008) which has tended to measure the measurable by focusing on statistical data while seemingly ignoring the lived experiences of those within the school. In the third cameo, the teachers at Woods Primary School were delighted that this had changed. The inspectors examined performance data and observed teaching, but they also asked children to talk about their experiences of teaching and learning.

The data from multiple OfSTED inspection reports have been collated at national level to provide further comparative statistics and develop thematic reports on specific issues, such as reading (OfSTED 2010d). This information is then distributed to schools to inform practice. In essence, inspections have aimed to provide a vehicle for education professionals to be accountable to, and learn from, each other.

Assessment, accountability, parents and children

The most profound aspect of assessment and accountability remains in the teacher's relationship with parents and children. For primary school teachers, the moral imperative to be accountable for pupil progress by assessing the social, emotional and cognitive needs of individual learners, far outweighs the legal necessity to account for their practices through national testing (GTC 2009: 12).

Fundamental to this is the partnership that teachers develop with parents – the children's primary educators – to build a holistic learning experience, where home and school work in unison. Most schools seek to break down pre-conceived barriers by engaging with parents towards a common goal. It is not unusual for teachers to arrange home-visits on children's entry to school, for parents to work in classrooms supporting children's learning as volunteers or as paid and trained teaching assistants, for parents to attend meetings to learn more about curriculum initiatives, or for them to support their children's reading or homework activities outside school hours.

Teachers are legally accountable to parents too (Directgov 2010) and transparency is essential. Teachers must write an annual report on each child, with details of national assessment results and comparative data at the end of each Key Stage. Parents must be given an opportunity for consultation with the teacher and they have the right to see their child's educational record. Schools have a duty to consult with parents when an application for a statement of special needs is made for an individual child. They are also required to produce a Home–School Agreement and their governing bodies must provide parents with an Annual Governors' Report, which includes comparative data from the national tests.

For their part, parents have a legal responsibility to ensure their child receives an education. They are encouraged, but not required by law, to take part in parent–teacher consultations and the more formal aspects of the school's life such as the governing body and the views of parents and pupils are sought by OfSTED during school inspections.

The relationship between teachers and children forms the starting point for all dimensions of assessment and accountability. National tests seek to measure what children know and understand – they are an assessment *of* learning. The results of the tests provide a summary of children's learning at a given point but teachers, working collaboratively with children, use day-to-day assessment to judge and improve the quality of learning. They use assessment *for* learning. It is through this approach that teachers engage children in the learning process and provide them with the tools to become autonomous learners.

Black and Wiliams' (1998) extensive literature review highlighted the benefits of formative assessment through peer- and self-assessment and the role of transparency in this process. To enable transparency and learning, teachers should share or develop learning objectives and success criteria with children, use lessons' plenaries to review and consolidate learning, and work with them to set individual and group targets in relation to the curriculum and children's previous, personal performance (Clarke 2001). Involving children actively in the learning process is beneficial to all and, as the Woods Primary School OfSTED inspection showed, if children are aware of their learning and have ownership of their next steps, they are more likely to benefit from the learning experience and be able to discuss the experience with confidence.

Conclusion

Accountability in education has moral, legal and financial dimensions (Headington 2003) and the data that form its basis rest, for the most part, on the outcomes of end of Key Stage tests and OfSTED inspections. The wealth of data made available through these two sources may be providing a level of transparency, through sampling teaching and learning in schools, but does it give a full and accurate account?

Being accountable – being answerable to others and taking responsibility for one's actions – suggests the need for building trust. The relationships that teachers have with children, their parents and other professionals serve to instil trust. All parties work together to provide children with effective learning experiences, and the relationships that develop through this shared goal are central to the moral dimension of accountability. Building the trust of those who are distanced from this, and whose focus is on the financial and legal dimensions of accountability, is more problematic for teachers who remain concerned that tests and inspections do not reflect the quality of teaching and learning in schools.

Prompted by this concern, many schools across the country developed strategies designed to improve the outcomes of tests and inspections. The detrimental aspects of these strategies, and particularly their wash-back on to teaching and learning, have long been recognized by research. Other schools maintained their belief that the quality of teaching and learning would shine through without employing additional strategies. They valued assessment *for* learning and refused to be swayed by an over-emphasis on testing and the assessment *of* learning.

It is gratifying that the government has at last acknowledged the impact that accountability has had on schools (DfE 2010b), though it is unlikely that testing and inspection will be removed in the foreseeable future. The challenge for teachers continues to be in using assessment at a range of levels to demonstrate accountability to many, while upholding the trusting relationship they develop with children that is so fundamental to the quality of teaching and learning.

Questions to Promote Thinking

1   Is formalized national assessment necessary?
2   Would it be possible for education professionals to demonstrate accountability without national assessment?
3   Should parents be more accountable to teachers?
4   Are children really involved in decisions about the learning process?

References and suggested further reading

Black, P. and Wiliam, D. (1998) *Inside the Black Box*. London: King's College.

Clarke, S. (2001) *Unlocking Formative Assessment*. London: Hodder and Stoughton.

Daugherty, R. (2009) National Curriculum assessment in Wales: adaptations and divergence, *Educational Research*, 51(2): 247–50.

DES (Department of Education and Science) (1988) *National Curriculum Task Group on Assessment and Testing: A Report*. London: DES.

de Waal, A. (ed.) (2008) *Inspecting the Inspectorate: OfSTED Under Scrutiny*. London: Civitas.

DfE (Department for Education) (2010a) *Achievement and Attainment Tables: Primary Schools Key Stage 2*. Available online at: http://www.education.gov.uk/performancetables/ primary_09.shtml (accessed 27 October 2010).

DfE (2010b) *The Importance of Education: The Schools White Paper 2010*. London: HMSO.

DfE (2010c) *Assessing Pupils' Progress*. Available online at: http://nationalstrategies.standards.dcsf. gov.uk/primary/assessment/assessingpupilsprogressapp (accessed 28 November 2010).

DfES (Department for Education and Skills) (2003) *Every Child Matters: Change for Children in Schools*. Nottingham: DfES.

Directgov (2010) *Parental Rights in Education*. Available online at: http://www.direct.gov.uk/en/ Parents/ParentsRights/DG_4002948 (accessed 27 October 2010).

Drake, S. (2008) Inspection today, in A. de Waal (ed.) *Inspecting the Inspectorate: OfSTED Under Scrutiny*. London: Civitas.

GTC (General Teaching Council) (2009) *General Teaching Council for England Survey of Teachers 2009: TNS Report*. Available online at: http://www.gtce.org.uk/documents/ publicationpdfs/survey09tns_rpt (accessed 28 November 2010).

Harlen, W. (2006) The role of assessment in developing motivation for learning, in J. Gardner (ed.) *Assessment and Learning*. London: Sage.

Harlen, W. (2007) *Assessment of Learning*. London: Sage.

Harrison, C. and Howard, S. (2009) *Inside the Primary Black Box*. London: GL Assessment.

Headington, R. (2003) *Monitoring, Assessment, Recording, Reporting and Accountability: Meeting the Standards*, 2nd edn. London: Fulton.

Kingdon, M. (1995) External marking: the KS2/KS3 tests in 1995, *British Journal of Curriculum and Assessment*, 5(2): 12–17.

Lawson, J. and Silver, H. (1973) *A Social History of Education in England*. London: Methuen.

Maclure, S. (1992) *Education Reformed*, 3rd edn. London: Hodder and Stoughton.

OfSTED (Office for Standards in Education) (2010a) *OfSTED: About Us*. Available online at: http://www.ofsted.gov.uk/Ofsted-home/About-us (accessed 28 November 2010).

OfSTED (2010b) *Inspection Reports*. Available online at: http://www.ofsted.gov.uk/Ofsted-home/Inspection-reports (accessed 27 October 2010).

OfSTED (2010c) *The Framework for Inspection of Schools*. Available online at: http://www.ofsted.gov.uk/Ofsted-home/Inspection-reports/Schools (accessed 27 November 2010).

OfSTED (2010d) *Reading by Six: How the Best Schools Do It*. Manchester: OfSTED.

QCDA (Qualifications, Curriculum and Development Agency) (2010a) *National Curriculum in Action*. Available online at: http://curriculum.qcda.gov.uk/key-stages-1-and-2/assessment/nc-in-action/index.aspx (accessed 26 November 2010).

QCDA (2010b) *National Curriculum: Values, Aims and Purposes*. Available online at: http://curriculum.qcda.gov.uk/key-stages-1-and-2/Values-aims-and-purposes/index.aspx (accessed 27 November 2010).

Shorrocks-Taylor, D. (1999) *National Testing: Past, Present and Future*. Leicester: British Psychological Society.

Swaffield, S. (ed.) (2008) *Unlocking Assessment: Understanding for Reflection and Application*. Abingdon: Routledge.

TES (Times Educational Supplement) (2008) *Ofsted Slams Teaching to the Test*, 25 July 2008. Available online at: http://www.tes.co.uk/article.aspx?storycode=6000653 (accessed 27 November 2010).

Wyse, D., McCreery, E. and Torrance, H. (2008) *Cambridge Review Research Briefing 3/2: The Trajectory and Impact of National Reform: Curriculum and Assessment in English Primary Schools*. Available online at: http://www.primaryreview.org.uk/publications/research_briefings.php (accessed 26 November 2010).

7

JANE WATERS AND TRISHA MAYNARD
Organizing the classroom: indoors and out

Summary

This chapter promotes three principles to guide the beginning teacher's organizational strategies for indoor and outdoor environments in the primary school. We suggest that organization should:

- maximize children's autonomy as learners within the space as well as their sense of ownership and responsibility;
- support and enhance both adult–child and child–child interaction;
- routinely attend to children's voices.

The extended cameos demonstrate enactment of the principles in learning situations and the chapter also considers application of the principles to the routines, rituals and ethos of the learning space.

Cameo 1

The Reception area is large and contains zones for different activity types (e.g. water play/exploration; mark making; junk construction; patterning) and an open 'free zone' to which children can bring items they wish to play with, or that can be set up to reflect children's interests. The water play area has been resourced with plasticine© and various objects that float or sink. Four children are playing independently in the water area and one girl (G) makes a loud exclamation. The teacher (T), who was observing play in the free zone, moves across to the water play area and the following interaction occurs.

G: Aah!

T: What happened to the plasticene©?

G: It fell!

T: It sank! How can we stop that plasticene© sinking, Jess? Jess, how can we stop it sinking?

G: Put something, put something in what floats, OK, then we'll put the plasticene© inside something what floats.

T: What could you find that floats?

G looks round the room, nearby there are shelves with various toys and objects on that can be placed in water.

T: What floats?

G: A boat!

T: A boat, what boat are you going to use? Do you want to use that boat?

T points to one of the boats on the shelf.

G: No . . . the big, the big yellow one, the really-est biggest one.

T: Will that fit in there?

G: Oh, maybe.

T: That one?

G: Yeah!

T: Or that one?

G: That one, the big one.

T: Put it in then.

T passes the big yellow boat to G.

G: OK. Put the plasticine© inside it . . .

G carefully places the lump of plasticine© inside the boat.

T: . . . and it floats!

T and G both smile broadly at each other.

T: What a good idea! That's a great idea!

NB: T did not plan for this outcome from the activity; her learning goal had been for children to explore how shape can change whether an object floats – by moulding the plasticine©, for example.

Following Jess's pleasure in her achievement, three other children approach the water area; retrieve boats from the shelves and begin to play. The teacher asks, 'I wonder if we can make the plasticine© look like a boat?' before she leaves the area. She adds a note to Jess's portfolio to reflect the understanding of the concept that Jess had demonstrated in the episode and also adds a note in her own files to ask the children at the end of the session how they got on with floating the plasticine©.

Cameo 2

Year 4 children are spending an afternoon in local woodland in order to explore what kinds of plants grow there and how they might be grouped as an introduction to a half-term of work focusing on life processes. They are getting ready to go out. Two days previously the children had decided upon friendship groups of three-four and, during an English language session, drawn up a list of items they wanted to take in order to explore the plants in the woodland. One child from each group has a rucksack that they collected from a large box on entry into the classroom and filled with items from the pre-prepared list. Specialist items such as magnifiers, sample pots and bug catchers were available from storage boxes placed on the tables at the end of the lunch period; non-specialist items such as scissors, pencils and rulers were collected from trays placed around the room. Children also collected items they had brought from home (notebooks, screw-top plastic jars) from their personal trays.

The children not involved in filling the rucksacks are in the changing area by the outside door of the classroom putting on their outdoor clothing. The teacher is marking the register as the children sit down outside, checking at the same time that they are suitably dressed and do not need to visit the toilet.

There is a buzz of excitement, activity and noise; a squabble breaks out over the one remaining bug catcher as two children both have this item on their list. The teacher intervenes by asking if they can think of a way to solve this problem. One child offers to share the bug catcher and take the second turn with it half-way through the afternoon. This child's group are rewarded with a house-point each for mature decision-making and helping to solve problems without argument.

When most of the children are seated outside, the remaining three children are asked to hurry and are given two minutes to finish getting ready. The class is asked to stand and line up either in pairs or singly ready to walk the half-mile to the woodland. The remaining three children join their groups and the teacher asks the front pair to lead the class out of the playground and to stop at the top of the drive in order for her to come to the front and lead them across the road. The teacher counts the children out of the playground and joins the children at the back until those at the front reach the top of the drive.

Introduction – underlying principles

As a beginning teacher it is important to recognize that the manner in which the learning space is organized impacts upon all the action that takes place within that space (see also Chapter 8). This may be referred to as the hidden – or implicit – curriculum (Meighan 1981) but this does not mean that it cannot be planned for in advance of action within the space. Before setting out to organize your learning space, you will want to consider one key question: what do you want children to learn – about themselves as people and as learners, about relationships and about the world and their place within it? Your answer will guide how you interpret the statutory curriculum as well as how you organize the areas in which this curriculum is experienced (see Chapter 5).

There are three principles advocated in this chapter and exemplified in the cameos. The principles are drawn together as a result of contemporary thought concerning the nature of the learning child, the nature of effective practice and the position of the child as a participant in society. Rather than promote the idea that organization – of itself – offers solutions to beginning teachers, we wish to promote the notion that the principles underlying organizational processes demarcate children's experiences in the classroom.

The first principle is that since children are viewed as competent individuals and learners (Dahlberg et al. 2007; see also Chapters 9 and 11), classroom organization should maximize children's autonomy as learners within the space as well as their sense of ownership and responsibility. As Moyles (2007) points out, across the primary school years, children will be developing independence in thinking, confidence and in their actions. The second principle is that, since we know the significance of talk in children's learning (Howes and Smith 1995; Alexander 2010) – and that young children learn effectively while engaging with others in episodes of shared thinking, particularly with trained adults in schools (Sylva et al. 2010) – the organization should support and enhance both adult–child and child–child interactions. The final principle is that, in line with the United Nations Convention on the Rights of the Child UNCRC (United Nations 1989), children's voices should routinely be heard – and responded to – as part of the organizational approach to learning and teaching in any setting (see Chapter 18). These three principles also reflect the evidence-based pedagogic principles of the *Teaching and Learning Research Programme* (TLRP/ESRC 2010).

In the first cameo, the children are free to move to where they have an interest and the teacher looks for and responds to children's exploration and interest. She does not impose her learning goals but responds to opportunities for them to be supported as a result of children's interaction with each other and their environment. The resources to stimulate children's interests and enquiry are readily available as are those that may be called upon to develop thinking or solve problems. Thus young children are supported in developing their independence and self-regulatory skills (see Chapter 10) as well as having meaningful and engaged interaction with adults in the setting.

Cameo 1 can be seen as exemplifying a number of the QTS standards – for example, Q14 ('Have a secure knowledge and understanding of their subjects/curriculum areas and related pedagogy to enable them to teach effectively across the age and ability range for which they are trained'); Q25b ('Build on prior knowledge, develop concepts and processes, enable learners to apply new knowledge, understanding and skills and meet learning objectives'); Q30 ('Establish a purposeful and safe learning environment conducive to learning'); and Q31 ('Establish a clear framework for classroom discipline to manage learners' behaviour constructively and promote their self-control and independence').

It also links to the following EYPS standards: S07 ('Have high expectations of all children and commitment to ensuring that they can achieve their full potential'); S08 ('Establish and sustain a safe, welcoming, purposeful, stimulating and encouraging environment where children feel confident and secure and are able to develop and learn'); S09 ('Provide balanced and flexible daily and weekly routines that meet children's needs and enable them to develop and learn'); S11 ('Plan and provide safe and appropriate child-led and adult-initiated experiences, activities and play opportunities . . . which enable children to develop and learn'); S14 ('Respond appropriately to children, informed by how children develop and learn and a clear understanding of possible next steps in their development and learning'); S16 ('Engage in sustained shared thinking with children'); and S27 ('Listen to children, pay attention to what they say and value and respect their view').

In cameo 2, the trip – and children's participation in the planning and organization of it – had been carefully planned in advance. By asking the children to organize themselves into friendship groups and drawing up lists of what they felt they would need in order to explore the woodland, the teacher implied that the children's choices and ideas were valued, that the manner in which they explored the woodland was theirs to control, albeit with a specific brief. By telling the children before lunch exactly how the afternoon session was going to run and how they were going to collect the resources they had on their lists, the teacher facilitated a smooth, organized start to an exciting afternoon. (She also ensured that she was not spending her lunch break organizing all this for the children.) By rewarding the children who resolved the problem of the bug catchers, the teacher used her organizational strategies to reinforce messages about which kind of behaviour was respected and expected in her classroom.

Cameo 2 exemplifies the following QTS Standards: Q1 ('Relationships with children and young people'); Q25a ('. . . use a range of teaching strategies and resources'); Q30 ('Establish a purposeful and safe learning environment conducive to learning and identify opportunities for learners to learn in out-of-school contexts'); and Q31 ('Establish a clear framework for classroom discipline to manage learners' behaviour constructively and promote their self-control and independence').

Both cameos imply respect for children's choices (see Chapter 18) – the mechanisms for hearing and responding to children's voices and choices are routinely embedded in the organization structure of the spaces described as well as the planning for learning. We can see how, in cameo 1, the EYPS and QTS standards identified are enacted through organizational and pedagogical approaches that support children's choices and independence while maximizing opportunities for effective interactions to take place. In cameo 2, the rights of the children to be participants in decisions that affect them and the QTS Standards identified are effectively enacted as a matter of day-to-day routines and rituals established as part of the organizational fabric of the learning space.

It is important to note that the apparent ease of this organization as described in the cameos does not occur overnight and that by planning – at the start of the year – what kind of learning environment and child participation you want, you can build towards these goals (see Chapter 5). It is not possible to impose autonomy and responsibility on children when they are used to being told exactly what to do all the time. Many beginning teachers expect that children will respond positively to such opportunities without realizing that the skills involved in taking responsibility and participating with autonomy have to be learned (Moyles 2007). Children can only learn these skills if they are able to practise them and are recognized and rewarded for their actions.

So how are these principles enacted in the way the classroom is organized?

In the classroom setting the three principles outlined above will be reflected in the way the teacher organizes the use of the space, the organization of resources and what goes on the walls and for what purpose. For example:

- *Organization of space* – is there a flexible approach to the organization of tables and chairs so that these can support a range of pedagogic strategies (Alexander 2010; Sylva et al. 2010) as appropriate, for example, individual, pair, group and whole-class learning? Is there room for children to move around the classroom safely and freely? Does the space encourage collaboration and communication?

- *Resources* – are resources accessible and clearly labelled? Are children given responsibility for selecting and putting away resources, and for maintaining and organizing them as appropriate?

- *Documentation/display* – could the classroom environment be described as 'rich' in supporting children's learning and a positive sense of self-as-learner? Does it reflect current interests? Does it demonstrate recognition of what children bring from home – their 'funds of knowledge' (Moll et al. 2001)? Does it support parents' understanding of pedagogical approaches adopted in school (Brooker 2010)? Is what is on the walls meaningful or simply decorative? Who engages with this material – children/parents?

But the principles will also be reflected in how the teacher manages classroom activities. Routines, rituals and rules that are fair, carefully explained and clearly communicated, provide a framework that supports positive behaviour and the smooth running of classroom activities and within which children can demonstrate their autonomy and sense of responsibility. For example:

- *Routines, rituals and rules* – are there clearly communicated expectations for entrances and exits, the beginning and end of activities? Are there systems in place – for example, for when children don't know what to do; finish their work; want to go to the toilet or go outside – that support children's autonomy, choice and sense of responsibility?

Finally, the principles may be demonstrated through the kind of ethos established within the classroom – how far children are shown that they are valued and respected and encouraged to value and respect others. For example:

- *Ethos* – how far are children allowed to manage their own time and activities? Are they encouraged to listen to and be respectful to others? How do the adults in the classroom demonstrate their respect for children? Are behaviour management strategies positively focused?

Moving outdoors

Moving between one space to another can be a flashpoint for behaviour management for children of all ages (Safran and Oswald 2003). Note how the physical organization of the transition space (Figure 7.1) supports children's autonomy in making safe and orderly transitions from indoors to outdoors.

Figure 7.1 The physical organization of the transition space supports children's autonomy

Such organization also supports young children's choice to move their activity from indoors to outdoors and vice versa thus meeting the EYPS Standards S11 ('Provide safe and appropriate child-led and adult-initiated experiences, activities and play opportunities in indoor, outdoor and in out-of-setting contexts, which enable children to develop and learn'); and S19 ('Plan a safe environment and employ practices that promote children's health, safety and physical, mental and emotional well-being').

The outdoor environment

Organization of the outdoor environment may be a specific challenge due to the physical constraints of what is already in the outdoor space, the size of the space as well as the routines that are already established within the school about the use of the space (Tovey 2007). However, the principles of considering how the organization supports children's autonomy and participation as well as maximizes the opportunity to work with others are still applicable. Figures 7.2 and 7.3 show a space in Iceland in which young children's exploration is invited by the materials present and supported by the scale of the space; the opportunity for interaction focused on children's interests and activity is present. The loose parts (Nicholson 1971) in this space are central to its richness since they afford (Gibson 1979; Fjørtoft 2001, 2004) various and multiple uses.

Figure 7.2 Outdoor space in Iceland (1)

Figure 7.3 Outdoor space in Iceland (2)

White (2008) suggests that young children in an outdoor space should have the chance to engage in ten key experiences. Some of these support children's autonomy and participation, for example, playing for extended periods of time in an environment full of 'irresistible stimuli' (2008: 9) in which children are in charge of their play. White also highlights that children need 'challenge and risk within a framework of security and safety' (2008: 10). Engaging in risk-taking in a 'safe' space can sound like a contradiction. EYPS S19 requires that practitioners provide a safe environment and employ practices that promote children's health, safety and physical, mental and emotional well-being. The requirement for safety does not mean that children cannot undertake appropriate challenges – and these may include small-scale risks. Indeed, *not* to provide for such challenges is arguably neglecting aspects of children's well-being (Stephenson 2003; Sandseter 2007, 2009; Tovey 2007). The organizational issues in providing for children's appropriate risk-taking is to ensure that all staff – and children – are knowledgeable about and confident of the rules for use of the space and the procedures for dealing with minor injury. These may include routinely checking the first aid box is well stocked (or allocating this task to a child) and establishing routines of action with the children in case of an accident.

In particular, practitioners must be confident the school management structures fully support the provision for, and organization of, children's activity. It is important for children to receive consistent messages about what they can and cannot do in their learning spaces (Waters and Begley 2007) – and why – by the establishment of a few clear rules to which everyone is required to abide. For example, if you want to climb the tree, you should let an adult know before you start. Such an approach respects children's interests while supporting safe activity. Play Wales (2005) suggests that open and honest discussion within the staff team about these issues can help build a mutually supportive team in which staff can confidently support children's choices to challenge themselves physically. Such discussion supports EYPS: S20 ('Recognise when a child is in danger or at risk of harm and know how to act to protect them').

As children move through KS1 and into KS2, the outdoor space is more likely to be used as a resource for specific aspects of content-based curricular learning. However, the organizational principles of maximizing children's autonomy, supporting interaction and encouraging responsibility still apply; when you read cameo 3, try to identify where (and how) the principles are being enacted.

Cameo 3

Year 6 children are putting into action a school council decision to improve the recycling facilities on the school site. This involves making a plan of the site and surveying other classes to decide which facilities are needed and where they would best be located. The class is working in pre-arranged groups, each of which has a specific task to undertake during the outdoor geography session. The composition of the groups has been decided by the children and the tasks, broadly negotiated during the previous geography session during whole class discussion, have been carefully structured by the teacher and written on task sheets.

Before leaving the classroom, the children have already decided what they need to take out with them to complete the task. They also know that they have been trusted to work independently on their task but that if they need support, then one of the group should walk to find the teacher, who may be working with another group, to explain the problem. The children know that they will have to sit and watch the other groups if they do not carry out the task sensibly; they also know that the teacher rewards responsible class behaviour with 'joke time' or a 'silly quiz' at the end of the day.

One group is finding out where the borders of an area of rough ground along the side of the playground actually lie. There are old logs and a couple of small shrubs obscuring the border in places. Two of the children in this group call the other members over to show them some fungus growing on the old log in a damp and dark area of the rough ground. The children are excited and start shouting that the fungus is poisonous; soon a group of eight children have gathered. The teacher goes over to the border area and asks what is going on. A number of the children explain that they have found poisonous fungus on the log. The teacher asks all the children to move away and sit down nearby, then asks one child to show her the fungus. Having looked at it carefully, the teacher asks, 'How can we tell if the fungus is poisonous?' and chooses three children to share their ideas. She then asks one child to go and get one of the class cameras and take a few photos of the fungus so that they can look it up later. The rest of the children are asked to complete their tasks.

On returning to the classroom after the outdoor session, the children sit down and place their plans on their tables. The teacher asks how the session has gone. One group says they needed more time to complete their plan and are told that they can do this either during lunchtime if they want to or during 'finishing off time' the following day. The teacher tells the class she is pleased with their sensible behaviour and they will have a 'silly quiz' later; she also tells them that one group has found something very interesting while doing their plan. The photos of the fungus are relayed through the interactive white board for the class to see. The children begin to offer their own experiences of seeing fungus and there is some argument on one table about whether it is actually poisonous. The teacher raises her hand and the class quietens; she suggests that they do a mini-project on fungus. The children are asked to do some research at home to bring in for the project table and the teacher offered to set up the microscope so they can explore the fungus in more detail. The class respond positively to this suggestion.

In the days that follow, five children bring in information about fungi and add it to the project table – a fixture in the classroom. Once it has been established that the fungus in the border area is not poisonous, a small section is broken off and placed under the microscope. The art session the following week is based on pattern and texture in nature and a number of the children use the underside of the fungus as a starting point for their pattern design.

In cameo 3, the children are aware of the organizational routines and the rewards and consequences for different types of behaviour. The teacher had established some key rules for talking – 'Anyone may be asked to give an opinion or answer'/'When I raise my hand I want you to listen.' Note that the rewards appeal to the children and are age/group appropriate. Star charts rarely inspire Year 6 children but the chance to engage in informal games/quizzes at the end of the day often meet with a positive motivational response. The teacher responds fairly and firmly to situations as they arise, recognizing and responding to children's interests as well as maintaining a focus on the task in hand. The project table is a negotiated space – one in which the children know they can have an input; this motivates some to undertake research at home when they are interested in the current mini-project. The teacher trusts the children to undertake tasks responsibly and demonstrates this in her expectations of behaviour; this supports the children's growing independence.

Cameo 3 exemplifies QTS: Standard 30 ('Establish a purposeful and safe learning environment conducive to learning and identify opportunities for learners to learn in out-of-school contexts').

Conclusion

By suggesting three principles to guide your organization, rather than providing lists of what should and shouldn't be present and where it might be placed, this chapter aims to encourage you, as a beginning teacher, to embrace organization as a process through which important understandings about children as learners, participants and competent individuals are enacted. This approach is in line with Moss and Dahlberg's consideration of quality in which they call for 'technical and managerial practice' to be put 'in its place, as subservient to democratic, political and ethical practice' (2008: 9). How you organize your learning spaces is part of your 'repertoire' of pedagogic strategies and provides an opportunity for you to enact evidence-based pedagogic principles (TRLP/ESRC 2010). In short, we encourage you to enact the principles through your organization of space, interaction, routines and rituals in order to create an ethos in which children know not only that you have high expectations of them but also that they are active participants within the learning community.

Questions to Promote Thinking

1. Consider the layout of one part of your indoor and outdoor area. Ask yourself:
   (a) Who is this organized for?
   (b) In what way(s) can children take more control in this area?
   (c) What messages about learning might the children be receiving from this organizational strategy?
2. Consider your routines and rituals. Ask yourself:
   (a) Are consistent messages being promoted to the children?
   (b) How do you engage children's participation in your routines?
   (c) How do your routines and rituals reflect respect for children's developing autonomy and independence?

References and suggested further reading

Alexander, R. (ed.) (2010) *Children, their World, their Education.* Abingdon: Routledge.
Brooker, L. (2010) Learning to play in a cultural context, in P. Broadhead, J. Howard and L. Wood (eds) *Play and Learning in the Early Years.* London: Sage.
Brooker, L. and Broadbent, L. (2007) Personal, social and emotional development: learning to be strong in a world of change, in J. Riley (ed.) *Learning in the Early Years*. London: Sage.
Dahlberg, G., Moss, P. and Pence, A. (2007) *Beyond Quality in Early Childhood Education and Care: Languages of Evaluation,* 2nd edn. London: Falmer Press.
Fjørtoft, I. (2001) The natural environment as a playground for children: the impact of outdoor play activities in pre-primary school children, *Early Education Journal,* 29(2): 111–17.
Fjørtoft, I. (2004) Landscape as playscape: the effects of natural environments on children's play and motor development, *Children, Youth and Environments,* 14(2): 21–44.
Gibson, J.J. (1979) *The Ecological Approach to Visual Perception.* London: Lawrence Erlbaum Associates.
Howes, C. and Smith, E. (1995) Relations among child care quality, teacher behaviour, children's play activities, emotional security, and cognitive activity in child care, *Early Childhood Research Quarterly,* 10(4): 381–404.
Johnston, J. and Halocha, J. (2010) *Early Childhood and Primary Education: Readings and Reflections*. Maidenhead: Open University Press (in particular, Chapter 17: Learning Places).
Meighan, R. (1981) *A Sociology of Educating.* Orlando, FL: Holt.
Moll, L., Amanti, C., Neff, D. and Gonzalez, N. (2001) Funds of knowledge for teaching: using a qualitative approach to connect homes and classrooms, *Theory into Practice,* XXXI(2): 132–41.
Moss, P. and Dahlberg, G. (2008) Beyond quality in early childhood education and care – languages of evaluation, *New Zealand Journal of Teachers' Work,* 5(1): 3–12.
Moyles, J. (2007) Getting it sorted! Organising the classroom environment in J. Moyles (ed.) *Beginning Teaching Beginning Learning in Primary Education,* 3rd edn. Maidenhead: Open University Press.
Nicholson, S. (1971) How NOT to cheat children: the theory of loose parts, *Landscape Architecture,* 62(1): 30–4.
Play Wales (2005) *Richer Play in Schools: A Guide for Schools Wishing to Improve Play Opportunities for Children and Young People.* Play Wales: Cardiff. Available online at: http://www.playwales.org.uk/downloaddoc.asp?id=55andpage=67andskin=0 (accessed 16 November 2010).
Prasad, S. (2000) *Spaces and Places*. UpStart! 03. London: DfEE Publications.
Safran, S.P. and Oswald, K. (2003) Positive behavior supports: can schools reshape disciplinary practices? *Exceptional Children,* 69(3): 361–73.
Sandseter, E.B.H. (2007) Categorising risky play – how can we identify risk-taking in children's play? *European Early Childhood Education Research Journal,* 15(2): 237–52.
Sandseter, E.B.H. (2009) Children's expressions of exhilaration and fear in risky play, *Contemporary Issues in Early Childhood,* 10(2): 92–106.
Stephenson, A. (2003) Physical risk-taking: dangerous or endangered? *Early Years: An International Journal of Research and Development,* 23(1): 35–43.
Sylva, K., Melhuish, E., Sammons, P., Siraj-Blatchford, I. and Taggart, B. (2010) *Early Childhood Matters: Evidence from the Effective Pre-school and Primary Education Project.* London: Routledge.

TLRP/ESRC (Teaching and Learning Research Programme/Economic and Social Research Council) (2010) *Evidence-Informed Pedagogic Principles*. Available online at: http://www. tlrp.org/themes/themes/tenprinciples.html (accessed 20 October 2010).

Tovey, H. (2007) *Playing Outdoors: Spaces and Places, Risk and Challenge*. Maidenhead: McGraw-Hill.

United Nations (1989) *Convention on the Rights of the Child*. (1989). Geneva: United Nations. Available online at: http://www.un.org/documents/ga/res/44/a44r025.htm (accessed 4 February 2011).

Waters, J. and Begley, S. (2007) Supporting the development of risk-taking behaviours in the Early Years: an exploratory study, *Education 3–13*, 35(4): 65–77.

White, J. (2008) *Playing and Learning Outdoors: Making Provision for High-Quality Experiences in the Outdoor Environment*. Abingdon: Routledge.

8

THEODORA PAPATHEODOROU
Creating a positive learning
and behaviour environment

Summary

Over the years, we have witnessed increasing concerns about challenging behaviours in educational settings. Although most of these behaviours relate to low-level disruption that interferes with the learning process, children's anxiety, loneliness, unhappiness, depression and out-of-school antisocial behaviours are also evident. There are many complex factors that may account for such trends but, increasingly, the learning environment which the children inhabit, both indoors and outdoors, and the encounters that it affords, are one aspect that needs serious consideration.

This chapter provides an overview of current concerns about behaviour in schools and discusses research findings which demonstrate how the schools' physical environments inhibit or enable positive behaviours. A discussion of the characteristics and elements of enabling outdoor spaces follows, with reference to children's perspectives. The case is made for articulating a pedagogy of space to enable children's overall and long-term well-being.

Excerpt

School built environment and discipline

. . . further research should be undertaken to identify those design features which are supportive to good discipline and order within school . . . design briefs for any new building should take account of the outcomes of this research so that whenever school buildings are being designed or renovated, the potential of the environment to improve behaviour and discipline is a priority for architects, school managers and local authorities (Steer 2005: 96).

Cameo 1

The challenges and potential of school playgrounds

All: We need bigger playground, because all we have, . . . about six classes in a 'tomb' [crowded space] and people are hit by those playing.

Betty: There are tennis balls . . . and people are hit with those, of course . . .

Sally: There are little squares . . . Miss lets us play football . . . and they aren't meant to be for football . . . or headers and catchers.

Betty: It's meant to be for people who want to play this game and the teacher doesn't stop it . . .

Ross: . . . does sometimes . . . I've got my ball taken off for playing football.

Mat: The playground is boring.

Ross: I don't like uprighters [monkey bars] . . .

Mat: They put those bloomin' uprighters . . . Do you know how high they are?

Ross: I would change the playground to take it back as it was; a swimming pool.

Eddie: Yeah . . . but they've got rid of it. They put like a cover up . . .

Steve: Yeah. We . . . we all pupils teach each other . . . yeah.

Sally: The little ones should be more out because when they are older they are going to do it . . . aren't they? Old boys should help the young ones with football skills.

All: Yeah, yeah, yes.

Betty: I like the garden most. They've got ponds there . . . they've got fish there. In the summer, Miss P. does a club where you help. You clean things out and you set plants . . . It's nice.

All: Yeah, yeah, yes.

(From an interview with primary school children, Papatheodorou 2002)

Cameo 2

Making the school a better place for children

We are currently carrying out a whole school research entitled 'The way I see it' from the children's perceptions (at last!). The children were asked to draw pictures and to write alongside their pictures:

- things that make me feel good in the playground after dinner;
- things that make me feel not so good in the playground after dinner;
- someone who helps make me feel better in the playground and how they make me feel better.

My children have only been at school three weeks but it was interesting to find that the things that made them feel not so good in the playground were not things that had actually happened but things that they were afraid might happen such as fights or having no-one to play with. Other things that made them feel good included 'When Jodie collects acorns with me' and it was interesting to find certain members of the class being repeatedly named as being liked to play with. The result of this is intended to highlight areas for improvement in the playground at this particular time of day to make it a better environment for the children (a teacher's account – personal communication with the author, 2009).

Introduction

The excerpt and two cameos illustrate awareness of the importance of the physical environment which educational settings provide for their pupils. The excerpt refers to recommendations 3.9.1 and 9.3.2, *Behaviour for Learning* (Steer 2005). These recommendations are of particular importance as they explicitly acknowledge the influence of the physical environment on school discipline and call for further research. The first cameo provides further evidence of the importance of the physical environment. It comes from two interviews conducted with groups of pupils in the final two years of a primary school, which participated in an international social inclusion research project. At the time of the interviews, the school was struggling to achieve the expected outcomes set out at national level. In interviewing the pupils about their experiences in their local community and school, noisy neighbourhoods, lack of amenities for play and recreation and the physical environment of the school were the main issues raised. When asked what they would like to change, the pupils unanimously agreed that this would be the school playground, highlighting its limitations and challenges as well as its potential (Papatheodorou 2002). The second cameo comes from a reception class teacher and demonstrates how consultation with young children can help schools gain insights about pupils' perspectives on the school environment and use them as the basis for creating spaces *for* children.

Starting from the issues raised in these cameos, I will first provide an overview of concerns about behaviour and discipline in schools; then discuss research related to the influence of the built and outdoor environments on children's behaviour and overall well-being. I will continue by exploring the features and characteristics of outdoor spaces from children's perspectives and conclude the chapter by making the case for developing a pedagogy of space or considering space as a key parameter of pedagogy.

Behaviour in schools

Since the publication of *The Elton Report* (Lord Elton 1989), concerns about children's behaviour in educational settings has remained constant (Steer 2005). Most of these behaviours are perceived as low-level classroom disruption that interferes with the learning process and/or irritate teachers, and poor behaviour exhibited during recess in the playground (Steer 2005, 2009; Blatchford and Baines 2006; OfSTED 2009). Increasingly, however, there are serious concerns about behaviours such as unhappiness and depression and out-of-school antisocial behaviours (Sharp et al. 2006; OfSTED 2008; Layard and Dunn 2009).

These concerns have led educators and policy-makers to consider strategies and good practice about discipline and behaviour management. UK government officials call for more adult authority in schools and zero tolerance. In a recent article in the national press, the Secretary of State for Education in England, Michael Gove, expressing his views about behaviour in education, argued that 'Unless there's good discipline teachers cannot teach and children cannot learn . . . it is crucial that adult authority in the classroom is restored and teachers feel safe so they can get on with the job' (Gove 2010: np). This kind of discipline is compatible with notions of control of others and associated with negative ideas of authoritarian practices (Martin and Norwich 1991). It assumes a unidirectional influence from teachers and school on pupils and creates a division and confrontational position between them.

Researchers for many years have been arguing that pupils do not require to be controlled: instead they need to be respected as intelligent persons who have the right to be involved in any decision which shapes their lives (Cooper and Upton 1990). They have recommended that educators should engage with actions that enhance the probability of pupils – individually and in groups – to develop effective behaviours that are personally self-fulfilling, productive and socially acceptable and provide a caring, happy, relaxed and productive environment (Martin and Norwich 1991).

The introduction of programmes such as Nurture Groups, Behaviour4Learning and Social Emotional Aspects of Learning (SEAL) reflect more caring and compassionate responses to children's challenging behaviours (EPPI Centre 2004; National Primary Strategy 2005; Reynolds et al. 2009; DCSF 2010). They are underpinned by affective and caring philosophies and aim to strengthen protective factors such as children's capacity to self-regulate emotions and behaviours, problem-solve, make meaningful friendships and develop trusting relationships that may ameliorate negative influences of children's stressful living situations (Webster-Stratton and Reid 2007). They acknowledge that children's social and emotional competencies do not unfold automatically; rather they are strongly influenced by the child's learning environment (Kramer et al. 2009; see Chapter 7).

While these programmes reflect a step towards more compassionate educational practices, they also have certain limitations. First, they assume a unidirectional influence from schools/teachers on pupils, underestimating pupils' agency. Second, good behaviour is seen as instrumental for curricula learning and for schooling rather than behaviour being an end in itself. As a result, the nurturing of pupils' social, emotional and behavioural predispositions has become an additional curricula area to be taught (Ecclestone and Hayes 2009).

Either advocating more adult authority and zero tolerance or the introduction of therapeutic programmes, behaviour and its challenging manifestations are seen as residing *within* the individual. Both approaches emphasize schools' and teachers' duties and responsibilities to *control* or *condition* children's behaviours. The school sets the goals and the conditions under which they could be achieved, almost assuming a passive role from the pupils. The fact that pupil learning takes place all the time and in all places – often informally – is largely ignored. Learning takes place as much in the classroom and under adult-controlled conditions as in the outdoors and during unplanned, self-motivated and self-directed activities and endeavours (see Chapter 10). It is within these ideas that, in the next section, I will provide an overview of research findings that demonstrate the impact of the physical environment, both built and outdoors, on children's behaviour.

The built environment

Initial research on the influence of the physical environment on pupils focused mainly on classroom variables such as spatial density, crowding and play and learning resources. Such research revealed that, in classrooms with high spatial density, there were more incidents of aggressive interactions and less pupil socialization than in classrooms with low spatial density (Loo 1972; Aiello et al. 1979). Large indoor and outdoor play areas afforded more interaction, friendly behaviours and social groupings and less troublesome behaviours; children displayed greater vigorous activity and made more unusual and creative use of play equipment. Children of all ages, who experience crowded conditions, reported feeling tense, annoyed, frustrated, experiencing discomfort and elevated levels of stress, with boys being more susceptible to negative consequences (Aiello et al. 1979; Papatheodorou 2002).

Reduction of resources did not seem to have a detrimental effect on children's behaviour and interactions, at least in the short term: instead children tended to make more varied use of those available. On the other hand, permanent limited resources per child created stressful situations, leading to more aggressive behaviours. Playgrounds with good facilities and resources enabled development of children's motor control and were reported as conducive to cooperation and communication, while poorly resourced playgrounds led to 'territorial' claims and conflicts, friction, boredom or inappropriate play choices which attracted unwanted attention from teachers (e.g. being caught in the classroom during break time; the football taken away). In general, such research findings are indicative of the impact of crowding and lack of appropriate resources on pupils' physiological, psychological, behavioural and social behaviours.

The outdoors

Recent research from disparate disciplines – medicine, social and health psychology, architecture and education – has provided further evidence about the impact of the physical environment (especially access to outdoor spaces and natural environments) on children's overall health, psychological and social well-being. Access to outdoors is associated with reduction of stress, release of tension, enhancement of wider well-being (Berto 2005) and lower or less severe symptoms of hyperactivity (Taylor et al.

2001). Exposure to natural elements relates to children's increased affective, imaginative, creative and cognitive functioning (Wells 2000).

In schools, pupils involved in active playtimes show improvement of physical fitness that enables the brain to recycle chemicals that are important for concentration, long-term memory and recall of information (Conley and Muncey 1999; see also Chapter 2). They develop social skills such as collaboration, communication, setting rules and following rules, leadership skills, positive self-concept, mood, emotional state and mental function (Hoy and Clover 2007). Physical activity is also the means for children to test and stretch their abilities, e.g. strength, flexibility, balance and co-ordination (Hewes 2005; Frost 2006).

Sandseter (2009) makes the case for the benefits of children's risky play that involves great heights, speed, dangerous tools and elements, rough and tumble play and getting out of adult sight. Children find risky play fun, exciting and thrilling. It offers them opportunities to explore and test possibilities, to learn about and assess risk, confront their own fears and phobias and gain competence and evaluate the strength of others in a peer group. As Sutton-Smith (1997) claims, risky play becomes the ground where children can actualize their potential. Of course, calls for more risky play are not easily reconciled with teachers' professional responsibilities for ensuring children's safety. Litigation arising from accidents also is a prohibiting factor in including or promoting risky play in schools.

The school grounds: an undervalued educational resource?

The characteristics and features of the physical environment and the way they impact on pupils' experience on behaviour and learning remain a neglected area of educational study. Most school buildings are designed with a nineteenth-century mind-set, despite research evidence (Burke, cited in Birkett 2001; Young 2001). This may be due to the fact that the physical environment is taken as something that is *fixed*, an *unchangeable* given, made available to users without any prior analysis of need or consideration to its function (Jamieson et al. 2000). Even when the importance of the school environment is acknowledged, the recommendations focus on the built environment with emphasis on attractive and stimulating classrooms (Steer 2005: 76) rather than considering the potential and function of the whole school's physical environment.

The physical environment – and especially the outdoors and playgrounds – have not yet been conceptualized as platforms for learning. Instead, they are seen as places where children release excess or suppressed energy during playtime and where troublesome behaviours mostly occur (Blatchford and Baines 2006). Concerns about health and safety have gradually led to practices where playgrounds are either governed by many rules and regulations or controlled by adults who largely condition children's play and interactions (Papatheodorou 2002). Curricula overload and attempts to minimize poor behaviour have also been contributing factors in significantly reducing the duration of break times in schools and children's time spent outdoors in general. It is estimated that, since the 1970s, children's overall playtime in schools has decreased by as much as 50 per cent and this time decreases further as children get older (Blatchford and Baines 2006). In out-of-school hours, parents also reported that children spent most of their time indoors, despite the fact that the outdoors was their own most memorable place in childhood for play for doing things or for just being with siblings and friends (Papatheodorou 2010).

Researchers have argued that outdoor spaces are conducive to child-initiated play which requires skills that are above and beyond those displayed in adult-directed play. Child-initiated play in particular, offers children opportunities for initiative, problem-solving and decision-making and the development of pro-social and social skills (Pellegrini, cited in Gleave 2009). As a result, some researchers have called for careful site planning that offers such opportunities and, at the same time, incorporates an academic component in their use (Layton 2001). Others, however, point out that adult-designed spaces have been unsuccessful in meeting the needs of children who show preference for less managed spaces (Hart et al., cited in Gleave 2009).

Through children's gaze

Gaining access to children's views can be informative in terms of their likes and dislikes as well as concrete suggestions for design aspects and elements of space and its functioning. Children express a strong preference for outdoor spaces that have natural features (e.g. leaves, trees, mud, grass, leaves and fresh air) and provide stimulation and opportunities to feel, do things and reflect, to co-operate and collaborate, to be active and have fun and to be safe and feel relaxed (Papatheodorou 2002; Groves and McNish 2008).

Children see themselves in the outdoors as being active, creative and engaging in collaborative and self-managed endeavours rather than contained and controlled. They like spaces which offer opportunities to actualize their potential and where they can exercise their agency and autonomy; spaces for which they have a sense of ownership, feel proud of their accomplishments and get messages for an 'I can do' attitude. They like spaces that can be transformed, as a result of their actions and interactions and, in the process, enjoy little journeys of discovery (McGavin 2001). These experiences and interactions transform space into a place which has particular meaning for its inhabitants. Children envision their school grounds as a living and changing system that either facilitates or obstructs interactions and actions and, at the same time, conditions how they feel, think and behave (Malaguzzi, cited in Gandini 1998: 166). It is these actions and interactions that determine children's relation, connection and bonding with the school as their place.

Children clearly identify two aspects of the physical environment as being important: the *stimuli* being present and the *interactions* that are enabled. Educators in Reggio Emilia refer to those two aspects of educational space as *content* and *container*, with the first being associated with educational stimuli and messages it contains and the latter with the social interactions it affords (Filippini, cited in Gandini 1998). It is the use of space as both *content* and *container* and their dynamic interaction that offers children the opportunity to make meaning of their experience and construct their own learning.

The importance of the school physical environment, and especially the outdoors, as an educational resource is now beyond any doubt. It is evident that unsuitable learning environments have a negative influence on pupils, leaving them feeling stressed, alienated or neglected and may lead to inappropriate and disruptive behaviours and poor academic performance. Environments that are carefully planned and provide access to nature and outdoor activities contribute positively to children's cognitive and behavioural functioning. They enable pupils to understand themselves and others, to develop trusting and respectful relationships and co-construct knowledge (Gandini 1998). As Pouler has argued, the space is neither innocent nor neutral. It has a performative effect on its inhabitants. It either works for or against them. It enables or prohibits what may occur. It lays down the law and implies a certain order: it commands and locates bodies (cited in Jamieson et al. 2000). It is, therefore, of no surprise that Malagguzi, the founder of the Reggio Emilia pre-schools, has referred to the learning environment as the third educator (cited in Rinaldi 2006).

The pedagogy of space

Developments in the design of space and pedagogy have yet to reach alignment with each other. Knowledge about the function of educational space has not been incorporated into theories of pedagogy nor have pedagogical principles been taken into account to develop educational spaces that provide appropriate stimuli and enable interaction. Yet, space has the potential to provide stimuli that address the holistic needs and potential of children, especially their overall well-being in the long term. It can offer experiences that address psychomotor, affective and cognitive aspects of human development (i.e. actions, feeling and thoughts) in an integrated way rather than separately and in a fragmented manner. The social skills acquired, especially in children's early years, can become a protective factor that can minimize both internalized and externalized behaviours (Henricsson and Rydell 2006).

The neglect of the physical environment of the school may be due to the fact that it is an aspect of the school ecosystem that it is difficult or expensive to change or because its impact is not always immediately observable or measurable. Zins and colleagues (cited in Kramer et al. 2009) observe that schools often hesitate to initiate and implement programmes with no direct effect on academic performance. Notwithstanding these challenges, the design or the best use of existing design, especially of outdoors space, should be reconceptualized to ensure diverse and necessary stimuli are ever present and carefully structured to enable the participation of each and all pupils (Doughty 2001). The school physical environment may be conceptualized as one variable of universal provision aiming to enable children to realize their uniqueness and their relationships with others, their health, safety, enjoyment and achievement and well-being mandated in statutory requirements and policies related to children in England (e.g. *Every Child Matters*: DfES 2003; Early Years Foundation Stage: DfES 2007).

Some researchers argue for a greater involvement of children in the design process and/or wider consultation with them to elicit ideas for the best use of space available (Burke 2005). Such a participatory approach also allows adults to gain better understanding of children's views and experiences and enables children to exercise their agency as intelligent and responsible citizens (Keenan 2007). Instead of creating learning environments *for* children, educators should work with children to co-create spaces which, to recall Rasmussen (2004), become children's places.

Conclusion

This chapter makes no claim to offer a blueprint for outdoor spaces but has offered research findings, some of which may be challenging, some controversial and some idealistic. I am well aware that many schools, and especially early years settings, do not have newly designed and purpose-built premises but all educators can work with children (as in the second cameo above) to make a children's place from the space available. Some starting points to working with children may include:

- the uniqueness and potential of a 'given' space;
- reconciling safety concerns with the potential of the space;
- use of space by children of different ages.

Questions to Promote Thinking

1   Audit the play resources available in your playground and review its design: how do they meet the needs of children from their point of view?
2   Review the school policy and regulations with children: how do they support or inhibit flexible and creative use of the school playground?
3   Are there ways for spending more time outdoors during breaks, without compromising curricula learning? Consult children and discuss their suggestions with them.

References and suggested further reading

Aiello, J.R., Nicosia, G. and Thompson, D.E. (1979) Physiological, social and behavioral consequences of crowding on children and adolescents, *Child Development*, 50: 195–202.

Berto, R. (2005) Exposure to restorative environments helps restore attentional capacity, *Journal of Environmental Psychology*, 25(3): 249–59.

Birkett, D. (2001) The school I'd like, *Guardian Education*, 16 January.

Blatchford, P. and Baines, E. (2006) *A Follow-up National Survey of Breaktimes in Primary and Secondary Schools: Final Report to Nuffield Foundation.* Available online at: http://www.breaktime.org.uk/NuffieldBreakTimeReport-WEBVersion.pdf (accessed 15 January 2011).

Burke, C. (2005) Play in focus: children researching their own spaces and places for play, *Children, Youth and Environments*, 15(1): 27-53.

Conley, S. and Muncey, D.E. (1999) Organizational climate and teacher professionalism: identifying teacher work environments' dimensions, in H.J. Freiberg (ed.) *School Climate: Measuring, Improving and Sustaining Healthy Learning Environments.* New York: Routledge.

Cooper, P. and Upton, G. (1990) An ecosystemic approach to emotional and behavioural difficulties in schools, *Educational Psychology*, 10(4): 301–21.

DCSF (Department for Children, Schools and Families) (2010) *Inclusion Development Programme: Supporting Children with Behavioural, Emotional and Social Difficulties: Guidance for Practitioners in the Early Years Foundation Stage.* Nottingham: DCSF.

DfES (Department for Education and Skills) (2003) *Every Child Matters: Change for Children in Schools*. Nottingham: DfES.

DfES (2007) *Statutory Framework for the Early Years Foundation Stage: Setting the Standards for Learning, Development and Care for Children from Birth to Five*. Nottingham: DfES.

Doughty, D. (2001) Playgrounds: the final frontier, *Times Educational Supplement*, 2 February.

Ecclestone, K. and Hayes, D. (2009) Changing the subject: the educational implications of developing emotional well-being, *Oxford Review of Education*, 35(3): 371–89.

EPPI (Evidence for Policy and Practice Information [and Co-ordinating Centre]) (2004) *A Systematic Review of How Theories Explain Learning Behaviour in School Contexts*. Review conducted by the Behaviour Management (Canterbury Christ Church University College) Review Group. London: EPPI-Centre, Social Science Research Unit, Institute of Education. Available online at: http://eppi.ioe.ac.uk/EPPIWebContent/reel/review_groups/TTA/BM(CCC)/BM(CCC)_2004 review.pdf (accessed 3 January 2011).

Frost, J. (2006) *The Dissolution of Children's Outdoor Play: Causes and Consequences*. Available online at: http://www.ipema.org/Documents/Common%20Good%20PDF.pdf (accessed 15 January 2011).

Gandini, L. (1998) Educational and caring spaces, in C. Edwards, L. Gandini and G. Forman (eds) *The Hundred Languages of Children. The Reggio Emilia Approach – Advanced Reflections*. Greenwich, CT: Ablex Publishing.

Gleave, J. (2009) *Children's Time to Play: A Literature Review*. London: Play England, Available online at: http://www.playday.org.uk/pdf/Childrens-time-to-play-a-literature-review.pdf (accessed 12 January 2011).

Gove, M. (2010) I've upset schools: reform isn't easy, *Sunday Express*, 11 July. Available online at: http://www.express.co.uk/posts/view/186212 (accessed 3 January 2011).

Groves, L. and McNish, H. (2008) *Baseline Study of Play at Merrylee Primary School*. Glasgow: Forestry Commission Scotland.

Henricsson, L. and Rydell, A.M. (2006) Children with behaviour problems: the influence of social competence and social relations on problem stability, school achievement and peer acceptance across the first six years of school, *Infant and Child Development*, 15: 347–66.

Hewes, P. (2005) *Let the children play: Nature's answer to early learning*, Canadian Council on Learning, Early Childhood Learning Subject Knowledge. Available online at: http://www.ccl-cca.ca/pdfs/LessonsInLearning/Nov-08-06-Let-the-Children-Play.pdf (accessed 15 January 2011).

Hoy, W.K. and Clover, S.I.R. (2007) Elementary school climate: a revision of the OCDQ, in W. Hoy and M. Di Paola (eds) *Essential Ideas for the Reform of American Schools: A Volume in Research and Theory*. New York: Information Age Publishing.

Jamieson, P., Fisher, K., Gilding, T., Taylor, P.G. and Trevitt, A.D. (2000) Place and space in the design of new environments, *Higher Education Research and Development*, 19: 221–37.

Keenan, C. (2007) Meeting youth where they live: participatory approaches to research with marginalised youth engaged in urban agriculture, *Children, Youth and Environments*, 17(3): 198–212.

Kramer, T.J., Caldarella, P., Christensen, L. and Shatzer, R.H. (2009) Social emotional learning in the kindergarten classroom: evaluation of the Strong Start curriculum, *Early Childhood Education Journal*, 37(4): 303–9.

Layard, R. and Dunn, J. (2009) *A Good Childhood: Searching for Values in a Competitive Age*. Harmondsworth: Penguin.

Layton, R. (2001) The great outdoors, *American School and University Magazine*. Available online at: http://asumag.com/mag/university_environmental_great_outdoors/ (accessed 25 October 2009).

Loo, C.M. (1972) The effects of spatial density on the social behaviour of children, *Journal of Applied Social Psychology*, 4: 372–81.

Lord Elton (1989) *The Elton Report: Discipline in Schools*. London: HMSO.

Martin, M. and Norwich, B. (1991) The interaction of research findings on classroom management into a programme for use in teacher education, *British Educational Research Journal*, 17(4): 333–51.

McGavin, H. (2001) Don't forget your bucket and spade, *Times Educational Supplement*, 27 July.

National Primary Strategy (2005) *Developing Children's Social, Emotional and Behavioural Skills: A Whole-School Approach*. London: DfES. Available online at: http://www.behaviour4learning.ac.uk/attachments/b0ce71d4-e114-46ae-8d32-804ad854aa69.pdf (accessed 3 January 2011).

OfSTED (Office for Standards in Education) (2008) *TellUs3 National Report*. Available online at: http://www.ofsted.gov.uk/Ofsted-home/Publications-and-research/Browse-all-by/Documents-by-type/Statistics/Other-statistics/TellUs3-NationalReport/(language)/eng-GB (accessed 12 January 2011).

OfSTED (2009) *The Exclusion from School of Children Aged Four to Seven*. London: OFSTED. Available online at: http://www.ofsted.gov.uk/Ofsted-home/Publications-and-research/Browse-all-by/Documents-by-type/Thematic-reports/The-exclusion-from-school-of-children-aged-four-to-seven (accessed 3 January 2011).

Papatheodorou, T. (2002) How we like our school to be . . . pupils' voices. *European Educational Research Journal*, 1(3): 445–7.

Papatheodorou, T. (2010) *Sensory Play*. Research Report submitted to Play-to-Z, Chelmsford: Anglia Ruskin University.

Rasmussen, K. (2004) Places for children: children's places, *Childhood: A Global Journal of Child Research*, 11(2): 155–74.

Reynolds, S., MacKay, T. and Kearney, M. (2009) Nurture groups: a large scale, controlled study of effects on development and academic attainment, *British Journal of Special Education*, 36(4): 204–12.

Rinaldi, C. (2006) *In Dialogue with Reggio Emilia: Listening, Researching and Learning*. London: Routledge.

Sandseter, H.B.H. (2009) Children's expressions of exhilaration and fear in risky play, *Contemporary Issues in Early Childhood*, 10(2): 92–106.

Sharp, C., Aldridge, J. and Medina, J. (2006) *Delinquent Youth Groups and Offending Behaviour: Findings from the 2004 Offending, Crime and Justice Survey*. London: Home Office Online Report 14/06. Available online at: http://rds.homeoffice.gov.uk/rds/pdfs06/rdsolr1406.pdf (accessed 3 January 2011).

Steer, A. (2005) *Learning Behaviour: The Report of the Practitioners' Group on School Behaviour and Discipline*. Nottingham: DfES. Available online at: http://publications.education.gov.uk/eOrderingDownload/1950-2005PDF-EN-02.pdf (accessed 3 January 2011).

Steer, A. (2009) *Learning Behaviour. Lessons Learned: A Review of Behaviour Standards and Practices in Our Schools*. Nottingham: DCFS. Available online at: http://www.teachernet.gov.uk/_doc/13514/8208-DCSF-Learning%20Behaviour.pdf (accessed 3 January 2011).

Sutton-Smith, B. (1997) *The Ambiguity of Play*. Cambridge, MA: Harvard University Press.

Taylor, A.F., Kuo, F.E. and Sullivan, W.C. (2001) Coping with ADD: the surprising connection to green play settings, *Environment and Behaviour*, 33(1): 54–77.

Webster-Stratton, C. and Reid, M.J. (2007) Strengthening social and emotional competence in young children who are socioeconomically disadvantaged, in W.H. Brown, S.L. Odom.

and S.R. McConnell (eds) *Social Competence in Young Children: Risk, Disability and Intervention*, Baltimore, MD: Brookes Publisher.

Wells, N.M. (2000) At home with nature: effects of 'greenness' on children's cognitive functioning, *Environment and Behaviour*, 32(6): 775–95.

Young, G. (2001) Space rage, *Guardian Education*, 9 January.

9

ALINE-WENDY DUNLOP
Moving in, on, up and out: successful transitions

Summary

This chapter considers transition to school as a joint enterprise shared by the teacher, children and parents. Two illustrative cameos highlight similarities and differences between children at school entry as they take part in learning and teaching, access curriculum, form relationships, settle into the new environment of the classroom and respond to their new teacher. A case is made for the usefulness of theories as tools to help this transition process and attention is given to the ongoing nature of transition with a particular focus on children's agency, teacher collaboration and parental participation in the process.

Cameo 1

Christopher was described by Mrs Wilkins, the head of his private nursery, as a 'quiet wee boy' who had made progress in his time at the nursery which he had attended since he was 18 months old. In the year before school entry he was in a small group with five other children. There were many adult-supported activities, some choice but with a limited range of options and a gentle preparation for school programme which included colouring in, cutting out, glueing and sticking and working collectively on art activities – all children took part and no choice was given. Christopher joined in and responded happily to adult requests despite many of the activities being very sedentary. He had a particular friend whom he liked to sit beside for stories and play within the small outside space. Pre-school assessments highlighted Christopher's interest in stories and a need for one-to-one time with adults in order for him to stay focused on the task. The head of the nursery said she found it challenging to build relationships with the local primary schools. At 4 years 9 months old, Christopher entered his new primary class knowing few others. He settled very quickly and, according to his teacher, mixed well with others, could carry out simple instructions, often had to be reminded to participate but enjoyed telling his news to the class. At the end of his first year in school, he required his teacher to act as scribe, worked quite well with numbers 1-10 often requiring the teacher's support, needing encouragement to express himself through art work but enjoying using a range of media. He remained easy with other children and very happy with his class teacher.

Cameo 2

Jasmine made the most of her entry to nursery class at 4 years old and, although initially she spoke little in English, she was very composed and made thoughtful choices about what to do with her time. She was always still working at a self-chosen activity when it was pick up time. Quiet, self-contained and self-assured – and very interested in making, drawing and enjoying books and stories – Jasmine intruded very little on others in her nursery class. Her persistence in the everyday tasks she set herself are well summed up by her attention to detail in making spring flowers for her mother at Easter time. In her home culture, Easter was not celebrated but she listened with interest to Easter stories and was intrigued by the spring blossoms that her teacher brought into the art area. After three attempts to make the perfect tulip, she retrieved the first attempt from the bin and re-worked it to her satisfaction. Pre-school assessments revealed her skills with phonics, number and word recognition. On the school induction day she met two teachers who were to job-share her new entrant class: Primary 1 (Scottish system). Jasmine started school at 5 years and 5 months. She made friends easily and soon she and Rachel were inseparable. Both always exceeded teacher requests and, when asked to draw a park scene, their pictures were the most vibrant and skilled in the class. Jasmine regretted that she didn't have much choice in school and said there were no books like at nursery – 'At least there are in the bookshelf, but you have to concentrate on the reading book and you can only choose a story book if you get all your work done.' She was co-operative and fitted in, taking responsibility in the class and moving easily to Primary 2.

Introduction

The introductory cameos illustrate the individuality of new school entrants while highlighting some of the differences children find between their pre-school experience and primary education: differences to which children gradually adjust. Current concepts of starting school see young children's transitions as a process rather than an event. In this chapter a focus is taken on four examples of transitions as a continuing process:

- moving into a new setting;
- moving on in that setting;
- moving up through the system represented in that setting;
- moving out of it to the next stage of education.

The chapter is, therefore, sequenced to look at the beginning teacher's role in supporting children in each phase of the transitions process: the child's start in the education system in prior to school settings away from home; the ways in which children's experience changes over time; looking ahead to new transitions with children; supporting the departing child's contact with the next stage of education (see Table 9.1).

Throughout the chapter, transitions are seen as a positive tool in the development of teaching and learning approaches including relationships, class environment, curriculum and pedagogy. The two cameos are used to illustrate these elements of transitions and to support continuity. A focus is taken on children's growing sense of competence, the challenges and opportunities that transitions provide to children, parents and teachers and the benefits inherent in the new/beginning teacher developing a concept of transitions as a way of classroom/school life to support teaching and

Table 9.1 Four examples of transitions as a continuing process

The children's roles	*The beginning teacher's role*
1 Moving into a new setting	
Child's start in an educational setting away from home	Benefits of the beginning teacher developing a concept of transitions as a way of classroom/ school life
Enactive and iconic approaches to representation	Reflecting on the classroom environment and habitual ways of being together
Intent participation	
2 Moving on in that setting	
The ways in which children's experience changes over time leading to a growing sense of competence	Forming a classroom community of practice with a focus on social and academic participation
Meaning makers and symbol users – progression through play and learning	Trusting children's strengths, scaffolding learning through guided participation
3 Moving up through the system	
A growing sense of agency, building transitions capital and transitions ease	Using transitions capital to look ahead to new transitions with children
Challenges for children	Challenges for teachers and parents
4 Moving out	
Children and teacher working collaboratively and on a sliding scale of novice, apprentice, practitioner and expert to make links with the next stage of education and the next teacher	

learning: together the beginning teacher and the beginning children move along the sliding scale of novice, apprentice, practitioner – and often expert – in making transitions work for them. Set in the context of the two children's transition's trajectories, three key concepts inform the discussion. These are:

1 children's agency;

2 teacher collaboration;

3 parental involvement.

The socio-cultural nature of learning provides opportunities to understand transitions as the entry to, acquisition of and shaping of a whole new culture – undertaken by children and their teacher with the help of supportive parents.

Key ideas drawn from researchers such as Rogoff, Corsaro and Bronfenbrenner (1979; 1986) inform the discussion which focuses on the transition trajectories of children as they build 'transitions capital' (Dunlop and Fabian 2007) and transitions ease (Dunlop 2010) on their journey in, on, up and through early childhood education and, in due course, out of the particular classroom and stage of education. Children's engagement in school, in social relationships and in their learning place them firmly in a collective enterprise with each other and their teachers as they create meaning together (Bruner 1986). The examples are early years related but the concepts apply across early years, primary and secondary schooling.

What matters at times of transition?

Embarking on the development of teaching and learning approaches including relationships, class environment, curriculum and pedagogy with a new entrant class as a beginning teacher gives a unique opportunity to co-construct their practice with the children's collaboration. Most children arrive in school with pre-school group experience: they have expertise to offer. They need to find a classroom with both recognizable features as well as new interest. They expect to learn to read and write, sometimes immediately, but they move into this with greater ease from a basis of the familiar – for example, an accessible story area, opportunities to play, time to talk with the teacher and build relationships – often achieved effectively through child–teacher discussion of their transition reports or portfolios if these are passed on. It may be helpful to sit near a friend in the early days and to be able to sustain the independence acquired in pre-school by having real opportunities to choose from class activities and areas as well as to be free to manage their personal needs such as visits to the toilet and enjoying their snack without a rush.

Transitions studies provide good insights into approaching work with an entrant class – such studies may be grouped broadly into three paradigms: (1) those that focus mainly on the individual development and readiness of the child for school; (2) those that, on the other hand, look more at the school context(s), systems and structures to find answers to ease transitions; and (3) those that combine to consider development in context with a focus on the interpersonal and socio-cultural (Dunlop 2009, 2010).

Many transitions researchers have made use of Bronfenbrenner's (1979) ecological systems theory to aid understanding of transitions (Fabian and Dunlop 2002,

2007; Dunlop and Fabian 2007). Engaged by the way in which he placed human development in context and asserted the interrelated and dynamic nature of the different contexts occupied by the child (in the present case home, pre-school and school), transitions researchers have also found that interpretations of Bronfenbrenner's ecological systems theory need not focus only on the individual child, but allow consideration of children collectively. A systems approach can offer a space to juxtapose, for example, human development in context with socio-cultural theory and sociologies of childhood. Elder (1998) too, focuses on change over time, seeing people not simply as the products of their experience but as producers of culture. In focusing on *timing in lives*, Elder proposes that 'the developmental impact of a succession of life transitions or events is contingent on when they occur in a person's life' (1998: 3). When several different transitions occur in tandem, this can disrupt the timing and duration of normative transitions: in early childhood it is, therefore, important to work collaboratively with families and to develop relationships that allow the sharing of events that may impact on children's day-to-day experiences. Elder and Bronfenbrenner both concern themselves with agency and the capacity to act and influence the life course.

Empirical work such as Corsaro and Molinari's (2008: 261) focuses on children's collective experiences and their shared agency. They highlight that children find differences between pre-school and school, including:

1   The requirements of order, control and rules in the classroom; how closely linked to pre-school?
2   Classroom and educational activities – the more structured tasks related to instruction in the more advanced educational activities.
3   The demands of a new and more differentiated peer culture.

They argue that expectations of what school will be like are based on pre-school priming events: 'Priming events involve activities in which children, by their very participation, attend prospectively to ongoing or anticipated changes in their lives' (Corsaro and Molinari 2008: 263).

Alderson (2003), in her discussion of 'Institutional rites and rights' considers the contribution of childhood studies, indicating that such studies tend to 'meet [children] in their everyday contexts and relationships where they have expert knowledge' (2003: 27), while the Cambridge Primary Review (Alexander et al. 2009) urges teachers to 'Respect children's experience, voices and rights. Engage them actively and directly in decisions that affect their learning' (2009: 12).

Shared beginnings

Beginning teachers, whether newly qualified or new to the particular school situation, share with the incoming children the experience of being new. From this perspective it is helpful to think about how teacher and children may be able to work through these changes together. However, the nature of transitions in education is that they are ongoing and consequently it may be helpful for the beginning teacher to adopt the view that transitions are a way of life (Brooker 2008) both for adults and in the daily lives of children.

As a newcomer with class teaching responsibilities, these may overwhelm any desire to take a wider view. In this chapter an emphasis is placed on the importance of theories as tools which can support teacher and child in the classroom setting. This relationship of theory and practice can be argued to support teachers' career-long learning to the benefit of children's learning. According to Donaldson:

> The capacity of the teacher should be built not just through extensive 'teaching practice' but through reflecting on and learning from the experience of support-ing children's learning with all the complexities which characterize twenty-first century childhood. The 'craft' components of teaching must be based upon and informed by fresh insights into how best to meet the increasingly fast pace of change in the world which our children inhabit.
>
> (2011: 4–5)

Bulkeley and Fabian (2006) assert the importance of the child's emotional well-being as a buffer that supports children's capacity to cope with such changes at times of tran-sition. Denham (2006) makes a connection between positive emotional expressive-ness, enthusiasm, the ability to regulate emotions and behaviours and social emotional well-being and successful learning.

The importance of bringing together a knowledge of children, a respect for their contribution, insights about the child and about childhood, allows an acknowledge-ment that times of transitions present opportunities, can emphasize common experi-ences between pre-school and school, as well as the differences that new children and new teachers take into account as they shape shared routines in the new classroom cul-ture. A culture that includes stories, drawing, discussion, shared play, folios, literacy, special events, production of routines, friendships, expectations, play and changes in the peer culture as children make new friends and judge with whom to play and work. Used to making such decisions in pre-school, children can bring this independence into the primary school as part of their contribution. Emerging from this discussion are some informative ideas to work from as teacher and children settle in together: the concept of transition trajectories, children's agency, teacher collaboration, parental participation and theories as tools.

A concept of transition trajectories lets us acknowledge that successful transitions may take time, that children deal differently with transitions and that prior experience needs to be taken into account as well as the particular dispositions of each child. In shaping classroom routines a balance needs to be struck between group cooperation and managing individual responsiveness. Tables 9.2 and 9.3 show how Christopher and Jasmine move *in, on, up and out* of the new entrant class: their particular trajec-tories differ.

Children's agency is promoted through real opportunities to make decisions, for example, as Ladd (1990) highlighted – whom to work with, whom to play with, who to be friends with and whom to avoid – illustrating self-regulation, the importance of choice, perspective taking, imagination and creativity. Building on what children offer, it is possible to see how adjustments for one may be helpful for all. Children's concern with rules, children's understanding of what is expected from them in school, the need to find ways of entering activities and play and also of leaving them (Corsaro 1979) show that each situation offers opportunities to exert agency.

Table 9.2 Christopher's trajectory

	Transitions trajectories	Children's agency	Teacher collaboration	Parental involvement	Theories as tools
Christopher on entry – Relationships with trusted adults in nurturing environment – as transition approaches school practice activities and paper-based tasks predominate					
IN	Only one from nursery going to particular primary school – peer relationships	Exerted a quiet agency in insistence on contact with adults	Quite separate – moved from a private nursery in a different area. Came to induction day – no visit from school. Children from many 'feeder' pre-schools attended induction day at school	Working parents who had enjoyed the support of pre-school – managed work flexibly for settling in period. Attended the induction day	Sources of agency (Bruner 1986; Emirbayer and Mische 1998; Rogoff 2003)
ON	Nursery wanted to send on a report and photos but unsure how this would be received. They sent it nevertheless and directly to the class teacher who benefited from the report and had a good sense of pre-school practices	Christopher's personal agency continued into primary school – 'It's impossible not to warm to him. He's immature, gentle, sometimes lacking concentration but responsive and rewarding'	While there was no face-to-face contact between settings, Christopher's receiving teacher recognized his needs well and built on the messages in the short report from the nursery	Some concerns about Christopher managing in the cloakroom and playground and with the greater number of children	Children's dispositions – resilience, playfulness and reciprocity (Carr and Claxton 2002)
UP	A gradual process of increasing engagement in learning – deemed to need support. Responded to his first teacher in school who listened to the children in her class, was a singer, story teller and loved her class	Exerting agency through participation in discussion and in groups, and through his own sense of self-worth. Still not showing what he is capable of	Some teaching relief for class teacher meant a new relationship with a supply teacher. Christopher adapted well on the days this teacher was in class	Some diffidence about own school experience, not clear if parents picked up on school's views of Christopher needing support	Children's participation and voice. Socio-cultural theory (Rogoff 2003). Situated learning (Lave and Wenger 1991). Importance of the first teacher (Harrison 2007)
OUT	Very involved with peer group by end of first school year	Liked his teachers and later was very clear if he detected any lack of commitment	Records passed on formally and informally to the teacher taking the class the following year	Regular attendees at school parent meetings	Access rituals (Corsaro 1979)

Jasmine on entry – *Time to settle, to develop English and to make relationships in preschool class.*

	Transitions trajectories	Children's agency	Teacher collaboration	Parental involvement	Theories as tools
IN	A confidence in making peer relationships, going to school with friends	Shows focus, interest and persistence	Nursery class within school – potentially good opportunities for meeting together and sharing information	Jasmine's mother was very focused on her happiness and worried about juggling work and children	Transitions as a collective process (Corsaro and Molinari 2008) Priming events (Corsaro and Molinari 2000)
ON	Report from nursery class passed on and discussed – showing Jasmine to be focused, interested, engaged in her own learning, skilled	Quietly subversive – pursues tasks in her own way. Too workbook bound, not enough choice. Strong disposition to learn	There was a real need for collaboration as the new entrant class was staffed by job-share teachers who, though experienced, had never taught at this stage. They were supported by Christopher's teacher	Joined in with the arranged induction activities and attended parents' nights when she could. Missed the regular conversations with the nursery staff	Children's dispositions – resilience (Carr and Claxton 2002)
UP	Jasmine's own expectations were entirely pragmatic – she expected to manage herself and was not over-dependent on her job share teachers	Mature, scaffolding others, e.g. in shop play	Shared information from the nursery class contributed to a smooth start but none of the teachers was aware of Jasmine's exceptional and natural ability with phonics. The teachers worked on the colour 'red' – this had little interest for Jasmine	Brings and picks Jasmine up from school. Finds the new mothers in the playground unfriendly	The more able or experienced other (Vygotsky 1978) Agency in social and cultural contexts (Bruner 1986) Complex play (Smilansky 1990)
OUT	Her move to the next stage coincided with family change, a school move and her parents' separation. She navigated these multiple transitions capably with the mutual support of her older sister	Highly motivated but finding a lack of choice and opportunity to show her creativity as for a while at least there was an over-dependence on workbooks	High level job share collaboration. Two different planning styles. Shared planning midweek. Poor school leadership, but good stage leadership	Marriage breaks up and Ameena moves to another area because of the need to find a new home. The children move school	Parental participation (Dunlop 2003)

Teacher collaboration at times of transition takes several forms – teachers as stage partners supporting each other within settings with planning, record keeping, resources and development, mentoring of beginning teachers, working together across sectors to ease transitions through knowledge of each other's practices and how they affect children. Help from a member of nursery staff to ease children's entry to school can be very helpful in the earliest days.

Parental participation

Parents too are affected by their child's transitions and contribute in shaping successful transitions (Dunlop 2003). Where an individual worry or concern is identified, it is important to work with parents together to co-construct the transition, to know more about the social capital of the child and to understand what they are bringing with them to school. Parental disposition and their thoughts about appropriate roles at transition make an important contribution and help parents to feel involved in the process of transition to school.

Theories as tools

A number of theories to explain transitions help in understanding both the new teachers' experiences and those of the new entrant to a class. The concepts of rites of passage (van Gennep 1960) and rites of institution (Bourdieu 1990) help in recognizing the adjustments both adults and children are making, while intent participation (Rogoff et al. 2003), situated learning (Lave and Wenger 1991), learning in companionship (Trevarthen 2002), understandings of children's peripheral and intent participation (Rogoff et al. 2003), the importance of scaffolding learning (Vygotsky 1978) and of teacher knowledge of complex play (Smilansky 1968, 1990) all contribute to environments in which early educators arguably become more aware of the impact of their practices.

Tables 9.2 and 9.3 show how theories as tools for understanding transitions may be mapped onto children's everyday experiences. References are provided to explore such theories further. There is a Christopher and a Jasmine in many early childhood classes across the country.

Conclusion

This chapter has argued that beginning teachers and beginning children share a unique opportunity to make the most of the opportunities that transitions into school offer. Together they may shape the culture of the classroom into one that values children, affords them opportunities to contribute, recognizes both the agency of the child and of the teacher and encourages them to co-construct the early days of shared experience in a way that set them up as a community of learners – socially, emotionally and academically. In that way, they move into their first year together in school, on into the learning processes, up through new experiences and demands and out to the next stage of their school careers.

Children's engagement, learning, sense of belonging and deep involvement combine with the expectations teachers and children have of each other. As Peters says in her review of transitions: 'Hattie . . . reminds teachers, if they are going to have expectations they should make them challenging, appropriate and checkable' (Hattie 2009, cited in Peters 2010: 26). Further, Peters cites Thomson and Hall, suggesting:

> After moving to England from Australia, Thomson noted the impact that curriculum has on teachers' ability to incorporate children's existing funds of knowledge. Writing with Hall, she commented that in the current context of English schooling there was 'little official opening for family, local and community knowledge, despite ongoing research which suggests that the inclusion of such "funds" can be important "scaffolding" for children whose languages, heritages and ways of being in the world are not those valued in schooling'.
>
> (Thomson and Hall 2008: 87, cited in Peters 2010: 27)

With an interest in transitions firmly established, it is time to reflect on the strengths found in partnership. The importance of leadership for the transition process needs to be recognized (see Chapter 22). A review of transition practices (Fabian and Dunlop 2007) found a number of whole school approaches were helpful for children in transition and their parents. These included:

- schools having a named person, or a small team, to take responsibility and a strategic overview of the process;
- schools providing pre-entry visits for children and their parents that involve parents and children learning about learning at school as well as familiarization with the environment and people;
- schools having systems that allow for high quality communication and close interaction between family, pre-transfer settings and school, where information is both given and received about children's experiences;
- flexible admission procedures that give children and their parents the opportunity to have a positive start to their first day (Fabian and Dunlop 2007: 25).

Sharing the transition to school with children provides the beginning teacher with a real opportunity to know the children in the class well, to be responsive to their needs and rights and to build learning relationships that add to children's ease in transitions and to their transitions capital for their journey through education.

Questions to Promote Thinking

1   Think of examples of how you could build on directly from children's prior to school experience of curriculum: can you add these into your day-to-day planning?

2   Could you create transition cameos of children in your class that take account of children's agency, teacher collaboration across the Foundation Stage/early level of curriculum and parental participation?

3   How does theory work for you as a tool to inform your practices?

References and suggested further reading

Alderson, P. (2003) Institutional rites and rights: a century of childhood, Professorial Lecture, London, Institute of Education, University of London.

Alexander, R., Armstrong, M., Flutter, J., Hargreaves, L., Harrison, D., Harlen, W., Hartley-Brewer, E., Kershner, R., Macbeath, J., Mayall, B., Northen, S., Pugh, G., Richards, C. and Utting, D. (2009) *Children, their World, their Education: Final Report and Recommendations of the Cambridge Primary Review*. London: Routledge.

Bohan-Baker, M. and Little, P. (2004) The Transition to Kindergarten: A Review of Current Research and Promising Practices to Involve Families. Cambridge, MA: Harvard Family Research Project.

Bourdieu, P. (1990) Rites of institution, in *Language and Symbolic Power*, trans. P. Collier. Cambridge, Polity Press, and Cambridge, MA: Harvard University Press (orig. 1982), pp. 117–27.

Bronfenbrenner, U. (1979) *The Ecology of Human Development*. Cambridge, MA: Harvard University Press.

Bronfenbrenner, U. (1986) Ecology of the family as a context for human development: research perspectives, *Developmental Psychology*, 22: 723–42.

Brooker, L. (2002) Starting School: Young Children's Learning Cultures. Buckingham: Open University Press.

Brooker, L. (2008) *Supporting Transitions in the Early Years*. Maidenhead: Open University Press/McGraw-Hill.

Bruner, J. (1986) *Actual Minds, Possible Worlds*. Cambridge, MA: Harvard University Press.

Bulkeley, J. and Fabian, H. (2006) Well-being and belonging during early educational transitions, *International Journal of Transitions in Childhood*, 2: 18–31.

Carr, M. and Claxton, G. (2002) Tracking the development of learning dispositions, *Assessment in Education: Principles, Policy and Practice*, 9(1): 9–37.

Corsaro, W.A. (1979) 'We're friends, right?': children's use of access rituals in a nursery school. *Language in Society*, 8(3): 315–36.

Corsaro, W.A. and Molinari, L. (2000) Priming events and Italian children's transition from preschool to elementary school: representations and action, *Social Psychological Quarterly*, 63: 16–33.

Corsaro, W.A. and Molinari, L. (2008) Policy and practice in Italian children's transition from preschool to elementary school, *Research in Comparative and International Education*, 3(3): 250–65.

Denham, S.A. (2006) Social-emotional competence as support for school readiness: what is it and how do we assess it? *Early Education and Development*, 17(1): 57-89.

Donaldson, G. (2011) *Teaching. Scotland's future: Report of a Review of Teacher Education in Scotland*. Edinburgh: The Scottish Government.

Dunlop, A-W. (2003) Bridging children's early education transitions through parental agency and inclusion, *Education in the North*, 11: 55–6.

Dunlop, A-W. (2009) Transition methodologies: choices and chances, Paper presented at the Scottish Educational Research Association (SERA), November.

Dunlop, A-W. (2010) The theoretical foundations and some key results of transitions to school research in a Scottish context – one framework or many? Populating the theoretical model over time, paper prepared for the Starting School Research, Policy and Practice Event, Charles Sturt University, Albury, Australia, 12–15 October.

Dunlop, A-W. and Fabian, H. (eds) (2007) Informing Transitions in the Early Years: Research, Policy and Practice. Maidenhead: Open University Press.

Elder, G.H. Jr. (1998) The life course as developmental theory, *Child Development*, 69(1): 1–12.

Emirbayer, M. and Mische, A. (1998) What is agency? *American Journal of Sociology*, 103(4): 962–1023.

Esmée Fairbairn Foundation (2009) Introducing the Cambridge Primary Review. Available online at: http://www.esmeefairbairn.org.uk/ (accessed 18 January 2011).

Fabian, H. and Dunlop, A-W. (eds) (2002) *Transitions in the Early Years: Debating Continuity and Progression for Young Children in Early Education.* London: RoutledgeFalmer.

Fabian, H. and Dunlop, A-W. (2007) *Outcomes of Good Practice in Transition Processes for Children Entering Primary School. Working Paper 42.* The Hague, The Netherlands: Bernard van Leer Foundation.

Harrison, L. (2007) The supporting role of relationships in children's transitions into and through school. Paper presented at the International Research Conference: Transforming Transitions, Glasgow, Scotland, April.

Ladd, G.W. (1990) Having friends, keeping friends, making friends and being liked by peers in the classroom: predictors of children's early school adjustment, *Child Development*, 61: 1081–100.

Ladd, G., Herald, S. and Kochel, K. (2006) School readiness: Are there social prerequisites? *Early Education and Development*, 17(1): 115–150. DOI: 10.1207/ s15566935eed1701_6.

Lave, J. and Wenger, E. (1991) *Situated Learning: Legitimate Peripheral Participation.* Cambridge: Cambridge University Press.

Peters, S. (2010) *Review: Transition from Early Childhood Education to School.* Wellington: Ministry of Education, New Zealand. Available online at: http:// www.educationcounts.govt.nz/publications/ece/78823 (accessed 18 January 2011).

Petriwskyj, A., Thorpe, K. and Tayler, C. (2005) Trends in construction of transition to school in three western regions, 1990–2004, *International Journal of Early Years Education*, 13(1): 55–69.

Rogoff, B. (2003) *The Cultural Nature of Human Development.* New York: Oxford University Press.

Rogoff, B., Paradise, R., Mejía Arauz, R., Correa-Chavez, M. and Angelillo, C. (2003) First hand learning through intent participation, *Annual Review of Psychology*, 54: 175–203.

Smilansky, S. (1968) *The Effects of Sociodramatic Play on Disadvantaged Preschool Children.* New York: Wiley and Sons.

Smilansky, S. (1990) Sociodramatic play: its relevance to behaviour and achievement in school, in E. Klugman and S. Smilansky, *Children's Play and Learning Perspectives and Policy Implications.* New York: Teacher's College Press.

Trevarthen, C. (2002) Learning in companionship, *Education in the North: The Journal of Scottish Education*, New Series, 10: 16–25.

Van Gennep, A. ([1908] 1960) *The Rites of Passage.* London: Routledge and Kegan Paul.

Vygotsky, L. (1978) *Mind in Society.* Cambridge, MA: Harvard University Press.

PART 3
Ways of learning

10

DAVID WHITEBREAD AND PENNY COLTMAN
Developing young children as self-regulating learners

Summary

The aim of a good teacher should be to make themselves redundant! In this chapter we argue that, if we are to educate children properly, we must enable them to become independent, or what might more properly be termed self-regulating, learners. We examine the psychological research literature concerning the nature of independent, or self-regulated, learning and report the findings of a two-year research project exploring the development of self-regulated learning capabilities in young children.

Cameo 1

In a reception class, a group of children work together to solve a jigsaw puzzle. Initially the children all begin tackling the task separately, competing for pieces and hoarding. As the puzzle remains incomplete the children begin to cooperate, using non-verbal communication as they offer pieces to each other.

Eventually the children begin to talk to each other about the task. One child takes charge of the picture on the lid of the puzzle box, indicating to others where key elements of the picture should be located. Other children check these instructions, comparing the picture with the puzzle on the floor. As the puzzle reaches completion, children negotiate the correct positions of pieces, supporting each other as they reach a shared goal.

> **Cameo 2**
>
> A group of children in a reception class are working independently on individual writing tasks, when Polly pokes Rosie with a pencil. Rosie asks Polly to stop. When the poking continues, Rosie turns to Adam, who is sitting to the other side of her, for support.
>
> Adam prefers not to tackle Polly directly but, instead, approaches another child Angela, asking her whether or not she thinks that it would help the situation if he swapped seats with Rosie. Angela merely turns to Polly, explaining that poking with a pencil can hurt and that she should stop doing this to Rosie. Her calm approach successfully diffuses the situation and the children return to their writing.

Introduction

The aim of a good teacher should, of course, be to make themselves redundant. If we are to properly educate our young children, we must enable them to become independent, or what might more properly be termed self-regulating, learners. There is currently widespread interest in fostering 'independent learning' among young children, as attested by a number of publications (Featherstone and Bayley 2001; Williams 2003) and by recent official English government guidelines. In this chapter we examine the psychological research literature concerning the nature of independent, or self-regulated, learning and report the findings of a two-year research project exploring the development of self-regulated learning capabilities in young children.

What is meant by 'independent learning'?

The education policy context

Initiatives, circulars and curriculum documents from various government agencies over the past decade have offered a range of suggestions as to what independent or self-regulated learning might involve. In the revised QTS Standards, *Qualifying to Teach* (TDA 2006), for example, teacher trainees are required under Standard S3.3.3 to 'teach clearly structured lessons or sequences of work which interest and motivate pupils and which make learning objectives clear to pupils . . . [and] promote active and independent learning that enables pupils to think for themselves, and to plan and manage their own learning'.

In the *Curriculum Guidance for the Foundation Stage* (QCA/DfEE 2000), which established the new curriculum for children between 3 and 5 years of age, one of the stated 'Principles for early years education' (2000: 3) is that there should be 'opportunities for children to engage in activities planned by adults and also those that they plan and initiate themselves'.

There seems, therefore, to be strong commitment to independent learning: however, there is also a need for clear definition. In some policy guidelines (e.g. the *Early*

Years Foundation Stage (DCSF 2007), the emphasis is more on helping children with personal independence skills and becoming an independent *pupil*, i.e. being able to function in a classroom without being overly dependent on adult help. As we shall see below, research studies have also generally found that this is the dominant concern for many teachers. This is very distinct from the concern to help children to develop as independent *learners*, i.e. being able to take control of and responsibility for, their own learning. It is for this reason that the term 'self-regulation' is preferred, with its emphasis on the learner taking control and ownership of their own learning.

The context of the classroom

While a commitment to encouraging children to become self-regulating learners is very common among primary school teachers, at the level of everyday classroom realities there are a number of problematic issues. The need to maintain an orderly classroom, combined with the pressures of time and resources and teachers' perceptions of external expectations from headteachers, parents and government agencies, can often militate against the support of children's independence.

Evidence from a study across the FS and KS1 (Hendy and Whitebread 2000) very much supported this view. The early years teachers interviewed shared a commitment to encouraging greater independence in learning among young children but held a wide spectrum of views about the essential key elements within it and of their role in fostering the necessary skills and dispositions. There was a dominant concern, nevertheless, with the *organizational* element of children's independence, as opposed to any concern with cognitive or emotional areas. Perhaps most significant, however, was the finding that the children appeared to become more, rather than less, dependent on their teachers during their first few years in school.

What is clear, however, is that if primary school teachers are to successfully foster independent learning in their classrooms, an understanding needs to be developed of the skills and dispositions involved in self-regulated learning and of the pedagogical practices which are most likely to foster these. The remainder of this chapter will review the relevant research literature from developmental psychology before exploring research about educational practices which might be helpful in this area.

Psychological approaches to self-regulated learning

Within cognitive developmental psychology over the past 30 years or so there has been a very considerable body of research evidence related to the development of children as independent learners. Within the psychological literature this has been variously characterized as 'learning how to learn' (Nisbet and Shucksmith 1986), 'reflection' (Yussen 1985), 'self-regulation' (Schunk and Zimmerman 1994) and 'metacognition' (Metcalfe and Shimamura 1994), all of which are concerned with children's developing self-awareness and control of their own mental processing. What has emerged is a body of research and theory which suggests that it is this aspect of development which is crucially responsible for individual differences in children's development as learners.

The work has been inspired by two traditions within developmental psychology. First, is the socio-cultural tradition founded on the work of the Russian psychologist, Lev Vygotsky (1978, 1986). For Vygotsky, the development of children's learning was a process of moving from other-regulation (or performing a task while supported by an adult or peer) to self-regulation (performing a task on one's own). A considerable body of research work in recent years has investigated the processes by which adults support children's learning. This research has largely endorsed Vygotsky's approach. Adults encourage, instruct, ask questions, give feedback, and so on. These various forms of interaction combine so that the skilful adult provides what has been termed 'scaffolding'. Crucially, research has shown that a key characteristic of a good scaffolder is the ability to sensitively withdraw support as the child becomes able to carry out the task more independently (see Schaffer 2004).

Learning for Vygotsky can, therefore, be characterized as a process of internalization whereby the procedures for successful completion of a task are initially modelled and articulated by an adult or more experienced peer, with the child then gradually becoming able to talk themselves through the task. Finally, the child can fully self-regulate using internal speech or abstract thought.

The second tradition is the information-processing approach and, specifically, the early work in the 1960s and 1970s of Flavell on the development of children's memory abilities. In their seminal study, Flavell et al. (1966) found young children under the age of 7 years were capable of carrying out a taught memory strategy but incapable of producing that strategy for use spontaneously (or independently). This led to Flavell's (1979) development of a model of 'metamemory' and Brown's (1987) model of metacognition. In Brown's model, metacognition was characterized as consisting of three related elements:

- *metacognitive experience*: the online monitoring or self-awareness of mental processing, and reflections upon it;
- *metacognitive knowledge*: the knowledge which is gradually accumulated about one's own mental processing, tasks and cognitive strategies for dealing with tasks;
- *self-regulation*: the metacognitive control of mental processing, so that strategies are developed and used appropriately in relation to tasks.

There have been two significant later developments in this area of research. First, there has been a broadening of notions of self-regulation from these purely cognitive concerns to include emotional, social and motivational aspects. The work of Goleman (1995) on emotional intelligence, for example, is part of this trend. Understandings emerging from neuroscience also support a model which integrates emotional and cognitive aspects of self-regulation (see Chapter 2). The development of metacognitive and self-regulatory functions appears to be related to developments in the frontal lobes (Barkley 1997).

Second, there has been the recognition of metacognitive processes in very young children. In a very comprehensive overview, Bronson (2000) demonstrates that the development of metacognitive and self-regulatory processes is fundamental to the whole range of young children's psychological growth. She describes in detail extensive research which has explored the emotional, prosocial, cognitive and motivational developments in self-regulation throughout the different phases of early childhood.

In our own research (the Cambridgeshire Independent Learning, or CIndLe, project; Whitebread et al. 2005) we worked with 32 Foundation Stage teachers over two years and collected approximately 100 hours of video and numerous other occasional observations. From these data, 705 events have been recorded and documented which show evidence of self-regulatory and metacognitive behaviour. As the average duration of these events is a number of minutes – in some cases as long as 20–30 minutes – this average rate of incidence of around seven events per hour is a striking testimony of the pervasiveness of self-regulatory and metacognitive behaviours in children in the 3–5 age range.

As part of this project, a checklist of self-regulatory behaviours (CHecklist of Independent Learning Development, or CHILD, 3–5) was developed consisting of 22 statements describing the most common and significant achievements in cognitive, motivational, emotional and social areas of development within the 3–5 age group (see Table 10.1). A number of the statements from the checklist were evidenced with considerable frequency, some being present in as many as a third of all the recorded events. For example, the statements of abilities for which the most numerous observations were recorded included the following:

- can control attention and resist distraction;
- can speak about how they have done something or what they have learnt;
- can make reasoned choices and decisions;
- develops own ways of carrying out tasks.

Of these 705 self-regulatory events documented in the project, 582 (i.e. 82.6 per cent) contained an element of specifically metacognitive activity. This provides initial and substantial evidence of the clear ability of young children to engage in a wide range of metacognitive and self-regulatory activities.

Table 10.1 Checklist of Independent Learning Development 3–5

Statement	Exemplar event	Description
EMOTIONAL ELEMENTS OF INDEPENDENT LEARNING		
Can speak about others behaviour and consequences	Warning about paper clips	Three children are playing in the workshop area. A girl that appears to be leading the game is explaining the rest of the group how dangerous paper clips can be, modelling the correct way of using them
Tackles new tasks confidently	Counting to 100 Making big sums Counting backwards Counting forever	A sequence of events representing a clear progression in the way children spontaneously set up and solve increasingly more challenging mathematical tasks after being provided with enough cognitive structuring by the teacher

(Continued)

Table 10.1 (Continued)

Statement	Exemplar event	Description
Can control attention and resist distraction	Fixing a bike	A child has entered the workshop area and has decided that he is going to fix the bike that has been placed as part of the setting. The child remains on task for an extended period of time using different tools and checking the outcomes of his actions
Monitors progress and seeks help appropriately	Building a bridge	A group of children have decided to build a bridge to get to a castle but the bridge keeps falling down. The 'builders' actively seek the advice of other children who stop in front of the construction to see what is happening
Persists in the face of difficulties	Finding the screwdriver	A girl has entered Santa's workshop area. She is looking for the screwdriver to make some toys. She actively looks for it and asks for the other children's help. After 15 minutes where she appears to have been engaged in other activities, she finally finds it. 'I found the screwdriver!'

PROSOCIAL ELEMENTS OF INDEPENDENT LEARNING

Statement	Exemplar event	Description
Negotiates when and how to carry out tasks	Planning the game Playing in small group	A group of children have been encouraged to create a game using a hoop and a ball. The children actively discuss who is going to hold the hoop and who is going to throw the ball. They all agree they have to take turns. 'Otherwise it wouldn't be fair,' says one of the children. They try out the game before teaching it to the rest of the class
Can resolve social problems with peers	Negotiating number of children	Too many children are in the workshop area. A child becomes aware of the situation and acts as a negotiator trying to determine who can stay and who has to leave. He uses different questions to solve the problem: 'Who doesn't want to be here?', 'Who's been here the longest?'
Is aware of feelings of others; helps and comforts	Making cards	A girl helps a boy make a card. She doesn't 'do' it for him but has been asked to show him what to do. During the sequence she is very helpful and 'keeps an eye on him'. She does not take over, yet seems to take pride in the helping process
Engages in independent cooperative activities with peers	Three Little Pigs crisis	Children are playing Three Little Pigs in the role play area. A 'crisis' has been introduced. The Big Bad Wolf has stopped the electricity getting to the house. The children are exploring using torches and working out what to do

Statement	Exemplar event	Description
Shares and takes turns independently	Taking turns	A group of girls are playing a lottery game. They spontaneously take turns asking: 'Whose turn is it?' and reminding each other: 'It's your turn now!'

COGNITIVE ELEMENTS OF INDEPENDENT LEARNING

Statement	Exemplar event	Description
Is aware of own strengths and weaknesses	Counting beans with Jack	A girl is counting beans using a puppet (Jack). Being aware that there are too many beans to count, she decided to put some of the beans away so Jack can 'count them better'
Can speak about how they have done something or what they have learnt	Drawing a fire	Two boys sit side by side at the drawing table and discuss how to draw a fire. One says it is a zig-zag shape and draws an example, saying that his mummy told him it was like this. The other disputes this and says it goes little and then very big, drawing small downward lines and long vertical lines. They talk about how fire is spread and how the flames move
Can speak about planned activities	The castle	Two girls have decided that they want to make a castle in the play area. Being prompted by the teacher's questions they verbalize what they want to put in the castle, the materials they need and what to do first
Can make reasoned choices and decisions	Writing an animal story	Two boys collaborating on a story decide between them that they want it to feature a particular animal so send someone in search of a picture to copy
Asks questions and suggests answers	Skeletons	A group were interested in skeletons, and the Nursery Nurse helped them to draw around one another and copy pictures from books to fill in their skeletons. The children felt the bones in their bodies as they drew. They asked questions about the bones and in some cases one child answered another's question
Uses a strategy previously modelled	Peer support in writing	Two boys support another with his writing when they see him struggle. They communicate clearly, using strategies they have heard from their teacher, and are sensitive to his feelings
Uses language previously heard for own purposes	Writing messages	Two girls help a boy who also wants to write. They track what he is doing and point to an example of a message (written by a child) on the wall and draw attention to the individual letters, naming them for the boy

(Continued)

Table 10.1 *(Continued)*

Statement	Exemplar event	Description
MOTIVATIONAL ELEMENTS OF INDEPENDENT LEARNING		
Initiates activities	Making computers	Two children decide to make a computer out of a cardboard box. They work collaboratively together and persist when things don't go well, e.g. working out how to join the box (computer screen) to the table
Finds own resources without adult help	Goldilocks and the three bears	The children have decided to recreate the story of Goldilocks and the three bears. They have found three boxes of different sizes for the beds, three bowls and spoons for the bears and a pot to cook the porridge
Develops own ways of carrying out tasks	Making books	One child made a 'book' by sellotaping together three small sheets of computer paper. She drew simple illustrations and asked her teacher to scribe the story for her. It was a perfect story: 'The cat was lost. The flower was lonely. The dog had no friends. The sun came out and cheered them all up.' The book was read to the class and by four weeks later half the class had made books using the same method
Plans own tasks, targets and goals	Christmas wrapping	A group of children have turned the play area into Santa's workshop. They have decided that they are going to wrap presents; they have found resources, and they have negotiated their roles
Enjoys solving problems and challenges	Building a bridge	The teacher has set up a problem: the children need to get a treasure located at the other side of the room, crossing a river filled with crocodiles. The children decide to build a bridge and they cooperate to achieve their plan

More recent studies (Whitebread et al. 2009) have established that the CHILD 3–5 instrument is a highly valid and reliable observational tool and one which classroom teachers can use very effectively as a diagnostic tool to help them identify key areas in which children with poorly developed self-regulatory skills require support.

The pedagogy of self-regulation

Collins et al. (1989) provided an extensive review of approaches which they termed 'cognitive apprenticeship' models of teaching and learning whereby, using various techniques, adults help to make the processes of learning explicit to children, and encourage their self-regulation.

Several other useful pedagogical techniques deriving from this broad tradition have been investigated and developed with primary-aged children. These include:

- *Cooperative groupwork* (Forman and Cazden 1985): a range of techniques involving children in collaborative activities which oblige them to articulate their own understandings, evaluate their own performance and be reflective about their own learning (Figure 10.1).
- *Reciprocal teaching* (Palincsar and Brown 1984): a structured procedure which involves teachers modelling the teaching of a particular task to children who are then asked to teach the activity to their peers.
- *Self-explanations* (Siegler 2002): an instructional practice which requires children to give 'how' and 'why' explanations about, for example, scientific phenomena or the events in a story, and then asks children to give explanations of their own and an adult's reasoning.
- *Self-assessment* (Black and Wiliam 1998): a range of pedagogical ideas involving children's self-assessment of their own learning, including, for example, children making their own choices about the level of difficulty of tasks to be undertaken, and selecting their best work for reflective portfolios.
- *Debriefing* (Leat and Lin 2003): a range of techniques for reflecting upon an activity or piece of learning including 'encouraging pupils to ask questions', 'making pupils explain themselves' and 'communicating the purpose of lessons'.

Figure 10.1 Young children engaging in collaborative problem-solving: building a house for 'Paws'

In the UK, Brooker's (1996) analysis of her work with a reception class over a year provides an excellent example of this kind of work. She began, before the start of the school year and during the first term, by interviewing the children on a number of occasions, asking them, among other things, 'Why do children go to school?', 'What are you good at?', 'What do you like doing best?' and 'How do you think you learn things?' In the Spring term, she moved on to develop the habit of self-assessment, training herself to withhold the usual excessive praise bestowed on children of this age and instead asking them 'How do you think you got on then?' At the end of the second term she asked the children 'What would you like to learn next term, after the holidays?' and this began a final phase during which, by a process of constant discussion and negotiation, the children gradually acquired more and more ownership of the curriculum and procedures of the classroom. Progressively, as the year went on, their views influenced the content and organization of their school day.

Perry et al. (2002) have engaged in similar work with young children from kindergarten to Grade 3 in British Columbia, Canada. They employed extensive observations in classrooms and conducted interviews with teachers providing evidence of young children planning, monitoring, problem-solving and evaluating their learning mostly in relation to reading and writing tasks. The pedagogical elements which emerged as being most effective in promoting self-regulated learning in these classrooms involved the teachers in offering choices to the children, opportunities for the children to control the level of challenge in tasks and to evaluate both their own work and that of others. However, what Perry's detailed analysis of the classroom discourses of teachers who were highly effective in this area reveals is a complex and highly skilled set of practices whereby all kinds of instrumental supports were provided to enable the children to develop independent learning skills and dispositions. The use of co-operative ways of working, together with an evaluative style that was non-threatening and which focused on understanding, were two significant elements in these support structures.

Within the CIndLe project we also explored effective pedagogies to encourage aspects of self-regulation. What became clear was that we needed to think broadly and look at the overall ethos of the classroom: this led to organizing the classroom in ways which gave children access to resources, allowed them to make choices and gave them responsibility for the activities in particular areas of the classroom. We also needed to examine the ways we interacted with the children, making sure that we asked more genuine open-ended and more challenging questions, that we explicitly discussed learning, emotions and self-regulation strategies and that we engaged in sustained conversations with the children within which we explored and developed their ideas.

Finally, from this work emerged four underlying principles which tied together all of these practices in ways which explained their importance when considered in the light of what we know about children as learners:

1 Emotional warmth and security: attachment.
2 Feelings of control.
3 Cognitive challenge.
4 Articulation of learning.

Emotional warmth and security: attachment

Secure emotional attachments in young children have been found to be associated with a range of positive emotional, social and cognitive outcomes (see Chapter 3). The evidence also suggests that this emotional security is the product of the child experiencing early relationships which are emotionally warm, sensitive and predictable (see Durkin 1995, for a review).

Cameo 3

Zac, in a nursery setting, is desperately keen to engage in some 'firemen' role play with his friend and clearly views the wearing of the fireman's outfit as an essential part of this. He successfully puts on the helmet but experiences much more difficulty with the jacket. Holding the coat upside down he attempts unsuccessfully to locate the sleeves. He twists the jacket this way and that, resulting in ever greater bodily contortions.

Zac's teacher does not intervene until he asks for help, as she is sensitive to his wish to persevere with the problems presented by the jacket. But she does offer encouragement through non-verbal interactions, remaining at hand to ensure he does not become distressed. Zac responds to the verbal encouragements of his teacher, maintaining determination and persistence.

At last the jacket is on, and Zac and his teacher enjoy a shared 'thumbs up' celebration of a goal achieved (Figure 10.2).

Cameo 3 is an excellent example of a teacher providing emotional support which enables a child to learn that perseverance can be a pleasurable experience and lead to a successful outcome. Often, in the absence of this kind of support, either the element of perseverance is lost as adults complete the task for the child, or pleasure is replaced by frustration and the task is abandoned. More generally, to provide emotional warmth and security in the classroom environment, teachers can do the following:

- provide a model of emotional self-regulation, talking through their own difficulties with the children;
- show that they appreciate effort at least as much as products;
- show an interest in the children as people and share aspects of their own personal lives;
- negotiate frameworks for behaviour with the children which are seen to be fair and supportive.

Feelings of control

Feeling in control of their environment and their learning is fundamental to children developing confidence in their abilities and the ability to respond positively to

Figure 10.2 Thumbs up!

setbacks and challenges. Human beings are quite literally control freaks. An early experiment carried out in California by Watson and Ramey (1972) involved the parents of 8-month-old babies being given special cots which came complete with attractive and colourful 'mobiles'. The parents were asked to put their babies in the cots for specified periods each day for a few weeks. In some of the cots the mobiles either did not move, or moved around on a timed schedule. But in other cots the mobile was wired up to a pillow, so that the mobile would move whenever the baby exerted pressure on the pillow. At the end of the experiment, the parents of the babies who had experienced these 'contingency mobiles' wanted to pay the research team large amounts of money to keep the cots because their babies had enjoyed these so much.

Cameo 4

Being a photographer

Thomas's nursery class is visited by a photographer. The children are taken into the school hall where they are arranged for a group photograph. On returning to his classroom, Thomas collects a digital camera and persuades a group of friends to act as subjects for his photography. He arranges his 'group' and uses the language of the photographer to encourage smiles. Some children are happy to comply and agree to sit as asked, waiting until Thomas has taken his photo, but others rearrange themselves and wander off. Regardless of these varied responses the 'photographer' sticks to his task (Figure 10.3).

Figure 10.3 The photographer

Here is a good example of a teacher allowing sufficient flexibility for a child who has been inspired by a particular experience to pursue this interest. Allowing opportunities for child-initiated activities enhances children's sense of ownership of and responsibility for their own learning. Other practices which are helpful in giving children this feeling of control include:

- making sure that children have access to a range of materials for their own purposes;

- giving children the opportunity to make choices about activities;

- understanding that a beautiful teacher-made role play area or display may not be as valuable for the children's learning as one to which children have contributed;

- adopting a flexible approach to timetabling which allows children to pursue an activity to their satisfaction, avoiding unnecessary interruptions.

Cognitive challenge

Children spontaneously set themselves challenges in their play and, given a choice, will often choose a task which is more challenging than the task which an adult might have thought was appropriate. Providing children with achievable challenges, and supporting them so they can meet them, is the most powerful way to encourage positive attitudes to learning and the children's independent ability to take on challenging tasks.

Cameo 5

Eliminating the poachers

As part of a year R project on rainforests, a jungle role play area has been created by the teacher and children together. The area is used by the teacher to promote a number of problem-solving discussions and activities. A process is developed of children discussing and 'playing out' their suggested solutions, exploring consequences and evaluating strategies.

One problem is that poachers have entered the jungle, killing and capturing the rainforest animals. What could be done to solve this problem?

As children offer ideas, the class is encouraged to listen carefully to them and then to act upon them. Children make a range of suggestions, including dressing up like animals to frighten the poachers and making a helicopter to spot and trap them. The teacher values every suggestion, giving particular credit to ideas which develop those of other children.

Cameo 5 shows the teacher taking children's proposed solutions to a challenging and engaging set of problems and helping them to think through and develop their ideas. The activity is set up to be highly collaborative, with the children working in teams. The children are, therefore, encouraged to take intellectual risks in an emotionally supportive context. More generally, teachers can:

- require children to plan activities;
- consider whether activities planned to be carried out individually could be made more challenging as a collaborative group task;
- ask more genuine, open-ended questions that require higher order thinking, e.g. why?, what would happen if?, what makes you say that?
- give children opportunities to organize activities themselves, avoiding too early adult intervention.

Articulation of learning

Finally, it is clear that if children are going to become increasingly aware of their own mental processing, the processes of thinking and learning need to be made explicit by adults and the children themselves need to learn to talk about and to represent their learning and thinking. The significance of this articulation of learning has been demonstrated by much research (see Mercer and Hodgkinson 2008, for a very useful collection of studies in this area). In current research, we are investigating the impact of developing children's abilities to talk productively to solve problems in groups. Early results show a significant improvement in self-regulation in 5–6-year-olds.

Cameo 6

The Giant's Castle

A nursery practitioner takes an opportunity to photograph a group of children as they engage in a self-initiated role play, packing a rucksack with cameras, binoculars and a map. The children explain that they are going to find a Giant's Castle and go outside to embark on their adventure.

Later the practitioner shows the children the photographs taken earlier encouraging them to talk about their memories, reliving a shared experience through conversation. 'How did you use the map to help you to find the Castle?', 'What did you see through the binoculars?'

In this episode the teacher is using the immediacy of the digital camera technology to stimulate an extended conversation with a group of children. As she was not an active participant in the children's imaginative play, she is able to ask genuine questions and stimulate the children to reflect upon their thinking and decision-making during the activity. Other strategies which are effective in stimulating children to talk about their learning include:

- peer tutoring, where one child teaches another;
- involving children in self-assessment;
- making learning intentions explicit when tasks are introduced, or discussed either while the children are engaged in the task, or afterwards in a review session;
- modelling a self-commentary, which articulates thinking and strategies, for example, when solving a mathematical problem.

Conclusion

There are structural reasons why facilitating genuinely self-regulated learning in early years and primary classrooms is not straightforward. However, we believe that it is possible and, certainly, the teachers involved in our projects have managed to achieve outstanding results and developed their practice. Our experience has been that whenever a teacher moves to give young children more responsibility for their own learning, or allows them to be more involved in decisions regarding the running of the classroom, or the organization of the curriculum, these teachers have always been deeply impressed by the response from the children, and have seen the benefits for the children's motivation and learning very quickly. When they enter school, the vast majority of young children are voracious in their enthusiasm for life and for learning. Sadly, for many, the experience of schooling diminishes rather than supports these appetites. Education has become, for too many of our children, something which is done *to* them, rather than *with* them. We hope that some of the ideas in this chapter will help readers to make the educational experience in their classrooms one which genuinely supports young children's development as confident and self-regulated learners.

If you would like to know more about the CIndLe project you can access further details, downloadable versions of publications and an order form for the CD-based training resource produced by the project team at: http://www.educ.cam.ac.uk/cindle/index.html.

Questions to Promote Thinking

1 How can we involve primary school children in making decisions about their learning and the organization of learning in their classrooms?
2 How can we support and encourage the children in our classes to become risk-takers in learning, adopting a positive attitude to mistakes and enjoying taking on difficult challenges?
3 How can we encourage exploratory talk in our classrooms, and how can we organize ourselves as teachers so that we spend more time in genuine discussions with children about their ideas?

References and suggested further reading

Barkley, R.A. (1997) *ADHD and the Nature of Self-control.* New York: Guilford Press.
Black, P. and Wiliam, D. (1998) *Inside the Black Box: Raising Standards through Classroom Assessment.* London: Kings College School of Education.
Bronson, M.B. (2000) *Self-Regulation in Early Childhood.* New York: Guilford Press.
Brooker, L. (1996) Why do children go to school?: Consulting children in the Reception class, *Early Years: An International Journal of Research and Development,* 17(1): 12–16.
Brown, A.L. (1987) Metacognition, executive control, self-regulation and other more mysterious mechanisms, in F.E. Weinert and R.H. Kluwe (eds) *Metacognition, Motivation and Understanding.* Hillsdale, NJ: Lawrence Erlbaum.
Collins, A., Seely Brown, J. and Newman, S.E. (1989) Cognitive apprenticeship: teaching the crafts of reading, writing and mathematics, in L.B. Resnick (ed.) *Knowing, Learning and Instruction.* Hillsdale, NJ: Lawrence Erlbaum.

DCSF (Department for Children, Schools and Families) (2007) *Early Years Foundation Stage.* London: DCFS.

Durkin, K. (1995) Attachment to others, in *Developmental Social Psychology: From Infancy to Old Age.* Oxford: Blackwell.

Featherstone, S. and Bayley, R. (2001) *Foundations of Independence*. Market Bosworth: Featherstone Education.

Flavell, J.H. (1979) Metacognition and cognitive monitoring: a new area of cognitive developmental inquiry, *American Psychologist*, 34: 906–11.

Flavell, J.H., Beach, D.R. and Chinsky, J.M. (1966) Spontaneous verbal rehearsal in a memory task as a function of age, *Child Development*, **37**: 283–99.

Forman, E.A. and Cazden, C.B. (1985) Exploring Vygotskian perspectives in education: the cognitive value of peer interaction, in J.V. Wertsch (ed.) *Culture, Communication and Cognition: Vygotskian Perspectives.* Cambridge: Cambridge University Press.

Goleman, D. (1995) *Emotional Intelligence.* New York: Bantam Books.

Hendy, L. and Whitebread, D. (2000) Interpretations of independent learning in the Early Years, *International Journal of Early Years Education*, 8(3): 245–52.

Leat, D. and Lin, M. (2003) Developing a pedagogy of metacognition and transfer: some signposts for the generation and use of knowledge and the creation of research partnerships. *British Educational Research Journal*, 29(3): 383–416.

Mercer, N. and Hodgkinson, S. (eds) (2008) *Exploring Talk in School.* London: Sage.

Metcalfe, J. and Shimamura, A.P. (eds) (1994) *Metacognition: Knowing about Knowing.* Cambridge, MA: MIT Press.

Nisbet, J. and Shucksmith, J. (1986) *Learning Strategies.* London: Routledge and Kegan Paul.

Palincsar, A.S. and Brown, A.L. (1984) Reciprocal teaching of comprehension-fostering and comprehension-monitoring activities, *Cognition and Instruction*, 1: 117–75.

Perry, N.E., VandeKamp, K.J.O., Mercer, L.K. and Nordby, C.J. (2002) Investigating teacher-student interactions that foster self-regulated learning, *Educational Psychologist*, 37(1): 5–15.

QCA/DfEE (Qualifications and Curriculum Authority/Department for Education and Employment) (2000) *Curriculum Guidance for the Foundation Stage.* London: QCA/DfEE.

Schaffer, H.R. (2004) *Introducing Child Psychology*. Oxford: Blackwell.

Schunk, D.H. and Zimmerman, B.J. (1994) *Self-Regulation of Learning and Performance.* Hillsdale, NJ: Lawrence Erlbaum.

Siegler, R.S. (2002) Microgenetic studies of self-explanation, in N. Granott and J. Parziale (eds) *Microdevelopment: Transition Processes in Development and Learning.* Cambridge: Cambridge University Press.

TDA (Teacher Development Agency) (2006) *Qualifying to Teach.* London: TDA.

Vygotsky, L.S. (1978) *Mind in Society.* Cambridge, MA: Harvard University Press.

Vygotsky, L.S. (1986) *Thought and Language.* Cambridge, MA: MIT Press.

Watson, J.S. and Ramey, C.T. (1972) Reactions to response-contingent stimulation in early infancy, *Merrill-Palmer Quarterly*, 18: 219–27.

Whitebread, D., Anderson, H., Coltman, P., Page, C., Pino Pasternak, D. and Mehta, S. (2005) Developing independent learning in the early years, *Education 3–13*, 33: 40–50.

Whitebread, D., Coltman, P., Pino Pasternak, D., Sangster, C., Grau, V., Bingham, S., Almeqdad, Q. and Demetriou, D. (2009) The development of two observational tools for assessing metacognition and self-regulated learning in young children, *Metacognition and Learning*, 4(1): 63–85.

Williams, J. (2003) *Promoting Independent Learning in the Primary Classroom.* Buckingham: Open University Press.

Yussen, S.R. (ed.) (1985) *The Growth of Reflection in Children.* New York: Academic Press.

11

MAULFRY WORTHINGTON
From astronaut to problem-solving: tracing children's symbolic meanings

Summary

A semiotic or 'meaning-making' perspective underpins children's symbolic play, enabling them to see that marks, symbols and other graphical representations can mean or 'signify' something. While the 'written' language of mathematics is integral to the subject, research has shown that children find this aspect of mathematics particularly challenging and is a problem that persists. This chapter traces the thread that links children's symbolic play with later calculations and problem-solving, highlighting their creative mathematical processes. This has relevance for mathematics throughout the Foundation stage and Key Stage 1 and has implications for 'written' mathematics in Key Stage 2.

Cameo 1[1]

Nursery – Nathan's astronaut

Nathan was busy tucking some pieces of green and purple paper beneath the flap of an envelope and securing it with masking tape (Figure 11.1). He explained that it was 'an astronaut', and announcing 'Blast off' lifted it above his head and moving his arm in an upwards, diagonal trajectory, made a 'whooshing' sound as he announced in an excited voice that it was 'flying to the moon'. Nathan then showed that by lifting the masking tape, the 'astronaut' could get out of his spacesuit (the envelope).

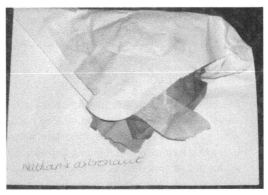

Figure 11.1 Nathan's astronaut

Cameo 2

Nursery – Isaac takes 'bookings for the campsite'

The nursery teacher Emma had set out musical keyboards for some children to play. Several telephones and old diaries had been left nearby and to Emma's surprise, rather than playing the instruments Isaac took a diary and announced he was 'taking bookings for the campsite'. His friend Oliver immediately responded, and picking up a phone said he'd like to stay for two nights. Isaac replied, 'No. I'll put you down for two million nights, but don't worry, it's only £1 a night.' He then made marks in his 'booking book' (a diary) and Oliver made his own symbols in another (Figures 11.2 and 11.3).

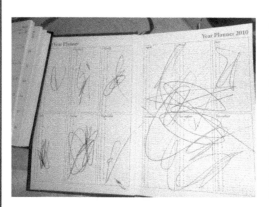
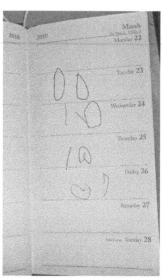

Figure 11.2 Isaac's bookings book   Figure 11.3 Oliver's reservations

Cameo 3

Nursery – 'Look! No chicken!'

Shereen was engaged in playing cafés, play that she had initiated. She drew some wavy lines on a notepad, asking her teacher 'I'm writing chocolate bar, what you want? I've got rice, chocolate, chicken?' (Figure 11.4). Emma replied that she'd have rice and handing Emma a bowl Shereen explained: 'There you go, it's 2, 1, 2' (referring to the price of a bowl of rice). Soon Shereen returned to see if she wanted anything else to eat, and referring to her notepad asked 'What you want: rice, chocolate, cake and chicken?' Emma said that she didn't want chicken and Shereen wrote something for 'chicken' and put a cross by it saying 'It says "x" – no chicken' (Figure 11.5).

After a while Shereen returned once more to see if Emma wanted anything else, and this time Emma said that she would have some chicken. Pointing to the 'x' she had written, Shereen said firmly 'Look! No chicken! You want mushroom?' and Emma agreed. Shereen added a tick by her drawing of a mushroom, explaining 'Look. A tick, that mean we got some', then added, 'You want ice cream? It's 3, 4.'

Figure 11.4 Shereen takes orders

Figure 11.5 Look! No chicken!

Introduction

During the past two decades research has revealed how a semiotic perspective through graphicacy supports children's understanding of the abstract symbolic language of mathematics (Carruthers and Worthington 2006, 2011; DCSF 2008). While symbolic (pretend) play and calculations might appear unconnected, these elements are inextricably linked through 'semiotics' that is the study of 'meaning making', enabling us to make and communicate our thoughts. We make meanings through a diverse range of signs or 'symbolic' tools' that enable us to perform 'psychological' tasks (Vygotsky 1978).

Symbolic play and graphicacy

In Vygotsky's view, symbolic play (particularly role-play) provides rich contexts for this meaning making. Children have a natural propensity for symbolic play which is seen as 'a leading factor in development' in childhood' (Vygotsky 1978) and it is valuable in two distinctive and related ways. First, children use 'symbolic tools' that help them come to understand how one thing can be used to mean or 'signify' something else, for example, using gestures, actions and speech, or artefacts that they substitute for other things and those they make (such as Nathan's astronaut), (e.g. Kress 1997; Worthington 2010a). Second, by building on their earliest awareness of relationships between objects in their meaningful play contexts, children come to understand that graphical marks and symbols can also be used to signify something, (Carruthers and Worthington 2011).

Imagination and symbolic play have been shown to underpin children's writing and drawing (Vygotsky 1983), research that Luria had begun in 1929 (Luria [1929] 1998): they also have considerable potential for children's understanding of the symbolic language of mathematics (van Oers 2005; Worthington 2010a). While the benefits of play have been well documented, this is no way to suggest that play should be used to 'prepare' children for the subjects of school.

In cameo 1, Nathan made personal meanings about astronauts through the materials he used, through using a combination of action and movement, the accompanying sound he made and through his verbal explanations. This example illustrates the complex multi-modal nature of young children's play and how children synthesize various means to best suit their purposes as they explore, make and communicate complex signs (Kress 1997; Pahl 1999). In this instance Nathan combined some elements from his everyday experience (of dressing and undressing), to signify new meanings (an astronaut removing his suit), with his knowledge of technologies and popular culture (e.g. Marsh 2004; Wohlwend 2009; Worthington 2010b). Nathan's lack of specific visual details in his astronaut was balanced by his actions and words, which were sufficient to ensure that others understood meaning.

Communicating mathematical thinking through graphicacy

Cameos 2 and 3 provide examples of young children making early explorations with marks and symbols, as they attach mathematical meanings to them in ways that made personal sense. Isaac's 'booking for the campsite' show that he knows it is advisable to book before going camping, and that reservations are written down. Isaac's scribble-marks appear to be *indications* of writing, rather than early written letters. Offering to book 'two million nights' and adding *'Don't worry – it's only £1 a night'* suggests that he knew that the real figure for one night's camping would be more than £1.00. Shereen's 'Look! No chicken!' emphasizes how rich children's self-initiated sustained play can be. Shereen's personal use of symbols provides evidence of how much she already knows about the power of graphical symbols and reveals her flexible use of symbols (Worthington 2009).

These two cameos highlight what has been described as 'funds of knowledge', a term that refers to children drawing on their rich personal knowledge from their home and community contexts in their learning (Moll et al. 1992) and in their play (Riojas-Cortez 2001). For example, Shereen drew on her personal knowledge of food – shopping, preparing and eating food as a family and eating out in restaurants and 'take-aways'. Isaac's experiences of camping with his family on many occasions supplied the cultural context for his 'bookings for the campsite' and Oliver was able to join in this play.

Vygotsky recognized the importance of personal relevance, arguing that 'writing should be *meaningful* for children, that an intrinsic need should be aroused in them, and that writing should be incorporated into a task that is *necessary and relevant for life*' (1978: 118, emphasis added) and from a mathematics perspective, this should also be so for written maths. Teachers' knowledge of children's home and cultural contexts, coupled with sensitive observations of their play will support increasingly rich play episodes. Cameos 2 and 3 show that in this nursery (where play and graphicacy are extremely well understood and supported), for these children play often arouses in them an 'intrinsic need' to communicate 'written' aspects of mathematics that are 'relevant for life'. In contrast, Gifford (2005) observed that a number of researchers (Munn and Schaffer 1993; Gifford 1995; Rogers 1996) have commented on the distinct lack of observable mathematics in either children's role play or – with the exception of block play – in wider aspects of their play. Brannon and van de Walle suggest that, 'It may be that for young children, *number is not automatically a salient dimension of the environment*' (2001: 75, emphasis added). Gifford explains: 'I began to conclude that children's role-play was concerned with the larger themes of life, like love and power, rather than mundane things like the price of potatoes' (2005: 2).

However, since numbers are embedded in children's everyday life, there does not appear to be any mechanism that would enable young children to 'select out' numbers in their play. This is borne out by the numerous examples we have of children exploring aspects of number in their play (e.g. Carruthers and Worthington 2006, 2011; Worthington 2010a), and in the DCSF publication *Children Thinking Mathematically* (2009) that we were commissioned to write. The implication of this is that rather than being 'optional extras', these dual aspects – making meanings in play and communicating mathematical meanings through graphicacy – need to be understood and valued by adults, and that children will naturally and spontaneously use number in their play where the culture supports their meaning making.

The importance of 'written' mathematics

Van Oers argues that one of the core concepts of mathematics 'is the concept of symbol. More importantly, however, symbols also function as means for regulation of the thinking process. They introduce new ways of organising in the course of thinking' (Van Oers 2000: 136). Vile refers to the 'inextricable connection with signs and mathematics. One might even say that mathematics consists entirely of a complex system of signs' (1999: 87). Yet we appear to have a long way to go if we are to resolve the difficulties children experience with 'written' mathematics that Ginsburg identified in 1977. In 1986, Hughes showed that in contrast to copying numerals without understanding, young children could draw on their own early understandings of symbols, although regretfully this interesting research had little impact on pedagogy. Since that time, numerous reports including OfSTED's have raised concerns about written mathematics including children's written methods, calculations and problem-solving every year since 2002. For example, OfSTED's (2008) report *Mathematics: Understanding the Score* emphasized:

The fundamental issue for teachers is how better to develop pupils' mathematical understanding. Too often, pupils are expected to remember methods, rules and facts without grasping the underpinning concepts, making connections with earlier learning and other topics, and making sense of the mathematics so that they can use it independently. The report raised concerns about 'pupils' reliance on formal written methods and a reluctance to use informal mental methods' emphasizing 'The best teaching gave pupils time to think'.

(OfSTED 2008: 5/21)

A recent report on young children's 'achievement' (assessed through the *Foundation Stage Profile*) showed that calculations was recorded as one of two strands with the lowest percentage of children achieving this (DfE 2010: 44), exceeded only by writing.

Children's own, informal representations

Terwel et al. explain that 'in designing representations, students learn how structuring processes develop . . . enhancing their capacity to generate new solution processes and to transform a representation according to changes in the situation, facilitating the construction of solutions to relatively new and unfamiliar problems'. Representations also 'play a major role in problem solving' (2009: 26–7).

However, the ways in which young children develop their understanding of written mathematics have not been a curricula focus, with the resulting 'passive' activities that Jo Boaler highlights. Boaler argues that it is the way in which mathematics is taught that causes problems,

> Students are forced into a passive relationship with their knowledge – they are taught only to follow rules and not to engage in sense-making, reasoning, or thought, acts that are critical to an effective use of mathematics. This passive approach, that characterises maths teaching in many schools, is highly ineffective.
>
> (2009: 36)

Boaler acknowledges the huge pressure that teachers are under, but argues that this narrow version of mathematics causes low achievement in England and fails to produce good performances in tests.

The evidence from current measures of attainment in England (DfE 2010), appears to confirm that the same is also true for younger children's experiences of written mathematics when they are 4 years of age. Vellom and Pape argue that 'typical' written mathematical tasks (i.e. those that involve one way of colouring-in, copying or completing) are 'seen as end results or "products"'. In contrast, 'in more realistic learning contexts, students may make sense of complex phenomena through their efforts to construct and through the use of graphical representations of these complex systems' (2000: 125) such as children's *mathematical graphics*, where *processes* of mathematical thinking are emphasized.

Creativity

Rich episodes of symbolic play and *children's mathematical graphics* reveal the highly creative processes that support children's cognitive development and their mathematical thinking (see also Carruthers and Worthington 2011). However, while the Early Years Foundation Stage (EYFS) emphasizes 'children's creativity must be extended by the provision of support for their curiosity, exploration and play . . . [including] mathematics', enabling children to 'explore many *processes*', and that 'children express their ideas *through a wide range of types of representation*' (DfES 2007: 104/105, emphasis added) – this is not generally what is understood by 'creativity' in education, a term that has become synonymous with the arts rather than wider aspects of learning.

Creativity in mathematics: Foundation and Key Stage 1

In 2000, we conducted a study of teachers and practitioners' understanding of creativity in mathematics, with those working with children from 3 to 8 years (see Carruthers and Worthington 2006). The main finding of this that almost all responses referred to specific resources or activities such as 'role play', patterns, constructions, shape, art, songs and rhymes and sand as 'creative': although children may sometimes explore these resources or activities in creative ways, they are no guarantee of creative learning.

This view of creativity continues to be widely held, for example, a recent report on creativity proposes:

> Problem solving reasoning and numeracy are supported as concepts of shape, size, line and area are used to classify and sort objects in the visual arts. Dance provides many opportunities to explore spatial concepts, and sequencing events and objects; for example, creating a pattern on a piece of clay helps children to understand patterns in mathematics.
>
> (Duffy 2010: 22)

Regretfully, once again, this appears to confirm the idea that certain activities and resources themselves ensure creativity. Davies and Howe challenge such 'myths about creativity' (2007: 250), arguing that play itself should not be deemed 'creative' and that the almost exclusive association between creativity and the arts needs reconsideration.

'Prescription stifles creativity'[2]

As children move through school, it appears to be common practice to present children with a particular method to use for calculations and to solve problems and while the National Strategies propose that 'Mathematics is a creative discipline' (DCSF 2006: 139), Cowley argues that 'even if learners are given the freedom to solve their own way, if later they are expected to adopt an apparently standard method, their own mathematics is diminished' (2010: 2). He continues, 'mathematics cannot be creative where prescribed methods are used to solve problems' since 'the problem has already been solved . . . the presentation of the problem without a method of solution is the only road to mathematics as a "creative discipline"' (2010: 4). These views concur with Boaler's (2009) and the following two cameos focus on children solving problems in which they were 'given the freedom to solve their own way'.

Solving problems – calculating with larger numbers

Cameo 4

Year 2 class – Alison's '99 times table'

Alison's class had been learning the 9 and 10 times tables and when asked 'Can you do the 99 times table?' greeted this question with laughter and replies of 'No!' After some discussion about how they might work out the '100 times table', the children felt more confident when their teacher then repeated her challenge to work out the '99 times table'.

At first Alison (Figure 11.6) chose to write '2 x 99', then after some crossing out wrote '99 + 99 = 20098'. Next she tried using tallies but soon found it difficult to keep track of them and wrote 'wrong' and 'no' next to the boxes she'd drawn around them. This example shows the various strategies Alison tried, including several she abandoned. Alison's teacher joined her, asking her if there was any other ways she could put something down to show 99. Alison hesitated and her teacher suggested she 'think about repeated addition': after beginning with 5 groups of 99, Alison moved to writing five groups of '100', adding them together and 'rounding up', then subtracting 5 to arrive at her answer.

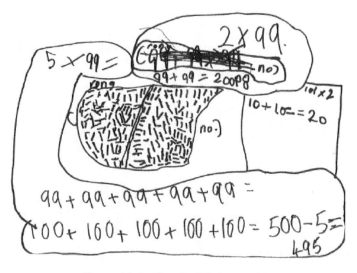

Figure 11.6 Alison's '99 times table'

For Alison, '20098' was a logical way to write '298': children often write numbers above 100 in this way as it appears logical to them and her crossings out shows genuine 'working out' in progress. The teacher's suggestion that Alison might think about repeated addition appeared to be a turning point, as she seemed immediately to make the connection between counting out '99' five times, and using a more efficient and less error-prone method in which she had confidence.

Cameo 4

Year 3/4 class: Miles and the nectarines

Miles's class was about to go on a residential trip and had planned a picnic to break the journey. Their teacher brought in a pack of three nectarines and asked if the children could help work out how many packs she would need to buy, so that each of the 26 children in the class could have a nectarine.

Miles reached for a piece of paper and placing it in front of him in 'portrait' format, drew a line across the width of the page. The way in which he had orientated his paper caused an initial problem since he soon discovered that he would run out of space on his line to make sufficient jumps of '3'. Using a highly adaptive strategy, Miles twice made jumps of '6' (doubling the 3) enabling him to resolve this problem (Figure 11.7).

Figure 11.7 Miles, calculating packs of nectarines

In their previous classes these children had been fortunate to have had rich experiences of play, and to develop and build on their earlier understandings of the abstract symbolic language of mathematics. They were confident in solving problems in their own, informal ways through their *mathematical graphics* and by Year 2 sometimes integrated some 'informal' taught methods by choice, when they felt they would be of use. In the National Strategies, these informal 'taught' methods include the valuable 'empty number line' and rounding up. In addition to the standard symbols such as '+' and 'x', both the empty number line and 'rounding up and subtracting' are symbolic tools and add to those they already have at their disposal.

Processes of mathematics

Thinking and communicating mathematically are significant aspects of early 'written' mathematics (Carruthers and Worthington 2008), yet they have largely been overlooked in curricula documents. In the EYFS (DfES 2007), 'communication', 'thinking' and 'language' (with the exception of mathematical vocabulary) are notable by their absence in the *problem-solving, reasoning and numeracy* section of the document. This is in direct contrast to *communication, language and literacy*, which has dedicated sections entitled 'language for thinking' and 'language for communication', and although 'using and applying mathematics' (DCSF 2006) is emphasized for mathematics in the primary school, OfSTED's repeated concerns show that children may not always have sufficient opportunities they need to 'use and apply' mathematics in their own ways.

The cameos of mathematics in this chapter show the creative *processes* of learning that children used. Cameos 2 and 3 relate directly to *Foundation Stage Profile* (FSP) point 8 'Uses developing mathematical ideas to solve practical problems'. The *Williams Maths Review* (DCSF 2008) raised particular concerns about this aspect of achievement and the low levels of attainment in 'calculations' (DfE 2010) are likely to be related to this. FSP point 8 in the EYFS relates closely to the various strands of 'Using and applying mathematics' in the National Curriculum (DCSF 2006) and includes:

Solving problems
Representing – analyse, record, do, check, confirm.
Enquiring – plan, decide, organise, interpret, reason, justify.
Reasoning – create, deduce, apply, explore, predict, hypothesise, test.
Communicate – explain methods and solutions, choices, decisions.

Cameos 4 and 5 provide evidence of many aspects of *using and applying mathematics*, revealing the thread that runs from Nathan's astronaut to children attaching mathematical meanings to marks as Isaac and Oliver did, and later to calculate and solve problems with larger numbers. They emphasize the continuing importance of *processes* of learning mathematics, throughout the Foundation Stage and the primary school.

Conclusion

Not only does mathematics matter but, so too, do play and graphicacy. Soler and Miller (2003) raise concerns about 'top-down pressures from statutory subject-based curricula' for both school and pre-school aged children, which have prompted 'ongoing struggles to incorporate traditional early years ideologies into recommended pedagogy' (Brooker and Edwards 2010: 43). However, Brooker and Edwards argue that while teachers have many tensions to deal with, 'Ultimately, the "struggle" described by Soler and Miller (2003) is not simply between different theories of learning but between different views of children.' They suggest that the most positive view of learners is to respect children as 'competent individuals who are capable of making meaning from their experience of the world, in collaboration with others and with the support of cultural tools' (Brooker and Edwards 2010: 44). Such views also require a shift away from seeing children's mathematics as full of 'mistakes', and to view and assess their emerging understandings from a positive perspective.

The authors of the *Williams Maths Review* emphasize that the 'United Kingdom is still one of the few advanced nations where it is socially acceptable – fashionable, even – to profess an inability to cope with the subject' (DCSF 2008: 3). The Review's final report acknowledges the significance of *children's mathematical graphics* in supporting their understanding of the abstract symbolic language of mathematics. However, diSessa et al. note, 'how rare it is to find instruction that trusts students to create their own representations' (1991: 156). This view is further reflected in a recent paper by Terwel et al. who propose that 'Although there have been positive changes in the past [two] decades, we believe that today, diSessa's statement holds true for many classroom practices' (2009: 28–9).

For too many children, when they move into school at the too-early age of 4 years (in England), the 'written' mathematics they are given often holds little meaning and fails to connect with their own understandings. Yet our accumulated research findings and recent empirical evidence from an increasing number of teachers and practitioners (Carruthers and Worthington 2011) show that young children will often readily make and communicate their mathematical meanings in play, and that this underpins their understanding of 'written' maths. Brooker and Edwards ask in the debate about play and subject teaching, 'Where are the children, and what do they make of their experiences?' (2010: 44). Our argument is that by focusing on children's symbolic play and their mathematical graphics children will be central in their learning cultures and in this debate.

Whether teaching in the Foundation Stage or in the primary school, it is hoped that the issues raised in this chapter will provoke critical reflection and an increased focus on children's mathematics, and will contribute to greater continuity for children's experiences of mathematics throughout the birth–11-years age range.

Questions to Promote Thinking

1   To what extent do teachers' observations throughout the Foundation Stage inform adults about individual children's interests and meaning making?
2   How do teachers in school build on and support children's meanings, thinking and graphicacy?
3   To what extent are the *processes* of children's 'written' maths recognized and understood, from Foundation Stage to KS1, and through KS2?

Notes

1   Cameos 1, 4 and 5 are used with kind permission of Sage Publications; cameos 2 and 3 are included with kind permission of Open University Press.
2   Cowley (2010: 3).

Useful website

Children's Mathematics Network: www.childrens-mathematics.net.

References and suggested further reading

Boaler, J. (2009) *The Elephant in the Classroom*. London: Souvenir Press Ltd.

Brannon, E. and van de Walle, G. (2001) The development of ordinal numerical competence in young children, *Cognitive Psychology*, 43: 53–81.

Broadhead, P., Howard, J. and Wood, E. (2010) *Play and Learning in the Early Years*. London: Sage Publications.

Brooker, L. and Edwards, S. (2010) (eds) *Engaging Play*. Maidenhead: Open University Press.

Carruthers, E. and Worthington, M. (2006) *Children's Mathematics: Making Marks, Making Meaning*. London: Sage Publications.

Carruthers, E. and Worthington, M. (2008) Children's mathematical graphics: young children calculating for meaning, in I. Thompson (ed.) *Teaching and Learning Early Number*. Maidenhead: Open University Press.

Carruthers, E. and Worthington, M. (2011) *Understanding Children's Mathematical Graphics: Beginnings in Play*. Maidenhead: Open University Press.

Cowley, R. (2010) Prescription smothers creativity in mathematics education. Getmaths: Available online at: http://www.getmaths.com/pdf/prescription.pdf (accessed 12 November 2010).

Davies, D. and Howe, A. (2007) What does it mean to be creative? in J. Moyles (ed.) *Early Years Foundations: Meeting the Challenge*. Maidenhead: Open University Press.

DCSF (Department for Children, Schools and Families) (2006) *Guidance Paper: Using and Applying Mathematics*. London: The National Strategies. Available online at: http://national-strategies.standards.dcsf.gov.uk/node/47324?uc=force_uj (accessed 17 September 2010).

DCSF (2008) *Independent Review of Mathematics Teaching in Early Years Settings and Primary Schools (The Williams Review)*. London: DSCF.

DCSF (2009) *Children Thinking Mathematically: PSRN Essential Knowledge for Early Years Practitioners*. London: The National Strategies.

DfE (Department for Education) (2010) *Achievement of Children in the EYFS Profile*. London: DfE. Available online at: http://publications.education.gov.uk/eOrderingDownload/DFE-RR034.pdf (accessed 17 September 2010).

DfES (Department for Education and Skills) (2007) *Early Years Foundation Stage*. London: DfES.

diSessa, A., Hammer, D., Sherin, B. and Kolpakowski, T. (1991) Inventing graphing: meta-representational expertise in children, *Journal of Mathematics Behaviour*, 10: 117–60.

Duffy, B. (2010) Using creativity and creative learning to enrich the lives of young children at the Thomas Coram Centre, In C. Tims (ed.) *Born Creative*. London: Demos.

Gifford, S. (1995) Number in early childhood, *Early Childhood Development and Care*, 109: 95–115.

Gifford, S. (2005) *Teaching Mathematics 3–5: Developing Learning in the Foundation Stage*. Maidenhead: Open University Press.

Ginsburg, H. (1977) Learning to count, computing with written numbers. Mistakes, in H. Ginsburg, *Children's Arithmetic: How They Learn It and How You Teach It*. New York: Van Nostrand.

Hughes, M. (1986) *Children and Number: Difficulties in Learning Mathematics*. Oxford: Blackwell.

Kress, G. (1997) *Before Writing: Rethinking the Paths to Literacy*. London: Routledge.

Luria, A.R. ([1929] 1998) The development of writing in the young child, in M.K. Oliveira, J. Valsiner and M.K. de Oliviera (eds) *Literacy in Human Development*. Stamford, CT: Ablex Publishing Corporation.

Marsh, J. (2004) The techno-literacy practices of young children, *Journal of Early Childhood Research*, 2(1): 51–66.

Moll, L., Amanti, C., Neff, D. and Gonzalez, N. (1992) Funds of knowledge for teaching: using a qualitative approach to connect homes and classrooms, *Theory into Practice*, **XXXI**(2): 132–41.

Munn, P. and Schaffer, H. (1993) Literacy and numeracy events in socially interactive contexts, *International Journal of Early Years Education*, 1(3): 61–80.

OfSTED (Office for Standards in Education) (2008) *Mathematics: Understanding the Score*. London: HMSO.

Pahl, K. (1999) *Transformations: Meaning Making in the Nursery*. Stoke-on-Trent: Trentham Books.

Riojas-Cortez, M. (2001) Preschoolers' funds of knowledge displayed through sociodramatic play episodes in a bilingual classroom, *Early Childhood Education Journal*, 29(1): 35–40.

Rogers, J. (1996) Children as apprentices to number, *Early Childhood Development and Care*, 125: 15–25.

Soler, J. and Miller, L. (2003) The struggle for early childhood curricula: a comparison of the English Foundation Stage curriculum, Te Whaariki and Reggio Emilia, *International Journal of Early Years Education*, 11(1): 57–67.

Terwel, J., Van Oers, B., Van Dijk, I. and Van den Eeden, P. (2009) Are representations to be provided or generated in primary mathematics education? *Educational Research and Evaluation*, 15(1): 25–44.

Thompson, I. (2008) *Teaching and Learning Early Number*. Maidenhead: Open University Press.

Van Oers, B. (2000) The appropriate of mathematical symbols: a psychosemiotic approach to mathematics learning, in P. Cobb., E. Yackel and K. McClain (eds) *Symbolizing and Communicating in Mathematics Classrooms: Perspectives on Discourse, Tools, and Instructional Design*. London: Lawrence Erlbaum Associates.

Van Oers, B. (2005) The potentials of imagination, *Inquiry: Critical Thinking across the Disciplines*, 24(4): 5–17.

Vellom, R.P. and Pape, S.J. (2000) EarthVision 2000: examining students' representations of complex data, *School Science and Mathematics*, 100: 426–39.

Vile, A. (1999) What can semiotics do for mathematics education? *Research in Mathematics Education*, 1(1): 87–102.

Vygotsky, L.S. (1978) *Mind and Society: The Development of Higher Mental Processes*. Cambridge, MA: Harvard University Press.

Vygotsky, L.S. (1983) The pre-history of written language, in M. Martlew (ed.) *The Psychology of Written Language*. Chichester: John Wiley & Sons Ltd.

Wohlwend, K. (2009) Early adopters: playing literacies and pretending new technologies in print-centric classrooms, *Journal of Early Childhood Literacy*, 9(2): 117–40.

Worthington. M. (2009) Fish in the water of culture: signs and symbols in young children's drawing, *Psychology of Education Review*, 33(1): 37–46.

Worthington, M. (2010a) Play is a complex landscape: imagination and symbolic meanings, in P. Broadhead, L. Wood and J. Howard. (eds) *Play and Learning in Educational Settings*. London: Sage Publications.

Worthington, M. (2010b) This is a *different* calculator – with computer games on, in J. Moyles (ed.) *Thinking about Play: Developing a Reflective Approach*. Maidenhead: Open University Press.

12

HELEN CLARKE AND KAREN PHETHEAN
Encouraging enquiry: exploring the world around us

Summary

A significant amount of research, within a constructivist framework, has revealed the complexity of children's ideas about scientific concepts – in other words, how children think their world works. Similarly, it is accepted that children employ a range of sophisticated skills as they formalize their investigations, take ownership of their lines of enquiry, work together in social construction of understandings and invite adults to take their place at the heart of child–adult interaction. We draw on case studies of children's exploration of the material world to illustrate the roles of children and adults as co-investigators in enquiries that cross subject boundaries. Children communicate their early ideas in many ways. We must hear the authenticity and integrity of children's voices. Observing and listening to children can support the provision of meaningful and relevant contexts in which learning can take place.

Cameo 1

In a nursery setting, 3- and 4-year-olds are exploring materials. They engage in a sequence of activities, designed by the adult, to encourage exploration, enquiry, reflection and talk. In glorious multi-sensory involvement, they poke, prod, rattle and shake objects to discover how the items behave. Prompted by the adult, they recall where they have met these materials before, what they already know about them, and how they might be categorized. They share their understanding in a myriad of ways; the adult listens respectfully and interprets their complex 'meaning making', ready to intervene with the next invitation to find out more.

Cameo 2

Children in a Year 3 class are about to undertake an investigation to prove that seawater is salty because it contains salt. Before they do anything they are encouraged to play with the resources that have been placed on the class tables – pebbles and stones of various sizes, sand, salt, water, beakers, sieves, funnels, filter paper, dishes. While the children play, the teacher watches and listens. After ten minutes the children sit on the carpet and their teacher reads them a story about a visit to the seaside in which a bucket of pebbles, sand and sea water are brought home following a lovely day out. In the story, an older brother implores his younger sister not to drink the seawater because it is salty and it will make her sick. The children in the class are asked by the teacher to help prove that the seawater is salty. The children recall their play; they begin to make connections with the pebbles, sand, salt and water with the bucket from the beach in the story. After some class discussion the children set off to investigate.

Introduction

The cameos above show a positive view which celebrates the amazing capabilities of learners. Young children, in particular, as they explore and make sense of their world reveal their growing understanding in surprising ways. A significant amount of research, within a constructivist framework, has revealed the complexity of children's ideas about scientific concepts. Children's exploration of the world is that of playful encounters with complex phenomena. Children learn through their interaction and exploration with that world – they are naturally curious. Enabling and supporting curiosity can foster the way in which children develop their reasoning skills, build experience and make sense of the complex world around them. Play and playful experiences can provide opportunities for children to sustain and develop their natural curiosity.

Early exploration of the world

Science begins with children's earliest acts of exploration: indeed, childhood is full of the 'beginnings of science' and is, thus, a 'springboard from which the next leap is taken' (de Boo 2000: 1). There has been extensive research into children's conceptions in science from a constructivist point of view (Driver et al. 1985; Osborne and Freyberg 1985; Harlen 2001; and, for materials, Russell et al. 1991). These studies have shown that learning outcomes depend on the environment and the prior knowledge, purpose and motivation of the learner. Learning involves the construction of meaning and is continuous and active. The research of Pulham (1998) and Clarke (2003) on children's understandings of materials showed that young children are willing and able to communicate their early ideas in science given an appropriate, investigative context, opportunities to express their meaning, and if their diverse modes of communication are 'heard' and valued. In cameo 1, Clarke (2003) celebrates the

Figure 12.1 A child's multi-sensory exploration of a familiar material

complexity of young children's intellectual growth in the context of their exploration of everyday materials.

In open exploration children develop their understanding of the properties of materials. They use their senses to find out, first hand, how materials respond. In Figure 12.1 the child explores dough by squashing, rolling, squeezing and moulding. Table 12.1 exemplifies complex thinking on the properties of materials.

Importantly, these responses illustrate the children's ability to suggest a range of properties for materials, demonstrating considerable expertise for this young age group. They draw on previous knowledge and experience in quoting examples from

Table 12.1 Children's ideas on the properties of materials

Object	Material	Children's (aged 3–4) comments	Property
Pie dish	Metal	I'm squashing it	Malleability
Spoon	Metal	That one is shiny	Reflectivity
Spoon	Wood	It makes a ticking sound	Sonority
Block	Wood	I can't break this	Strength

Source: Clarke (2003).

Figure 12.2 Children's categories for a range of materials
Source: Clarke (2003).

both their home and nursery environments. These young children also show their ability to sort objects accurately according to the materials from which they are made (Figure 12.2), (Table 12.2).

Table 12.2 Children's categories for a range of materials

Metal	Plastic	Wood
Bangle	Cup*	Box
Coin	Coin	Toy teddy bear puppet
Aluminium foil^	Doll	Shavings^
Brass jug	Polystyrene egg	Egg
Keys*	Slinky^	Rabbit serviette ring
Aluminium pie dish	Toy tractor	Spoon*
Spoon*	Spoon*	
Toy train		

Note: 21 objects, *denotes stereotypical objects, ^denotes objects selected as those more unlikely to be familiar to the children.
Source: Clarke (2003).

Making sense of the world

Interrelated processes affect this knowledge construction in young children. Kress et al. (2001) consider the multiplicity of modes of communication present in the classroom, where learners actively engage with several modes in a complex interaction. Bloom (1992) proposes a dynamic view of cognition where the contexts of meaning (episodic knowledge, metaphors, interpretive frameworks, and emotions-values-aesthetics (EVAs)) impact on general cognitive processes (categorizing, associating and inferring, elaborating and storytelling). He examines how the identified contexts of meaning influence the processes affecting the development of new knowledge and, crucially, meaning. Episodic knowledge refers to the verbalization of prior personal experiences, denoted by the mention of a specific setting and time. Metaphors act as a mechanism of comparison that 'link' different types of information, and enrich conceptual understanding. Interpretive frameworks describe how certain points of view, belief systems or knowledge influence the operation of various processes. Interpretive frameworks are also thought to affect and be affected by the other contexts of meaning in Bloom's typology. Bloom combines emotions, values and aesthetics into one category (EVAs) due to the difficulty of clearly distinguishing them as they appear in the children's speech.

Multimodal communication of early ideas

The complexity of young children's thought and communication suggests a rich landscape of representation beyond immediate speech, which includes modes such as actions, drawing, modelling, dancing and singing (Gallas 1995; Pahl 1999). Educators must access these methods of communication in order to reach fully the children's developing ideas. Even the 'silences' of young children, as they engage with a task, are an integral part of their learning (Gallas 1995; de Boo 2000), and provide 'space' for thinking.

If children are to be heard and understood, it is crucial to step back sufficiently from the standard science concept that is the focus of the activity and observe children's explorations in all their complexity. Children's narratives are not always heard, nor acted upon in the context of the school day, and hence, their potential as powerful tangents of thought is rarely tapped (Gallas 1995). Dialogues are a prerequisite for a dynamic classroom and a learner-centred approach. To adopt such an approach is to offer considerable power to the child, as illustrated in the examples above.

Emergent understanding

Children employ a range of sophisticated skills as they formalize their investigations, take ownership of their lines of enquiry, work together in social construction of understandings and invite adults to take their place in child–adult interaction. Employing enquiry skills enables children to move forward, and helps them to develop emergent ideas. The following example illustrates how two teachers changed their practice to fully engage children's skills of questioning, observation, recording and communicating in a social context.

The AstraZeneca Science Teaching Trust (AZSTT) and University of Winchester (2009) project, Teachers and Young Children Exploring their Worlds Together, supported practising teachers in developing their practice of science within the early years through appreciative enquiry in their own classrooms (Clarke et al. 2009). Cox and Noble (2009) researched and developed their practice in a Reception/Year 1 class. They recognized that the way they taught science was not getting the best from the children and decided to give the children more ownership of their learning. They developed a more open approach, one which takes into account and values the children's previous experience, knowledge and interests and listens to their talk. The context of their study was children's emergent science learning, again in the context of materials and their properties. The following summarizes their approach:

1   Introduce the broad theme (for example, materials) – the children have free time to explore a range of materials that have been put out for them.

2   Children make pictorial mind maps of everything they know about the theme. An adult scribes the children's ideas.

3   Children are asked individually what they would like to find out on this theme.

4   (a) Children are grouped into those with similar questions so they can work with an adult to find answers.

    (b) While some children are working with the adults, the others freely explore a selection of things set out and items they find in the classroom.

    (c) Children may go on a walk around the school to explore the theme (for example, materials around the school, electricity used around the school, shadows on the playground).

5   The children record what they have found out – in pictorial form, maybe with some attempts at writing.

6   The children communicate what they have found out to the group/class (for example, speak, show and talk about the picture, draw on interactive whiteboard, demonstrate).

Cox and Noble (2009) describe their approach as responsive to the needs of the children as individuals. They recognize that children's questions are thoughtful and important. In this way, emergent science is playful, holistic and rooted in the world around us. Adults provide the motivation and the scaffold for children to engage in exploration and interaction.

In such practice, practitioners are 'open to what may *emerge* in children's responses to each situation' (Ovens 2004: 19). 'It is only during the session, when the exact lines of enquiry are negotiated with the children . . . that the *precise objectives will emerge*, differentially and accurately related to *"where the children are"'* (Ovens 2004: 20). This 'authenticity' (Ovens 2004) is a feature of a 'child–adult' relationship (Clarke 2003) and focuses on ways to capture, respond to and develop children's ideas through practitioner/adult recognition of science opportunities and strategies to help adults follow and support early curiosity.

Emergent science also prompts practitioners to respond to children's unpredictable paths of learning and this becomes an essential part of fostering the natural curiosity of children. For both initial and post-qualification teachers, ongoing reflective practice is an essential attribute of a good teacher (Moyles 2010). Effective continuing professional development (CPD) lies at the heart of good practice in the classroom.

Developing enquiry

There is some cognitive value to the playful element in science. *Playing with ideas is, after all, what science is about* ... When we set up encounters between various chemicals, our expectations extend those of the child who has been given a paint box and tries mixing various colors just to see what comes out. In the same mood, the chemist asks himself what would happen were he to change the proportions or modify the sequence of the operations in a complex synthesis. Such a playful, childlike attitude can be extremely fruitful. Let us not be too embarrassed to acknowledge that *play is often what motivates us.*
(Laszlo 2004: 398, author's emphasis)

The role of enquiry in developing children's conceptual understanding is central to the development of *scientific literacy* (Harlen 2006: 6) and inherent as a key factor in good teaching (Richardson 2006). Chak (2007: 142) argues that children's natural curiosity is 'a key motivational force for the acquisition of knowledge' and as such is important in fostering positive attitudes and skills (Johnston 2005: 12). Curiosity is, therefore, linked with intrinsic motivation and the desire to find out (Johnston 2005; Harlen and Qualter 2009: 134–41), that it is 'instinctive' and that 'children want to find answers and make sense of the world' (Oliver 2006: 64). It is important, therefore, to sustain children's curiosity and desire to find out not only in the early years *but beyond* so that the attitudes and skills important to learning are embedded and develop into lifelong learning skills (Claxton 2008: 122; Alexander 2010).

Scientific enquiry uses process skills (observation, planning, predicting, hypothesizing, measuring, interpreting, concluding and evaluating) which help to explore and gain understanding of the world. Teachers should not only support these enquiry skills but recognize that children's learning is underpinned by the ideas they already hold as a result of prior experience (a constructivist perspective) and the importance of ascertaining those ideas to meet and match learning needs (formative use of assessment).

Cameo 2 provides an example of an enquiry-based approach in which the children are provided with a context for their learning and ownership of that learning. There is in the 'play' beforehand the opportunity for the children to have time to access their prior learning and ideas, to consider what they already know about the resources, mixing, separating, and to think about what they want to know and what they can do. Constructivism is at work. When the teacher reads the story to the children, the context of the story 'makes sense to them'; they are able to relate what they have just done to what is happening in the story; when the problem is then posed for

Table 12.3 Examples of talk: Bloom's framework (1992) (contexts of meaning), extended by Clarke (2003)

Processes	Children's talk
Episodic knowledge	Do you know when we went to our old house we saw someone painting the wood
Metaphors	Something hard like wood
	Plastic is like this (flicking pages of card)
	I put glitter on to make it look like snow
Interpretive frameworks	All these go together
	You can tell by feeling them
	You need to be strong to do this
EVAs	I like silver coins
	They're nice and metal
actions * – enactic	You can bang it with a hammer
	I can look right through it
	I'm still trying to break it
	I'm scratching it now
actions *- iconic	Bending (mime)
(mime)	He stroked it (gestures)
	With my hand like that (demonstrates)
(model)	I'm doing a window (make a book wood)
	I've made green sausages

them to investigate, the children are able to approach it with a sense of confidence and understanding that are relevant and meaningful *to them* and to their stage of learning. The children ask questions to clarify thinking, to find answers. For example, many of the children wanted to know what the filter paper could be used for. The teacher was able to demonstrate and explain its use and it was noticeable that not only did the children listen but the explanation as to how and why it is used was meaningful to the children because it was directly relevant to them. The children went off excitedly to prove that indeed seawater contains salt. Ownership of their learning continued into their recording (Table 12.3), (Figure 12.3).

In cameo 2, the teacher has the opportunity to identify the prior knowledge and understanding of the children as she listens to them play before the story and recognizes her input. Playing with the resources enables the children to explore and be naturally curious. The learning that follows the play is a shared negotiation involving the development of the children's curiosity into the questions that have arisen for them in the play and in the story and the teacher's facilitating and scaffolding their learning in answering questions they want and need to be answered.

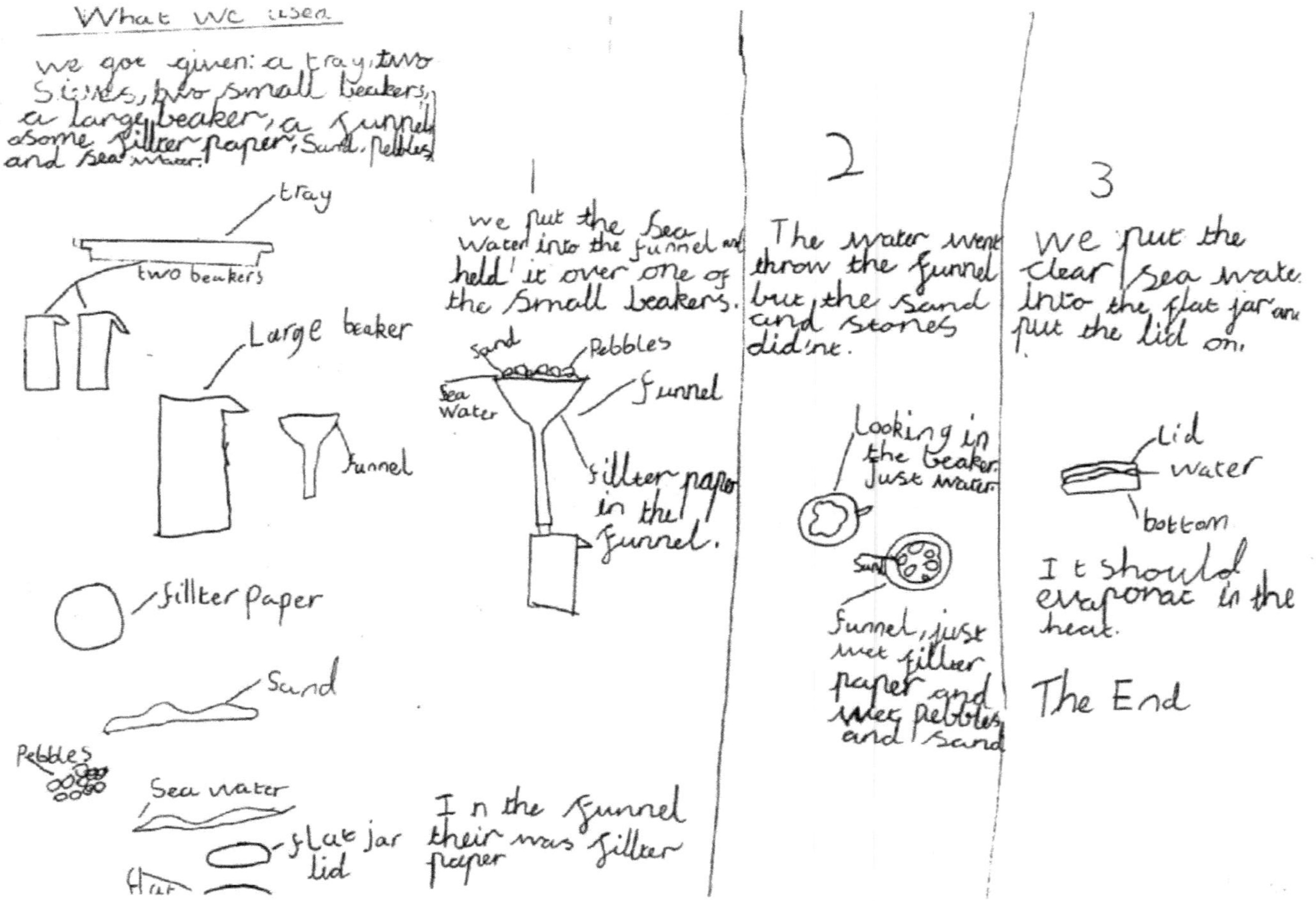

What we used

we got given: a tray, two
Stiroks, two small beakers,
a large beaker, a funnel,
some filter paper, sand, pebbles
and sea water.

tray

two beakers

Large beaker

funnel

filter paper

Sand

Pebbles

Sea water

glass jar
lid
(Hat)

In the funnel
their was filter
paper

1

we put the sea
water into the funnel and
held it over one of
the Small beakers.

Sand   Pebbles
        funnel
Sea
Water   filter paper
        in the
        funnel.

2

The water went
throw the funnel
but the Sand
and stones
did'nt.

Looking up
the beaker
Just water

funnel, just
wet filter
paper and
wet pebbles
and sand

3

We put the
clear sea water
into the flat jar an
put the lid on.

lid
water
bottom

It should
evaporate in the
heat.

The End

Figure 12.3 Salty Seawater, child's own recording of separate materials investigation

Playing in the world – a case for play-based enquiry in the Primary Science curriculum

The value of play in supporting the development and learning of young children has long been recognized (Bruce 2001; Moyles 2008). If children use play to explore their world, then we need to ensure that the opportunities for that play continue well beyond the early years in order that we encourage the curiosity, the playfulness identified by chemist Pierre Laszlo (2004) above for the scientists of the future. Schofield identifies the role of creativity in developing those skills of enquiry inherent to the scientist, skills which 'require creative attributes or qualities, which lead to playfulness, risk-taking, curiosity and self-awareness' (Schofield 2008: 10).

Play allows the individual to do the following:

- to create and explore a world that can be mastered, conquering fears while practising a range of different skills;
- to develop creativity through the development and use of imagination and fine and gross motor skills;
- to learn to work in groups, to share, to negotiate and to resolve conflicts;
- to practise decision-making skills;
- to move/progress at their own pace;
- to move on the road of self-discovery; following own lines of enquiry and having ownership of learning.

In their play, children are enabled to take the circuitous paths along which their learning may take them and in so doing create their own personal learning journeys. These learning paths are co-constructed as teachers respond to the unpredictability of the children's learning and thus foster their natural curiosity.

Science learning should be fun and interesting, engaging and stimulating the learner in a way that develops curiosity and enquiry from a sense of awe and wonder in the world around them. However, teaching science can be difficult when the resources and the nature of the activity are such that learners can be distracted, in the initial stages, by those resources. A free play session at the beginning of activities can make the most of learning situations creating not only a positive environment but an effective tool for enquiry and creativity – this is often an approach adopted within the early years (Brook et al. 2006). For older children, a free play session used in this way can be seen to 'P.R.E.P.' them for the work to follow – P.R.E.P. can develop and enhance pupil spontaneity and enthusiasm, to focus and support children's learning while supporting independence (Phethean 2008).

The case for P.R.E.P.

P.R.E.P. is an acronym, each letter representing the following characteristic (with their associated dictionary definition (Thompson 1998):

Play – enjoyment, fun, amusement, entertainment

Research – study, review, assessment

Exploration – fact-finding, experimental, searching, trial

Practice – carry out, rehearse, go through, run through.

If we look at each of these characteristics individually in terms of developing under-standing we can identify the dispositions of P.R.E.P. that support positive and effec-tive learning.

- *Play*: when children perceive learning to be fun and enjoyable, they will be actively engaged and focused – play is naturally a way in which children can express themselves.
- *Research*: learning involves a cycle of studying, reviewing concepts and ideas, and assessing what has been learnt and what needs to be done next (target setting).
- *Exploration*: learning involves finding out facts in a variety of ways – it may involve research and quiet study, searching for prior knowledge and understanding and for answers to questions, trialling or testing ideas, conceptions.
- *Practice*: carrying out an activity – 'doing', going through what you already know helps to build upon prior understanding.

In the concept of P.R.E.P., we have a term in which play or free play embodies learn-ing in a meaningful context in a situation that makes learning *relevant and meaningful* for the learner.

P.R.E.P. How and when?

It is suggested that P.R.E.P. is an unstructured, exploration time of 'Free Play' at the very beginning of a learning session – in particular, in sessions where equipment or practical resources of some kind are intended to be used. The timing of the session should be at the discretion of the teacher but no longer than 10 minutes. Classroom-based research (Phethean 2008) has found that 5–10 minutes is optimal in that it allows sufficient time for adequate exploration and involvement in the resources with-out the children becoming bored or frustrated.

Why P.R.E.P. anyway?

It is well recognized that there are certain situations in which children do not learn effectively:

- When faced with unfamiliar equipment or ideas, children can be anxious. If given the opportunity to 'play freely' first, they might develop a familiarity that will enable them to engage in more structured tasks with less fear of failure.
- If given a problem to solve or an idea to investigate, children may not know where to start or fully understand the problem that is to be solved. Through preliminary 'free play' (P.R.E.P.) children can access current schemas and develop mental pictures that place the enquiry or problem within a familiar context.

- Challenging and problem-solving tasks require the use of prior learning and higher-order thinking skills – some children need time to draw upon these ideas and experiences. As teachers, we can sometimes pre-empt children's thinking by giving ideas or solutions to them before they have time to access the experiences that initiate ideas, thereby depriving them of the opportunity to develop this skill, often children don't know where to 'look' for the idea. 'Free play' (P.R.E.P.) gives children an opportunity to gently draw on these ideas for themselves.
- P.R.E.P. within the context of a skilfully planned lesson can help create a sense of ownership that the teacher can utilize to engage children in challenging thinking.
- P.R.E.P. can enable children to pursue their natural curiosity and desire to learn and thus support intrinsic motivation and a desire to persevere with tasks.
- P.R.E.P. provides an opportunity for the teacher to watch and listen (with no intervention) considering the prior knowledge and understanding of the children which can support the 'pitch' of the lesson that follows.
- If children are given opportunities to explore freely unfamiliar objects and phenomena, they are encouraged to raise questions and take risks.

P.R.E.P. therefore can act to do the following:

- *Remove anxiety* – to engage in free play prior to an activity allows exploration and engagement in the resources reducing 'emotional' constraints to learning.
- *Contextualize learning* – free play allows children to put into context equipment and ideas and to help build on prior learning.

This is also important to:

- *Access memory* – free play allows time in a non-threatening way for children to revisit ideas (remember past activities) and build on prior learning.
- *Initiate ownership* – free play allows time to develop questioning and investigative skills so that children feel that they want to go on and discover/learn more.
- *Provide assessment opportunity* – free play allows the teacher time to watch and evaluate, identifying misconceptions and areas in which the lesson to follow will need to focus.

After P.R.E.P., children appear more confident and empowered (*less anxious*) to tackle a task and consequently what they learn is truly learnt (*contextualized*) (Phethean 2008).

The importance of providing free play (P.R.E.P.) before a focused teaching session lies in the way in which it creates an environment that is conducive to maximizing learning – making individuals feel safe and secure and prepared to take risks that they otherwise may not have done and in so doing extended their scientific understanding and reasoning.

A Year 6 class is about to embark upon a revision lesson about forces and measuring forces. The teacher has placed a range of different forcemeters on group tables. She gives them 10 minutes play with the forcemeters. She watches as the children explore – placing as many pencil cases on a hook as they can; dragging a car across the room; pulling a range of classroom resources and watching the scale change (Figure 12.4). The children in their play raise questions – what is this? Why are there two scales? What is the 'g', what is the 'N'? The teacher listens. The play is brought to an end and the teaching begins – children sit on the carpet full of questions they want to be answered by their teacher.

Figure 12.4 Playing with the forcemeter

Conclusion

In cameo 3, the teacher uses a P.R.E.P. session to elicit prior knowledge in the context of a *revision* of concepts and resources with which the children should already be familiar because they have been 'taught' them before. It is clear through their play that the learning undertaken in past years had not been 'real' to them. Following their play, the children take ownership of their learning – they want to know and they ask their teacher questions and the answers to those questions prompt more questions. There is active dialogue between teacher and the children and as they ask questions, they are learning. The children want to know because they have played with the equipment; they are following their own lines of enquiry and the teacher goes along with them. The children complete their formal end of year assessment six months later – a question appears asking them to name the piece of equipment in Figure 12.4 (a force-meter) and then questions related to its use follow. Every child in the class who had played, remembers and the question is addressed confidently – and accurately. Year 6 children played and through their play, their curiosity sparked interest and a desire to know and to learn.

From the early years to Year 6 (and beyond) the curiosity of children helps them to explore their amazing world. Teachers are privileged to spend time in the company of children making sense of their world. 'Most of the learning described here seems light-hearted, playful. It is. But it is also monumentally serious' (Duckworth 1996: xii).

Questions to Promote Thinking

1   How do you know that the children in your class are curious in their learning? What characteristics displayed by the children show that they are intrinsically motivated and engaged in their learning?
2   How might you use a P.R.E.P. session to support your teaching?
3   In a KS2 class, does P.R.E.P. present a pedagogical challenge – for you? – for your school? How might this be addressed?

References and suggested further reading:

Alexander, R. (ed.) (2010) *Children, their World, their Education.* Abingdon: Routledge.

AstraZeneca Science Teaching Trust and University of Winchester (2009) *Fostering Curiosity in the Early Years.* Continuing Professional Development Unit. Available online at: http:// www.azteachscience.co.uk/resources/cpd/fostering-curiosity-in-early-years-science/view-online.aspx (accessed 20 November 2010).

Bloom, J. (1992) The development of scientific knowledge in elementary school children: a context of meaning perspective, *Science Education,* 76: 399–413.

Brook, C., Young, K., Mordecai, S. and Phethean, K. (2006) Purposeful play? Teachers and young children exploring their worlds together, In H. Clarke, B. Egan, C. Ryan and L. Fletcher (eds) *Teachers and Young Children Exploring Their Worlds Together.* Research in Action Occasional Papers 2005–6, Early Years Science. Winchester: University of Winchester.

Brooker, L. and Edwards, S. (eds) (2010) *Engaging Play.* Maidenhead: Open University Press.

Bruce, T. (2001) *Learning through Play.* London: Hodder and Stoughton.

Chak, A. (2007) Teachers' and parents' conceptions of children's curiosity and exploration, *International Journal of Early Years Education,* 15(2): 141–59.

Claxton, G. (2008) *What's the Point of School?* Oxford: Oneworld Publications.

Clarke, H. (2003) Encouraging young children to talk about materials: reflections on the influence of context on young children's expression and development of scientific ideas, unpublished PhD thesis, University of Southampton.

Clarke, H., Egan, B., Ryan, C. and Fletcher, L. (eds) (2006) *Teachers and Young Children Exploring Their Worlds Together*. Research in Action Occasional Papers 2005–6, Early Years Science. Winchester: University of Winchester.

Cox, A. and Noble, H. (2009) Emergence, in AstraZeneca Science Teaching Trust and University of Winchester, *Fostering Curiosity in the Early Years*, Continuing Professional Development Unit. Available online at: http://www.azteachscience.co.uk/resources/cpd/fostering-curiosity-in-early-years-science/view-online.aspx (accessed 28 November 2010).

de Boo, M. (ed.) (2000) *Laying the Foundations in the Early Years*. Hatfield: Association for Science Education.

Driver, R., Guesne, E. and Tiberghien, A. (1985) *Children's Ideas in Science*. Milton Keynes: Open University Press.

Duckworth, E. (1996) *The Having of Wonderful Ideas and Other Essays on Teaching and Learning*, 2nd edn. New York: Teachers College Press.

Egan, B., Clarke, H., Fletcher, L. and Ryan, C. (eds) (2008) *Innovative Practice: Teachers and Young Children Exploring Their Worlds Together*. Research in Action Occasional Papers 2005–6, Early Years Science. Winchester: University of Winchester.

Fletcher, L., Ryan, C., Phethean, K. and Clarke, C. (2009) *Fostering Curiosity in the Early Years*. AstraZeneca Science Teaching Trust/University of Winchester Continuing Professional Development Unit. Available online at: http://www.azteachscience.co.uk/resources/cpd/fostering-curiosity-in-early-years-science/view-online.aspx (accessed 20 November 2010).

Gallas, K. (1995) *Talking Their Way into Science: Hearing Children's Questions and Theories, Responding with Curricula*. New York: Teachers College Press.

Harlen, W. (2001) *Primary Science: Taking the Plunge*. Portsmouth, NH: Heinemann.

Harlen, W. (ed.) (2006) *ASE Guide to Primary Science Education*. Hatfield: Association for Science Education.

Harlen, W. (2009) Enquiry and good science teaching, *Primary Science ASE*, 106: 5–7.

Harlen, W. and Qualter, A. (2009) *The Teaching of Science in Primary Schools*, 5th edn. Abingdon: Routledge.

Johnston, J. (2005) *Early Explorations in Science*. Maidenhead: Open University Press.

Kress, G., Jewitt, C., Ogborn, J. and Tsatsarelis, C. (2001) *Multimodal Teaching and Learning: The Rhetorics of the Science Classroom*. London: Continuum.

Laszlo, P. (2004) Science as play, *American Scientist*, 92(5): 398. Available online at: http://www.americanscientist.org/issues/pub/2004/5/science-as-play/4 (accessed December 2010).

Lucas, B. and Claxton, G. (2010) *New Kinds of Smart*. Maidenhead: Open University Press.

Moyles, J. (ed.) (2008) *The Excellence of Play*, 3rd edn. Maidenhead: Open University Press.

Moyles, J. (ed.) (2010) *Thinking about Play: Developing a Reflective Approach*. Maidenhead: Open University Press.

Oliver, A. (2006) *Creative Teaching Science*. London: Fulton.

Osborne, R. and Freyberg, P. (1985) *Learning in Science: The Implications of Children's Science*. Portsmouth, NH: Heinemann Educational.

Ovens, P. (2004) A SANE way to encourage creativity, *Primary Science Review*, 81: 17–20.

Pahl, K. (1999) *Transformations: Children's Meaning Making in a Nursery*. Stoke-on-Trent: Trentham Books.

Phethean, K. (2008) When are you too old to play? *Primary Science*, 105: 12–15.

Pulham, S.M. (1998) Developing and using a range of contexts to explore young children's ideas about materials. MPhil thesis, King Alfred's College, Winchester.

Richardson, I. (2006) What is good science education? in W. Harlen (ed.) *ASE Guide to Primary Science Education*. Hatfield: Association for Science Education

Russell, T., Longden, K. and McGuigan, L. (1991) *Materials*. Liverpool: Liverpool University Press.

Schofield, K. (2008) Curriculum change: what it means in the primary classroom, *Education in Science*, 228: 10.

Thompson, D. (1998) *The Concise Oxford Dictionary*, 9th edn. London: Oxford University Press.

13

RACHAEL LEVY
New technologies in the primary classroom

Summary

The aim of this chapter is to invite beginner teachers and other practitioners to consider the ways in which children now engage with aspects of digital technology in their lives, with a view to informing their classroom practice. The goal is to demonstrate that it is important for teachers to cultivate a positive ethos around the use of digital technology in the classroom, which recognizes the ways in which developments in the technological landscape influences how children today learn, as well as the content of their learning. This chapter concludes that it is now part of the early years and primary practitioner's role to help children to make the most of this changing environment and encourage them to develop skills and confidence in handling all twenty-first-century texts.

Introduction

There is no doubt that new technology has had a major impact on the ways in which we now work, shop, communicate, socialize and engage in recreation. For many adults today who have witnessed this technological development, such changes have been met with a mixture of fascination and awe, often laced with the fear of being unable to keep up with this rapid rate of progress. Yet for children, particularly those of primary school age, there is nothing 'new' about technology. Indeed there is a wide body of evidence to suggest that from birth, young children are immersed in an environment that is rich in media and technology (Marsh et al. 2005) and that interactions with digital technology are now an inherent component of family life (Plowman et al. in press).

This raises questions for primary school teachers, regarding the ways in which technology should be utilized within the classroom. However, the aim of this chapter is not to provide newly qualified teachers with an 'instruction manual' on how to use technology within the primary classroom. Rather this chapter invites teachers to recognize the ways in which young children are now engaging with such technologies in their everyday lives and consider the implications this has for practice across the primary school age range.

To begin, teachers now find themselves in the unprecedented situation of teaching a curriculum to children who are already immersed in a digital culture. This of course raises questions with regard to the ways in which digital technology is acknowledged and indeed should be utilized within the classroom. For example, computer technology is no longer regarded as being the focus of a weekly ICT lesson but is now used to support many curricular and non-curricular activities both inside and outside the classroom. However, before teachers can really think about how technology is viewed and used within the classroom, it is important to give some thought to the ways in which they view the children themselves as participants in 'the digital age' (Marsh 2005). With this in mind, the first section of this chapter explores the concept of children as 'digital natives' (Prensky 2009) and invites practitioners to consider this construct in the light of their own practice.

Children as 'digital natives'

In recent years, authors have used a variety of terms to describe 'digital age' children. For example, the term 'Cyberkids' was adopted by Holloway and Valentine (2003), while others have used terms such as 'Net-generation (Tapscott 1998) to describe children today. However, Prensky's (2001) assertion that young children are 'digital natives' has provoked particular interest. Should children be regarded as 'native' users of digital technology? And are there any dangers in viewing children as a 'native community' to the digital age?

These are important questions for teachers to consider. First, if children are regarded as being 'native' users of digital technology, then this suggests that there is something homogenous about the skills and the ways in which children develop skills in handling aspects of digital technology. Yet it has been argued that teachers cannot assume that all children develop digital skills similar to one another. For example, both Facer et al. (2003) and Holloway and Valentine (2003) argue that each child's interaction with digital technology is unique to that particular child. They further claim that the ways in which computers impact upon children's lives is dependent on the individual social structures in place within children's homes. This suggests that teachers need to have an awareness of the variety of digital skills that are brought into the classroom while, at the same time, remaining alert to the fact that some children will need to be actively taught how to use certain aspects of digital technology and be encouraged to develop particular digital skills.

This point was emphasized by Bearne et al. (2007: 28) who pointed out that there is evidence of 'teachers making assumptions that students know how to access, interpret and critically analyse internet texts' and concluded that it is important that such skills are taught in school. While this is important for all primary school (and indeed secondary school) teachers to acknowledge, this may have particular implications for teachers working in KS2. For example, a child may demonstrate considerable skill in using certain software packages but may never have developed the ability to use search engines effectively, or have learned how to navigate a web page in order to retrieve needed information. It is, therefore, important that teachers recognize that while many children will bring a variety of digital skills with them into the primary classroom, there still exists a need to ensure that all children are offered opportunities to develop their skills in handling digital technology.

Clearly, the teaching of digital skills in the primary classroom is not a straightforward issue. First, this may be derived from the fact that while ICT continues to exist as a subject within the National Curriculum, it is now recognized that as a general requirement, teachers should provide pupils with opportunities to apply and develop their ICT capability in all subjects (except physical education and the non-core foundation subjects at KS1 (DCSF 2008): there is currently, however, little guidance on how this can be achieved.

It is becoming increasingly recognized that digital technology extends far beyond the use of computers alone. Indeed, it is now common to see equipment such as iPods and flip cameras as well as interactive whiteboards and televisions in primary classrooms. As a consequence, it is not easy to provide recommendations as to how teachers should be using digital technology within the primary classroom in any specific sense. However, as already discussed, it does seem to be crucial that children are afforded the opportunities to handle a variety of digital media. So what are the implications of this for teachers entering the profession today?

This issue was recently brought to our attention in the work of Prensky (2009) who speaks of the concept 'digital wisdom'. In brief, Prensky's notion of 'digital wisdom' can be described as the capacity to capitalize on the rapidly changing landscape of technology by 'wisely' making use of one's knowledge about the advancing digital world. Prensky argues forcibly that the potential affordances of the digital age are by no means confined to the actual technology but are embedded within 'the relationship between mind and machine' (2009: 4). Prensky appears to be arguing that for children, and indeed adults, to be successful in modern society, there is a need to not just learn how to physically use the technology but to develop a competence and confidence around technology in general.

At first glance, it may seem like quite a challenge for newly qualified teachers to encourage their children to develop confidence and competence in using a range of digital media. However, this is perhaps less to do with the development of specific digital skills and more to do with cultivating a particular ethos around the use of digital technology in the classroom. It is important for teachers to recognize that children are indeed growing up in a world that is changing rapidly and this does have an impact on *how* children learn, as well as influencing *what* they learn. To illustrate this point further, the next section looks specifically at the issue of literacy learning and examines the ways in which teachers can cultivate a positive environment that recognizes the impact of digital technology on children's interactions with text today (see also Chapters 15 and 17).

Literacy, text and digital technology

As modern communication systems continue to change and develop, schools are being urged to recognize the shift in 'textual landscapes' (Carrington 2005) occurring as a result of this. As Marsh and Singleton (2009: 1) point out, recent research into literacy and technology has tended to follow two avenues of enquiry: the first 'seeking to determine the ways in which literacy needs to be redefined in a digital age', while the second has been concerned with investigating how 'technology can enhance learners' skills, knowledge and understanding in relation to the reading and writing of print'.

First, it must be recognized that the concept of 'text' has undergone radical change in recent years. Whereas the term 'text' has generally been used to describe paper-based media such as books, newspapers and magazines, as well as passages of print within these media, it has been argued that we can no longer confine a definition of 'text' to these contexts. For example, Bearne (2004: 16) claims that we 'need to redefine what "literacy" involves [and] . . . note new uses of the term "text"', that include digital and screen media.

It has been noted that young children entering the schooling system today are often able to make meaning from a variety of digital and screen texts within the context of their home and social environments. For example, Wohlwend (2009) observed children in early years classrooms who were longing to play with the new technologies and media that were part of their everyday out-of-school experiences. To illustrate this, she provided the example of one young boy who, frustrated by the lack of digital technology in the classroom, chose to make his own mobile phone out of paper, complete with a numeric key pad and LCD screen. Bearne et al. (2007: 11) also reported that 'very young children show expertise in on-screen reading, even where homes have no computers' because the handling of such texts is now part of many children's cultural discourse.

Even though teachers cannot make assumptions about the specific digital skills children acquire outside of the school environment, schools cannot ignore the fact that children are growing up in a world where digital texts and multimedia are commonplace. As a consequence, redefining the term 'literacy' means that teachers must also consider what it means to be a 'reader' and 'writer' of text in modern society. Has the prevalence of digital technology changed the ways in which children learn to make sense of the texts they are exposed to at school and at home?

Levy (2009a) investigated this issue in a study of 12 young children (aged 3–6) exploring their perceptions of reading. The study examined the ways in which these children were interacting with screen texts and using them to develop strategies to make sense of a whole variety of symbolic representations, including print. Levy discovered that the children in her study were not only able to transfer their 'meaning-making' skills from the home into the school setting but that even the youngest children were developing skills which allowed them to *use* print within the context of the computer, even though they were not yet print-literate. What is more, the children in this study all seemed very comfortable with the fact that they were *using* the printed prompts alongside pictorial and symbolic images to make sense of the texts, rather than accurately decoding them.

Cameo 1

Young children using printed prompts and images to read screen texts

The following passage relates to a research activity with 3–6-year-old children, who were observed using the computer in the classroom to access and play a variety of web-based games.

> Most of the children clearly understood the meaning of many symbols on the computer although the language they used to describe the symbols was unique to each individual child. For example, it was evident that the 'e' symbol for *Internet Explorer* had meaning for Huda even though she did not fully comprehend the function of the internet. She reported that the sign 'means *CBeebies*' which she explained 'have lots of games there – and puzzles'. Moreover Simona reported that the *timer* symbol 'means you have to wait', while Joseph stated that the same symbol meant 'don't touch it' . . .
>
> Many of the children reported that they understood the meaning of printed prompts appearing on screen even though they could not decode the print. For example, the options *'Play'* or *'Play again?'* were reported to be 'Start' or 'Go'. The *'Home'* icon was often recognized by the children and reported to mean 'Back' or 'Stop'. Finally, many of the children were observed clicking on the icon *'Games'* which appeared regularly on screen. As Joseph pointed out, this particular icon was often distinctive because of the colour surrounding it. He reported that he knew this said *'Games'*, 'because it's orange and it's got writing on it' (Levy 2009a).

Levy's work suggested that young children entering the school system today may be using their interactions with screen texts in the home to develop holistic strategies and skills to help them make sense of a whole range of sign and symbol systems, including print. This contrasted somewhat with further findings from the same study in relation to the children's perceptions of book reading. Without exception, all 12 children reported that they believed that print in books needed to be rigorously decoded. What is more, a number of children also appeared to be inhibited by the presence of print in books and in reading scheme texts in particular (Levy 2009b). Yet these same children seemed to be largely comfortable in using print within the context of the computer. These results indicated that, through their interactions with digital technology, young children may be learning *how to read*, within a context that is meaningful, motivating and free from proficiency grading.

The findings from this study support the assertion raised earlier in this chapter that the presence of digital technology in modern society does have an impact on how children learn. This highlights the need for teachers not only to offer children opportunities to interact with digital technology and new media from their earliest years in school but also to embrace and value the variety of ways in which children themselves develop strategies to make sense of all texts.

If teachers are to facilitate the development of children's confidence in handling text, they must recognize that young children today are exposed to a wide variety of different texts including those of screen *and* paper-based media. In a recent review of research into technology and early childhood settings, Burnett (2010: 16) concluded that it is now apparent that 'complex interactions . . . occur between children, technology, and their wide-ranging experiences of literacy'. Burnett appears to be arguing that literacy is now a multimodal concept and involves interaction between the skills and strategies used to make sense of, and produce, traditional and new media texts. This suggests that one aspect of a teacher's role today is to help children to build a healthy relationship between their interactions with paper and screen texts. In order to achieve this, it is important that teachers view the relationship between digital and traditional media as reciprocal and mutually supportive.

An important aspect of primary classroom teaching today is the cultivation of a positive ethos around the use of digital technology. That is not to say that traditional constructions of text and literacy should be replaced by digital media. Rather, teachers should encourage children to value and enjoy the wide range of texts that are now available to them and support them as they develop strategies to handle texts in general. However, in order for teachers to be able to support children's own interactions with digital texts, there is a need for teachers to gain a deeper understanding of the various ways in which children interact with texts in their homes.

Using digital texts in the home

As stated earlier, there is now an extensive body of evidence that young children are engaged with media and technology-based activity from their earliest years. In the UK, Marsh et al. (2005) conducted a survey of 1,852 parents of children aged from birth to 6 and concluded that many young children were competent users of digital technologies and that parents felt that their children gained knowledge and skills in the use of such technologies from a very young age. Similar findings have been reported in the USA (Rideout et al. 2003).

In terms of the ways in which children interact with digital texts outside of school, there is now a wealth of research to suggest that digital technology is intrinsic to the social practices and cultural lives of children today (Davies and Merchant 2009). As Levy and Marsh (in press, 2011) point out: 'Whereas in previous eras children may have simply accessed favourite Internet sites, often media-related, to play games, there is now evidence that children are using social networking sites to interact with others in online play.'

What is more, there is strong evidence to suggest that issues of identity formation and self-expression are also deeply embedded in children's digital text use in the home. For example, having investigated the ways in which children are producers of online digital texts, Dowdall (2009) discovered that children are creating highly sophisticated profile pages in online social networking sites. She reported that these pages are: '[D]igital . . . texts where still and moving images, words, sound and graphics are combined to create a representation of the owner for members within their online social network to view and communicate with' (2009: 43).

Not only are these texts complex in nature but, Dowdall argued, they are 'highly purposeful, powerful and of consequence to the creator' (2009: 43). Further research has revealed that sites such as *Flickr* (Davies 2006) and *Facebook* are very popular with early adolescents in particular, as a means of creating a personalized identity to be presented within a social networking community. Similarly, Marsh (in press) also discovered that even very young children are also engaged in using popular virtual worlds such as *Club Penguin, Barbie Girls* and *Webkinz*.

The implications of this for primary school teachers are many. However, there are two connected issues that need to be considered. First, this has implications for the ways in which teachers expect children to use texts in the classrooms, especially in relation to literacy teaching. The second issue is related to teachers' own attitudes towards digital technology and their confidence in handling such texts themselves in the classroom.

Children's interactions with digital texts are often social in nature and closely linked with issues of identity formation. Given that the curriculum still tends to prioritize paper-based media over digital text and that children's interactions with multimodal texts goes largely unrecognized in the literacy curriculum (Marsh 2003; Bearne 2004; Levy 2009a), teachers must acknowledge that a disparity may exist between the ways in which children use texts in their homes and the ways in which they are expected to read, produce and interact with texts in the classroom. Levy (2008) discovered that young children in her study were using the contexts of play, popular culture and digital texts in order to develop broad and inclusive definitions of reading. Yet as the children progressed through their early years of schooling, these valuable constructions became eroded by the dominant culture of school. As a consequence, these children came to believe that 'reading' was the decoding of print within reading scheme texts. Moreover, many of these children were observed losing confidence in their own abilities to make sense of texts as they did not believe that their own 'home' interactions with texts were authentic 'reading'.

This supports the assertion that it is vital that teachers create an ethos of support and inclusion around the use of digital technology in the primary classroom. In particular, it has been acknowledged that the ways in which children read multimodal texts goes largely unrecognized in the literacy curriculum and its assessment (Bearne 2003, 2004; Marsh 2003; Levy 2009a). This issue is illustrated in cameo 2, which presents an account of a 10-year-old boy's home literacy practices which occur largely through the medium of his interaction with digital and multimodal texts. Even though Alex claims to 'hate' literacy at school, he is deeply engaged with the reading and production of a wide variety of texts in his home. What is more, much of this includes a substantial element of print literacy.

Cameo 2

Alex's use of digital texts in his home

The following passage was written by the mother of a 10-year-old boy in connection with her son's engagement with various texts within the home environment.

Alex is a 10-year-old (year 5). We are having dinner together as a family. I ask Alex what he has done at school that day. He pushes food around his plate and mumbles, 'Boring boring literacy!' When I ask him why literacy was boring, he tells me that he 'hates' literacy and that he cannot 'do it'. I do not pursue the conversation, as I am used to hearing that he dislikes literacy at school. Later that night Alex rushes downstairs and asks me how to spell the word 'tremendous', because he is having a conversation on *Facebook* with a friend about Lady Ga-ga and wants to spell the word correctly. During the course of the evening Alex also downloads a set of 'cheats' from the internet which he reads and then uses to support his gaming on the play station. Before going to bed, Alex and his brother plan a 'horror story' which they act out. They take it in turns to record each other with Alex's flip camera, each taking different roles in the story. The boys download the film onto the computer and show it to their father and me. As Alex gets ready for bed that night, he becomes distracted with an *Asterix* book which is lying in his room. He reads the book in deep concentration for almost 15 minutes. As I am saying goodnight to Alex, he tells me again that he is not looking forward to going to school tomorrow because he hates doing literacy.

This cameo highlights the growing need for teachers to find ways in which to accommodate and build upon children's own interactions with digital media. As children's home text use becomes increasingly multimodal in nature, it is important that schools are aware that unless such interactions become more valued within the school context, the disparity between home and school literacy practices will continue to grow. Newly qualified teachers entering the primary school classroom have a unique opportunity to introduce a 'holistic' approach to the teaching of literacy that both recognizes and values the variety of different strategies children use to read and produce texts today. The extent to which teachers are able to promote this ethos within classrooms depends also upon their own confidence; confidence in using technology within the context of everyday classroom activity as well as having the confidence to allow children to learn for themselves. Given that further studies have suggested that many teachers feel challenged once children move into fluid networked spaces and begin exploring their own paths (Burnett 2009; Merchant 2009), this may be a particular issue for newly qualified teachers.

In terms of teachers' own use of digital technology, researchers have provided excellent examples of ways in which new media practices can support children's learning (Gillen 2009). Despite this, it is clearly difficult for all teachers to use resources, such as 3D visual worlds, within their classroom practice. As Merchant (2009: 4) rightly points out, using such resources in classrooms 'places additional demands on teacher time and planning'. He argues that teachers also need time to 'build their confidence and to experiment with new approaches' (2009: 4). However, Merchant further asserts that it is necessary for teachers to invest this time if they are to respond effectively to the demands of the digital age.

Conclusion

This chapter has raised a number of issues for students and new teachers to consider with regard to the role of new technologies in the primary classroom. It has been highlighted that while teachers cannot make assumptions about children's individual digital skills, they must also recognize that developments in technology are having a great impact on the ways in which children today learn to read and write and learn to *learn* within the context of their everyday lives. Part of the primary school teacher's role is to help children to make the most of this changing environment by encouraging them to develop confidence in their abilities to handle twenty-first-century texts. However, rather than implying a value judgement between the domains of print and digital text, this chapter has stressed that primary school teachers need to help children to develop their own healthy relationships with both. It has been further argued that this can be facilitated by encouraging children to capitalize on the skills and strategies they develop in their out-of-school interactions with digital and multimodal texts and build upon these within the school context.

Never before have children been exposed to such variety and complexity in text use and never before have teachers had so many opportunities to support children's learning through the context of digital technology. It therefore seems logical to suggest that teachers must now consider it part of their job to encourage children to enjoy the range of texts that are available to them both inside and outside of school. In order to achieve this aim, it is also important that teachers take responsibility for developing their own confidence in handling digital media.

Questions to Promote Thinking

1 In your view, how has the prevalence of digital technology changed the ways in which children learn to make sense of the texts at home and school?
2 How can teachers capitalize on children's exposure to digital technologies?
3 What skills do you need to learn in order to engage effectively with children of the digital age?

References and suggested further reading

Bearne, E. (2003) Rethinking literacy: communication, representation and text, *Reading Literacy and Language*, 37(3): 98–103.

Bearne, E. (2004) Multimodal texts; what they are and how children use them, in J. Evans (ed.) *New Ways of Reading, New Ways of Writing; Using Popular Culture, New Technologies and Critical Literacy in the Primary Classroom*. New York: Heinemann.

Bearne, E., Clark, C., Johnson, A., Manford, P., Mottram, M. and Wolstencroft, H. (2007) *Reading on Screen*. Leicester: UKLA.

Burnett, C. (2009) Research into literacy and technology in primary classrooms: an exploration of understandings generated by recent studies, *Journal of Research in Reading*, 32(1): 22–37.

Burnett, C. (2010) Technology and literacy in early childhood educational settings: a review of research, *Journal of Early Childhood Literacy*, 10(3): 247–70.

Carrington, V. (2005) New textual landscapes, information, new childhood, in Marsh, J. (ed.) *Popular Culture, New Media and Digital Literacy in Early Childhood*, London: RoutledgeFalmer.

Davies, J. (2006) Affinities and beyond!! Developing ways of seeing in online spaces, *ne-learning, Special Issue: Digital Interfaces*, 3(2): 217–34.

Davies, J. and Merchant, G. (2009) *Web 2.0 for Schools: Learning and Social Participation*. New York: Peter Lang.

DCSF (Department for Children, Schools and Families) (2008) *National Curriculum Key Stages 1 and 2: ICT in Subject Teaching*. Available online at: http://curriculum.qcda.gov.uk/key-stages-1-and-2/learning-across-the-curriculum/ictinsubjectteaching/index.aspx (accessed 24 November 2010).

Dowdall, C. (2009) Impressions, improvisations and compositions: reframing children's text production in social network sites, *Reading*, 43(2): 91–9.

Facer, K., Furlong, J., Furlong, R. and Sutherland, R. (2003) *Screenplay: Children and Computing in the Home*. London, RoutledgeFalmer.

Gillen, J. (2009) Literacy practices in Schome Park: a virtual literacy ethnography. *Journal of Research in Reading*, 32(1): 57–74.

Holloway, S.L. and Valentine, G. (2003) *Cyberkids: Children in the Information Age*. London: RoutledgeFalmer.

Levy, R. (2008) 'Third spaces' are interesting places; applying 'third space theory' to nursery-aged children's constructions of themselves as readers, *Journal of Early Childhood Literacy*, 8(1): 43–66.

Levy, R. (2009a) 'You have to understand words . . . but not read them'; young children becoming readers in a digital age, *Journal of Research in Reading*, 32(1): 75–91.

Levy, R. (2009b) Children's perceptions of reading and the use of reading scheme texts, *Cambridge Journal of Education*, 39(3): 361–77.

Levy, R. and Marsh, J. (in press, 2011) Literacy and ICT in the early years, in D. Lapp and D. Fisher (eds) *The Handbook of Research on Teaching the English Language Arts*, 3rd edn. Mahwah, NJ: Lawrence Erlbaum Associates.

Marsh, J. (2003) One-way traffic? Connections between literacy practices at home and in the nursery, *British Educational Research Journal*, 29(3): 369–82.

Marsh, J. (2005) Introduction: children of the digital age, in J. Marsh (ed.) *Popular Culture, New Media and Digital Literacy in Early Childhood*. London: RoutledgeFalmer.

Marsh, J. (in press) Young children's play in online virtual worlds, *Journal of Early Childhood Research*.

Marsh, J., Brookes, G., Hughes, J., Ritchie, L, Roberts, S. and Wright, K. (2005) *Digital Beginnings: Young Children's Use of Popular Culture, Media and New Technologies*. Sheffield: Literacy Research Centre, University of Sheffield.

Marsh, J. and Singleton, C. (2009) Editorial: Literacy and technology: questions of relationship, *Journal of Research in Reading*, 32(1): 1–5.

Merchant, G. (2009) Literacy in virtual worlds, *Journal of Research in Reading*, 32(1): 38–56.

Murphy, K., De Pasquale, R. and McNamara, E. (2003) Meaningful connections: using technology in the primary classroom. Available online at: http://journal.naeyc.org/btj/200311/techinprimaryclassrooms.pdf (accessed 14 January 2011).

Plowman, L., McPake, J. and Stephen, C. (in press) The technologisation of childhood? Young children and technology in the home, *Children and Society*.

Prensky, M. (2001) Digital natives, digital immigrants, *On the horizon, 9(5)*. MCB University Press. Available online at: http://www.marcprensky.com/writing/Prensky%20-%20Digital%20Natives,%20Digital%20Immigrants%20-%20Part1.pdf (accessed 24 November 2010).

Prensky, M. (2009) *From Digital Immigrants and Digital Natives to Digital Wisdom*. Available online at: http://www.innovateonline.info/pdf/vol5_issue3/H._Sapiens_Digital-__From_Digital_Immigrants_and_Digital_Natives_to_Digital_Wisdom.pdf (accessed 7 May 2010).

Rideout, V.J., Vandewater, E.A. and Wartella, E.A. (2003) *Zero to Six: Electronic Media in the Lives of Infants, Toddlers and Preschoolers.* Washington, DC: Kaiser Foundation.

Tapscott, D. (1998) *Growing Up Digital: The Rise of the Net Generation.* New York: McGraw-Hill.

Willett, R., Robinson, M. and Marsh, J. (eds) (2009) *Play, Creativity and Digital Cultures*. London: Routledge.

Wohlwend, K. (2009) Early adopters: playing new literacies and pretending new technologies in print-centric classrooms, *Journal of Early Childhood Literacy*, 9(2): 117–40 (see www.ecl.sagepub.com/cgi/content/abstract/9/2/117).

14

CARRIE WESTON AND ELIZABETH MARSDEN

The relationship between physical development and learning in the early years and primary classroom

Summary

This chapter considers the centrality of movement, physical learning and activity within the history and development of early years educational practice. The teaching of movement to children within PE lessons is then explained and examined. Highlighting the importance of physical activity in learning, the classroom and curriculum-based context are also explored. This allows the primary school practitioner to understand and draw upon physical, active learning in daily teaching.

Introduction

The journey from birth to maturity is a period of rapid physical and intellectual development, none more so than in the early years of life. To perceive physical and cognitive development as separate areas of growth is to overlook the central role of the physical in learning, exploring and making sense of the world. Indeed, it can be argued that physical and intellectual growth cannot be considered as anything but one, due to the embodied nature of existence (i.e. that we all experience life and learning within our bodies). This chapter will consider how practitioners working with young children can use movement and the relationship between physical and cognitive development to enhance learning opportunities for children in the early years.

To say that children are active in their learning is probably to state the obvious. It takes little more than casual observation to witness that babies and young children use physical movements to explore surroundings and objects, to form relationships, to express emotions and to seek both pleasure and comfort. From the moment of birth, it is through movement and the physical self that children learn about the world around them. As they grow, understanding and awareness develops from the *physical* nature of experience and interaction. Of course, this is not news! The importance of play, toys, space and opportunities for children to move and explore are universally recognized. However, little attention is given to maximizing the potential of children to learn through their physical being. Generally, we do not teach children to reach out, grab, crawl, walk, run and jump. It is assumed that these things just happen, that children develop motile capacities as part of their natural growth and maturation. Yet, if we accept that there is an inextricable link between physical and cognitive development, then the importance of maximizing motile potential through teaching movement becomes apparent. In order to capitalize on movement as a vehicle for learning, children need to know and experience their bodies, their physical capabilities and their embodied self in relation to their environment and other beings.

This chapter will also consider how to promote opportunities for children to gain mastery of their own bodies, understand how different parts move and feel, explore how much force or resistance is required at the right time and how to physically relate to, and interact with, others. In doing so, the child will be considered as an embodied, physical learner.

Cameo 1

A Year 1 class of 28 children are seated on the carpet in the book corner to listen to a story. There is very little room so the teacher reminds the children to cross their legs and fold their arms. Some of the children at the back are kneeling so that they can get a better view of the pictures in the book. Some children have difficulty keeping their legs crossed, others lean and sprawl. The teacher stops reading on several occasions in order to remind children not to lean on each other and to bring the attention of some children back to the story.

Reflect for a moment:

- Have you ever noticed a time when children are restrained within their learning environment?
- What can happen on these occasions?
- How can the teacher better use the space?
- How long can Year 1 children sit still with their legs crossed (in Scotland, this is referred to as having one's legs 'in a basket')?
- How can the teacher position herself so that all the children can see?

Beginning with the familiar

The importance of the physical nature of learning is readily found within established theories and practices concerning early years teaching and learning. It is likely that both students and practitioners will be familiar with the emphasis on physical space, action and movement in the history and development of early childhood pedagogy. However, a brief appraisal with this emphasis in mind serves to reposition the familiar and allows us to focus on the centrality of physical movement in learning. In the following swift journey through major influences on practice in early education, count how often physical activity and movement is a central feature.

Let's start with Pestalozzi (1746–1827). Building on the philosophies of Rousseau (1712–1778), Pestalozzi saw education as more than the development of academic skills. Like Rousseau, he believed in stages of development and saw that the natural inclination of young children to move and be active could be harnessed in their physical learning. Pestalozzi's ideas were brought to the UK in 1816 by the Scottish industrialist Robert Owen. Concern for the physical welfare and education of the children of poor factory workers led Owen to establish factory schools which promoted kindness, equality and physical activity at the heart of their practice.

The German educator, Froebel (1782–1852) was, like Owen, first introduced to teaching through the Pestalozzi tradition. Froebel believed that young children should come together in a 'kindergarten' where they could be encouraged to grow personal, social and physical skills ready for academic learning. Similarly, in the United States, Dewey (1859–1952) advocated that education for young children must be active and interactive, emphasizing that young children learn by *doing*. This is echoed in the work of Erikson (1904–1994), who describes the 5-year-old child as energetic and ready to learn. This energy, in Erikson's view, is best used in an activity to increase confidence and autonomy in learning.

At the same time, the educational value of space to allow activity and movement for young children was a salient feature of the nurseries established by the Christian Socialist sisters Rachel and Margaret McMillan (1859–1917 and 1860–1931 respectively). Having worked extensively with children in inner-city environments, they noted the relationship between poor physical and poor intellectual development in young children and identified the need for them to have space and opportunity for physical movement in order to enhance both learning and well-being. Margaret McMillan saw the child's need for movement as crucial to development; 'to move, to run, to find things out by new movement, to feel one's life in every limb; that is the life of early childhood' (cited in Curtis 1963: 333). Like the McMillan sisters, Steiner (1862–1925) believed that young children needed space and freedom to develop self-expression, creativity and morality. Steiner established schools for the children of factory workers in Austria and left the legacy of Steiner schools worldwide.

Much of the work of Susan Isaacs (1885–1948) also centred on a belief in the importance of play and space, plus gentle guidance in the educational development of young children. Based on both Dewey and Froebel's philosophies of interest led, active and interactive educational experiences for young children, Isaacs' writing had an impact on provision in early years education throughout the 1930s and 1940s. Similarly, Maria Montessori (1870–1952) understood that children use their senses to explore and learn from the world around them. Physical movement, particularly manual dexterity, and the enjoyment of educational experiences were regarded by Montessori as central to children's learning and are essential aspects in Montessori schools today.

The legacies of both Piaget (1896–1980) and Vygotsky (1896–1934) stress the importance of creating an environment in which children are stimulated to actively explore and learn. Piaget saw physical development as linked to intellectual growth and the child's physical interaction with the environment as integral to learning. Differing from Piaget, Vygotsky placed great emphasis on the role of social interaction in learning; language and social interaction are essential experiences and, without these elements, learning is less effective and less purposeful (Vygotsky 1978). Children are context-embedded, using body language and their environment in order to achieve this social interaction.

Vygotsky's theories had a great impact on the work of Jerome Bruner (1966) and Barbara Rogoff (1990) and influenced Loris Malaguzzi's (1920–1994) Reggio Emilia kindergarten education system in Italy. According to Malaguzzi, those working in the early years should not, primarily, transmit knowledge but enable young children to develop active relationships between others and their environment. Using the active world of the child as the starting point of learning is a central feature of the educational philosophy of Jerome Bruner. Bruner also emphasizes the importance of play, not in the 'free play' sense of Froebel, McMillan, Steiner and Isaacs, but in the sense that games are 'practice in mastery' (Bruner 1986) of skills for adult life.

In a project for the Froebel Institute, Athey (1990) considered how children acquire knowledge, starting from Piaget's theory of motor schemas. Athey's work concludes that children construct understanding through sequences of actions which have meaning for the child within the context in which they take place. Athey's view is that repeated patterns of actions indicate the development of schemas, a notion similar to that found in David's review of brain research (David 2003) and what neuroscience can tell us about early childhood development. Contemporary research suggests that, from birth, the child's active experience of their environment influences and strengthens the development of neural connections within the brain. The greater the capacity for physical interaction and stimulation, the stronger and more complex the neural networks become.

So, even such a brief amble through theories of early learning highlights that the *physical* plays a crucial role in children's development. There are clear and established common threads recognizing that physical and cognitive development are closely intertwined during the early years as children move to explore, play and make sense of the world and people around them.

However, a word of caution. It needs to be noted that often strategies in teaching and learning are justified on the grounds of *developmentally appropriate practice* (DAP: see Bredekamp and Copple 1997). In other words, an understanding of children which presumes they are ready to do particular things at particular ages. Within this, there is a danger that assumptions are made about the universal nature of child development and what is appropriate, based on an understanding of a predominantly western childhood (Corrie 1995; Adams et al. 2004; Yelland 2005). Practices within early education also need to reflect the diverse and unique configurations of childhood, the rich cultural, ethnic and social differences which comprise contemporary society.

It could be argued that physical education, and the teaching of movement in particular, offers a unique opportunity to reflect the individuality of the child as a learner. Just as the experience of *embodiment* (the physical reality of being, thinking and doing within one's own body) must be a personal one, so the development of motile capacity to move, feel and interact is implicitly relevant and meaningful to the embodied individual. In providing opportunities for physical movement development within the early years, the practitioner is enabling and extending the unique embodied experiences of the child through developing the motile capabilities which will enhance the active processes of learning.

What is movement education?

We have already noted that there is a general tendency to expect children to crawl, walk, run, jump and throw automatically when their physical development reaches a certain level of maturity. It is true that most children follow a pattern of physical and motor development that allows the general motor skills to mature (Haywood and Getchell 2009). We could ask, therefore, what is the point of physical education (PE)? For many of us, PE at school, especially secondary school, was a time of near horror. We remember having to strip off to pants/shorts and t-shirts and being 'made' to run around outside in the freezing weather while brandishing some sort of implement for hitting a very hard ball and desperately trying to avoid being hit ourselves. Or perhaps one of the worst memories might be that of entering a dark and gloomy gymnasium full of terrible looking boxes, ropes, beams and wall bars upon which you were just expected to happily leap, climb, roll and balance (Figure 14.1). This would then be followed by the dreaded communal shower!

If your experience of PE was even vaguely similar to that above, it is not surprising that you might not look forward to becoming acquainted with it again. In the present climate, PE covers a wide spectrum of activities, beliefs and values. Some regard it as exercise and fitness training which is strongly related to physical health and obesity control; others think of it only as competitive games and sports. In fact, it

Figure 14.1 There's more to observation than meets the eye!

is a very broad church and may involve dance, athletics, swimming, outdoor activities, games of all types and gymnastics. Physical education is underpinned by motor development, motor skills acquisition, health-related activity and movement education.

Educating children physically should always include movement education and yet, in our highly competitive world, this most basic aspect of physical education is often forgotten. Good movement education for children in their early years has a very definite pedagogical foundation. Traditional PE and games has a subject- and skills-based pedagogy while movement education has a child-centred pedagogy. This is important to remember as we often fall back on old experiences when we are working in areas in which we are unfamiliar or uncomfortable. Movement education is fully inclusive as it challenges children to solve open-ended tasks carefully set by a teacher who is familiar with the children's abilities and the environment in which they will work. The aims of movement education are concerned with providing children with the opportunity to explore what their bodies can do; how to use space; when to employ different movement dynamics or qualities and how to relate physically with others, with gravity and sometimes with equipment and apparatus. It does, in fact, allow children to become physically literate (Haydn-Davies 2005; Whitehead 2010). As confidence and experience grow, children will learn more movement 'vocabulary' and be able to create their own movement sequences and movement stories.

Teaching movement

The most important skills required by the teacher of movement education are the ability to observe movement (Marsden 2010); an understanding of movement principles (Laban 1998) and some knowledge of the teaching points for basic movement skills (PEA UK 2003, 2008).

Cameo 2

There are 30 children aged 9–10 years old in class. They are changed and ready to start a 30-minute movement class in the gym. The teacher has mats, hoops, cones and benches organized at the sides of the gym. As soon as the children enter the gym, they are told to sit quietly and listen. The teacher goes through all of the safety rules and the aims of the lesson. She allows the children to warm up for 3 minutes but stops them frequently and insists they sit while she tells them they are too noisy. She then spends 10 minutes organizing the equipment before allowing the children to start work. She rotates the groups so that everyone has a turn with the equipment but she does not give anyone any teaching points. Some children demonstrate while the others watch and the teacher tells them that they have done well but she has not said why. When all the equipment has been returned, the children sit still until they are allowed one at a time to line up at the door.

Reflect for a moment:

- What percentage of the lesson do you think the children were actually moving?
- Why do you think the teacher wanted the children to sit still so frequently?
- Did the children learn anything about movement?
- How would you improve this lesson?

Movement of any kind is very transient and so the teacher will need to remember what happened and then use some kind of tool with which to analyse in order to gauge whether the child is answering the task, needs assistance to improve, and is safe. 'Elastic Boxes' (Figure 14.2) can be successfully used both to analyse movement and to aid in planning balanced movement lessons *ad infinitum*. It is a visual summary of *Laban's Principles of Movement* (Laban 1998). The boxes are 'elastic' because they are not definitive and there is room to add more types of movement vocabulary as required, e.g. in the BODY box, falling and rising is not present nor is kicking.

Using one box at a time, any movement, motor skill or sequence can be analysed by circling the observed movement vocabulary. It seems daunting at the beginning

BODY	SPACE
Actions:	**Levels:**
Stepping, jumping, rolling, sliding, vaulting,	High/Medium/Low
twisting, turning, swinging, balancing, gesture,	**Directions:**
stillness	Left – right
Parts of body:	High – deep
Can lead, can support, can relate, can move	Back – forwards
symmetrically, can move asymmetrically	**Extensions:**
Body shape:	Near – far
Arrow, ball, pin,	**Air and floor patterns:**
Wall, screw	Straight, curved, twisted, angular
DYNAMICS/ EFFORT	RELATIONSHIPS
Time:	**With other people:**
Sudden/quick.....................sustained/slow	Alone/Partner/Small group/Large group
Weight:	**With apparatus:**
Strong/heavy....................light/fine touch	The floor/Small (mats, benches)/Large
Space:	(climbing materials, ropes, boxes)
Direct/straight............flexible/circuitous	**With equipment:**
Flow:	Small (balls, hoops, cones, etc.)
Bound.................................free	Large (tunnels, goals, weights, etc.)

Figure 14.2 Elastic Boxes: a framework for observing movement

but with practice, any observer can become highly skilled and speedy at analysing. The teacher of early years children will find this fascinating as, over time, a clear picture of each child's learning of movement vocabulary will become clear. As in literacy when children are learning new vocabulary, it is the teacher's aim to introduce more words that the children have not yet experienced or may be finding difficult. Similarly, the Elastic Boxes can extend the children's movement vocabulary and thus also help you plan future lessons. If your class are poor at space awareness both in PE and in the classroom and around the school, you can choose to take elements of the SPACE box as your main aim for a sequence of movement lessons. In the first lesson, you can choose one element from each of the three remaining boxes as sub-aims and then by changing one of the sub-aims each lesson, you can have a completely different lesson. This will further extend the children's vocabulary of movement while still keeping the main emphasis on spatial awareness. Thus, by inter-changing different elements over the years, you can plan lessons *ad infinitum* and give the children a wide experience of movement vocabulary. This is especially useful because as humans, we tend to have our favourite ways of moving and we never naturally experience all the possibilities or learn all the movement vocabulary of which we are capable.

Children with SEN or additional support needs are especially at risk of never experiencing a wide range of movement vocabulary.

Cameo 3

David is aged 6 years old and has cerebral palsy which has affected his legs and he uses a walking frame. He is a bright, sociable and creative boy and his classmates like him very much. He is able to join in with everything except PE. In PE lessons his classroom assistant takes him through a prescribed set of physiotherapy exercises on a mat in a corner of the gym.

Reflect for a moment:

- How do you think David feels during PE?
- How do you think his classmates feel?
- What could you do to include him in the PE lesson?
- How can you give David the opportunity to be creative physically?
- How can you give David the responsibility for taking care of a partner?

Like David in Cameo 3, children with SEN or additional support needs may be given limited exposure to gym space and be assigned specific physiotherapy-style 'exercises'. Their creative and exploring opportunities are denied for fear that they might injure themselves. But by using *Laban's Principles of Movement* and the Elastic Boxes for planning and observing, they can be encouraged to expand their movement vocabulary; explore new physical spaces; learn to be responsible for a partner and create new movement stories. Veronica Sherborne worked with children of all ages and all abilities and disabilities and came to the conclusion that all children have two basic needs. First, they need to feel at home in their own bodies and, second, that they need to be allowed to form relationships. Sparkes, a very experienced physical education teacher who had watched Sherborne's brilliant and innovative work through three decades, wrote:

> To understand the Sherborne approach to movement teaching is to understand movement in the context of early child development and to engage oneself in an analysis of the teaching method . . . It is a way of working that sets out to give confidence, to engage the participant in non-judgemental teaching, to develop an individual's self-esteem and to ensure both consolidation and progression in personal learning.
>
> (2001: xi)

Sherborne's work, now internationally recognized as *Sherborne Developmental Movement* (www.sherbornemovement.org) was solidly based on *Laban's Principles of Movement* and research has shown that it is especially useful for developing movement vocabulary and social development of early years children in mainstream school (Marsden et al. 2004); for strengthening parent–child bonding in disaffected early years children (Filer 2007); for focus and concentration of children with autism (Astrand 2007; Konaka 2007) and for enabling early years teachers to plan child-centred, holistic and balanced lessons (Weston 2010).

The inter-connected curriculum

Through developing movement capabilities within PE, children's potential to learn through physical action and interaction is enhanced. In the classroom context it is important to consider opportunities for movement, physical experiences and 'doing' within learning in order to capitalize on how actions support and enhance children's understanding. In this way, the movement teaching of the PE lesson can enhance the learning experience of the classroom in an inter-connected, seamless curriculum.

Using physical learning and movement within the classroom context is also inclusive practice. While the earlier section of the chapter evidenced that all children will benefit from a physical and active dimension within learning, for some children it is an essential aspect of their learning style. Often known as 'kinaesthetic' learners, some children (and adults too) learn best through hands-on, practical experience; touching, feeling and doing (see Gardner's (1983) 'multiple intelligences' and Kolb's (1984) *Experiential Learning Theory*). Offering physical experiences within classroom learning will meet the needs of kinaesthetic learners, but at the same time will enhance the learning of *all* children.

Utilizing physical movement within active learning offers the opportunity for some exciting, innovative teaching. In a recently observed lesson, a class of 7-year-olds were estimating lengths and measurements using straws. The teacher then stopped the lesson and the children arranged the desks and chairs in a horseshoe, affording plenty of space in the middle of the room. The children carried on estimating, now using body parts. They guessed how many footsteps it took to cross the carpet; how many children lying head-to-foot would measure the room; how many handspans measured a friend's height. When a particularly innovative method of measuring was thought of, the children sat in the horseshoe and watched the inventor carry out the measurement while they made guesses. As the lesson progressed, one child recalled that her father had told her how cats measure the width of spaces using their whiskers. This prompted a new activity, using the straws to make whiskers and trying out the cat-theory. Children crawled through chair legs and under tables, discovering that turning and twisting or slithering on bellies allowed them to get through spaces without squashing their whiskers. This led to discussions about height as well as width – did cats use their ears for judging spaces too? There was considerable disappointment when it was time for lunch, but a wealth of activities for the teacher to return to another time and an incredible amount of varied and unforgettable learning.

Conclusion

This chapter has reviewed the importance of movement and physical activity in the learning and development of children. In doing so movement teaching has been highlighted and explored. As well as children becoming confident in their own bodies and using their motile capacities, the link between movement and the classroom experience is also established. Being able to utilize the physical within learning is integral to inclusive practice and offers a wealth of opportunities. Finally, just observing any school playground should serve to remind us that children are naturally physically active. We must not overlook the sheer pleasure and enjoyment that children derive from activity and movement, but should seek to foster it.

Questions to Promote Thinking

1 Think about the physical environment of your classroom. How are the desks and chairs arranged?
2 Can they be easily moved to create space and opportunity for movement and activity?
3 For example, is there room within their working space for the children to manipulate objects connected to their learning or use body language in their interactions?
4 Look at the learning outcomes planned for a lesson.
5 Can any of these be met through physical learning experiences?
6 How can movement, touch, doing or experiencing be brought into the lesson?
7 Could experiences from PE be utilized and re-visited within the classroom context to aid and support learning?

Useful websites

PEA UK (2003) www.observingchildrenmoving.co.uk (children aged 3–7) (accessed 21 January 2011).
PEA UK (2008) www.observinglearnersmoving.co.uk (children aged 7–14) (accessed 21 January 2011).

References and suggested further reading

Adams, S., Alexander, E., Drummond, M.J. and Moyles, J. (2004) Inside the Foundation Stage: Recreating the Reception Year. London: ATL (Association of Teachers and Lecturers).
Astrand, B. (2007) Adapted relationship play and children on the autistic spectrum, in E. Marsden and J. Egerton (eds) *Moving with Research*. Stourbridge: Sunfield.
Athey, C. (1990) *Extending Thought in Young Children*. London: Paul Chapman.
Bredekamp, S. and Copple, C. (1997) *Developmentally Appropriate Practice in Early Childhood Programmes*. Washington, DC: NAEYC.
Bruner, J.S. (1966) *Toward a Theory of Instruction*. Cambridge, MA: Belknap Press/Harvard University Press.
Bruner, J.S. (1986) *Actual Minds, Possible Worlds*. Cambridge, MA: Harvard University Press.
Corrie, L. (1995) Vertical integration: teachers' knowledge and teachers' voice. *Australian Journal of Early Childhood*, 20(3): 1–5.
Curtis, C. (1963) *The History of Education in Great Britain*. London: University Tutorial Press.
David, T. (2003) *What Do We Know about Teaching Young Children? Professional User Review based on BERA Academic Review*. Canterbury: Christ Church University College.
Filer, J. (2007) Bonding through developmental movement play, in E. Marsden and J. Egerton (eds) *Moving with Research*. Stourbridge: Sunfield.
Garder, H. (1983) *Frames of Mind: The Theory of Multiple Intelligences*. New York: Basic Books.
Haydn-Davies, D. (2005) How does the concept of physical literacy relate to what is and what could be the practice of physical education? *British Journal of Teaching Physical Education*, 36(3): 43–48.
Haywood, K. and Getchell, N. (2009) *Life-Span Motor Development*. Champaign, IL: Human Kinetics.
Kolb, D.A. (1984) *Experiential Learning*. Englewood Cliffs, NJ: Prentice Hall.
Konaka, J. (2007) Developing social engagement through movement: an adapted teaching approach for children with autistic spectrum disorder, in E. Marsden and J. Egerton (eds) *Moving with Research*. Stourbridge: Sunfield.
Laban, R. (1998) *The Mastery of Movement*, 5th edn. London: Northcote House.
Marsden, E. (2010) Observation of pupils in PE, in S. Capel and M. Whitehead (eds) *Learning to Teach Physical Education in the Secondary School*. London: Routledge.
Marsden, E., Weston, C. and Hair, M. (2004) Innovative and inclusive physical education, paper presented at the BERA Conference, Manchester Metropolitan University, September. Available online at: http://www.leeds.ac.uk/educol/documents/00003898.htm (accessed 21 January 2011).
Rogoff, B. (1990) *Apprenticeship in Thinking: Cognitive Development in Social Context*. New York: Oxford University Press.
Sparkes, J. (2001) Foreword, in V. Sherborne, *Developmental Movement for Children*, 2nd edn. London: Worth Publishing.
Vygotsky, L.S. (1978) *Mind in Society*. Cambridge, MA: Harvard University Press.

Weston, C. (2010) Researching quality: the case for PE in the early years, paper presented to BERA Conference, University of Warwick, September.

Whitehead, M. (2010) *Physical Literacy throughout the Life Course.* **London: Routledge.**

Yelland, N. (2005) *Critical Issues in Early Childhood Education.* Maidenhead: Open University Press.

15

LIZ CHAMBERLAIN AND JACQUELINE HARRETT
The power of story

Summary

This chapter explores the role of story in developing and understanding young children's communication development. It explains the significance of listening to stories and rhymes before considering the importance of engaging with the 'tune on the page' (Barrs and Cork 1992). The role of traditional tales will be introduced as a means of demonstrating the centrality of story to the lives of all children. The chapter will consider the practical application of story in the classroom and how, by putting story at the heart of the curriculum, teachers can support children's ways with words, understanding of language and provide opportunities for performance. The final message stresses that by encouraging children to develop their oral skills, teachers are able to view children's literacy development in a more holistic way.

Cameo 1

Rufsana, an elective mute, watches carefully and listens intently, during a storytelling. Her head to the one side, she follows the gestures and mimics them, smiling slightly. At the end of the story she is with a group of others in a quiet room off the classroom. She listens to the other children re-telling their versions of the story. 'Do you want to try?' Rufsana nods and with much gesture and great hesitancy, she whispers the main points of the story and grins widely.

Introduction

In teaching there are moments that are etched on your memory. This was one of those moments. Rufsana had joined the class from another school three weeks previously. She had not made any oral contact with anyone but waited and watched. Although it was obvious from her physical response that the story was having an impact the fact that it opened the doors for this child to communicate demonstrates the power of story.

Making sense of the world

Oral storytelling is an ancient tradition and a vital part of many cultures. What all stories attempt to do is to make sense of the world and to give meaning to aspects of our lives (Bruner 1986). Wells (1989) suggests that we are all engaged in telling stories; narrating our way through life and making links through what we observe, read and engage in. Paley (1991) highlights how nursery children make sense of their own lives through the constant commentary and narration of the mundane, or the exciting aspects of their young lives. Through the construction of stories or 'storying', it enables even very young children to make meaning of the world they inhabit (Wells 1989: 194).

Children are familiar with the genre of narrative long before they begin reading about stories in books. They 'learn to make sense of the world through constructing their own stories' (Grainger 1997: 9). By building on this early learning and thinking, teachers can create storytelling classrooms, allowing children to experience the interchange between speaking and listening and cross the bridge into reading and writing. As storytellers, children soon learn to shape their own tales where they 'catch bits of memory that might turn into story' (Gillard 1996: 33).

One familiar routine in the early years classroom is the sharing of stories and rhymes that, over time, children learn by heart. It is through the constant re-telling and re-visiting of stories that children become more aware of knowing how language works and in doing so become more confident and skilled when the time comes to use it in their own telling. By engaging with familiar stories children can learn to imitate and explore language and become familiar with the subtleties of word play and transfer this ability when creating and enjoying their own stories. Corbett (2006) promotes the telling of stories as a way into writing and suggests that as children learn stories by heart, they engage with the repetitive patterns of language found in many favourite stories. In doing so, they build up a bank of known stories, which introduces them to new vocabulary and extends their storytelling experience. He suggests that as children move through each class they can be introduced to new stories that further extend their repertoire from which they can draw on in their own writing. As children begin to imitate the stories they hear, they can begin to innovate on the characters, settings or themes until they develop a confidence in inventing their own stories.

However, while 'memorization is central' (Egan and Nadaner 1988: 100) the aim of storytelling is not to create an oral culture, which becomes merely a system of remembering and repeating the all and forgetting the detail but is valued as a tool to support meaning making. The unique aspect of the telling of a story is that it provides children with the opportunity to explore their reactions and experience of their world. As children learn to tell and share their stories, they become familiar with the subtleties of word play and become experienced as story-makers. As Grainger suggests, narrative is 'central to early learning and thinking and teachers can build on this' (1997: 33). By learning stories, children can inter-change between speaking and listening, reading and writing and in doing so develop a competence in their spoken language.

There are benefits to all areas of the English curriculum, as by becoming more playful with their own word play children begin to engage with the 'tune on the page' which in turn supports their reading development (Barrs and Cork 1992). Margaret Meek talks about 'the spellbinding of the oral tale is a necessary prelude to "being lost in a book"' (1991: 185). Through listening to and telling stories, children quickly grasp the concept of drama and suspense as well as insights into characters and setting. Therefore if children are secure in their knowledge of story, it can help them as they enter the rich world of the written text. Research also suggests that good comprehenders are able to use their story knowledge to tell structurally coherent stories (Cain 2003: 348). Therefore, practising storytelling and experiencing story learning can support children in developing comprehension and in so doing, improve their reading skills.

While storytelling is enjoying a resurgence in primary classrooms, it is important to remember that it sits not only within a specific strand of English but also provides essential cross-curricular experiences (Wells 1989; Grainger 1997). For children to hear stories that link to history, as in the story of the Fire of London or in geography through the oral re-telling of *Eco-Wolf* (Laurence Anholt and Arthur Robins), the benefits to all areas of children's learning can be realized.

Developing story knowledge

What is unique about storytelling is its ability to cross cultural divides. For example, across the regions of the UK familiar tales are told that draw on the Welsh, Irish, Scottish and English traditions, illustrating the importance of identity and belonging. By honouring the re-reading and retelling of tales, the classroom therefore becomes an environment that invites stories and the sharing of personal histories (Gillard 1996: 35). This is especially important for children who bring with them different cultural experiences drawing on different languages, ethnicity or from sometimes overlooked backgrounds, such as children from the traveller community.

Story is central to different cultures and becomes the unique voice in sharing past experiences and passing onto new generations. This can be illustrated through the Somali language, which until the 1970s had no formal written form so the gift of the spoken word, traditionally delivered in a poetic style, was crucial. Within the Aboriginal culture, the song-lines across Australia were formed long before maps or the written language explained the history of the land and the traditions of generations. It was the spoken word and the narrative structure that enabled communities to tell stories that shared messages and warning. In a sense, the familiar tales that teachers share with children in their classes have their histories rooted in an ancient oral tradition.

Jack Zipes (1995: 5) is clear about the importance of story being central to the human experience crossing cultural boundaries and backgrounds: 'It is crucial for giving children a sense of story and an ability to play with story as they may later play with their lives.' In *Creative Storytelling,* he shares the origins of familiar tales told in the classroom and explores children's responses and meaning making through their own re-telling. He suggests that stories such as The Gingerbread Man and Red Riding Hood can give children a sense of the familiar and that they can benefit from being able to interpret and share their ideas behind the meaning of the different stories.

Cinderella is a favourite KS1 text among practitioners and with its various film forms is usually a well-known story long before children come to school. Teachers can extend this experience by finding stories from other cultures that share a similar theme. For example, *Mufaro's Beautiful Daughters* (John Steptoe) which is set in Africa, tells the familiar story of a king in search of a wife who has to resort to wily guiles to find out the true nature of the two daughters, one mean and one dignified. While in Vietnam, the story of *Tam and Cam* takes the familiar telling beyond the traditional fairytale ending and sees the comeuppance of the wicked stepmother in quite a different way. More recent versions of the story include *Prince Cinders* (Babette Cole) and *Cinder Boy* (Laurence Anholt and Arthur Robins) and are sure to engage a new generation of children by playing with the known characters and twisting the familiar ending. By giving children the experience of exploring the similarities and differences between stories, they are able to engage with some very complex themes in quite a different way. In developing story knowledge, children need to be given experiences of listening and engaging with stories as well as sharing and re-telling their own.

The teller and the listener

Storytelling is often used as a blanket term to cover both oral stories and their written counterparts. Writers are described as good storytellers when what is meant is that they are able to write a story convincingly.

Storytelling is often linked with drama as it requires many of the same performance techniques and, while engaging in storytelling and drama, 'learners can develop and transform their perspectives' (Grainger 2003: 106). Storytelling requires much from the performer – the teller. Enabling children to become storytellers encourages them to improvise and become more creative and gives them ownership of a story. In retelling a story, tellers have poetic licence to change and adapt. This permits freedom from the constraints of the printed word and enables storytellers to alter or exaggerate different parts of stories according to their audiences.

Grugeon and Garder (2000: 2) claim that 'telling a story is a unique and personal performance'. Storytelling by its very nature is ephemeral. Active listening and audience response are encouraged and allow children to extend and explore narrative in unique and personal ways. One could argue that story-reading achieves the same objectives but the dynamics used vary.

Children who listen to heard and read versions of stories also learn that it is the print version that does not change. The fact that a story can change is an important fact to remember. As Corden (2000) pointed out, a story may be told many times with embellishments and elaborations, or alternatively, simplified to meet the needs of an audience. With oral storytelling, children learn about language but also realize that they are experiencing something different and special – something that can never really be recaptured. Corden (2000: 147) believed that storytelling can help to make explicit differences between spoken and written language as, by telling and retelling to each other, children begin to understand how language works.

However, one cannot deny the value of story-reading. Phinn (2004) stresses that having access to exciting, imaginative and well-structured stories is essential for children who are learning to read. Good picture books that encourage interaction with text are important for them to develop a love of literature. Sharing and talking about picture books with children is invaluable to an understanding of literacy. Work by Poulson (2003) also indicates that teachers who have knowledge and love of children's literature have beneficial effects on their literacy development. Teachers who read to children and display enthusiasm encourage not only speaking and listening but also pre-reading and reading skills. Interaction with texts and the ability to access them is bound to have some impact on their understanding and responses to narrative.

One of the many benefits of books is the durability. They may be treasured and visited time and time again and then pages explored in more detail each time, not only words but pictures encouraging children to read. Oral stories cannot, by their nature, perform the same act. Oral stories, while sometimes magical in the interaction they demand, are never quite as polished or crafted in the same way as final versions that writers have worked on many times. Reading with fluency and expression is part of a performance element of reading aloud, enabling listeners to become lost in the story.

Although the oral and the written are intertwined in many ways, it is important to make a distinction between these two discrete forms of storytelling and story-reading. Oral storytelling uses voice as the main implement of delivery combined with other non-verbal communication such as eye contact and gesture. With story-reading the main implement is a written text, sometimes a picture book with attractive illustrations. The common factor in both cases is the story. The fiction of story could be a reflection of the realities of life, or pure fantasy as an escape from those realities.

Grugeon and Garder's comment on the difference between written and oral stories is worth reflecting upon: 'Perhaps that is the difference between reading and telling; reading is a process of sharing and interpreting a text that someone else has produced but telling a story is a unique and personal performance' (2000: 2).

In the context of storytelling and story-reading the line between the two modes can sometimes appear nebulous. Both entail performances using voice and expression necessary to engage children. Children may then retell stories, copying the tones and rhythms of their teacher. Speaking and listening skills are aided by this performance element. Children learn to listen actively, make connections in their imaginations, re-tell and take ownership of stories by re-inventing them. Adding the 'what if?' factor to storytelling and story-reading enables children to take ownership and add parts to the story or leave out the areas they regard as superfluous. They become masters of the narrative and gain confidence in their ability to structure stories through imitating the patterns they have heard. Even young children, given enough exposure to story, soon realize that stories usually begin in certain ways – 'Once upon a time . . .', 'One day . . .' and will often end with a final sentence such as '. . . and they all lived happily ever after' or even simply, 'The end'.

In the classroom

When children talk about stories and act them out, they are building knowledge of story structure and presenting versions and interpretations. This is vital as it helps them to orally re-draft before attempting mark-making or writing. Fisher et al. use the term 'oral rehearsal' to help children understand the distinctions between spoken and written language 'reducing the mental demand of writing' (2010: 69). From examination of children's re-tellings we are able to ascertain what they know about language in general and narrative in particular. Children who are confident in storytelling can use their own ideas to produce something unique.

The following is a story told by 6-year-old George who was a lively storyteller and had grasped the idea that invention was encouraged. The context was a large inner city multicultural primary school and George was in a mixed class of Year 1 and Year 2 children, 6- and 7-year-olds. Following a telling of *The North Wind and the Sun* George produced his version.

> One day there was a big, it was a peculiar day in the sky, because the sun and the wind were having an argument about which was better then there was big, then they both said okay, whoever can blow that man's jacket off he was climbing up the hill, he was stronger so the wind blew and blew until it caused a bit giant tornado and then the sun shone so hot, that the man got so hot that he took his jacket off at the top of the hill and there was snow on top of the hill that was melting right down it was so hot and the wind said oh damn you win once again you haven't seen the last of me and he was such in a bad temper that he blew himself right away and he was never seen again only in them windy countries.

This transcription, without the imposition of punctuation, does not do justice to the child's voice or give an impression of his excitement and ability to hold an audience by maintaining eye contact and using gesture, tone, pitch and timing. However, from this we can see that George is a sophisticated user of language. He introduces the word 'peculiar' to describe the sky and other elements not in the original such as 'tornado' and the snow on the top of the hill. He also uses character voice and vocabulary not in the original: 'Oh damn, you win once again you haven't seen the last of me'. (I should never use 'damn' in a class of children!) George was aware of audience and storytelling conventions with his opening of 'One day . . .' and the closing remarks '. . . and he was never seen again'. Repetition of 'so hot' also conveys the atmosphere he is trying to create and a contrast to the snow which was melting. It is a masterly tale displaying one child's confidence in using oral language to draft a story.

Even children with less developed vocabulary than George understood and used the conventions of beginning, middle and end in their re-tellings. Sana was barely 6 when the following story was recorded. English was her second language but her re-telling displays her ability to listen actively and use the language of the oral story she had heard. Sentences such as: 'the leaves on the trees were dancing like yo-yos' stem directly from the oral tale told to the class. The fact that she remembered this particular section indicates that it had resonated with her experience and she was able to visualize it:

> Once the wind and the sun were having an argument to see who could take the horseman's cloak off first the wind blew that the leaves on the trees were dancing like yo-yos next the waves went over the boats and the boats sank then the sun smiled and the flowers opened the sun the sun made the man hot so he took his cloak off and went to sleep.

The use of words like 'first', 'next' and 'then' illustrate the knowledge Sana has about sequencing of narrative and how stories depend on one action following on from, or being a consequence of, another. She has also given a conventional beginning and obvious end to her story.

Children respond to stories in different ways and sometimes drawings tell us what they have understood. *The Owl and the Woodpecker* is a traditional tale retold in picture book format by Brian Wildsmith. Following an oral version of this story, children were given the opportunity to draw or write their visualizations of the story. The story is about an owl who disagrees with his neighbour, a woodpecker. Owl becomes so disruptive that all the animals of the forest gather to decide what to do. In the oral version a woodcutter starts to cut down the tree where Owl is sleeping but leaves as a storm approaches. Woodpecker warns Owl who escapes before the tree crashes to the ground. Ben's drawing (Figure 15.1) shows a simple outline with the owl in his tree trying to sleep while the woodpecker is busy tapping away on the tree next to it.

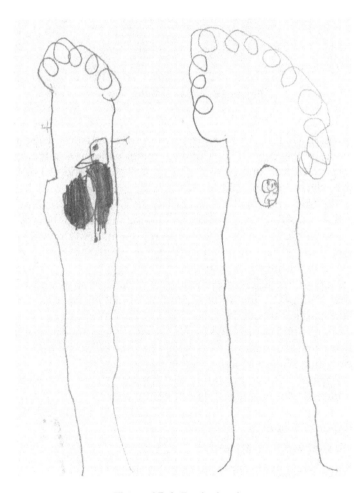

Figure 15.1 Ben's drawing

Figure 15.2 Joseph's drawing

Joseph's version (Figure 15.2) requires more interpretation as he has tried to capture sequences in this story. This is quite complex as it has several passages from the story incorporated into one picture. On the left we see the owl and the woodpecker with the owl complaining about the noise the woodpecker is making. The next section shows the tree where owl sleeps during the day, the house representing his home. The next section shows the woodcutter sawing the tree. In the final section, on the right, the woodcutter is leaving. The house represents Owl's new home. The tortoise is a mystery as it was not mentioned in this particular story but appears in another story told to this group previously.

Joseph is aware of the different elements that make up a story and has an understanding of the drama. The inclusion of houses brings his own experience to his pictorial interpretation of the narrative.

When listening to oral stories, children realize that there is a gap that they need to fill through their own imaginations. As children become older and have more experience of narrative, they should be able to do this more readily.

A group of Year 5 children by adding the 'What if?' element were able to change and adjust traditional tales by suggesting different scenarios.

- What if Rapunzel had greasy hair?
- What if the Wolf was vegetarian?
- What if Snow White made apple pie from the poison apple?
- What if Cinderella didn't fancy the Prince?

One of the group, Christopher, when questioned about an element in his story responded, 'I made it up!'

Giving children the opportunity to be able to take narratives, change them and gain ownership of them is important in developing their knowledge of how language works and the power of story.

Conclusion

This chapter has suggested that the power of story needs to be realized within the primary classroom and considered a central theme of a child's literacy experience. In order for this to happen there are some key points for teachers to remember including:

- introducing different versions of the same story;
- learning stories by heart to develop a bank of stories;
- developing a knowledge of story structure to support reading comprehension;
- experiencing a sense of performance and an awareness of an audience.

By valuing the stories children tell, teachers can further develop activities that support speaking and listening, reading and writing in a meaningful way and in so doing, ensure within their classrooms 'the ordinary becomes the extraordinary' (Zipes 1995: 6). That's the power of story.

Questions to Promote Thinking

1 How can talk help children understand narrative?
2 Why is it important to consider the difference between storytelling and story-reading?
3 How does the oral experience offer the teacher a more holistic way of viewing a child's literacy potential?

References and suggested further reading

Barrs, M. and Cork, V. (1992) *The Reader in the Writer*. London: CLPE.

Bruner, J. (1986) *Actual Minds, Possible Worlds*. London: Harvard University Press.

Cain, K. (2003) Text comprehension and its relation to coherence and cohesion in children's fictional narratives, *British Journal of Developmental Psychology*, **21**: 335–51.

Corbett, P. (2006) *The Bumper Book of Storytelling into Writing at KS1*. Strathfield, Australia: Clown Publishing.

Corden, R. (2000) *Literacy and Learning Through Talk*. Buckingham: Open University Press.

Egan, K. and Nadaner, D. (1988) *Imagination and Education*. Milton Keynes: Open University Press.

Fisher, R., Larkin, S., Jones, S.J. and Myhill, D. (2010) *Using Talk to Support Writing*. London: Sage.

Gillard, M. (1996) *Storyteller Storyteacher.* Maine: Stenhouse Publications.

Goodwin, P. (2001) *The Articulate Classroom: Talking and Learning in the Primary School.* London: David Fulton.

Grainger, T. (1997) *Traditional Storytelling.* Warwickshire: Scholastic.

Grainger, T. (2003) Exploring the unknown: ambiguity, interaction and meaning making in classroom drama, in E. Bearne, H. Dombey and T. Grainger (eds) *Classroom Interactions in Literacy.* Oxford: Oxford University Press.

Grugeon, E. and Gardner, P. (2000) *The Art of Storytelling for Teachers and Pupils: Using Stories to Develop Literacy in Primary Classrooms.* London: David Fulton.

Harrett, J. (2004) *Tell Me Another* ... Hertfordshire: UKLA.

Meek, M. (1991) *On Being Literate.* London: Bodley Head.

Paley, V.G. (1991) *The Boy who Would Be a Helicopter.* Cambridge, MA: Harvard University Press.

Phinn, G. (2004) *Your Readers and Their Books: Suggestions and Strategies for Using Texts in the Literacy Hour.* London: David Fulton.

Poulson, L. (2003) The subject of literacy: what kind of knowledge is needed to teach literacy successfully?, in E. Bearne, H. Dombey and T. Grainger (eds) *Classroom Interactions in Literacy.* Oxford: Oxford University Press.

Tyrrell, J. (2001) *The Power of Fantasy in Early Learning.* London: RoutledgeFalmer.

Wells, G. (1989) *The Meaning Makers.* Portsmouth, NH: Heinemann.

Zipes, J. (1995) *Creative Storytelling.* London: Routledge.

PART 4
Influences on children's learning

16

JANE PAYLER AND JAN GEORGESON
Social class and culture: building bridges

Summary

This chapter revisits the concept of inclusion and the underlying principle of 'valuing diversity' when applied to social class. For children from working-class families with low socio-economic status, their backgrounds are sometimes portrayed as deficient, requiring compensation, rather than something to value. While this may be understandable, given the long-standing and seemingly intractable social class differentials in educational attainment and health outcomes, we argue that this deficit model is neither appropriate nor helpful. What therefore does a critically reflective teacher or early years professional need to know in order to help *all* children to learn and develop fully? We consider theoretical explanations and practical strategies to help approach the home backgrounds of children less as deficient and more as rich sources of context for learning and development.

Cameo 1

David is just 4 years old and is one of the youngest in his Reception class. According to his mother, David's parents have had a stormy relationship in the past. David recently moved out of his grandparents' home where he lived with his mother from birth to live with both parents in a house near to the school. David's teacher, Clare, finds him to be a handful in the classroom: he is not making good progress and his behaviour can be challenging. Many children bring in drawings, colourings and toys from home to show to their classmates. These are shared at whole group time on the mat with Clare's encouragement. Here, Clare also asks the children about their weekend and evening activities with their families. Hannah went to the zoo; Aisha went to visit her grandmother; Ben had a friend to tea and they played in the paddling pool in the garden. Their offerings are praised and talked about with interest. David brings in a drawing that he says he has done at home and shows Clare; it is of matchstick men fighting and looks like an adult's drawing of an imaginary battle scene. Clare asks him, incredulously, if he drew it himself, probing: '*You* did it? Or was it your Daddy?' He says he did it himself and describes excitedly how the men are beating each other. 'Very nice', says Clare, turning away and raising her eyebrows to the LSA. He is not invited to show it at circle time.

Cameo 2

Suzy is a newly qualified teacher of a Year 5 class where there are several children who are struggling with reading. Their reading books come back from home unread, but Suzy is determined that they should not be disadvantaged by their parents' lack of engagement with helping their children to read. She plans carefully to make sure she has time to spend with them on their reading books, often missing her lunch break to fit them all in. But she has noticed how reluctant they are to join her, mumbling through the text and answering with single words her attempts to involve them in the story. They are just as quiet in class discussions, yawning all the way through and staring out of the window. After school she attends a session led by her SENCo examining some new reading materials which the school has been asked to trial. To her dismay, they are all about really boring topics, garishly presented. Suzy finds them totally unappealing, makes an excuse and leaves early.

That evening, in the supermarket, she spots two of her reluctant readers, Darren and Callum, over by the newspaper kiosk. Muttering to herself about what on earth are their parents doing letting them out so late, she notices they are pointing at the headlines on the back pages and arguing heatedly; she can't follow the argument but from the odd word it's clear it's something to do with football. She carries on with her shopping, sighing to herself; typical . . . if only they could show the same enthusiasm in school . . .

Then she remembers the new reading materials – weren't they all about football? It just might be worth trying them out with Darren and Callum next week . . . The results are startling; as soon as they see the books, they pick one out and they're off – really working hard at the phonics and discussing the pictures. They even agree to read a second book at the same sitting.

Introduction

In cameo 1, witnessed by one of the authors during research in the Reception class, David is bringing his home activities (presumably completed with an adult) into the classroom, just as are other children in the class. However, his world and the values implied in his chosen contribution do not match well with the ethos of the setting. The setting is a Church of England primary school with a predominantly owner-occupied housing estate as its catchment, although close to a large local authority housing estate. Clare is concerned to help David to improve his behaviour in class and focusing on 'fighting' as exciting and fun appears on the face of it to offer little progress towards this. Equally, sharing talk of a battle scene with other 4–5-year-olds is unlikely to fit well with the expectations of the parents of other children in the Reception class, or of the staff. Clare's decision is understandable, but during a year of research, the author did not witness David bring in any other drawings or offerings from home. But using children's everyday knowledge, their *horizontal discourses,* can provide an effective way of helping them to make sense of new learning in the early years setting or in school, easing their understanding of *vertical discourse.* We pick up this point later in the chapter as we explain the terms and share ideas on how this can create bridges between home culture and educational culture, the type of bridges eventually used by Suzy, the teacher in cameo 2, which was based on teachers' actual responses to new reading materials. If we are to make such bridges available for all children, we need to be open to the potential of all aspects of their home culture, even if these don't always fit in with our own value systems.

Meeting the standards

Primary teachers and early years professionals (EYPs) are required by their professional standards to understand how children's backgrounds and home cultures help to shape their development and learning. Consider the following (Table 16.1):

Table 16.1 QTS/EYPS Standards (1)

QTS	Q18 Understand how children and young people develop and that the progress and well-being of learners are affected by a range of developmental, social, religious, ethnic, cultural and linguistic influences
EYPS	S2 Knowledge and understanding of the individual and diverse ways in which children develop and learn from birth to the end of the Foundation Stage and thereafter

In addition, teachers and EYPs should ensure that their own professional practice provides optimal conditions for every child's development, as stated in the standards shown in Table 16.2.

Table 16.2 QTS/EYPS Standards (2)

QTS	Q1 Have high expectations of children and young people including a commitment to ensuring that they can achieve their full educational potential and to establishing fair, respectful, trusting, supportive and constructive relationships with them
	Q19 Know how to make effective personalized provision for those they teach, including those for whom English is an additional language or who have special educational needs or disabilities, and how to take practical account of diversity and promote equality and inclusion in their teaching
EYPS	S7 Have high expectations of all children and commitment to ensuring that they can achieve their full potential
	S12 Select, prepare and use a range of resources suitable for children's ages, interests and abilities, taking account of diversity and promoting equality and inclusion
	S18 Promote children's rights, equality, inclusion and anti-discriminatory practice in all aspects of their practice

Including all children

Allan (2008) argues forcefully that inclusion for all children is not meant to be a narrow technical exercise of identifying need and then applying the appropriate remedy. She criticizes the lack of discussion of values in the more 'cookbook' approach to inclusion and points out that 'inclusion *is and should be* a struggle' (2008: 19, author's italics). This can sit uncomfortably on the shoulders of new professionals trying to demonstrate competence in front of experienced colleagues. The educational textbooks on inclusion which they might have encountered on their course are full of 'bland platitudes about students who are "different"' and 'portray idealised versions of classroom life and of children benefiting from interventions' (Allan 2008: 19). The reality can be very different and beginning teachers, lacking in confidence, can find themselves blaming their own inexperience when the interventions suggested in the textbook do not work.

Inclusion can lead us into difficult territory: making decisions about who to help and how to help them takes us back to why we became teachers in the first place. We need to be fully aware of our own value systems, while at the same time recognizing and respecting the value systems of the families we are working with – and those of our colleagues. But that in itself is not enough: we need also to keep to the fore the realization that certain ways of doing, being and saying are much more compatible with our educational system, particularly as children move through into national testing. Teachers have to perform a delicate balancing act, combining an understanding of the social and cultural capital that each child brings from their home background with an awareness of the knowledge, dispositions and attitudes that are likely to make it easier for these children to succeed in our society. To do this without seeming hypocritical – one minute valorizing a child's cultural heritage and the next encouraging them to be interested in something else – poses an intellectual challenge of some subtlety. There are two qualities that can support us in this demanding task; respect for others' way of life, and a deep and clear personal understanding about the purpose of education.

Exclusion on the basis of social class is not prohibited by legislation (unlike discrimination on the basis of disability, race or gender); indeed the privileged classes are inclined to conclude that we are now living in a 'classless society'. Reay argues, however, that class 'infuses the minutiae of everyday interactions' and to deny this is dangerous, leaving social class as a 'zombie stalking' our schools (Reay 2006: 288). Having high expectations of all children and helping them to reach their full potential requires deeper understanding and more concerted effort to engage equally with each child's culture than might initially be assumed. This can be made more difficult if it is implied that some cultures are in need of remediation because they are a source of disadvantage for the child. For children from working-class families with low socio-economic status, their backgrounds have been more recently identified as something less to value and rather more to be seen as deficient, requiring compensation. For example, in a speech made before he became prime minister, David Cameron clearly forecasts his government's intention to target support to parents in poorer households with a view to making them more like middle-class parents:

Of course there's a link between material poverty and poor life chances, but the full picture is that that link also runs through the style of parenting that children in poor households receive . . . Because the research shows that while the style of responsible parenting I've spoken about today is more likely to occur in wealthier households, children in poor households who are raised with that style of parenting do just as well.

(Cameron 2010)

So what are the aspects of children's outcomes related to social class that engender this deficit model?

Children's life chances

There can be no doubt that for a very long time social class has been linked not only to lower income, but also to far poorer health, shorter life expectancy and lower educational achievement. These are not new problems and they are not insubstantial. Let's take a closer look at what this means in real terms.

Connolly (2006), reporting on data from 1997, 1999 and 2001, showed clearly that social class and ethnicity continued to have a substantial influence on educational attainment. Of children from higher professional backgrounds, 79 per cent gained five or more A*–C grade GCSEs compared to just 31 per cent of children from routine occupational backgrounds (2001 Youth Cohort Study of England and Wales, cited in Connolly 2006: 9). By comparison, 69 per cent of Chinese children gained these qualifications, while 36 per cent of Black children did so. The popular simplistic notion from the last decade of boys failing and girls succeeding is challenged by figures showing that 72 per cent of boys from higher professional backgrounds attained 5 high grade GCSEs compared to 36 per cent of girls from routine occupational backgrounds (figures from 2001, cited in Connolly 2006: 10). More recent figures from 2009 show the pattern to remain the same. Using eligibility to free school meals as a proxy for socio-economic disadvantage, the data showed that 54 per cent of children not eligible for free school meals achieved five or more A*–C grade GCSEs compared to 27 per cent of those who were eligible for free school meals (DCSF 2009: 7).

Poorer life chances are not confined to educational attainment. Detailed evidence from The Black Report (1980), The Whitehead Report (1987) and The Acheson Report (1998) have shown that greater levels of ill-health and shorter life expectancy are also strongly associated with social class. The most recent findings from The Marmot Review (2010) confirm that the problem remains and that the cost of not reducing these inequalities is excessively high:

Consider one measure of social position: education. People with university degrees have better health and longer lives than those without. For people aged 30 and above, if everyone without a degree had their death rate reduced to that of people with degrees, there would be 202,000 fewer premature deaths each year.

(Marmot 2010: 3)

While the Review team acknowledge that the gradient in health is unlikely to be removed, they assert that its gradient should be reduced through concerted effort. Two of the six policy objectives for action to address the problem are significant to teachers and early years professionals, the first being 'Give every child the best start in life': 'To have an impact on health inequalities we need to address the social gradient in children's access to positive early experiences. Later interventions, although important, are considerably less effective where good early foundations are lacking' (Marmot 2010: 16).

The second is to '. . . enable all children, young people and adults to maximise their capabilities and have control over their lives' and:

> to achieve equity from the start, investment in the early years is crucial. However, maintaining the reduction of inequalities across the gradient also requires a sustained commitment to children and young people through the years of education. Central to this is the acquisition of cognitive and non-cognitive skills, which are strongly associated with educational achievement and with a whole range of other outcomes including better employment, income and physical and mental health.
>
> (Marmot 2010: 18)

Addressing inequality of children's life chances then, is something that should concern teachers and EYPs. It is certainly something that concerns politicians, and successive governments have launched strategies to 'widen participation' and 'narrow the gap', but with only modest success (Field 2010; Sullivan et al. 2010). Connell (1994) noted the tendency for 'education to be represented in political rhetoric as a panacea for poverty' but cautions against the use of compensatory programmes targeted exclusively at 'the poor'. He argued that 'compensatory programs may even reinforce the patterns that produce inequality', especially in the contexts of 'policies to increase competitive pressures which reinforce the advantages of the privileged and confirm the exclusion of the poor'. He recommended instead that more attention should be paid to the practical experience of teachers as they work in areas of disadvantage, so that we build culturally sensitive knowledge about what to teach and how.

Tobin (2005) also highlights the importance of developing an informed understanding about which pedagogical approaches and curriculum content are relevant, through teachers working in partnership with parents, rather than by assuming that a particular approach will better compensate for children's disadvantage. For example, when consulted, parents argued that, contrary to the school's expectations, it was more beneficial for their children to be taught in English, not Spanish (their home language) as this would speed their learning of English and place them in better positions in school and the future job market. Parents were also quite happy to take responsibility for ensuring that their children knew about their cultural background, believing that it was the school's role to teach them about mainstream culture (Tobin 2005: 430–3). There are clearly no simple solutions and no quick fixes, but by improving our understanding of the issues involved, we can all play a part in ensuring that we make the most of every child's background as a fund for learning.

Understanding the processes at work

It might help to look a little more closely at some of the everyday processes through which children from different family backgrounds end up with different ways of looking at the world. Because our brains need experience to develop, early experience has a major role to play in shaping our cognitive resources. Hasan (2005) points in particular to the importance of early language experience in setting children on different learning trajectories (see also Chapter 2 by Goswami):

> Our most precious biological assets – the plasticity of our brain and its potential for forming billions of connections – make us uniquely dependent on the social for turning that powerful brain into a usable mind . . . Through centuries of evolutionary trial and error, the human brain is predisposed to make sense of symbols and, among the various symbolic systems, language . . . proves crucial in the enterprise of linking the biological and the social . . . So, if we wish to answer our question—why and how does social location intervene in constraining what is learnt by whom? —we will need a theory that is sensitive to the complex interactions of language, culture and consciousness, for although learning is achieved by individual minds, the minds themselves are fashioned socially.
>
> (Hasan 2005: 215)

Hasan's work offers a detailed way of linking educational and home settings by considering how, as they take part in ordinary day-to-day communication, children pick up their understanding of how society works and their own pathway through it. From her extensive field study on mother–child talk in the home, she concludes that it is here, in the early years, that children learn about their own culture's values and power structures. The qualities conveyed in communication are so 'everyday' that they become invisible, but a close analysis of communication can reveal ways in which values are transmitted, to which children become accustomed.

For example, Hasan investigated how the role of women in different subcultures can be learnt by children as they participate in everyday conversations with their parents. Read the two extracts that follow and think about the understanding which the young child is developing about the role and status of women in society:

Child: Pop home?

Mother: No they're all out. They're all at work.

Child: Bob and Mark are working.

Mother: Yes Bob's at work. Mark's at work. Everybody's at work.

Child: I not at work.

Mother: No. You're only little.

Child: Youse at work?

Mother: I don't work. I look after you. [. . .] Who'd look after you if Mummy went to work?

Child: And you forgot my painting!

Mother: Did you do a painting? You didn't tell me . . .

Child: Well you should've looked on those cupboards.

Mother: Oh, I know, but I'm such a forgetful mother you should know by now you have to tell me you have to remind me about these things because my brain doesn't work too well sometimes.

(Hasan 2005: 262)

Taken by themselves, it might be argued that these are just one-off exchanges that don't have particular import. But all day, every day, the drip, drip, drip of messages that what women do in looking after children is not work, that a women who forgets has a defective brain rather than too many things to remember, can leave children with a very different picture of the role of women than (we might imagine) that of classmates whose mothers works 8 a.m.–6 p.m. in a prestigious job in the city and whom they see for 'quality time' for an hour before bedtime.

Hasan encourages us to look at Bernstein's theory of language codes to help us understand the role of language in shaping the way we understand the world, and of revealing this to others. The term code 'refers to a set of organizing principles behind the language employed by members of a social group' (Littlejohn and Foss 2008: 318). Bernstein's work offers a way of considering children's access to contexts for learning and teaching in relation to their home background, and how they are positioned within these contexts. He encourages us to think about who decides which codes are used in school and how strongly other codes should be resisted. When the codes of 'school' and 'home' are strongly separated, some children will find it hard to feel like 'fish in water' at school and this 'often means that the images, voices and practices the school reflects make it difficult for children of marginalized classes to recognize themselves in the school' (Bernstein 1996: 29: see also Brooker (2002) on children from Bangladeshi communities settling into their Reception class in an inner city school with a broad cultural mix).

Here, children can have two barriers to overcome: first, recognizing what is required of them in the ways of schooling and then being able to interact, produce or perform as they are expected (Bernstein 1996: 31–2).

Overcoming barriers

Bernstein's work helps us to understand differences between what children know and can do in relation to their home contexts (what they bring with them) and what is expected in 'schooled' forms of learning (Bernstein 1999). He refers to 'horizontal discourse' to describe the set of characteristics of knowledge formed outside school (or outside educational) contexts; for children, this is mainly home. Horizontal discourse is a set of loosely connected practices, ways of knowing and acting that are 'situated' in particular contexts: 'The form of knowledge usually typified as everyday, oral or common-sense knowledge has a group of features: local, segmental, context dependent, tacit, multi-layered, often contradictory across contexts but not within contexts' (Bernstein 1996: 170). Examples might include sharing a story book, 'writing' a ticket for the pretend bus, recognizing and using environmental print. Horizontal discourse is meaningful to the child and contextualized by the social situation. Bernstein contrasts this with 'vertical discourse', which is the label he uses to describe the set of knowledge and practices associated with abstract, educated ways of knowing and acting: 'A vertical discourse takes the form of a coherent, explicit, systematically principled structure, hierarchically organized, or it takes the form of a series of specialized languages' (Bernstein 1996: 170–1). Examples might be phoneme–grapheme correspondence, rules of apostrophe use, recognizing how commas, connectives and full stops are used. The constructs of vertical and horizontal discourse can be helpful to teachers and early years professionals. Researchers have suggested (see, for example, Bourne 2000; Moss 2001) that using children's horizontal discourse might be a way to help them to recognize and begin to make use of vertical discourse, with its high currency in education. In the past, there has rightly been an emphasis on 'starting from the child' and incorporating children's interests, at least in the early years. However, it requires a concerted effort on the part of teachers and EYPs to do the following:

- make use of *every* child's experiences and interests;
- go beyond acknowledging these to using them as bridges to ensure that *all* children can see the links to learning and how the learning is relevant to the child.

Marsh and Millard report on 'encountering the sheer delight of school children when they were allowed to relate their own interests to their work in school' (Marsh and Millard 2001: 8) in their work on using popular culture in literacy teaching in primary schools.

Learning without limits

Teachers and EYPs clearly have a duty to help children to reach their full potential and to have high expectations of all children. Yet it can often be difficult to step outside our own preconceptions and interpretations to see the potential within, sometimes masked by language or cultural differences. Critical professional reflection and thoughtful, creative planning can help. The following steps offer a structure:

- *Reflect*: think about knowledge, skills and interests shown by the child in their everyday ideas and daily life experiences. How can you encourage them to share these?
- *Critique*: think about any assumptions or value judgements you are making about the children's experiences and potential based on what children say, the way they say it or what they don't say; challenge them. Are you making the most of *all* children's home and wider experiences?
- *Plan*: with high expectations: How can the children's everyday interests and ideas be used to create routes into vertical discourse; what opportunities are there to *embed* learning in the things children know, enjoy and can do? How can this be taken forwards to *extend and enrich* learning for all?

Practical strategies

Let's return to cameo 2 to see what Suzy tried with her reluctant literacy learners.

Cameo 3

Suzy was as delighted as the boys were with their new-found interest and success in reading: she did some research on the internet and came up with more suggestions for activities based on football. She worked with Darren and Callum to write down one of their 'arguments' about who would make the best manager. This they turned into a short play, which they performed for an end-of-term event. The boys had persuaded their parents to come along and the parents spoke to her afterwards about their sons' renewed enthusiasm for school; 'It's about real things, now, they say, important stuff.' Callum's father commented on how his son was now getting hold of the newspaper at home before he could, and was eager to discuss the latest transfer rumours with him when he got in from work. Suzy realized how wrong she had been to dismiss football as trivial: for some families it provided a shared focus, which was clearly linked to family-based literacy activities.

For younger children, using their ideas and experiences for role play, such as a Chinese takeaway or visit to MacDonald's, can provide meaningful contexts in which to embed language, literacy, numeracy and problem-solving (how to make a menu or write down an order, how to wrap a meal so that it stays hot until you get home).

Conclusion

By 'listening' to all children's experiences and interests and engaging with them respectfully, new teachers and early years professionals can begin to ensure that the home backgrounds of children are seen less as deficits and more as rich sources of context for learning and development. Embedding learning in those contexts and making the links to principled knowledge explicit can help children to learn with enjoyment and without limits.

Questions to Promote Thinking

1   Do you talk about discrimination by social class or is it a 'zombie' stalking your school too?
2   Can you think about something that a child has told you about which you ignored because it didn't fit in with your ideas about what is important? How might you have instead used it to provide a bridge between home and school learning?

> 3   Or to what extent should we just accept that middle-class ways make
>   it easier for children to move through the education system? We can't
>   change society, so should we therefore just aim to change children to
>   make it easier for them fit in with society?

References and suggested further reading

Allan, J. (2008) *Rethinking Inclusive Education; the Philosophers of Difference in Practice.* Dordrecht: Springer.

Bernstein, B. (1996) *Pedagogy, Symbolic Control and Identity: Theory, Research, Critique.* London: Taylor and Francis.

Bernstein, B. (1999) Vertical and horizontal discourse: an essay, *British Journal of Sociology of Education*, 20(2): 157–73.

Bourne, J. (2000) New imaginings of reading for a new moral order: a review of the production, transmission and acquisition of a new pedagogic culture in the UK, *Linguistics and Education*, 11(1): 31–45.

Brooker, L. (2002) *Starting School:Young Children Learning Cultures.* Buckingham: Open University Press.

Cameron, D. (2010) Supporting parents, speech delivered at Demos' launch of The Character Inquiry; 11 January 2010. Available online at: http://www.conservatives.com/News/Speeches/2010/01/David_Cameron_Supporting_parents.aspx (accessed 13 November 2010).

Connell, R.W. (1994) Poverty and education, *Harvard Educational Review*, 64(2): 125–49.

Connolly, P. (2006) The effects of social class and ethnicity on gender differences in GCSE attainment: a secondary analysis of the Youth Cohort Study of England and Wales 1997–2001, *British Educational Research Journal*, 32(1): 3–21.

DCSF (Department for Children, Schools and Families) (2009) *GCSE Attainment by Pupil Characteristics, in England 2008/09.* Available online at: http://www.dcsf.gov.uk/rsgateway/DB/SFR/s000900/index.shtml (accessed 11 November 2010).

Field, F. (2010) The Foundation Years: preventing poor children becoming poor adults. Available online at: http://povertyreview.independent.gov.uk/final_report.aspx (accessed 13 November 2010).

Hasan, R. (2005) The ontogenesis of ideology: an interpretation of mother–child talk, in J. Webster (ed.) *Language, Society and Consciousness: The Collected Works of Ruqaiya Hasan,* vol. 1. London: Equinox.

Littlejohn, S. and Foss, K. (2008) *Theories of Human Communication*, 9th edn. Belmont, CA, Thomson Wadsworth.

Marmot, M. (2010) *Fair Society, Healthy Lives: Strategic Review of Health Inequalities in England Post 2010.* The Marmot Review. Available online at: http://www.marmotreview.org (accessed 10 July 2010).

Marsh, J. and Millard, E. (2001) *Literacy and Popular Culture.* London: Sage.

Moss, G. (2001) On literacy and the social organisation of knowledge inside and outside school, *Language and Education*, 15(2/3): 146–61.

Reay, D. (2006) The zombie stalking English schools: social class and educational inequality, *British Journal of Education Studies*, 54(3): 288–307.

Sullivan, A., Joshi, H., Ketende, S. and Obolenskaya, P. (2010) *The Consequences at Age 7 of Early Childhood Disadvantage in Northern Ireland and Great Britain. A Report to the*

Northern Ireland Office of the First Minister and Deputy First Minister. Available online at: http://www.ofmdfmni.gov.uk/the_consequences_of_childhood_disadvantage_in_northern_ireland.pdf (accessed 13 December 2010).

Tobin, J. (2005) Quality in early childhood education: an anthropologist's perspective, *Early Education and Development*, **16(4): 421–34.**

17

JEAN CONTEH
Empowering learners from 3–11 through language diversity and bilingualism

Summary

Through the stories of learners and their teachers at home, in their communities and in formal learning settings, this chapter illuminates key principles for thinking about the role of language in learning, for *all* pupils from 3 to 11 years, including those categorized as 'EAL learners'. Through exploring the two strands of language diversity and bilingualism and language learning strategies based on the *KS2 Framework for Languages* (DfES 2002), it illustrates ways in which practitioners can build on the full range of their pupils' language resources for learning across the whole curriculum. Reference is made to research and theory for what they show us about the best practices to empower learners and open out their opportunities to succeed.

Cameo 1

'Performing identities' in maths

Sameena,[1] aged 8 (and in Year 3), is very proud that she gained level 3 in her KS1 maths SATs (the expected level is 2). In the following extract from an interview, she describes how she uses her knowledge of Punjabi to answer her class teacher's 'hot mental' questions at the start of the daily maths lesson. The children were asked to count in fives from 20 to 40:

> We had to count in fives, so I did it in my head in Punjabi then I said it out in English. . . . Eek, do, teen, cha . . . twenty-five . . . chey, saat, aat, nor. . . . Thirty . . . . Eek, do, teen, cha . . . . . thirty-five . . .

In trying to demonstrate how the counting in Punjabi is going on silently in her head while the performance of the English numbers is producing the answers her teacher requires, she varies the pitch of her voice, almost whispering when she says the numbers in Punjabi and saying those in English aloud. She repeats the counting from 1 to 4 and then from 6 to 9 in Punjabi, saying the relevant number in English in between, keeping the numbers in both languages in sequential order. In this way, she accomplishes the task, in English, set by the teacher. In her skilled performance, she is demonstrating what is coming to be described as 'translanguaging', a concept fully examined by Blackledge and Creese (2010: 210–15). Sameena is focused on finding the answer to her teacher's questions in order to affirm her identity as a good learner of maths and she has worked out a strategy for herself that gets the job done satisfactorily.

Cameo 2

Biliteracy and reading

It is lunchtime. In a Year 3 classroom (different from the one above), three 8-year-old children are looking together at a dual-language book and talking to a visitor about the books they like to read. One child goes to the class library shelf, finds a book, brings it back to the group and opens it. Everyone begins looking carefully at the book and the following conversation ensues:

01 3 children together (spelling out) khargosh . . . khargosh

  Visitor: the rabbit. . .

  Yasmin: khargosh . . .sh . . .sh . . .em. . . gha . . . gha

  Nahida: ghu . . . ghu . . .

05 *Yasmin:* khargosh . . . gha . . .

  Nahida: heh . . . spell it out . . . gha . . .

  Yasmin: what's carrot in Urdu? . . . ghajar

  Nahida: ghajar . . .

  Anwar: ghajar . . .

10 *Yasmin:* ghajar . . .

  Nahida: ghajar . . . sh . . . shawk se   kah raha hai . . .

  Yasmin: it means . . . rabbit is eating . . .

  Nahida: the rabbit is eating happily the carrot

  Visitor: the rabbit is happily eating the carrot

15 *Nahida:* eating the carrot

  Yasmin: yeah . . . miss.

(Conteh 2003: 46–7)

As well as English, Yasmin, Nahida and Anwar all speak Punjabi and Urdu. They are simultaneously learning to read and write in two scripts: Urdu at home and English at school. The book that Yasmin chose was a reading primer in Urdu. On the page, there is a picture of a rabbit eating a carrot and several lines of Urdu text. The children's reading shows evidence of their biliteracy (Datta 2007). They are becoming biliterate in different ways and for different purposes. At school, like almost every other KS2 pupil in England, they are learning to read in English using the approaches embodied in the *National Literacy Strategy*, which encourage the reader to engage in a range of active, sense-making strategies. They all got good level 2s in their KS1 SATs. At home, they are learning to read in Urdu using very formal, repetition and rote-learning approaches. What is interesting about their reading behaviour is the way in which they seem to be transferring the strategies they have learnt from their lessons in reading in English to their reading of the Urdu text. Their learning to read in one language seems to be supporting their learning in the other.

Introduction

These brief cameos are both taken from small-scale, longitudinal, classroom-based research. Sameena, Yasmin, Nahida and Anwar are all bilingual learners. They all live in a multilingual city in the north of England, typical of many British cities. England has for many years undeniably been a multilingual country. But more recently, because of changes in the EU community and its composition such as the inclusion of the 'A8 accession states' in 2004, we have seen great increases in the number of bilingual children, and the languages they speak, in our schools. The latest figures show that almost 14 per cent of pupils in schools now have a first language other than English and around 300 languages are spoken by these pupils (DCSF Standards Site 2009). These are some of the pupils usually categorized as 'learning English as an additional language' (EAL).

Language learning and the whole curriculum – weaving the strands together

Language and learning

Donaldson (1986) gives some fascinating examples of young children engaging in activities where they think in complex ways and make judgements that are subtle and sophisticated. She challenges the sequential, biologically-grounded model of development established by Piaget and shows how learning is embedded in language and in the learner's culture in the people and things that surround them in their homes and communities. Donaldson's work – like that of many other researchers since – shows how young children use whatever comes to hand (literally, in many cases) as tools to help them to learn in multi-sensory ways. From the start, language is one of those many tools, gradually growing in importance as children gain experience of how it works and how they can use it. Thus, there are intimate links between language and learning (Gee 1994).

As children move outside their homes and immediate communities and into more formal learning settings, language takes on more and more importance. They begin to learn how to do a great many new things, and the language they need becomes more self-referential and specific. Donaldson (1986) writes about how children progress from learning which is strongly 'embedded' in the surrounding contexts to learning which is 'disembedded' and much more dependent on the language in which it is framed. As they progress through their primary schooling, children have to learn to talk, read and write in very specific and specialized ways. Many of these school tasks demand that children use language which they do not have to use in any other parts of their lives. They have to learn to write answers to questions rather than say them, to write instructions for other people, to report on things they have done, to summarize ideas from texts, to write lists of correctly spelt words, to argue, to persuade . . . the list goes on.

Most of the tasks children do in school are done in writing. Their attainment is almost always assessed through writing. Despite this, their actual learning is mostly done through talk. Talk is a central element in the way that children actually learn. Not only do they need to *learn to talk*, children also need to be able to *talk to learn* across the whole curriculum. From the seminal work of Barnes (1992) and others, many researchers have demonstrated the importance of collaborative talk for children's learning. Mercer (1995) indicates that such talk is a means for people to think and learn together. The word 'together' is important: children's learning needs to be interactive and dialogic (Mercer and Littleton 2007). Teachers and learners need to negotiate and construct mutually supporting contexts in order for the dialogues to be productive and beneficial to learning.

Work by researchers such as Barnes and Mercer shows the importance of talk, particularly group discussion, in the processes of learning, and suggests ways in which classrooms can be organized and activities planned to facilitate interaction. Other studies show the specific ways in which classroom dialogues can support cognitive development in individual learners. Wells and Chang-Wells (1992) provide examples of talk from multilingual classrooms which offers children the opportunity for 'collaborative sense-making' with their peers.

Using the key concept of 'internalization' from the Vygotskian sociocultural model of learning, Wells and Chang-Wells argue that 'literate thinkers', are able to 'exploit the symbolic potential of external representation as an aid to the construction of inner meaning' (1992: 69) whether in speech or writing. In other words, talk develops thinking, which underpins literacy – and literacy is the main route to learning and academic success in our education system.

Being yourself: language, culture and identity

Besides being an essential tool for learning and academic success, language is an inextricable part of our personal and social lives, of the cultures we live in and of who we are our identities. In complex ways, our identities are formed from the activities we do every day and the conversations we have with the people around us. Through this, we also develop a sense of where we belong, and how we identify with the social worlds that surround us. There is a great deal of evidence (e.g. Conteh 2003) to show that, if pupils have a sense of belonging and being valued in their classrooms, their attitudes to learning will be much more positive and their achievements will improve.

The need to belong; to 'be yourself' is deeply entrenched in even the youngest pupils in school. On BEd and BA (QTS) courses, we ask our first-year students to write autobiographical accounts of events that are important to them as young learners. One year, Rukshana, a lively and enthusiastic bilingual student, wrote about her experiences as a 5-year-old Punjabi speaker beginning school unable to speak English. Very few other pupils in her class could speak Punjabi, and everything went on around them in English. One day, Rukshana was working with another Punjabi-speaking child when the teacher approached and held an object in front of her, saying something in English. Her friend whispered to her in Punjabi that she was to name the colour of the object, so Rukshana declared 'neela' (*blue*). This resulted in the teacher sending the other child away and continuing to talk in words that Rukshana did not understand. She continues the story:

> The teacher left me staring blankly at the other children. Every one of them was doing something; playing, reading, working or talking in English. I sat back and felt sorry for myself . . . This was a day that I felt so many emotions inside me. Feelings that I had never experienced before. I did not want to be myself.

After this inauspicious start, the story ended happily for Rukshana. She did eventually succeed in school and went on to become a very good teacher. But there are many pupils who may not have been so fortunate.

The links between identity, language and culture are strong. The same words are used in different ways with different meanings in different cultural settings. As teachers, we can learn much from our pupils and their families. An example from my own children shows this. My two children were born in Sierra Leone in West Africa and we came to live in England when they were 7 and 10 years old. My daughter's 70-year-old teacher was approachable and friendly. She went off to the town library, found some Sierra Leonean stories and asked me to go into the class and teach the children a bit of Mende, a language that my daughter spoke. The only concern she had was that my daughter seemed to find it difficult to use science equipment such as the large plastic weighing scales. This was not really surprising as she had never seen anything like them before, let alone handled them. When the teacher asked her to balance the two sides of the scales, my daughter looked puzzled. She told me afterwards that she didn't realize what the teacher meant. Again, this was not surprising. In Krio, the Sierra Leonean lingua franca, 'to balance' means to carry something on your head.

When all this was explained to the teacher, she was relieved, pleased and fascinated all at the same time. At the time, I did not fully understand the importance of what she did for my daughter and for us as a family. Through her sensitivity and willingness to listen, the teacher showed us that she valued our culture and the 'funds of knowledge' that we brought to her class and her school. Gonzalez et al. (2005) and others have shown the vital importance of this for academic success. In the way she handled the confusion, the teacher valued my knowledge as a parent, affirmed my daughter's identity and so provided her with a positive environment for her learning.

Language and the curriculum from 3–11

In recent years, a vast amount of resources have been lavished on the curriculum in Foundation Stage and primary classrooms, much of it related to language and language learning. In the Early Years Foundation Stage (EYFS)(DCSF 2007) one of the 'six areas of learning', *Communication, language and literacy,* provides a strong focus for language development and learning. Language in different forms is clearly identified in the other five areas as a tool for learning and as evidence of learning. Practitioners are given guidance both in modelling many facets of language and in supporting learners in their growing capacities to use language in their learning. For example, in the *Mathematical development* area, they 'encourage children to talk about the shapes they see' (2007: 79), in *Knowledge and understanding of the world,* they 'discuss reasons that make activities safe or unsafe' (2007: 89) and in *Physical development,* they 'teach and encourage children to use the vocabulary of movement' (2007: 105).

As pupils progress into the primary curriculum, the holistic nature of their language learning begins to fragment. In the current form of the statutory National Curriculum (QCDA 2010), we have the subject labelled 'English' organized into two Key Stages, each with three programmes of study structured by language mode. Then we have clearly articulated targets for pupils' attainment in each mode. Alongside this, the non-statutory but highly prescribed literacy framework (DfES 2006a), provides extensive guidance material. But its units of work are organized year by year by text type grouped under 'narrative', 'poetry' and 'non-fiction'. Its learning objectives are presented as 12 strands, each focusing on different aspects of language use, such as 'listening and responding', 'understanding and interpreting texts', and so on. While the links with other areas of the curriculum may be embedded in these resources, they are often not easy for teachers to elicit and carry into their planning and teaching.

A document introduced in 2002 to support the introduction of modern foreign languages (PMFL) into primary schools, the *KS2 Framework for Languages* (DfES 2002), has brought new ways of thinking about language to primary pupils' and their teachers' attention. Children at KS2 are now expected to study a 'modern foreign language', but – as the framework makes clear – the approach is very different from secondary MFL teaching. Rather than developing proficiency in a specific language, PMFL is intended to be much more about helping children develop generic skills for learning, strategies for language learning and the positive values, attitudes and awareness that the language learning experience can provide. The framework does not prescribe specific languages; schools are free to choose, and can even use different languages for different parts of the framework. To facilitate this approach, the KS2 framework has two 'cross-cutting strands' of learning which underpin those more specifically related to oracy, literacy and intercultural understanding:

- Knowledge about language (KAL)
- Language learning strategies (LLS).

It is these, perhaps, which are intended to foster a distinctive 'primary language teaching' approach which, as Brown (2007) argues, needs to be 'inclusive of all learners', with the potential to stimulate children's creativity, broaden intercultural understanding and ensure an international dimension in learning and developing understanding across the curriculum. The Introduction to the framework, describing the *Intercultural understanding* strand, clearly shows this intention:

> Language competence and intercultural understanding are an essential part of being a citizen. Children develop a greater understanding of their own lives in the context of exploring the lives of others. They learn to look at things from another's perspective, giving them insight into the people, culture and traditions of other cultures. Children become more aware of the similarities and differences between peoples, their daily lives, beliefs and values.
>
> (DfES 2002: 8)

Going further, the Introduction points out the potential cognitive benefits, across the curriculum, for children of this approach to language learning:

> An important aim of language learning in KS2 is to familiarise children with strategies which they can apply to the learning of any language . . . Over the four years of KS2 children should have regular opportunities to identify and apply a range of *Language learning strategies*. By selecting and using different strategies, children develop awareness of how they learn and the ability to plan to use specific strategies for particular tasks. Strategies explored in language lessons can also be used for learning in other subjects.
>
> (DfES 2002: 9)

Given the right encouragement, children love doing the kinds of activities suggested in the KAL and LLS strands, and some of them are briefly explored in the following sections. Through them, community funds of knowledge can take a central place in the classroom and learning new languages is strongly linked to learners' personal and social experiences. The links with other official guidance for primary teachers in England, such as the cross-curricular *Excellence and enjoyment* strategy and the *Excellence and enjoyment for bilingual learners* material (DfES 2006b) are also strong.

Learning bilingually – synergy and creativity

There are many definitions of bilingualism and the one which perhaps best captures the expertise and experience of children like Sameena, Yasmin, Nahida and Anwar who began this chapter was developed by advisory teachers in Tower Hamlets. It captures the important links between language and social practice by defining bilingual pupils as those who:

> live in two languages, who have access to, or need to use, two or more languages at home and at school. It does not mean that they have fluency in both languages or that they are competent and literate in both languages.
>
> (Hall 2001: 5)

A study in 2003, in the city where the children in the cameos live, revealed the complex ways in which members of their communities use the wide array of languages and dialects at their disposal from their heritage in Pakistan or Bangladesh (Aitsiselmi 2004). Aitsiselmi illustrates the complications some of his respondents faced when asked to name the languages they spoke. One concluded by saying, 'We just call it apni zabaan' (*our language*). This resonates with the idea of translanguaging I introduced earlier which, Garcia (2009) suggests, promotes a language identity which is 'brighter and more intense' than a monolingual one.

Research into bilingualism and bilingual education by Cummins (2000, 2001) resonates with the view of languages in communities revealed by Aitsiselmi. It can lead us beyond the constraints of the current 'monolingualizing' ideology of the English system (Heller 2007; Conteh 2010) and encourage us to think differently about language pedagogy. Sameena, in her bilingual counting and Yasmin, Nahida and Anwar in their biliteracy, are demonstrating something of Cummins' theory of 'interdependence', which convincingly challenges the common-sense notion that, when learning a second language, the learner's first language should be avoided. Instead of focusing on the 'problems' of multilingual classrooms, we need to consider the possibilities of using the children's languages as resources for their learning of the English language and of literacy. Research by Kenner et al. (2008) is beginning to show that bilingual learners in primary classrooms are eager to use their home languages for learning, and that they can have positive benefits across the curriculum. Moreover, research in complementary learning settings such as Saturday schools (e.g. Conteh et al. 2007; Blackledge and Creese 2010) shows the range of ways that bilingualism can play out in classrooms and begins to map out possible 'bilingual pedagogies' including translanguaging and biliteracies. Finally, Conteh and Brock (2010) show how 'safe spaces' can and must be found to empower young learners to be and become bilingual in home, community and education settings in England.

Language diversity and learning for all pupils

The idea of language diversity as a resource for learning is often seen as relevant only in schools where pupils themselves may speak a range of languages besides English in their homes and communities. But it is equally relevant, though possibly in different ways, in schools where pupils may only speak English. These pupils are also members of a multilingual society, and – it could be argued – are placed at a disadvantage by their monolingualism, their opportunities for learning through language limited by the monolingual contexts that surround them. In a world where more people speak English as a second or foreign language than their native one (Centre for Applied Linguistics 2010), they are increasingly in the minority. A project run many years ago by The Schools' Council (1984; see Conteh 2003: 120–1) identified ways in which promoting awareness of language diversity and bilingualism could benefit schools where pupils have such limited experiences. It concluded that, at whole-school level, bilingualism offered:

- increased language awareness and knowledge about language;
- increased awareness of cultural diversity;

- a contribution to combating racism in school and wider community;
- improved communication between different groups.

Such benefits can be realized by promoting a welcoming, inclusive whole-school ethos where language and cultural diversity are mediated as important, interesting and valued aspects of the school community and the wider society (DfES 2004), where different languages are welcomed and regarded as a resource for the whole school community.

In the classrooms of such a school, children are interested in languages and confident to explore and try out different languages. I remember once going into a Year 3 classroom where a child came running up to me and asked, 'Miss, do you speak any languages?' He was eager to find out a new way to say 'good morning' so that he could surprise his teacher by answering in a new way when she called the register. Language diversity is a fascinating focus of study – even a phonics session can raise children's awareness of different accents and the ways people pronounce their vowel phonemes. Then they can set off as 'language detectives', to find out who says what and in which ways in their school. Many years ago, when I began working as a teacher in Bradford, a child asked me why I pronounced 'book' in a different way from the way she did. I replied that I did so because I came from Newcastle, not Bradford. A few days later, she came and told me that 'Mr Smith' pronounced 'book' in the same way as I did and, sure enough, he came from Newcastle.

In the KS2 Languages framework, the first Year 3 learning objective for IU is '3.1: Learn about the different languages spoken by children in the school' (DfES 2002: 19). This links with the KAL objective, 'recognize that many languages are spoken in the UK' (DfES 2002: 30) and the LLS, 'analyse and compare the language or languages with English' (DfES 2002: 30). These objectives lend themselves to a rich and wide range of activities that, besides promoting children's learning of different languages, can get them exploring their local communities and their wider society and developing global awareness and understanding. Some of the Year 3 teaching activities (DfES 2002: 37) illustrate this:

- Talk about the different languages they know or have heard around them through family members, friends, the media, in the neighbourhood or when visiting other countries.
- Talk about dialects and accents within the UK – different people may pronounce the same word differently or use different words.
- Children and teacher compile a list of languages spoken by children within the school. Locate the country/countries where these languages are spoken using maps, atlases and globes.
- Use Interactive Whiteboards to create a 'live and growing' resource of different languages, e.g. sound files of greetings in different languages.
- Create a welcome sign on the door of the classroom in the languages children know.

The objectives can be met in ways that include families and affirm their funds of knowledge as well as those of bilingual staff in the school. They can also be used with children younger than KS2. One of my former students, Suzanne Aston, working in a reception/year 1 class, developed a wonderful project, which she called the 'Name Tree' that would meet many of the Year 3 objectives (see Conteh 2003: 122–3). Beginning by showing the children a photo of her own daughter and explaining why she was given her name and what it meant, Suzanne gave her pupils and their families a powerful message about the aims of the project and motivated them to share their own knowledge. Every child was given a 'leaf' with their name on it and asked to provide an explanation on the other side of where the name came from and what it meant. These were then displayed on the large, colourful 'Name Tree' in the classroom. Many parents came in to share family stories, photos and other treasured possessions, in the process introducing a rich range of languages and cultural knowledge into the classroom. In this way, the community funds of knowledge become part of the curriculum for the children, and the learning entailed was genuinely dialogic and affirmative of the children's cultures and identities.

Questions to Promote Thinking

1   What do you think are the implications of research such as Donaldson's for assessing young children's understanding of particular concepts and learning generally?

2   How could you make the settings you work in reflective of the cultures and identities of your learners?

3   How might the idea of 'language diversity as a resource for learning' be activated in your own settings?

Note

1   To protect confidentiality, all names have been changed.

References and suggested further reading

Aitsiselmi, F. (2004) *Linguistic Diversity and the Use of English in the Home Environment: A Bradford Case Study.* Bradford: University of Bradford.

Barnes, D. (1992) The role of talk in learning, in K. Norman (ed.) *Thinking Voices: The Work of the National Oracy Project.* London: Hodder and Stoughton.

Blackledge, A. and Creese, A. (2010) *Multilingualism: A Critical Perspective.* London: Continuum.

Brown, J. (2007) Getting started with primary languages: advice, support and resources for a multilingual approach, *Race Equality Teaching*, 26(1): 33–5.

Centre for Applied Linguistics (2010) *A Global Perspective on Bilingualism and Bilingual Education.* Available online at: http://www.cal.org/resources/Digest/digestglobal.html (accessed 21 November 2010).

Conteh, J. (2003) *Succeeding in Diversity: Culture, Language and Learning in Primary Classrooms.* Stoke-on-Trent: Trentham Books.

Conteh, J. (2010) Making links across complementary and mainstream classrooms for primary children and their teachers, in V. Lytra and P. Martin (eds) *Sites of Multilingualism.* Stoke-on-Trent: Trentham Books.

Conteh, J. and Brock, A. (2010) Safe spaces? Sites of bilingualism for young learners in home, school and community. *International Journal of Bilingual Education and Bilingualism*. Available online at: http://www.informaworld.com/smpp/content~db=all~content=a9240 14542~frm=abslink?words=conteh|brock&hash=1850177570 (accessed 20 November 2010).

Conteh, J., Martin, P. and Helavaara Robertson, L. (eds) (2007) *Multilingual Learning Stories in Schools and Communities in Britain*. Stoke-on-Trent: Trentham Books.

Cummins, J. (2000) *Language, Power and Pedagogy: Bilingual Children in the Crossfire*. Clevedon: Multilingual Matters.

Cummins, J. (2001) *Negotiating Identities: Education for Empowerment in a Diverse Society*, 2nd edn. Ontario, CA: California Association for Bilingual Education.

Datta, M. (ed.) (2007) *Bilinguality and Literacy: Principles and Practice*, 2nd edn. London: Continuum.

DCSF (Department for Children, Schools and Families) (2007) *Early Years Foundation Stage*. London: DfES.

DCSF Standards Site (2009) *Ethnic Minority Achievement*. Available online at: http://www. standards.dfes.gov.uk/ethnicminorities/raising_achievement/whats_new/statistics/ (accessed 31 January 2011).

DfES (Department for Education and Skills) (2002) *Key Stage 2 Framework for Languages, Parts 1, 2 and 3*. Available online at: http://nationalstrategies.standards.dcsf.gov.uk/node/ 85274 (accessed 15 November 2010).

DfES (2004) *Aiming High: Understanding the Needs of Minority Ethnic Pupils in Mainly White Schools*. London: DfES Report 0416/2004.

DfES (2006a) *The Primary Framework for Literacy*. Available online at: http://nationalstrategies. standards.dcsf.gov.uk/primary/primaryframework/literacyframework (accessed 15 November 2010).

DfES (2006b) *Excellence and Enjoyment: Learning and Teaching for Bilingual Pupils in the Primary Years*. London: DfES Report 0013–2006PCK–EN.

Donaldson, M. (1986) *Children's Minds*, 2nd edn. London: HarperCollins.

Garcia, O. (2009) Imagining and enacting: educating for bilingualism in complementary schools, lecture delivered as part of ESRC seminar series: *Complementary Schools: Research, Policy and Practice*, University of Birmingham, 12 November.

Gee, J.P. (1994) First language acquisition as a guide for theories of learning and pedagogy. *Linguistics and Education*, 6: 331–54.

Gonzalez, N., Moll, L.C. and Amanti, C. (eds) (2005) *Funds of Knowledge: Theorising Practices in Households, Communities and Classrooms*. Hillsdale, NJ: Lawrence Erlbaum.

Hall, D. (2001) *Assessing the Needs of Bilingual Pupils: Living in Two Languages*, 2nd edn. London: David Fulton.

Heller, M. (ed.) (2007) *Bilingualism: A Social Approach*. London: Palgrave Macmillan.

Kenner, C., Gregory, E., Ruby, M. and Al-Azami, S. (2008) Bilingual learning for second and third generation children, *Language, Culture and Curriculum*, 21(2): 120–37.

Mercer, N. (1995) *The Guided Construction of Knowledge*. Clevedon: Multilingual Matters.

Mercer, N. and Littleton, K. (2007) *Dialogue and the Development of Children's Thinking*. London: Routledge.

QCDA (Qualifications and Curriculum Development Agency) (2010) *The National Curriculum*. Available online at: http://curriculum.qcda.gov.uk/key-stages-1-and-2/subjects/index. aspx (accessed 15 November 2010).

Wells, G. and Chang-Wells, G.L. (1992) *Constructing Knowledge Together: Classrooms as Centers of Inquiry and Literacy*. Portsmouth, NH: Heinemann.

18

MARY KELLETT
Accessing children's voice and experiences

Summary

This chapter begins with a brief overview of policy shifts, drawing on a children's rights framework and situating meaningful participation and voice in a legislative context. Content then embraces examples of practice that are effective in accessing children's lived educational experiences and which build capacity for pupil voice. Illustrations draw on a wide range of participation activity such as circle time and the mosaic approach for younger children, school councils and child-led research in the older age range. Challenging concepts are examined such as adult–child power relations, distributed leadership and accessing voice for the silent minorities.

Introduction

The past two decades have been characterized by a fundamental repositioning of the status of children in society spearheaded by the United Nations Convention on the Rights of the Child (1989) and its global focus on children's rights. Articles 12 and 13 compelled governments to find more effective ways of engaging with children through improved listening skills and better consultation processes. In recent years, there has been recognition that consultation alone is not enough (Sinclair 2004); there needs to be meaningful participation and involvement in decision-making processes. Participation is the act of doing and being involved while voice is the right to free expression of views that may, or may not emanate from participation. Young children begin to participate through everyday family practices but they need to learn how to self-advocate and educators need to provide opportunities for them to exercise agency and have a voice.

   Accepting that children's worlds are somewhat opaque to us, accessing their voice and experiences is neither straightforward nor without challenge. It took 15 years and some stinging criticism from the United Nations Special Summit on Children's Rights (United Nations General Assembly 2002) to finally prompt legislation that embedded the principles of the Convention. This was enacted in England in the 2002 Education Act and the *Every Child Matters* (ECM) Green Paper (DfES 2003) which identified five outcomes deemed to be important for children to lead happy lives – 'being healthy'; 'staying safe'; 'enjoying and achieving'; 'making a positive contribution' and 'achieving economic well-being'. The Green Paper was converted into legislation via The Children Act 2004 (DfES 2004). ECM has been a key driver in accessing children's voices and experiences. ECM put the child at the centre of provision – the notion of the 'team around the child' (Siraj-Blatchford et al. 2007) – that provides for children's needs from a holistic perspective and emphasizes well-being as human rights (Hartas 2008).

In 2008, the UK government announced new legislation relating to the expression of pupil views (Education and Skills Act, DCSF 2008):

> to place duties on governing bodies of maintained schools in England and Wales to invite the views of registered pupils about prescribed matters, and consider any views on those matters expressed by pupils (whether or not in response to an invitation) in light of their age and understanding.
>
> (para 199)

Despite this legislation and prior requirements that inspectors report on how schools seek and act on the views of pupils (OfSTED 2005), engaging children's voices remains a challenge (Leitch and Mitchell 2007). Traditional hierarchical adult–child power relationships in schools can result in tokenistic pupil voice for reasons of accountability (Wyness 2006; Robinson and Taylor 2007) rather than pupils' human rights. Smyth (2006) proposes a shift of emphasis in pedagogic and leadership approaches away from the focus on standards and accountability towards 'relational reforms' which address the emotional and personal needs of pupils thus engendering confidence, trust and respect. This remainder of this chapter focuses on examples of practice that are effective in accessing children's lived educational experiences and which build capacity for pupil voice.

The mosaic approach

The mosaic approach (Clark and Moss 2001) is a collection of child-friendly participation activities which creates a 'mosaic' of young children's experiences of their learning environments and has been used successfully in a variety of early years settings. Children are given disposable cameras with which to photograph particular aspects of their learning environments they like or dislike. The photos are used in child interviews as prompts to elicit discussion about experiences of different parts of their environment. Another aspect of the mosaic is a guided tour of their early years setting by a young child. This is an informative way of accessing children's experiences. The parts of a setting they choose to show to an adult and how they describe and explain these places to that adult divulges much about how they are experiencing it. Other parts of the mosaic approach include observation and getting children to draw maps or pictures of their settings. The power of the approach is in pulling together different sets of information which, in isolation, may only tell part of a story but when pieced together can provide a strong rendition of a young child's lived experiences.

Waller (2006) used the mosaic approach in a participatory study with young children about their experiences of an outdoor play area where they were given free time and space to play as they wished. The 3- and 4-year-olds were given digital cameras to film and record their perspectives by taking photos of their happy and special places. Through discussion of the photos with a practitioner they then created a learning story.

Cameo 1

Zachary's story

One morning red group visited the park shortly after a light snowfall. Zoe noticed some tracks in the snow made by birds. 'Look, look a goblin's footprint,' she said. A small group of children (Charleigh, Jessica and Zachary) came over to see the footprints. They followed the tracks and Zoe took a photograph on a digital camera. The children followed the track to a pump house where they stopped. 'I think he lives in there,' Zoe said – pointing to the pump house.

The children tiptoed over towards a blue door and then stopped. 'You go, Julie – we're scared!' Julie (a practitioner) knocked on the door. The children ran away. 'Don't worry – there is no one at home today.'

Following this, the children named the pump house the 'Goblin's House'. Zachary then collected some sticks and cleared some space on the ground. 'This is for the flowers to grow,' he said. He then placed the sticks around the flowers, as if to protect them. Zachary then said, 'There might be butterflies. I'm making a butterfly garden.' After a few seconds, he turned and pointed to the steps behind, 'You have to go right up there to see the ducks.'

Zachary drew a picture to represent the goblin's footprints. It is interesting to note that he also drew the Butterfly Garden, which is near to the 'Goblin's House' and is an area of the park to which he has consistently given attention.

(Waller 2006: 90–1)

All the learning stories, illustrated by the children's drawings and photos, were displayed in the nursery. They provided an admirable example of a young child voice in action.

Circle time

Circle time is a well-known activity used to develop self-esteem, strengthen social skills and promote well-being. However, circle time is also an excellent means of building capacity and creating opportunities for pupil voice and accessing children's experiences. It is popular in PSHE curricula in primary schools. Sitting in a circle enables children to see one another easily and also negates power differentials. Ground rules are established between teacher and pupils beforehand such as:

- only one person speaks at once;
- everyone has to listen with respect;
- everyone gets a turn to contribute;
- no negative comments are allowed.

Games and props help to facilitate child contributions. For example, passing a favourite toy or object around the circle. A child can make a contribution (or choose to pass) when holding the toy before giving it to the next person in the circle. Children can only talk when they are holding the toy. Themed prompts can be used to shape the session such as sentence completion e.g. I feel unhappy when . . ., I am afraid of . . ., I get embarrassed if . . ., I am most proud of . . ., etc. This approach can easily be adapted to accommodate advocacy themes that will begin to inculcate children towards participation in the pedagogical and social community of their school. Thus sentence completion themes might be, e.g. I like lessons which . . ., In the lunch break I would like to . . ., A good school rule is . . . or A bad school rule is . . ., etc.

School councils

The growth of school councils and the establishment of School Council UK as an empowering organization have done much to raise awareness about the potential for children to play a part in the leadership and management of schools. School councils have been a well-established component of secondary schools for many years now, less so in the primary sector until recently. When these work well, they are a good vehicle for active citizenship and provide opportunities for children to engage in decision-making, practise civil governance skills, develop responsibility and stimulate agency.

The best models are those which have councils for every class in the school and representation from each of those class councils on the main school council. In this way all children can be involved at some level. This requires a commitment to regular, formal meetings and systematic dissemination. An effective school council is pupil-led and concentrates on core issues of the school not adult-compliant topics that have been pre-determined. Innocuous examples that spring to mind are toilets, lunches, recycling and pupil behaviour. It is somewhat concerning that the School Council Handbook (DfES 2006) is littered with these kinds of examples. Active child citizenship should encompass all of school life. Teaching and learning are too often excluded from pupil voice.

Some schools allow a school council pupil representative to attend governors' meetings: others involve them in the appointment of staff. Here is an example of questions asked of a prospective deputy headteacher in an interview by primary pupils appears (Clay 2005: 52).

Cameo 2

Lauren: Welcome to our school council meeting. My name is Lauren and I am the chairperson. This is Rachel and she is the secretary.
We have taken a lot of time on these questions. John has the first question.

John: Why do you want to be a Deputy Headteacher?

Lauren: Charlie has the next question.

Charlie: What sorts of things will you do as a Deputy Headteacher?

Lauren: Maddie has the next question.

Maddie: Why do you really like this school?

Lauren: Jordan has the next question.

Jordan: What is the best thing in your classroom?

Lauren: Callum has the next question.

Callum: How do you tell people off?

Lauren: Joseph has the next question.

Joseph: Could you tell us about your rules in the classroom?

Lauren: Sharon has the next question.

Sharon: What sorts of subjects do you look after in your school?

Lauren: That's all of our questions. Do you want to ask us a question? Thank you for coming.

Children with learning difficulties

Despite all the ECM rhetoric, the voices of marginalized children and those with additional needs are still proving challenging to reach. Some children are not able to express their views in words, either because English is not their first language or because they have communication difficulties. The school experiences of children with learning difficulties were vividly depicted in Mencap's *Don't Stick It, Stop It!* research (2007) which revealed that 80 per cent of children with learning difficulties were being bullied at school. Findings showed that 60 per cent had been physically hurt by bullies and 36 per cent reported that the bullying did not stop even when they told someone. For 27 per cent of children with learning difficulties, the bullying lasted three or more years. How can teachers ensure they are giving *all* pupils a voice in order to understand experiences such as these? Children themselves can be powerful anti-bullying advocates and many schools have peer-run anti-bullying initiatives. However, much can be done within the regular classroom such as drawing up ground rules and codes of conduct that outlaw bullying. If children are involved in the creation of the rules and sign contracts to abide by them, they have a greater sense of ownership and are more likely to fulfil them. Bullying can be a topic for a circle time or a PSHE lesson. Puppetry is a valuable tool in facilitating voice. Finger puppets are easy to make and communication can be done entirely via the puppet characters. If there is something a child wants to convey that is distressing or embarrassing, the puppets provide a safe vehicle through which to communicate. Dolls and favourite toys can also become 'voices'. Providing graffiti boards or opportunities for children to chalk artwork on to playgrounds can be another vehicle for marginalized children's voices.

The London Borough of Newham and the North London Special Educational Needs Regional Hub is working with the Rix Centre on a research project in six primary schools called 'What constitutes good progress for children with Special Educational Needs?' The project uses multi-media advocacy technology to enable children to be more involved in their own learning and have more voice.

> We have been using talking mats, disposable cameras, computers, microphones and photo stories. The children enjoyed the use of cameras and this definitely helped with their engagement. We found we were able to engage the attention of most children for much longer than with their usual activities, often for up to an hour and with minimal support.
>
> (Gosia Kwiatkowska, the Rix Centre, www.rixcentre.org)

Other research (Kwiatkowska 2009) has included the co-construction of multi-media advocacy profiles produced as web pages which enable children with learning difficulties to express their likes and dislikes and voice their perspectives.

One must not assume that voice necessarily equates with empowerment. In fact, child voice initiatives in schools can be disempowering of some pupil groups especially where schools have implicit contracts that pupils speak 'responsibly, intelligently and usefully' (Bragg 2001: 73). This closes doors to pupils who do not have the language or presentation skills prized by the school and can reinforce existing divisive practices. The risk here is that voice becomes inextricably linked with privilege. Voice initiatives in schools can also be oppressively censorial if areas such as teaching and learning become forbidden areas of enquiry (Fielding 2001) and only comfortable, 'safe' issues are encouraged (Lodge 2005) where teachers' roles are never questioned (Devine 2002).

Children's rights

The status of children in educational contexts is closely bound up with a rights discourse. Devine (2002) supported by Wyness et al. (2004) maintains that the rights discourse in this context focuses primarily on children's right to education rather than on children's experiences within the system itself. Almost every aspect of the school experience is decided by adults (either parents or teachers) without children having any right to be consulted from how they must dress, which school they must attend, what they must study and for how long.

The notion of pupils as *school citizens* gives new meaning to transactional processes and shared decision-making. It is widely acknowledged (Lister 2007) that children's citizenship status cannot be the same as adults because children do not enjoy the same civil rights or suffrage. However, framing children's citizenship in these terms risks rendering it less equal and isolating it in what Cohen (2005) refers to as 'middle ground'. Equality does not prohibit difference and it is this very sense of difference that we must prize if children's citizenship in schools is to go beyond rhetoric and become agentic. Agency brings responsibility – does children's increased agency in schools encourage greater responsibility because of a sense of ownership in the decision-making processes? How might active citizenship be progressed in primary schools? Perhaps this will be achieved through the distribution of voting rights related to aspects of their learning environment and greater involvement in decision-making through democratic systems such as school councils. Inevitably there will be tensions if adult and child views are in conflict. The gritty reality of children voicing their opposition to education policy is a long way from consultations about what colour to paint the classroom walls or an imperative to renovate the toilets.

As yet, citizenship education is only compulsory in state secondary schools in England and Wales but Personal, Social, Health and Economic (PSHE) education became statutory in 2008 for all state schools in England and Wales. Interestingly, the nominated PSHE topics do not make any reference to voice or rights but creative teaching can do much to bring the concepts of participation and active citizenship into PSHE lessons. If citizenship is to be active and consequential in children's school lives, then there have to be spaces created in which citizenship capacity can be developed. Some of these processes do exist for older children (e.g. UK Youth Parliament, Funky Dragon in Wales, Scottish Youth Parliament, the Youth Forum in Northern Ireland and a number of youth forum groups) but for children aged birth–11, citizenship is still an evolving concept. One initiative which is doing much to advance active citizenship and give voice to children's perspectives is the enabling of children to undertake their own research (Kellett 2005).

Children as researchers

Children observe with different eyes, ask different questions, have different concerns and immediate access to a peer culture where adults are outsiders. The research agendas children prioritize, the research questions they frame and the ways in which they collect data are quintessentially different from adults. Child–child research generates nuanced data which provide valuable insights into our understanding of childhoods. There is an important link to political literacy and the notion of child researchers as advocates and protagonists (Kellett and Ward 2008). This emerges from two conceptual arenas of power and emancipation. Power issues relate to whose interests the research serves, who owns the research and whom the research is for. Emancipatory elements challenge the legitimacy of research which does not empower groups (in this case, children) who are either invisible or oppressed. Hence the interests of children are well served when they set their own agendas and lead their own research (Fielding 2004).

We cannot expect children to carry out quality research without quality training. Most adults could not undertake empirical research without some training.

The Children's Research Centre at the Open University, UK (http://childrens-research-centre.open.ac.uk) exists to provide tailored research training to children as young as 9 and support them to undertake their own research. Its website is host to over 100 original research studies by children.

Are boys and girls treated differently at school?

Helen Dandridge, aged 10, conducted some research into whether girls and boys were treated differently by teachers at their school (Dandridge 2008). After comprehensive training in research processes, she began her investigation by searching the internet for any opinions being expressed by children on this subject. On websites such as *BBC Newsround* (a children's topical news programme) she found some strong views being expressed that boys and girls were treated differently in school. Helen decided to find out whether this was true in her own school. She collected three complementary sets of data: a self-designed questionnaire for 9–11-year-olds, lesson observations and an analysis of the gender differences on the school's Golden Time Chart (Golden Time was a free choice activity period on Friday afternoons which was prized by pupils but Golden Time could be withdrawn by teachers for inappropriate behaviour). Questionnaire results showed that 86 per cent of pupils did not believe that teachers deliberately favoured one gender and 72 per cent believed that teachers did not choose girls to answer more questions in class than boys. However, 80 per cent of 11-year-olds thought that girls were chosen over boys to help with special jobs in the classroom and 63 per cent thought that teachers treated boys and girls differently as a response to their behaviour. The lesson observations – there were only three so caution needs to be employed in making any inferences – generated some different data (see Table 18.1).

When Helen analysed the Golden Chart Time sheet, she found many more boys being denied Golden Time than girls. Her research report concluded that boys and girls were treated differently at her school although she did not think this was any deliberate act on the part of teachers.

Child-led research can be influential at a local level. Helen presented her research to teachers and governors to raise awareness and succeeded in getting gender issues onto the school management agenda.

Table 18.1 Lesson observations

Lesson	Number of times girls picked to answer	Number of times boys picked to answer	Number of times girls told off	Number of times boys told off
English	9	3	4	19
Maths	18	5	5	14
Art	16	8	11	39

Enjoyment and achievement

Eleven-year-old Daisy Wooller investigated whether children's liking for a subject affected how good they were at it (Wooller 2005). She focused on the core subjects of English, maths and science. She surveyed 60 11-year-olds to find out how much pupils liked the three subjects, whether they thought they were good at them and what reasons they gave. Daisy's findings drew attention to children's perceptions that a subject being boring is a key factor in liking it or engaging with it.

> The main reason for pupils disliking a subject was they found the subject boring although another big factor was they didn't like the teacher . . . Some suggested that teachers should think of ways to make a lesson more interesting, maybe by having the class involved in the teaching.
>
> In English, the results showed that the more a pupil enjoyed a lesson, the more they felt able in that area and the pupils who disliked the subject felt less able at it. However, in maths and science, generally pupils felt that they were more able if they enjoyed it more, until it came to the pupils who strongly disliked the subject. It would seem that the pupils who strongly disliked maths and science thought they were fairly able at the subject.
>
> On the questionnaires, some children stated that they were unhappy about the fact that their teacher always chose the same people, because they knew that that student would get it right. Others felt that their teacher picked them to answer questions too often even though they didn't have their hand up because they didn't know the answer. Because of this, the children in Year 6 would like their teachers to choose people randomly and try not to pick the same people too often.
>
> If pupils came into a lesson with a positive attitude their performance may be affected by that and the same if they came into a classroom with a negative frame of mind. Also if the children just believed they could do something and put their mind to it, they could probably achieve a lot instead of just sitting there refusing to do any work, because they don't think they can do it. The pupils' performance is also affected by the environment they're working in; if there is lots of shouting and jumping around, no-one's going to get anything done.
>
> (Wooller 2005)

Some teachers may find Daisy's research challenging – even offensive – in its criticism of teachers' lessons which were perceived to be boring. If professionals can get past initial feelings of resentment and take the research at face value – that it is honestly reporting children's responses about issues that impact on their learning and not 'teacher-bashing' – then the insights from the research offer opportunities to develop new strategies and teaching approaches to engage pupils more effectively.

Children's perceptions of ideal teacher qualities

Mitchell Schofield, aged 11, researched the views of his peers about ideal teacher qualities (Schofield 2008). 'I chose this project because I wanted teachers to see what qualities their pupils really want in a teacher.' He carried out an initial questionnaire to help him create nine choice categories:

- sets fair homework;
- exciting;
- lots of activities;
- encouraging;
- happy and smiling;
- keeps control of the class;
- kind;
- fair to everyone;
- group work.

He then did individual interviews with his classmates to rank the categories. Mitchell chose a diamond ranking (Thomas and O'Kane 1999) so that children could give some categories equal ranking as per the shape of a diamond. The choice categories were written on cards and children were invited to place them on the diamond template from most to least important. Children could shuffle the cards around until they were happy with the final layout (see Figure 18.1).

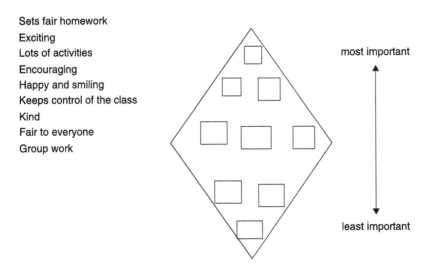

Figure 18.1 Diamond ranking template

Mitchell then attributed a score to each line of the diamond from 5 at the top (most important) to 1 at the bottom (least important)

5

4   4

3   3   3

2   2

1

and converted the results into a bar chart (see Figure 18.2) showing how his class-mates rated qualities of an ideal teacher.

Figure 18.2 Ranking of ideal teacher categories

Interestingly, keeping control of the class, closely followed by being a happy, smiley teacher, were ranked as the most important qualities in their ideal teacher.

Conclusion

I began with a rationale for accessing children's voice and experiences and went on to present examples of how this might be achieved in practice. It would appear that children want to be involved in decision-making processes about their education. They feel a sense of community in their schools and want to be actively engaged in transformative measures. The way forward is effective listening cultures that build into meaningful participation and empower child voice. We need 'the broadest and most inclusive constructions of meanings applied to the child's voice and its potential spheres of influence' (Hart 2002: 252). I would argue that a particularly powerful expression of child voice is evidence-based perspectives facilitated through child-led empirical research as illustrated by some of the cameos in this chapter.

Questions to Promote Thinking

1   Where are you on the listening → consulting → participation agenda?
2   What do you consider are the barriers and challenges to initiating children-as-researcher projects in primary schools?
3   Is there a danger that increased child voice, while reducing some of the adult–child power dynamics, may increase child–child power relations?

References and suggested further reading

Bragg, S. (2001) Taking a joke: learning from the voices we don't want to hear, *Forum*, 43(2): 70–3.

Clark, A. and Moss, P. (2001) *Listening to Young Children, The Mosaic Approach*. London: National Children's Bureau and Joseph Rowntree Foundation.

Clay, D. (2005) *Participation and School Councils Toolkit: Taking Part and Helping Our School*. London: School Councils UK.

Cohen, E. (2005) Neither seen nor heard: children's citizenship in contemporary democracies, *Citizenship Studies*, 9(2): 221–40.

Dandridge, H. (2008) Are girls and boys treated differently in school? Available online at: http://childrens-research-centre.open.ac.uk/ (accessed 12 October 2010).

Devine, D. (2002) Children's citizenship and the structuring of adult–child relations in the primary school, *Childhood*, 9(3): 303–20.

DCSF (Department for Children, Schools and Families) (2008) *Education and Skills Act*. London: HMSO.

DfES (Department for Education and Skills) (2003) *Every Child Matters: Change for Children in Schools*. Nottingham: DfES.

DfES (2004) *The Children Act*. London: DfES.

DfES (2006) *School Councils UK Handbook for Primary* Pupils. London: HMSO.

Fielding, M. (2001) Students as radical agents of change, *Journal of Educational Change*, 2: 123–41.

Fielding, M. (2004) Transformative approaches to student voice: theoretical underpinnings, recalcitrant realities, *British Educational Research Journal*, 30(2): 295–311.

Hart, S. (2002) Making sure the child's voice is heard, *International Review of Education*, 43(3–4): 251–8.

Hartas, D. (2008) *The Right to Childhoods*. London, Continuum.

Kellett, M. (2005) *How to Develop Children as Researchers: A Step by Step Guide to Teaching Research Process*. London: Sage.

Kellett, M. and Ward, B. (2008) Children as active researchers: participation and power sharing, in A. Moore and R. Mitchell (eds) *Power, Pedagogy and Praxis: Social Justice in the Globalized Classroom*. Rotterdam: Sense Publishers.

Kwiatkowska, G. (2009) *Personalisation and Learning Disabilities: A Review of Evidence on Advocacy and its Practice for People with Learning Disabilities and High Support Needs*. Report 24. London: Social Care Institute for Excellence (SCIE).

Leitch, R. and Mitchell, S. (2007) Caged birds and cloning machines: how student imagery 'speaks' to us about cultures of schooling and student participation, *Improving Schools*, 10(1): 53–71.

Lister, R. (2007) Inclusive citizenship: realizing the potential, *Citizenship Studies*, 11(1): 49–61.

Lodge, C. (2005) From hearing voices to engaging in dialogue: problematising student participation in school improvement, *Journal of Educational Change*, 6: 125–46.

Mencap (2007) *Don't Stick It, Stop It!* Available online at: www.mencap.org.uk.

OfSTED (Office for Standards in Education) (2005) *Guidance for Inspectors of Schools: Conducting the Inspection.* Available online at: http://www.ofsted.gov.uk (accessed 12 October 2010).

Robinson, C. and Taylor, C. (2007) Theorizing student voice: values and perspectives, *Improving Schools*, 10(1): 5–17.

Schofield, M. (2008) 11-year-olds' views on school subjects and ideal teacher qualities. Available online at: http://childrens-research-centre.open.ac.uk/ (accessed 12 October 2010).

Sinclair, R. (2004) Participation in practice: making it meaningful, effective and sustainable, ***Children and Society,*** **18(2): 106–18.**

Siraj-Blatchford, I., Clarke, K. and Needham, M. (2007) *The Team Around the Child: Multi-Agency Working in the Early Years.* Stoke-on-Trent: Trentham Books.

Smyth, J. (2006) When students have power: student engagement, student voice, and the possibilities for school reform around 'dropping out' of school, *International Journal of Leadership in Education*, 9(4): 285–98.

Thomas, N. and O'Kane, C. (1999) Discovering what children think: connections between research and practice, *British Journal of Social Work*, 30(6): 819–35.

United Nations (1989) ***Convention on the Rights of the Child.*** **Geneva: United Nations. Available online at: http://www.un.org/documents/ga/res/44/a44r025. htm (accessed 4 February 2011).**

United Nations General Assembly (2002) *A World Fit for Children.* Geneva: United Nations.

Waller, T. (2006) 'Don't come too close to my octopus tree': recording and evaluating young children's perspectives of outdoor learning, *Children, Youth and Environments*, 16(2): 75–104.

Wooller, D. (2005) Does how much you enjoy a subject affect how good you are at it? Available online at: http://childrens-research-centre.open.ac.uk/ (accessed 12 October 2010).

Wyness, M. (2006) Children, young people and civic participation: regulation and local diversity, *Educational Review*, 58(2): 209–18.

Wyness, M., Harrison, L. and Buchanan, I. (2004) Childhood, politics and ambiguity: towards an agenda for children's political inclusion, *Sociology*, 38(1): 81–99.

19

DEBORAH ALBON
Promoting children's health and well-being in primary schools

Summary

There are many professionals whose *raison d'être* is concerned with children's health – so much so that it would be easy to assume that the health of children is *their* job and not the role of the teacher. This chapter aims to challenge this view and will argue that teachers have a *crucial* role to play in promoting children's health, something which is also reflected in the TDA and EYPS standards. In doing this, the chapter will emphasize a positive conception of health and will consider some practical suggestions for promoting health in the Foundation Stage, Key Stage 1 and Key Stage 2 classrooms in England with a focus on the area of childhood obesity.

Introduction: What do we mean by 'health' and 'health promotion'?

When asked to define 'health', a negative definition would be one that emphasizes an *absence* of illness or disease. However, on further reflection, it is possible to see that the notion of 'health' is far more nebulous and open to multiple interpretations (Tones and Tilford 2001) owing to differences in people's cultural, economic and social situations as well as different perceptions of 'health' throughout the life course (Ewles and Simnett 1999). Further consideration therefore suggests that the concept of health means far *more* than mere absence of disease. A *positive* definition of health, then, is one that refers to a state of well-being.

This positive conception of health can be seen in the World Health Organization (WHO) definition of health:

> The extent to which an individual or group is able, on the one hand, to realise aspirations and satisfy needs; and, on the other hand, to change or cope with the environment. Health is, therefore, seen as a positive resource for everyday life, not an object of living, it is a positive concept emphasising social and personal resources, as well as physical capacities.
>
> (WHO 1984, cited in Ewles and Simnett 1999: 9)

Reene Dubos developed the term 'wellness' as an important concept in relation to health and she identifies six dimensions of health (Donatelle and Davis 1996). These dimensions reflect a holistic conception of health and refer to:

- physical health
- social health
- mental health
- emotional health
- environmental health
- spiritual health

Thus, the way 'health' is defined has *expanded* and become more holistic in recent years. It is also important to view health in terms of *inclusion* as a child with a disability can be very healthy, especially if the environment is adaptive and responsive to that child's individual needs.

The idea that environmental and structural factors impact on health is an important one. Children who live in families experiencing relative poverty, for instance, are less likely to eat a healthy diet because foods high in sugars and fat are cheaper and richer in energy when compared to foods such as vegetables and fruit (Acheson 1998). In addition, families living in poverty are more likely to include a parent suffering from depression and have lower rates of breast feeding, both of which have a negative impact on the health of children (Underdown 2002). Thus, inequalities of health are significant in determining the life chances of children as they grow and develop (The Marmot Review Team 2010).

Having considered briefly a range of ways that 'health' might be defined and the impact of health inequalities, we will now consider how this relates to health promotion.

Promoting health and well-being

There are many different models or ways of understanding health promotion. Naidoo and Wills (2000), for example, argue that there are five main approaches:

- *Medical or preventative* – This approach is 'expert'-led and often about disease prevention, e.g. immunization.
- *Behaviour change* – This tends to be a 'top-down' approach with a focus on individuals changing their lifestyles, for example, government campaigns about the cessation of smoking.
- *Educational* – This approach aims at educating people to enable them to make informed choices, for example, learning about nutrition.
- *Empowerment* – The locus of control in this approach moves away from health professionals to individuals and communities, who act as advocates for change, e.g. forming a group to campaign against heavy traffic or noise pollution near a school.

- *Social change* – This approach to health promotion involves challenging the structures that impact on health, for example, poverty. As we saw earlier in this chapter, poverty has serious implications for the health of children and their families.

We will return to these models of health promotion later in the chapter when we examine a few examples of teachers working to tackle issues relating to childhood obesity. However, first, it is important to consider why *teachers* should promote children's health and well-being.

Why should *teachers* promote children's health and well-being?

An easy answer to the question posed above is that the English Teacher Development Agency (TDA) and Early Years Professional Status (EYPS) Standards say this is a requirement! This can be seen in TDA Standard C22, which states that teachers need to 'know the current legal requirements, national policies and guidance on the safeguarding and promotion of the well-being of children and young people' (DfES 2002). The guidance that goes with this Standard tells teachers that they need to ensure they are mindful of their responsibilities for the health, well-being and safety of children and young people.

With regards to the EYPS Standards (CWDC 2009), Standard 5 requires candidates to have a secure knowledge and understanding of 'the current legal requirements, national policies and guidance on health and safety, safeguarding and promoting the well being of children and their implications for early years settings.'

In addition, EYPS candidates need to demonstrate that they can lead and support others to 'establish a safe environment and employ practices that promote children's health, safety and physical, mental and emotional well-being' (Standard 19).

We can see from these two sets of standards that promoting the health and well-being of children is embedded into the professional standards for teachers and early years' practitioners with EYPS, but it is important to develop a deeper understanding of why teachers should promote the health of young children. After all, the development of standards in teaching reflects what a society believes is important for a teacher to know and be able to do at a particular point in time.

Some of you reading this chapter may think that you have enough to do teaching other curriculum subjects, notably those of literacy and numeracy, or that there are a number of health professionals who have a particular training in the area of health that positions them as being the 'proper' people to be concerned with promoting the health of children. I want to challenge this perception on four grounds:

1   The conception of health outlined in the previous section is far broader than mere absence of disease: it includes our general sense of well-being. This is a vital prerequisite for *learning* to take place. In the area of nutrition, for instance, there is evidence that a nutritious diet plays an important role in our behaviour and learning (Dani et al. 2005).

2   Teachers have pedagogical skills that can be employed effectively as health edu-
    cators. Doctors and nurses, for instance, do not receive training on how children
    learn, how to organize the classroom environment for teaching and learning, or
    how to plan and develop the curriculum.

3   Teachers see children five days a week for much of the year. As schools
    are increasingly extending their provision to include activities such as breakfast
    clubs, homework clubs, after school and holiday provision, they have far more
    direct contact with children than any health professional will ever have with
    individual children, unless the children have a complex illness or disability.
    Thus, teachers are particularly well placed to support children in making healthy
    choices as part of their daily routine; to note any signals that the child may
    be unwell or unhappy; develop supportive relationships that encourage children
    about issues that concern them; and to embed health issues into the
    curriculum.

4   Teachers should not see themselves as dislocated from the many other profes-
    sionals that work with children and families. The *Every Child Matters* agenda in
    England (DfES 2003) makes clear the need for professionals to work together
    and this is crucial in the area of children's health and well-being. Chapter 4 of
    this book looks specifically at safeguarding issues and details the key role of the
    teacher in the network of professionals who come into contact with children
    and families. However, teachers might also work with health professionals, for
    example, in developing a healthy eating project or in promoting oral health. For
    teachers working in children's centres, health professionals may well be working
    on the same site on a daily basis.

The policy frameworks that underpin the role of schools in promoting children's health

There are many policies that identify schools as having a role in promoting children's
health and these are too numerous to mention in this brief chapter. The *Every Child
Matters* agenda (DfES 2003), for instance, has 'being healthy' as one of its five key
outcomes and places a duty on childhood professionals to work together to secure
positive outcomes for children and their families. My focus in this chapter, however,
will be to outline what is meant by a 'health promoting school' and the initiative
entitled the National Healthy Schools Programme (NHSP).

Healthy Schools Schemes were first seen in Europe in 1989. Croghan (2007)
argues that a health promoting school is considered to be one in which:

- time is allocated to health-related issues in the formal curriculum through subjects
  including home economics, physical education, social education and health
  studies;
- health remains the hidden curriculum of the school including staff/pupil relationships, school/community relationships, the school environment and the quality of
  services such as school meals;

- the health and caring services visit the school, providing a health promotion role in the school through screening, prevention and child guidance. These principles remain fundamental to achieving a health-promoting school.

(2007: 5)

The introduction of the NHSP in 1999 is an expression of the view that schools should play a wider role in children's health. It is a joint initiative between the Department for Education and Skills (DfES, now the Department for Education) and the Department of Health (DoH). The NHSP is viewed as a key delivery mechanism in *The Children's Plan* (DCSF 2007) and in *Healthy Weight, Healthy Lives* (DoH 2008) and aims to deliver the following:

- improvement in health and reduced health inequalities;
- raised pupil achievement;
- more social inclusion; and
- closer working between health promotion providers and education establishments.

The NHSP website http://home.healthyschools.gov.uk/ states the following:

We want all children and young people to be healthy and achieve at school and in life. We believe that by providing opportunities at school for enhancing emotional and physical aspects of health in the longer term, this will lead to improved health, reduced health inequalities, increased social inclusion and raise achievement for all.

The NHS Standard is based on evidence that healthier children perform better academically and that education plays an important role in promoting health particularly among children who are socially and economically disadvantaged.

The NHSP contains four main themes:

1 Personal, Social, Health and Economic (PSHE) education, including sex and relationships education and drugs education.
2 Healthy eating.
3 Physical activity.
4 Emotional health and well-being (including bullying).

Although many schools have achieved National Healthy School Status, this and personal, social and health education (PSHE) are not statutory. It is a pity that, at the time of writing this chapter, the clause to introduce PSHE education as a *statutory* subject in the National Curriculum in primary schools was removed during negotiations in the Children, Schools and Families Bill. Nevertheless non-statutory guidance does exist. Many primary schools are likely to have a designated PHSE coordinator and, as this chapter has shown, the professional standards for teachers and EYPs demonstrates that promoting the health and well-being of children is an integral part of their role.

How can teachers promote children's health and well-being in the primary school?

In thinking about the National Healthy Schools Programme we can see that a wide range of activities might come within its remit. Some of these might involve specific teaching (for example, teaching about a healthy diet; the importance of exercise or drugs education), other activities may be more linked to the hidden curriculum, such as the routines of meal times, snack times, playground times (such as physical activity, self-care in the sun, or safety on equipment), arrangements for personal hygiene and toileting, and so on. As the area is so vast, I aim in this final section to look at the role teachers can play in helping to combat childhood obesity as this is an area of national concern at the current time (Aylott et al. 2008; HPA 2009). I have chosen this area as it encompasses many aspects of the NHSP because it can involve PSHE education, healthy eating, physical activity as well as emotional health and well-being. In reflecting briefly on what is a huge and complex issue, I aim to show how teachers in the Foundation Stage and Key Stages 1 and 2 can develop their work to help to address this issue.

Before considering some short cameos of people working in these three stages, it is important to gain an understanding of obesity and some of the factors that are linked to it. Although obesity refers to being well above the weight expected for one's height and (for adults especially) having a body mass index (BMI) of over 30, precise ways of measuring obesity in children are difficult as they are still growing (Albon and Mukherji 2008). Waist measurement is also an indicator of the prevalence of obesity and it has been shown that waist measurements have been steadily increasing over time (Aylott et al. 2008). The prevalence of obesity in the UK is increasing and has been described as an 'epidemic' (Aylott et al. 2008). In 2004, about a third of boys (32.6 per cent) and girls (34.1 per cent) aged between 2 and 15 years in England were either overweight or obese. Furthermore, the rate of obesity is increasing across countries in the UK (HPA 2009).

The Marmot Review (The Marmot Review Team 2010) has, as one of its six key policy objectives that are aimed at reducing health inequalities, the need to ensure that each child has the best possible start in life. There is a strong correlation between poverty in the minority (or 'developed') world and obesity, which is further evidence of inequalities of health. The Marmot Review also stresses the need to tackle obesity at all stages of life because of the negative impact it can have on health.

The BMA Board of Science (2005) reports a number of health risks that are associated with inactivity and obesity in children. These include the development of metabolic syndrome in later childhood and adulthood, which relates to a cluster of conditions implicated in cardiovascular disease such as high cholesterol and high blood pressure. Obesity is also a key factor in the later development of coronary heart disease and type 2 diabetes. There is also evidence to suggest that obese children are at greater risk of discrimination and suffer psychological difficulties in childhood and later life (Viner and Cole 2005).

Obesity in children and adults is a significant financial burden to the National Health Service (HCPAC 2007) and *prevention* and *early intervention* are crucial as opposed to dealing with the consequences of obesity (Albon and Mukherji 2008).

Many different agencies need to be involved in any strategy to prevent obesity and these would include the Department for Education, the Department of Health, as well as Departments of Transport and Culture, Media and Sport. Voluntary sector organizations, local government, individual schools and early childhood provision also play a vital role. Tackling obesity, after all, involves both increasing physical activity through sport and in our daily lives as well as developing attitudes to eating that are healthful – it is a complex issue (Aylott et al. 2008).

What follows now are some cameos that show how teachers in the Foundation Stage and Key Stages 1 and 2 can develop their work in ways that are supportive of tackling childhood obesity.

Cameo 1

Sharon works as a teacher in a children's centre attached to a primary school (in the 3–5s' room). She has noticed that a number of the children in the Centre are already overweight and a number of parents have expressed the difficulty they face at home in encouraging children to eat fruit and vegetables as opposed to sweets and crisps. Sharon wants to encourage the children to eat a healthy diet and to work with parents in order to promote this.

The success of health promotion activities has been linked to the effectiveness of partnerships fostered between parents and practitioners (Mooney et al. 2008). Alongside this, increasingly early childhood practitioners (including teachers) are encouraged to listen to children's perspectives in order to develop a health promoting curriculum (Albon and Mukherji 2008). Sharon kept this in mind in developing the curriculum to promote healthy eating. Here are some of the activities Sharon decided to employ:

- growing vegetables in the garden (with parents, practitioners and children tending the plot) and using the food in cookery activities;
- developing a positive attitude to healthy food options such as making fruit smoothies; fruit kebabs; or dips to use with raw vegetables and offering these at snack times or at the beginnings and ends of meals;
- making a healthy recipe book with ideas shared between children, their families and the Children's Centre;
- eliciting children's and parents' perspectives on healthy food ideas for the Children's Centre menu, for example, having taster sessions and encouraging feedback;
- setting up a role play area as a shop selling healthy produce;
- including a range of stories with healthy food-related themes.

Cameo 2

Furqan works in a Year 2 classroom. He is worried that for much of the day the children seem to be inactive. Despite the efforts he puts in to his physical education planning, Furqan believes that the school could be regarded as an obesogenic (or obesity-producing) environment. This means that rather than obesity being purely the fault of individual lifestyle choices, the environment itself is an important contributing factor in the rise in obesity (Aylott et al. 2008). Here, we might think of the number of times we take a lift and not the stairs or the number of times we use a labour-saving device such as a vacuum cleaner or washing machine, which decades ago would have involved physical effort. Furqan is considering ways in which his school and, more specifically, his teaching can encourage children to be more active.

Furqan's concern over the obesogenic environment is one that is shared by many health commentators (Aylott et al. 2008). While PE is an obvious time when children can be encouraged to be physically active and can facilitate discussion about this, for the majority of the time, the children in Furqan's class are physically inactive. They might be sitting still in assembly, in whole class teaching sessions, or when engaged in small group or individual work. Many children travel to school by car and some do not take part in physical activity during break times, preferring to sit and talk with their peers.

Furqan decides that he will review his teaching in order to make it more active. He decides to take the curriculum outdoors and introduce sessions with a more physically active element. Here are two examples:

- In mathematics: using skittles and tallying on a chalk board to develop further the children's understanding of number bonds (10 skittles – how many are standing? How many have fallen?)
- In science: using movement to develop an understanding of how the solar system works (for example, children moving to represent the planets revolving round the sun at the various distances apart).

However, Furqan wants to take this work further. He encourages the school to develop a walking-to-school initiative and encourages the children across the primary school to talk to him about what they like and dislike about playground times and what they would like to see that would encourage greater physical activity. He also elicits the children's views about the local playground space beyond the school, as he rarely sees children playing there when he leaves the school to go home. The children tell him that much of the playground equipment is broken; there are dogs roaming and defecating in the play space; and the equipment that is not broken lacks challenge unless you are a small toddler. He encourages the children to write their comments in letters to the local council to lobby for improvements.

We can see from this that Furqan has gone beyond an 'educational' model of health promotion (as noted earlier in the chapter, using the model developed by Naidoo and Wills 2000) to one of *empowerment*, because the children are encouraged to campaign for improvements that could make a real difference to their health and the health of others. In eliciting children's perspectives, Furqan is also acknowledging children as having a unique knowledge about their lives *as lived now* (Kjorholt 2005).

Cameo 3

Tina works in a Year 5 classroom. She has noticed that the children are becoming increasingly aware of their own body shapes and have begun to tease each other about differences in weight and appearance. Tina wants to encourage the children to think about feelings associated with teasing and about body size more generally. As noted earlier, childhood obesity has been linked to increased prevalence of discrimination (Viner and Cole 2005) and this has implications for the mental well-being of children as well as their physical health.

Tina decides to put into practice some of the ideas suggested by Robinson (2006), who provides some interesting suggestions for lesson planning to support children's understanding of healthy eating at KS2. Robinson emphasizes the need for lesson planning to contribute towards the social, emotional and behavioural skills identified in the NHS Standard, such as solving problems alone and with others and understanding and valuing the differences between people. She suggests that teachers and health educators plan specific sessions to tackle issues such as the one above and we should remember that children from a very early age have constructed their own understandings about body shape and size (Dixey et al. 2001; Ludvigsen and Sharma 2004).

Robinson (2006) suggests that teachers encourage children to adopt a problem-solving approach to a particular dilemma story, such as the following:

Jane and her family have moved to a new house and today is Jane's first day at her new school. *How do you think Jane is feeling?* After lunch three children come over to Jane and tease her about the way she looks – her weight and her size. *How do you think Jane is feeling?* When the children are teasing Jane, *how do they feel?* Mehvish is with some friends on the other side of the playground. Mehvish sees Jane standing alone, looking down at her feet – upset. *What might Mehvish be thinking?* Mehvish comes over to Jane and wonders who she is and why she has joined the school. *What could Mehvish say to or ask Jane?* They exchange information about each other. *How do you think Jane is feeling now?* The three children who had initially teased Jane are still sniggering and pointing at her. *What might Mehvish and Jane say to these children? How might Jane feel now?*

(adapted from Robinson 2006: 172–3)

Tina encouraged the children to problem solve at various points in the story and later, to work in groups to develop the story into a play. In doing this, she hoped the children would develop some empathy with the various characters in the story. Children were also encouraged to think about the range of body shapes and sizes that could be regarded as 'healthy' and to reflect on the way the body shape and size of men and women are portrayed in the media.

Conclusion

This chapter has argued for a positive conception of health and asserts that teachers have a vital role to play in health promotion – the cameos reflecting issues relating to childhood obesity. Some of the policy initiatives in the area of promoting children's health and well-being in the primary school have been outlined and there is nothing to suggest that the pace and development of such initiatives will subside. Therefore, I will conclude by suggesting two further areas that I believe are crucial for any teacher: the need to keep up to date with policy developments and new writing on the subject; and second, the need to maintain a critical voice. In the models of health promotion discussed earlier in the chapter (Naidoo and Wills 2000), I noted how promoting health can also mean acting as *advocates for change*. Thus, another crucial role teachers can play in promoting the health of children is to lobby local and national governments on matters that affect children's health and well-being.

Questions to Promote Thinking

1. Consider the past week in your setting. What have you done (it may be a small interaction or a larger project) that has promoted the health of a child or group of children? What opportunities were missed and why? How can you ensure that promoting the health of children permeates your daily practice rather than being regarded as a one-off topic?
2. Explore the issue of childhood obesity further. Is your school involved in any initiatives in order to address this issue? In what way(s) is it involved?
3. To what extent do you see the role of the teacher as extending *beyond* the classroom? Some of the ideas contained in this chapter encourage you to think about your role as an *advocate* for change as many of the factors that impact on the health of children (and indeed adults) relate to wider structural issues such as poverty.

Useful websites

http://home.healthyschools.gov.uk/ A useful website to find out more about the National Healthy Schools Programme.
http://www.pshe-association.org.uk/ A useful website for those of you wishing to find out more about PSHE education.

References and suggested further reading

Acheson, D. (1998) *Independent Inquiry into Inequalities in Health Report*. London: HMSO.

Albon, D. and Mukherji, P. (2008) *Food and Health in Early Childhood*. London: Sage.

Aylott, J., Brown, I., Copeland, R. and Johnson, D. (2008) *Tackling Obesities: The Foresight Report and Implications for Local Government*. Sheffield: Sheffield Hallam University.

BMA (British Medical Association) Board of Science (2005) *Preventing Childhood Obesity*. London: BMA Publications.

CWDC (Children's Workforce Development Council) (2009) *Early Years Professional Status Handbook for Candidates (Annex)*. Leeds: CWDC.

Croghan, E. (2007) *Promoting Health in Schools: A Practical Guide for Teachers and School Nurses Working with Children Aged 3 to 11*. London: Sage.

Dani, J., Burrill, C. and Demming-Adams, B. (2005) The remarkable role of nutrition in learning and behaviour, *Nutrition and Food Science*, 35(4): 258–63.

DCSF (Department of Children, Schools and Families) (2007) *The Children's Plan: Building Brighter Futures*. Norwich: The Stationery Office.

DfES (Department for Education and Skills) (2002) *Qualifying to Teach: Professional Standards for Qualified Teacher Status and Requirements for Initial Teacher Training*. London: TDA.

DfES (2003) *Every Child Matters, Green Paper*. Nottingham: DfES.

Dixey, R., Sahota, P., Atwal, S. and Turner, A. (2001) 'Ha ha, you're fat, we're strong'; a qualitative study of boys' and girls' perceptions of fatness, thinness, social pressures and health using focus groups, *Health Education*, 101(4): 206–16.

DoH (Department of Health) (2008) *Healthy Weight, Healthy Lives: A Cross-Government Strategy for England*. London: DoH Publications.

Donatelle, R.J. and Davis, L. (1996) *Health: The Basics*, 4th edn. New York: Allyn Bacon.

Ewles, L. and Simnett, I. (1999) *Promoting Health: A Practical Guide*. London: Bailliere Tindall.

HCPAC (House of Commons Public Accounts Committee) (2007) *Tackling Child Obesity: First Steps*. London: The Stationery Office.

HPA (Health Protection Agency) (2009) *A Children's Environment and Health Strategy for the UK*. Didcot: HPA.

Kjorholt, A.T. (2005) The competent child and the right to be oneself: reflections on children as fellow citizens in an early childhood centre, in A. Clark, A.T. Kjorholt and P. Moss (eds) *Beyond Listening: Children's Perspectives on Early Childhood Services*. Bristol: Policy Press.

Ludvigsen, A. and Sharma, N. (2004) *Burger Boy and Sporty Girl: Children and Young People's Attitudes Towards Food in School*. Ilford: Barnados.

Mooney, A., Boddy, J., Statham, J. and Warwick, I. (2008) Approaches to developing health in early childhood settings, *Health Education*, 108(2): 163–77.

Naidoo, J. and Wills, J. (2000) *Health Promotion: Foundations for Practice*, 2nd edn. London: Bailliere Tindall.

Robinson, S. (2006) *Healthy Eating in Primary Schools*. London: Sage.

The Marmot Review Team (2010) *Fair Society: Healthy Lives*. Available online at: http://www.marmotreview.org/ (accessed 13 January 2011).

Tones, K. and Tilford, S. (2001) *Health Promotion: Effectiveness, Efficiency and Equity*. Cheltenham: Nelson Thornes.

Underdown, A. (2002) Health inequalities in early childhood, in C. Cable, L. Miller and G. Goodliff (eds) *Working with Children in the Early Years*, 2nd edn. Abingdon: Routledge.

Viner, R. and Cole, T. (2005) Adult socioeconomic, educational, social and psychological outcomes of childhood obesity: a national birth cohort study, *British Medical Journal*. Available online at: www.bmj.com/cgi/content/abridged/330/7504/1354 (accessed 25 July 2007).

PART 5

Working together

20

MARY SCANLAN
Reaching out: fostering partnership with parents[1]

Summary

This chapter explores the history of home–school partnership. It examines expectations and challenges for practitioners. It discusses work carried out by the Home–School Knowledge Exchange[2] (HSKE) project, which aimed to support teachers and parents to exchange the information they have about children's learning. Activities were designed which helped information to flow from the school to the home and vice versa. The chapter ends by proposing a different theorization of partnership, a conceptualization in which the child plays the key role.

Cameo 1

Vicki teaches in a small village primary nursery school which has an affluent catchment area. In most cases both parents work and the majority of the children attend for whole day sessions. Parents regularly attend parents evenings and are very keen to support their children's education. However, because parents are very busy, it can be difficult to find opportunities to communicate and discover what they would like to know about supporting their child's learning.

Cameo 2

Mark teaches a Year 1 class in a busy inner city primary school. The school catchment includes a centre for refugees and asylum seekers. Mark is on friendly terms with the parents he sees but many children are brought to school by friends, neighbours and childminders. School events such as curriculum evenings are very poorly attended.

> **Cameo 3**
>
> Megan is a NQT who has just started teaching a Year 4 class in a suburban setting. She is new to the area and is still getting to know the staff and children in her school. She would like to find out about the home lives of the children and also ensure that parents know they are welcome to come into school and support children in the classroom.

Introduction

The need for settings and parents to work together has been acknowledged for some time. The Plowden Report (CACE 1967) emphasized the key role that parents played in their child's learning, and policy of the last Labour government continued to highlight that importance. *Every Child Matters* (DfES 2003: 39) stated: 'Parenting has a strong impact on a child's educational development, behaviour and mental health.' Later policy stressed the need both to ensure better communication between home and school and also to create opportunities to involve parents, particularly fathers (DfES 2007).

Professionals working with children need to demonstrate that they can meet certain Standards, many of which are concerned with parental involvement. For example practitioners wishing to gain Early Years Professional Status must demonstrate through their practice that they meet and that they can lead and support others to do the following:

S29: Recognise and respect the influential and enduring contribution that families and parents/carers can make to children's development, well-being and learning.

S30: Establish fair, respectful, trusting and constructive relationships with families and parents/carers, and communicate sensitively and effectively with them.

S31: Work in partnership with families and parents/carers, at home and in the setting, to nurture children, to help them develop and to improve outcomes for them.

S32: Provide formal and informal opportunities through which information about children's well-being, development and learning can be shared between the setting and families and parents/carers.

(CWDC 2010)

The current *Standards for Teachers* (TDA 2007) also acknowledge that working with parents is an important area. Teachers are expected to do the following:

Q.4. Communicate effectively with children, young people, colleagues, parents and carers.

Q.5. Recognise and respect the contribution that colleagues, parents and carers can make to the development and well-being of children and young people, and to raising their levels of attainment.

Q.6. Have a commitment to collaboration and co-operative working.

Q.24. Plan homework or other out-of-class work to sustain learners' progress and to extend and consolidate their learning.

There have been many theorizations of parental partnership. Pugh and De'Ath (1989) studied 130 early years settings and developed a framework which identified different dimensions of involvement (Table 20.1). Epstein (1995), in the United States, identified six areas within home school partnership where opportunities exist for collaboration. These were: parenting, communicating, volunteering, learning at home, decision-making and collaborating with the community. Epstein acknowledged that there were challenges in each area. In the area of communication, for example, challenges might include: considering the needs of parents who do not speak English, reviewing the quality of communications and establishing two-way communication. Additionally analysing the impact of home–school partnership can be problematic. Desforges and Abouchaar (2003) carried out a wide-ranging review of the literature on the effect of parental involvement on children's achievement. They looked at two aspects of involvement: spontaneous paternal interactions and planned interventions (e.g. by schools). They found that the former supported the child indirectly, through factors such as having high expectations, but acknowledged that factors such as socio-economic status and confidence impacted on this interaction. They also stated that it was impossible to draw any firm conclusions regarding the literature on planned interventions due to methodological weaknesses in research designs.

Docking (1990) highlighted the fact that some practitioners also have concerns about their work with parents and identified five areas where problems might arise (see Figure 20.1) Other commentators such as Dyson and Robson (1999) have questioned whether some initiatives have overlooked or undermined family practice,

Table 20.1 Dimensions of parental involvement

Type of involvement	Characteristics
Non-participation	Parents not involved in children's learning.
(a) Active	(a) Actively decide not to participate.
(b) Passive	(b) Factors prevent involvement – lack of confidence, etc.
Support	Parents support the setting (but only when invited to do so and from outside the setting).
Participation	Parents involved within the setting.
(a) As helpers	(a) Helping in the setting, hearing readers, etc.
(b) As learners	(b) Attending family literacy classes, etc.
Partnership	Demonstrated by shared values and mutual respect.
Control	Parents make decisions and determine practice.

Source: Pugh and De'Ath (1989)

Ideological *Traditions about professional boundaries*	
Psychological *Feeling threatened by having one's practice scrutinized*	
Political *Lack of resources and personnel*	
Professional *Lack of training in working with parents*	

Figure 20.1 Partnership: possible problematic areas for practitioners

imposing school-based values on communities and thus further marginalizing some families. There has also been some criticism regarding the phrase *'hard to reach'* as this perhaps promotes a deficit view of families. An alternative credit model is proposed which suggests that parental participation might be increased if societal barriers are removed. This model questions whether schools might be termed as 'hard to reach' settings, and if so, what they might do to remedy this.

Most commentators who write about this area for practitioners stress the importance of communication (Dunhill et al. 2009). The following discussion draws on work carried out by the Home–School Knowledge Exchange (Hughes et al. 2004) project which explored the knowledge parents and teachers have of children's learning and how this knowledge might be shared and built on both at home and school. A key theme of the work was the issue of *directionality* in home school communication.

Finding out what parents want to know – making DVDs

One of the starting points of the HSKE project (Feiler et al. 2007) was finding out what information parents and teachers wanted to share regarding children's literacy learning in Key Stage 1. Both parties identified the working of the literacy hour and in particular reading as a joint concern. Therefore one of the first activities was making a DVD which focused on this area and which included: the whole class sharing of the 'Big Book', group work, a guided reading session, a child receiving individual support with their reading and the plenary session. Every DVD was accompanied by a booklet which gave parents information on strategies to support and extend their children's reading in the home, for example, 'When your child brings home a new reading book, talk about the pictures together, before he/she reads it for the first time.'

Personalized DVDs have many advantages. Schools can choose the content to reflect the needs of parents and/or their own priorities. They can be an opportunity for parents, who for a variety of reasons cannot visit during the school day, to see everyday classroom life. Schools might target parents who cannot attend setting-based events such as curriculum evenings. However, the content needs to be carefully planned by the teacher for example ensuring that every child appears. Practical issues need to be addressed such as who will do the filming – use might be made of adult help in the classroom or older children in the school. Permission needs to be gained from all participants and parents need to be informed about plans for the finished DVD. It can also be useful to provide an opportunity for parents and teachers to watch the finished version together, so that parents can ask questions. Schools might arrange screenings at different times, in order that parents who worked might attend. Refreshments can be offered to help create a welcoming atmosphere.

The responses to the project DVDs were positive. Parents commented that they felt more able to support their child's learning, for example, after watching one which focused on reading, a parent commented, 'I learnt a lot from that, because I never used to read a story first, I'd just open the book and start to read it . . . but if you've read the book and you look through the pictures and you explain the story, by the time you get to read it then you're more into it, aren't you?'

Another common parental response was appreciation of having a record of their child's time in the classroom and this was especially true for parents who for various reasons did not go into school, 'It's always good to see how it works in the classroom, because that's not an opportunity you'd normally have, is it, unless you were a helper.'

Response to Cameo 1

Vicki might find it useful to send home a short questionnaire to find out what the parents of the children in her nursery would like to know about how to support their child's learning. She might then consider ways of communicating with them and sharing practice perhaps by making a DVD or producing other materials, such as booklets, which could be used at home to support areas identified by parents.

Reaching out to all parents – the supermarket display

As has been seen from evaluations of national initiatives such as Sure Start (National Audit Office 2010), there can be challenges in meeting the needs of *all* parents and carers. Some parents do choose to be active non-participants in home–school partnership and this decision needs to be respected. However, if participation is universally low, schools might usefully question whether they themselves might be labelled as a 'hard to reach setting'.

In many schools the sharing and celebration of children's achievements (parents' evenings, class assemblies, etc.) are carried out in the setting. There are normally practical reasons for this, e.g. familiarity for parents, children and teachers. Frequently these meetings happen at times which are decided by, and convenient to, the school. However, for some parents these settings and times are far from suitable. In many families both parents work, many in jobs with very little access to flexible hours. For some parents, their own experience of school can make return visits problematic. For them, school is not seen as a 'neutral' space, but as somewhere that can evoke very powerful memories and feelings. Additionally changes in society mean that many children are now cared for by nannies, childminders and family members. Many of these important figures in a child's life remain unacknowledged by some schools and while many might not welcome formal partnership, some might appreciate the chance to informally partake on an ad hoc basis.

So it might be helpful to consider other locations where this sharing might take place. Some schools have obvious alternatives such as community centres. For others, it is more difficult, and care has to be taken that any chosen venue is suitable for all parents (which might, for instance, rule out pubs and clubs). The project set up a display, to share the work that had been done at school, in a local supermarket. This was designed as a casual 'drop in' event, accessible both to parents who would not necessarily feel comfortable coming into school and those whose lifestyles precluded attendance at school-based events. To attract as wide an audience as possible, it was open from before school started until late in the evening. The supermarket was chosen to host the event because it was opposite the school and many parents used the car park when picking up and dropping off children. The display itself contained books that children had written with parents (see below) and the DVD and booklets of the class literary hour. Individual and class photographs of the children working on the activities were also shown together with some of the written work produced.

The atmosphere was very different to a more conventional 'school-based' event, as there were no set attendance times and indeed no pressure or obligation to be present. Refreshments were offered to parents and children and the event was open to friends, the wider family and community. Children were invited orally at school and parents received a written invitation with the teacher issuing invitations personally whenever this was possible. In the past this school had struggled with parental engagement and school-based events such as curriculum workshops had attracted less than 20 per cent of parents. However, attendance at the supermarket event was impressive

Figure 20.2 Parents at the supermarket display

with over 60 per cent of the parents visiting. Many came on more than one occasion and brought along friends and relations, and it was noteworthy that many fathers attended (see Figure 20.2). It was clear that this activity was accessible in a way that perhaps more conventional school-based activities might not be. For example, one parent, who had English as an additional language, heard about the display through her extended family and visited on three separate occasions. Parents and children were pleased that the children's work was being displayed to a wider audience, 'I think he was quite proud of seeing his like work displayed, because there was a picture of the Bagpuss he'd drawn . . . I think it gives them a sense of pride in their work doesn't it?'

The teacher taking part in these activities highlighted the fact her participation had supported her professional development. She had built up a portfolio of the ideas generated and the resources used and had gained confidence in her work with parents.

Response to Cameo 2

Perhaps Mark might offer to meet parents at the centre for refugees and asylum seekers rather than expecting them to come into school for parents evenings and curriculum events. Parents might feel more comfortable in this setting particularly if they have family and friends to support them. He might also ask the local authority to provide translators to help those parents who have EAL.

Finding out about the children you teach

Disposable cameras and shoeboxes

If we reflect on the nature of the partnership discussed so far, it might be seen as rather one-sided with the school still the dominant partner and the information flow remaining in the conventional school to home direction. To achieve true partnership (Pugh and De'Ath 1989) activities needed to be more equitable and encourage the flow of knowledge from the home to the school at the same time as the more conventional school to home direction. In her work, Moss (2001) used cameras to capture literacy learning in the home because photographs provide immediacy and a level of detail which young children might find hard to record in other ways. They are an excellent means of conveying the intimacy of the home in the school setting.

Children in the project were given a disposable camera and were asked to use it over a school holiday. It was felt that this gave them more opportunities to take photographs than during a normal school week. The activity supported the curriculum as children were asked to take photographs that linked to forthcoming topics, e.g. the local area and living things, as well as things/places/people that were important to them. When the photographs were developed, parents and children were given an opportunity to look through them and remove any that they did not wish to be in the public domain. They were then used in a variety of ways to promote writing. One school sent the photographs home together with brightly coloured card and parents and children were asked to write about what was happening in the photographs. These were then used to make an eye-catching display in the school corridor (see Figure 20.3). A second activity involved inviting parents into the classroom to take part in a writing workshop using the photographs to make books with their child. This activity was designed to allow parents (who held most information about the photographs) to feel that they, not the teacher, could most fully support their child's learning even though the activity was carried out in the context of the school. Children responded positively to the presence of their parents in the classroom, one child noting his father's support had been 'Fun . . . he helped me. He reminded me what I could write and what things were and when they were.'

Teachers noted the enthusiastic response of the children, who had particularly enjoyed having their own cameras and had been excited to get their photographs back. A teacher who had linked the activity into a topic on *living things* commented

Figure 20.3 Writing carried out at home

that it was a wonderful way to start a project. Similarly the school which had focused on *the local area* was amazed by the depth of knowledge displayed by the parents. Another teacher commented that an outcome of the whole process had been 'a better bond with the parents; they treat me more as a friend than a teacher'.

However, in asking children to reveal their out-of-school lives in this manner, practitioners need to be sensitive in ensuring that the information brought in is respected. They also need to accept that some families will choose not to participate. Additionally it is important to recognize that some parents might feel a sense of unease at being invited into the classroom to help with writing and alternative activities might be more successful, for example, those based on other curriculum areas such as art (for example, making photograph frames).

True partnership – shoeboxes

In the following section the activities are described which encouraged the exchange of knowledge in a more innovative direction – from the home to the school. In their research on motivating literacy learning in a nursery Marsh and Thompson (2001) constructed media boxes (with the help of parents) containing examples of popular culture, such as *Bob the Builder*.

Building on this idea, the project used shoeboxes as a summer holiday activity designed to help children introduce themselves to their new teacher. Pupils took home boxes accompanied by a letter which asked parents to encourage their child to fill it with artefacts such as photos, toys, postcards, books or magazines, writing and anything else which was special to them. Importantly the class teacher also took part in the activity by filling her own box over the summer, giving the children information about her 'out-of-school life'. She put in a tennis racket key ring (she played tennis), a pair of chopsticks (she loved Chinese food), and other personal items. As well as this sharing of personal information, the boxes were then used in the curriculum. The teacher planned the week's literacy work around them using the contents of her box to model activities (Greenhough et al. 2005). A previous summer literacy activity at this school had been to keep a scrapbook of holiday events and while the response rate for this had not been very high (20 per cent), the shoebox activity had been far more successful in terms of engagement (90 per cent) (see Figure 20.4).

In a second school, the boxes were used when the class teacher went on maternity leave and the children filled boxes for her replacement. The contents of the boxes did

---

Response to Cameo 3

Megan might plan activities which allow children to share aspects of their home lives in the classroom, for example, a project on favourite toys. She could also consider how artefacts from homes might be used in the curriculum (e.g. using family photographs for history). She might also invite parents in to school to support children's learning in subjects they are knowledgeable about, e.g. the local area.

Figure 20.4 The contents of a holiday shoebox

differ on this occasion, as in many cases the children put in important personal items such as baby clothes and photographs of grandparents. Parents responded positively to the use of shoeboxes citing the enjoyment the children had experienced, 'That was really good fun . . . and it was really nice for Mrs K. because it gave her a chance to get to know the children a bit better.' Children also liked being able to let the teachers know about their interests – 'She learned what cartoons I liked.'

Marsh (2003) has questioned the extent to which early years settings impose their own literacy practices on the home without acknowledging family practice in the setting, a process she terms 'one-way traffic'. With this in mind, one school decided to use the shoebox idea both to allow parents access to the curriculum and to promote creative writing. The children took shoeboxes home over the Christmas holidays, accompanied by a letter which explained,

> We are interested in finding out more about what motivates children to write, and also to produce high quality written pieces. The idea of the shoebox is for each child to be able to use it to collect items they think would be a good and motivational stimulus for writing.

Parents were asked to talk to their child about what they had chosen to put in. Back at school, children took it in turns to present their contents to the class, explaining both why they had chosen the artefacts and how they planned to use them in their writing. Then they worked independently or collaboratively to produce texts. When the writing was complete, the work was word-processed and spiral bound. The finished books went home together with a letter for parents, jointly composed by the teacher and children. This explained the sort of writing that had been inspired by the boxes and thanked parents for their support. Children found the activity motivating: one child commented that he had put in his box, 'Pictures and models, things that help me in my writing'.

For other children the activity promoted self-esteem, as they had an area of interest or expertise that could be shared with the whole class. The teacher acknowledged her surprise at one child, 'because he's not one who does often contribute to [the class discussions] . . . when he had things to talk about that he cared passionately about . . . he did a very good presentation'.

The class teacher stated that the activity had been highly enjoyable and that the class had been motivated and engaged. She also commented that the contents of the shoebox had provided 'a literacy breakthrough' for some children. These breakthroughs were in areas such as length of composition, organization of writing and motivation and inspiration. Interestingly parents seemed to have had a clear understanding regarding their involvement in the activity. One parent later recalled 'They came home with a box with the intention of putting anything interesting in it that might stimulate some creative writing . . . which I thought was a great idea actually.'

Although the focus of the research described above was literacy in KS1, all the activities described can be adapted to use across different age ranges and in other subject areas such as mathematics in KS2 (Winter et al. 2009).

Conclusion

It is perhaps time to review the historical conceptualization of parental partnership (e.g. Pugh and De'Ath 1989) and propose an alternative conceptualization which stresses the importance of the child. MacLeod (2004) conceptualized the idea of the agency of the child to describe the part the child can play in the research process. In this model: 'children themselves bring the social, cultural and linguistic worlds of their homes and communities into the classroom' (2004: 248). Activities such as those described above allowed children agency to present aspects of their out-of-school identities in the classroom and led to motivation and engagement (Scanlan 2010). Child engagement can perhaps be seen as the key to successful home school work, as Edwards and Alldred note, 'Children and young people could be just as active in discouraging, evading and obstructing their parents' involvement as they could in its promotion' (2000: 445).

In this new theorization of home–school partnership, rather than the conventional pairing of teacher and parent, a triad of parent–teacher–child is proposed with the child moving between the different social worlds of home and school. In this conceptualization, knowledge flows between the different settings with the child as mediator. The child, rather than the parent or teacher, is seen as the key player. They act as the conduit, through which information is passed, but their role is not merely passive as they also select and act upon this information. It must be acknowledged that while home–school partnership has benefits for practitioners and parents the main beneficiary must be the child. If this is true, then acknowledging their place in a new conceptualization of partnership can perhaps seen as essential to future home school practice.

Questions to Promote Thinking

1   How might teachers find out what information parents in their schools would like to know?
2   What kinds of information might teachers want to share with parents?
3   Why might teachers consider making a DVD of their classroom practice?
4   What means do teachers have to access the home lives of the children they teach?
5   In what ways might photographs be used?
6   What appropriate out-of-school areas (pubs, clubs, community centres and local libraries, etc.) might teachers use to share work with a wider audience?
7   In what other ways might schools recognize the vital part home plays in a child's life?
8   How can teachers acknowledge the out-of-school interests and achievements of the children they teach in the curriculum?

Notes

1   The use of the word 'parents' in this chapter includes all natural parents and any person or carer who has parental responsibility for a child.
2   The Home School Knowledge Exchange (HSKE) project was funded by the ESRC (reference number L139 25 1078).

References and suggested further reading

CACE (Central Advisory Council for Education) (1967) *Children and their Primary Schools (The Plowden Report).* London: HMSO.

CWDC (Children's Workforce and Development Council) (2010) *On the Right Track; Guidance to the Standards for the Award of Early Years Professional Status,* London, CWDC. Available online at: http://www.cwdcouncil.org.uk/assets/0000/9008/Guidance_To_Standards.pdf (accessed 1 December 2010).

Desforges, C. and Abouchaar, A. (2003) *The Impact of Parental Involvement, Parental Support and Family Education on Pupil Achievement and Adjustment: A Literature Review.* Nottingham: DfES.

DfES (Department for Education and Skills) (2003) *Every Child Matters.* London: DfES.

DfES (2007) *Every Parent Matters*. Nottingham: DfES.

Docking, J. (1990) *Primary Schools and Parents*. London: Hodder and Stoughton.

Dunhill, A., Elliott, B. and Shaw, A. (2009) *Effective Communication and Engagement with Children and Young People, their Families and Carers*. Exeter: Learning Matters.

Dyson, A. and Robson, E. (1999) *School, Family and Community: Mapping School Inclusion in the U.K.* Leicester: Youth Work Press.

Edwards, R. and Alldred, P. (2000) A typology of parental involvement in education centring on children and young people; negotiating familiarisation, institutionalisation and individualisation, *British Journal of Sociology of Education*, 21(3): 435–55.

Epstein, J. (1995) School, family, community partnerships: caring for the children we share, *Phi Delta Kappan*, 76: 710–12.

Feiler, A., Andrews, J., Greenhough, P., Hughes, M., Johnson, D., Scanlan, M. and Yee, W.C. (2007) *Linking Home and School Learning: Primary Literacy*. London: RoutledgeFalmer.

Greenhough, P., Scanlan, M., Feiler, A., Johnson, D., Yee, W.C., Andrews, J., Price, A., Smithson, M. and Hughes, M. (2005) Boxing clever: using shoeboxes to support home–school knowledge exchange, *Literacy*, 39(2): 97–103.

Hughes, M., Pollard, A., Claxton, G., Johnson, D. and Winter, J. (2004) *The Home-School Knowledge Exchange Project*. Available online at: http://www.tlrp.org/proj/pdf/Hughesposter.pdf (accessed 10 December 2010).

MacLeod, F. (2004) Literacy, identity and agency: linking classrooms to communities, *Early Child Development and Care*, 174(3): 243–52.

Marsh, J. (2003) One way traffic? Connections between literacy practices at home and in the nursery, *British Educational Research Journal*, 29(3): 369–82.

Marsh, J. and Thompson, P. (2001) Parental involvement in literacy development: using media texts, *Journal of Research in Reading*, 24(3): 266–78.

Moss, G. (2001) Seeing with the camera: analysing children's photographs of literacy in the home, *Journal of Research in Reading*, 24(3): 279–92.

National Audit Office (2010) *Sure Start Children's Centres: Memorandum for the Children, Schools and Families Committee*. London: National Audit Office.

Pugh, G. and De'Ath, E. (1989) *Working Towards Partnership in the Early Years*. London: National Children's Bureau.

Scanlan, M. (2010) Opening the box: literacy, artefacts and identity, *Literacy*, 44(1): 28–36.

TDA (Teacher Development Agency) (2007) *Professional Standards for Teachers; Why Sit Still in Your Career?* London: TDA.

Winter, J.C., Andrews, J.C., Greenhough, P.M., Hughes, R.M., Salway, L. and Yee, W.C. (2009) *Improving Primary Mathematics: Linking Home and School*. London: RoutledgeFalmer.

21

ANN BURNETT AND ALISON CLOSS
Education of children with long-term
health issues

Summary

This chapter starts by illustrating the wide range of children who have health issues in four cameos that also describe briefly the measures that schools, teachers and others implement to support full participation in education by these children. The legal position of such children in school is outlined and official guidance with which school staff should be familiar (and to which they must adhere) is identified. The importance of education, teachers and collaboration with families and other professionals for children with long-term health issues is then established. The chapter lists other measures and developments that teachers and schools will find facilitate inclusion for children with health issues. Many of these are good for *all* children. Finally it looks at the well-being of teachers and how this may be safeguarded.

Introduction

Many beginning and student teachers in early and primary education will already have encountered pupils with recognizable health issues; a child with eczema, others just returned to school after chickenpox or surgery, and some who use inhalers for asthma. They may also have noticed a sad and withdrawn child or one who has been formally diagnosed as having Attention Deficit Hyperactivity Disorder (ADHD). Perhaps some have thought about the implications of these children's conditions for their education or for their family and home life but others may hardly have registered it, believing that, although promoting positive health is part of every teacher's role (see Chapter 19), 'ill health' – whether physical or mental – is a 'problem for families and for medical personnel'. Students and teachers in special schools/centres may have had wider experience and acquired a better understanding.

Many children with health issues have special educational needs or additional support needs (SEN in England, Wales and Northern Ireland and ASN in Scotland) and/or disabilities. However, research some years ago (Bolton 1997; Closs and Norris 1997) established that they often miss being identified as having SEN/ASN. Recently this was also found to be so in relation to identification as disabled (Porter et al. 2010).

As a result, some lack the support they need, so their education suffers and their health may be at further risk. While in some cases children with health issues attend special schools/centres because their range of needs *may* be better met there, others attend special school simply because mainstream schools and centres have failed to meet needs that could have been met by good collaborative working between schools'/centres' staff, other professional services and the children's families (see also Chapter 23).

Cameo 1

Caitlin (8), oldest of four children, attends a city school in a socio-economically disadvantaged area. She is of low average ability and particularly enjoys stories and music. Her parents are unemployed and live in damp rented accommodation. Caitlin's mother has some learning difficulties and their home-life is disorganized. Caitlin has asthma and uses inhalers. She has twice had life-threatening attacks at home, once requiring resuscitation in the ambulance taking her to hospital. Caitlin's teacher gets on well with her parents although she was initially judgemental about Caitlin's clothing and cleanliness. She worries about Caitlin possibly having an acute asthma attack in school and wants to help all she can. She respects Caitlin's ability to manage her own inhalers and has told her so.

The experienced Deputy Head Teacher and the authority's local School Welfare Officer are good allies for home and school, as is the school nurse who checks Caitlin's breathing levels weekly. The entire school staff has had asthma-awareness training through the community health service (there are many inhaler-users in school). Caitlin has an annually reviewed Healthcare Plan that includes Emergency Procedures with which *all* staff are familiar and for which the Deputy Head Teacher, class teacher and a special needs assistant have further training annually. Spare inhalers are kept in a known accessible place and checked for being within date. A special access phone number can be used to activate emergency medical services. The school, school doctor, asthma clinic paediatrician and family GP have supported the family's application for priority placement on the Council Housing list.

Cameo 2

Sean (4) attends full-time nursery school during term-time and a children's centre during the holidays. He is hyperactive, unable to focus on anything for more than seconds. He clutches the same nursery toy throughout every day. His parents are drug users, living apart. Sean is on the local authority 'At Risk' register and lives with his mother; his father has limited supervised access. Sean's family is supported by the local social services. His older sister is additionally

supported by the Child and Adolescent Mental Health (CAMH) team after referral by her school for violent behaviour. Sean has sustained violent tantrums
if frustrated, hitting himself repeatedly, then sobbing in prolonged deep distress. His speech is virtually incomprehensible, he has been aggressive to other
children and to staff and needs very clear adult direction. Sean is placed in a
small group of children with a high staff ratio and a structured programme of
few activities to help him sustain his focus longer. Two members of staff have received instruction in using 'gentle restraint' to prevent Sean damaging himself or
others. There are monthly case meetings at the Social Work office, also attended
by Sean's parents, a representative of the CAMH team, the nursery's senior
teacher, the children's centre manager and the educational psychologist. All
work hard to support the parents' role but also monitor Sean's and his sister's
mental and physical well-being very closely. Recently his mother came to the
Nursery School open day for the first time and played at the sandpit with Sean
when encouraged to do so.

Cameo 3

Ashad (10) is an able boy from a privileged family, just returned after a long
absence from his leafy suburban school. His school-work is still ahead of most
peers but at times he is 'off task' and has memory lapses. His friendships are
recovering slowly. He has had chemotherapy for a recurrence of Leukaemia, four
years after the first diagnosis, and was too ill to attend school. He has lost his
hair and much weight although he also looks rather bloated. He does not talk
with classmates or his teacher about his illness experiences; this has been respected. His future is uncertain; he and his parents are fearful. His younger sister,
Amira, has become demanding at home and withdrawn in school. Although
Ashad seems glad to be back at school, he has had unexplained absences and
has asked to go home frequently, complaining of a 'sore stomach'. The school
supported Ashad during his absences by staying in touch through letters, recorded
messages and videos. His classmates took it in turns to make weekly phone
calls. His teacher visited him in hospital, with his parents' consent. Ashad replied
to messages but only spoke and wrote about non-illness matters. The school had
no previous experience of in-hospital education but responded promptly to requests for liaison, supplying Ashad's record and some textbooks to the hospital-
based teachers. His class teacher liaised with them about the class's progress in
each curricular area. The hospital teachers sent regular reports to his school and
frequently spoke with his parents during their daily visits to Ashad. When Ashad
first came home, he had a local authority home-visiting teacher who liaised with
hospital and school and provided six hours weekly of home tuition until Ashad
was fit to return to school. The hospital's Leukaemia home liaison nurse visited
school to prepare staff and pupils for Ashad's return; she calls now every second
month. She spends some individual time with Ashad's young teacher whose

mother had died of cancer and who was upset about Ashad's illness and his parents' anxiety. Ashad sees the Clinical Psychologist at the hospital for informal counselling about his hopes and fears when he returns for medical check-ups. The Head Teacher reminded all pupils at assembly about their 'Golden Rules' for ensuring that *all* pupils were made to feel included, valued and welcome, using Ashad and a returning Traveller family as illustrations. She also knew about *Contact-a-Family* and its meeting days for siblings of children with special needs and suggested tactfully to Ashad's parents that Amira might find them useful, something they were pleased to take up. The school SENCo is organizing a transition-planning meeting to ease Ashad's transition to secondary school next year.

Cameo 4

Samantha (6) attends a large village school, and was previously a cheerful child from an apparently happy family, progressing well and popular with her peers. She has a football-mad brother, David (11). Over the previous six months she had become very withdrawn, sometimes sitting on her own crying silently, neglecting her work, doing nothing in 'free choice' time. She had a nervous 'tic' at the side of her face and compulsively pulled hairs from her scalp. Samantha's experienced class teacher was initially sympathetic and encouraging but gradually became impatient. Letters home enquiring about Samantha's apparent distress brought no answer. David appeared to be behaving normally. Samantha then deliberately tore up a painting she had done for an exhibition and had several episodes of encopresis (soiling herself). Her class teacher was disgusted and suggested to Samantha that she might have to go back to Nursery School if she soiled herself again. He later overheard classmates 'teasing' Samantha about her mum running away, her dad being drunk and about being a 'dirty girl' – the teasing seemed well established. He realized that he had misjudged the situation, apologized to Samantha for not being more understanding and asked what he could do to help. This marked a turning point, leading to the long, slow recovery of Samantha's mental health in which the school staff – especially her class teacher – played a belatedly constructive role during and after her parents' divorce. The SENCo persuaded Samantha's parents to agree to a qualified child counsellor talking with Samantha about her grief and sense of loss, and ensured that Samantha knew that, although she and her feelings were unique, many children had divorced parents. David refused any help or discussion, insisting he was 'fine' although this seemed unlikely. The opportunity for counselling was left open to him. The school took its anti-bullying policies and practices more seriously, ensuring that 'teasing' was never viewed as harmless. Samantha's class teacher, at his own request, attended an in-service course on 'distressed and isolated children' and was later instrumental in setting up a support network of staff in school and external experts to work with pupils in developing a more positive ethos in the school and buddy and peer support groups.

The legal position and official guidance: education in and out of school, medication and healthcare plans in schools

There is some variation across the four countries of the UK in the legal entitlements within education of children with health issues and in the official guidance on educational matters, as Table 21.1 shows. The notes refer to the guidance itemized below Table 21.1.

The giving of medication in school is not mandatory on school staff and is a contentious issue. Responsible authorities may offer insurance indemnity to school staff who follow their guidance in giving medication or treatment to pupils. This

Table 21.1 Guidance on entitlement/right

Entitlement/right	England	Wales	Scotland	Northern Ireland
School education	Yes	Yes	Yes	Yes
Assessment for possibly having SEN/ASN	Yes	Yes	Yes	Yes
Out-of-school education (e.g. in hospital, special centre or at home)	Yes 1	Yes 5	Yes 2	Yes
Specified minimum hours of out-of-school education	Yes 1	Yes 5	Yes 2	No
Medication/medical treatment in school with Healthcare and Emergency Plans (if needed)	Yes 4	Yes 5	Yes 3	Unclear, currently under discussion
Assessment for possibly being 'disabled' (under DDA Act 2005 and Equality Act 2010)	Yes 6	Yes 6	Yes 6	No

Notes

1 DfES (2002) Access to Education for children and young people with medical needs. London: Department for Education and Science. Available at: http://publications.education.gov.uk/default.aspx?PageFunction=productdetails&PageMode=publications&ProductId=RB393&.

2 SEED (2001) *Circular No 5/200: Guidance on the Education of Children Absent from School through Ill-health.* Edinburgh: Scottish Executive Education Department. Available at: http://www.scotland.gov.uk/Resource/Doc/158331/0042883.pdf.

3 Scottish Executive (2001) *The Administration of Medicines in Schools.* Edinburgh: Scottish Executive. Available at: http://www.scotland.gov.uk/Resource/Doc/158301/0042868.pdf. (Some local authorities also issue more detailed guidance.)

4 DfES/Department of Health (2007) *Managing Medicines in Schools and Early-years Settings.* London: DfES/DoH. Available at: http://publications.education.gov.uk/default.aspx?PageFunction=productdetails&PageMode=publications&ProductId=DFES-1448-2005. (This guidance is general. All local authorities or schools *must* also produce detailed guidance in line with this national advice.)

5 Welsh Assembly Government (2010) *Guidance Circular 003/2010 Access to Education and Support for Children and Young People with Medical Needs.* Cardiff: Welsh Assembly. Available at: http://wales.gov.uk/docs/dcells/publications/100603medguideanceen.pdf.

6 XX Website for Equality Bill Code of Practice (due in December 2010).

necessitates regular training for staff volunteers, and a clear documented system for storing medication, securely but accessibly, and for recording the process. A variety of pro-formas have to be completed by parents and school. Giving medication is a natural extension of school staff's duty of care, and of teachers' *in loco parentis* role in schools. It enables children's inclusive education and makes their lives safer and more normal. Many school staff *do* volunteer and *do* develop the necessary skills, confidence and empathy – even those who previously felt very anxious or sick at the thought!

The school's doctor and/or nurse work with school staff and parents to ensure the system is practicable and safe. All collaborate to develop, monitor and review healthcare plans and, where necessary, emergency plans for any child whose health condition requires this. Increasingly now, children themselves are involved in planning; they are capable of developing responsibility for their own medication and should be encouraged in this – diabetic children as young as 5 may inject their own insulin. A child's age, ability, sense of responsibility and reliability, availability of a safe private area for giving and receiving medication and of trained school staff to supervise, will decide how schools work with their individual pupils within the guidance that applies to their country, authority and school.

These and other pro-health measures, for example, banning peanuts because a pupil has life-threatening anaphylactic responses to them, are almost always accepted by the school community – adults and children – when the reasons are presented calmly and rationally by a health professional or well-informed senior member of staff. Children are very accepting of situations that may initially make adults anxious or resistant. The authors of this chapter have seen happy busy mainstream classes where a pupil is dependent on oxygen from a portable cylinder, or a pupil fed through a stoma (a tube directly into the stomach), or a child eye-points using a word board instead of talking, or another has arms and legs bandaged because of acute eczema. Such inclusion helps all pupils grow into more tolerant and humane adults who recognize that we *all* have needs at some time in our lives.

Some children with more severe and complex health conditions may be assessed as having SEN/ASN and may meet the criteria for having a Statement of Needs (or Co-ordinated Support Plan in Scotland). They may also be assessed under the Disability Discrimination Act 1995 or the Equality Act 2010 which replaces it (Northern Ireland is not yet included in this Act). The DDA defines a person (adult or child) as disabled if he/she has 'a physical or mental impairment which has a substantial and long-term adverse effect on his/her ability to carry out normal day-to-day activities'. A Code of Practice for Schools for the Equality Act is currently out for consultation (EHRC 2011). To comply with existing duties schools and local authorities must:

- not treat disabled children and young people less favourably, without justification, for a reason which relates to their disability;
- take reasonable steps to ensure that disabled children and young people are not placed at a substantial disadvantage compared to other children and young people who are not disabled; and
- plan strategically for and make progress in:

o   improving the physical environment of schools for disabled children and young people;

o   increasing disabled children and young people's participation in the curriculum;

o   improving the ways in which written information is provided to children and young people.

Children with long-term health conditions therefore have all the educational rights that *all* children have, plus some additional rights. Schools should have the relevant guidance in their 'Official Circulars' Folder; all teachers, other key school staff and student teachers in their final training year should be familiar with them. Do ask to see the school's file of official guidance when you are on student placement or first employed.

The importance of education

Readers of the four cameos may wonder if education has any place at all in such troubled lives. Might the children not be better off in an entirely therapeutic environment with health personnel rather than teachers? However, for their parents and for the children with significant and enduring health issues, even those nearing the end of their lives, education may still be important for the *same* reasons as for other families. Academic success is still possible for some children with very serious health issues, long absences and troubled lives. Other children may take longer but still make progress through positive teacher support and a carefully planned and accessed curriculum. Education may also be important in *different* ways for children with health issues:

- School is a shared arena with their peers. Teachers – not medical and social work personnel – are the main weekday significant adults for most children, and learning is what all children do. Education is therefore some kind of 'normalization' in their 'different' lives.
- It is a source of potential friendships even if children with mental health issues and children frequently absent find friendships hard to form.
- It can be a distracting and satisfying activity in times of trouble and distress.
- It provides a structure and 'tracks' along which children progress, offering some areas of certainty while their emotional and/or physical health is uncertain or poorly.
- Having their children at school offers parents a degree of respite and normalization that enables them to be better parents and carers when children come home.

Teachers' collaboration with other professionals, parents/carers and children

Collaboration underpins education and the other social, health, familial and emotional dimensions of the lives of children with health issues and their families, as we saw in the profiles. This is not a job for a traditional '*me* and *my* class in *my* room working in *my* way' teacher (we can all recognize a little bit of this teacher in ourselves) but rather for a calm, listening, learning, sharing, flexible, empathic, organized, resourceful and imaginative person who recognizes the need for collaboration. This cannot be achieved immediately or quickly by many beginning teachers but being willing and fully committed to working *towards* that level of competence and humanity is deeply important.

Team-working allows members to support each other in compensatory and complementary ways as well as the children whose holistic development is their shared aim. Many teachers in special and early education and even some in mainstream already have a small classroom team of teacher and assistant/s. Those with pupils with additional needs will also have more visits from parents, carers, and from education, social service or health personnel intermittently making inputs, seeing the relevant children or liaising with teachers. Mutual flexibility and shared understanding of each other's work enable the necessary collaboration and liaison.

Much has already been said in Chapter 20 that is of great value to teachers about working with parents of children with health issues. Having a child with a serious health issue in the family involves extra work and worry (Eiser 1993). Little wonder that many parents are tired and stressed. The kind of issues that teachers may particularly want to discuss with parents or carers may include 'bad' behaviour, a possible new symptom, some difficulties in learning, a regression in skills . . . These are depressing for teacher and parent alike and not a good starting point for parent–teacher partnership. Skilled teachers learn to ask questions and to listen to the responses, 'How are *you*? How do you think Ron's doing? Can we share some good things that have happened? Would you like to compare our worries about Ron? You start!'

Children also have views on their own lives and want to share them but only with people who are trusted. Trust is not easy to establish with children who have difficult backgrounds or have experienced trauma, loss or abuse of any kind, leading to mental health issues. Those with physical health issues may believe that few teachers understand or empathize with their condition. Children like fairness, genuineness, a kind sense of humour and respect, but some children are not ready to like or respect anyone very much. Their world to date has not nurtured trust or respect in them, so patience, genuine care, quiet stamina and a measure of optimism laced with realism are required from their teachers. The quality of teaching and learning in classrooms owes much to the quality of relationships between teachers and pupils (Morgan and Morris 1999).

Teachers' importance and what else they can do to help

Teachers are key to the necessary activities and collaboration in the education of children with health issues. Despite this central position, some decisions may be taken by medical personnel that directly impact on classroom practice – what a child may do, and when and how he/she may do it. However, teachers probably rank second to parents or carers in terms of time spent with the child in early years and primary education. This puts them in a strong position to establish a close and constructive relationship with children with health issues – except that there are another 15, 20 or even 30 children all looking for the same commitment at the same time! This *is* hard for children and for teachers but, over time, good working and personal relationships may be achieved, although sadly not in every case as we warned above. *It is vital never to give up on any child.*

What else can teachers do?

- Be prepared to learn about the child *and* about his/her health issue/s, any related behaviours or emotions, any treatment being given and possible side-effects. Liaison with involved health professionals and family helps up-date knowledge. Reading material and websites of national and local support agencies are helpful although not all are of equal value. Ask for parents' and health professionals' evaluations.

- Work towards understanding how health (both negative and positive aspects) and treatment may impact on a child's learning and use this knowledge in curriculum planning, implementation and regular reviews.

- Develop and implement strategies to promote inclusion of *all* children in both classroom and on visits and excursions. Remove any barriers in organization and practice that may exclude any child.

- Monitor health discreetly and record and notify appropriately any changes.

- Monitor absence and encourage attendance.

- Observe necessary confidentiality and avoid *any* gossip about any pupils or families – a very serious abuse of trust – but learn from experienced colleagues in school and in health and social services what information *must* be shared in the best interests of children. Think about the ethics of your actions.

- Try to nurture developing friendships between children with health issues and their healthy peers.

- Emotional and aesthetic aspects of education and sensitive interpersonal communication are vital to the children we have been discussing – think how to develop them creatively in your work.

What can schools do to help?

Every school should have a regularly up-dated policy and plan for increased inclusion. Inclusion, however good the policy document, simply cannot be implemented unless the school also continuously nurtures a positive ethos (Closs and Cowie 2005) that places the well-being of all its pupils, their families and carers and all school staff at the forefront of its aims and listens to them. Those with health issues – and their siblings – may need even more focused attention. Implicit within inclusion is a positive approach to accessing and individualizing the curriculum for pupils who need this, including those with more serious health issues.

While we have stressed the importance of class teachers, many responsibilities for education and school health systems are managerial, as set out in the official guidance listed earlier. They address issues such as naming school and health service/social work contacts to facilitate communications between the various services and with parents. Effective communication with parents from children's earliest education usually pre-empts possible breakdown in home–school relations and reduces anxious visits and phone calls. Extra efforts from education and health services to create trust can bring 'absent' parents more willingly to school.

We come finally to one of every school's prime duties, looking after and supporting their own 'frontline' teachers, who face the greatest challenges. You will be among them, needing and deserving support. You should never hesitate to ask for it. Being new in any job is hard, being new to teaching and a class of children is very hard. Having children in your class with mental health issues brings extreme challenges (Jackson 2002) while a child with a deteriorating terminal medical condition can make even the most resolute teacher question their fundamental beliefs.

Even those teachers with the highest and strongest ideals may notice how the child they wanted to help seems, as time passes, to become an 'inconvenient' pupil and perhaps, yet later, becomes a 'bad' pupil. This slide in our perception of children who have health issues – we saw it in the cameo about Samantha when her previously supportive teacher became an angry teacher as Samantha's overt symptoms of mental distress grew – results from our feelings of inadequacy and frustration that we cannot 'fix' the situation so that our pupils are happy, learn well and behave. Teachers tend to judge themselves by how their pupils learn and behave (Brown and McIntyre 1986). When pupils are not learning and/or behaving well, teachers feel they must either blame themselves or their pupils. Yet, in most cases, neither choice is correct or productive. The best way forward is through additional blame-free support for both teacher and pupils from listening and supportive colleagues.

Asking for and accepting help is a sign of professional wisdom, not weakness. Any good teacher at some stage in their career, or with certain pupils such as those with health issues, may need support. Eventually, they will be able to offer that support to others.

Questions to Promote Thinking

The cameos present four very different children and family backgrounds, schools, teachers and health conditions.

1   Consider the kinds of health dimensions listed in Chapter 19 and see which are most relevant to each of the children and whether several or many dimensions are involved in relation to each child.
2   You might also identify in the cameos some of the issues to do with attachment and relationships described in Chapter 3 and reflect on the responses of the various people involved with the profiled children at school level. Which were useful? empathic? timely? skilled? imaginative? collaborative? made children feel safer? supported their education?
3   Did any of the staff develop professionally or personally as a result of their experiences? What might have supported these children, their siblings, their parents, their teachers and their education better?
4   Are there some issues that are common to some of the children's stories and do these common issues carry messages for teachers?

Useful websites

www.youngminds.org.uk Youngminds is the children's mental health charity which publishes many information leaflets for professionals, parents and children.
www.cafamily.org.uk/medicalinformation/conditions/azlistings/a.html Contact-a-Family is a charity for all children with any kind of special or medical need and their families. It produces a *Directory of Medical Conditions* (also identifying related support organizations).

References and suggested further reading

Bolton, A. (1997) *Losing the Thread: Pupils' and Parents' Voices about Education for Sick Children.* London: NAESC/PRESENT.
Brown, S. and McIntyre, D. (1986) How do teachers think about their craft?, in P.M. Denicolo and M. Kompf (eds) *Teacher Thinking Twenty Years On: Revisiting Persisting Problems and Advances in Education.* Lisse, The Netherlands: Swets and Zeitlinger.
Closs, A. (ed.) (2000) *The Education of Children with Medical Conditions*. London: David Fulton Publishers. This book addresses the education of children who predominantly have serious physical health conditions, including those that are life-threatening or life-shortening, and features the voices of young people themselves, parents and siblings. Chapter 8 advises how children's education can be made more effective while Chapter 13 looks at schools and the death of pupils, fortunately a rare occurrence.
Closs, A. and Cowie, M. (eds) (2005) *Ethos is Here to Stay: A Handbook of Printed and Electronic Resources to Help All Schools to Develop a More Positive Ethos.* Edinburgh: Scottish Schools Ethos Network. Available online at: http://www.ethosnet.co.uk/resources_otherdocuments.htm (accessed 20 January 2011)
Closs, A. and Norris, C. (1997) *Outlook Uncertain: Enabling the Education of Children with Chronic and/or Deteriorating Conditions.* Edinburgh: SOEID/Moray House Institute of Education.
DCSF (Department for Children, Schools and Families) (2010) *Targeted Mental Health in Schools Project: Using the Evidence to Inform Your Approach: A Practical Guide for Headteachers and Commissioners*. London: DCSF. Available online at: http://publications.education.gov.uk/eOrderingDownload/00784-2008BKT-EN.pdf (accessed 20 January 2011). This report is concerned with the mental health of 5–13-year-olds in special and mainstream schools and units and advises on effective interventions.
EHRC (Equality and Human Rights Commission) (2011) *Draft Codes of Practice for Schools: in England and Wales; in Scotland.* Available online at: http://www.equalityhumanrights.com/uploaded_files/EqualityAct/draft_code_of_practice_schools_eng_wales.pdf and http://www.equalityhumanrights.com/uploaded_files/EqualityAct/draft_code_of_practice_schools_scotland.pdf (accessed 5 February 2011).
Eiser, C. (1993) *Growing Up with a Chronic Disease: The Impact on Children and Their Families.* London: Jessica Kingsley Publishers.
Farrell, P. and Harris, K. for DfE (2003) *Access to education for children with medical needs: a map of best practice*. Manchester: Manchester University/Department for Education. Available online at: http://www.teachernet.gov.uk/_doc/3757/Access%20to%20Education%20for%20Children%20with%20Medical%20Needs%20-%20-%20A%20Map%20of%20Best%20Practice.doc (accessed 20 January 2011).
Jackson, E. (2002) Mental health in schools: what about the staff? *Journal of Child Psychotherapy*, 28(2): 129–46.

Morgan, C. and Morris, G. (1999) *Good Teaching and Learning: Pupils and Teachers Speak.* Buckingham: Open University Press.

Porter, J., Daniels, H., Martin, S., Hacker, J., Feiler, A. and Georgeson, J. (2010) *Testing of Disability Identification Tool for Schools.* London: Department for Education.

Wilson, P. (2003) *Young Minds in Our Schools.* London: Youngminds. This book introduces mental health and its varied manifestations, explaining when teachers should be worried. It offers ways forward – teachers' willingness to listen to and respect the views of children themselves and to work with others, being most important

22

CARRIE CABLE
Exploring leadership in the classroom

Summary

This chapter focuses on the role of teachers and other practitioners as both leaders and as members of teams within their settings. In the majority of primary schools and early years settings, adults are not working alone but are part of a network of people with different roles and responsibilities and, at any one point in time, a teacher might assume different roles in different groups and teams. Some of these roles are illustrated in the four cameos in the first half of this chapter, showing how the ability to work with colleagues is key to becoming a successful teacher. The different ways of engaging in leadership revealed in the cameos are then discussed.

Introduction

One of the tasks that teachers feel they are often least prepared for is working with other adults both inside and outside the classroom. Traditionally the school-based element of pre-service or initial teacher education emphasized the role of the lone worker. A focus on assessing the performance and judging the competence of the student teacher during lesson observations or observations of practice tended to reinforce this, especially when other adults were asked to leave the room during observations. The ability of an individual teacher to manage a large group of children and to promote their learning is still considered one of the most important professional skills for a teacher.

However, teachers working in primary schools and especially in the early years quickly realize that the reality is somewhat different. In the majority of primary schools and early years settings adults do not work alone. They are part of a network of people with different roles and responsibilities (see Chapter 23). They are also members of a number of teams. As a result the ability to work with others in constructive, collaborative and cooperative ways is a key attribute that requires skills, knowledge and understanding of how to work as a member of different groups and teams and how to engage in leadership.

Cameo 1

The classroom team

Marianna, in her first year of teaching, talks about the range of people she works with and her role in an early years classroom.

I'm the class teacher in Room 1 and we have nine people as part of our team. So we've got a nursery nurse and two lunchtime supervisors; also an early years practitioner, and then in the extended team we have two people who come for our PPA time and a member of the outreach team does that as well. And there's somebody from the local university who works in our class as well one day a week. So we have a real mixture of different personalities and levels of experience. As the team leader, my role encompasses managing all the members of the team and making sure that everybody is fully briefed and understands the planning, the teaching and the objectives on a weekly basis and from a wider perspective in terms of the long-term planning and what we're trying to achieve with the progression of the children. There are currently 30 children in the class but we have some new children coming and going. Really a big part of our role is providing an environment for the children to feel like they wish to explore and personalise their own learning and have an enjoyable time with us.

Within a classroom or unit, teachers are likely to work with a range of other practitioners or colleagues. Some may have specific responsibilities for working with children identified as having additional needs, e.g. learning support teachers or assistants. Others may have specific responsibilities for working with children who are new to English or developing their ability to learn through the medium of English, e.g. bilingual support teachers or assistants. Many schools now employ teaching assistants (TAs) who have general roles which include supporting children's learning, supporting teaching through the preparation of resources or carrying out administrative tasks such as photocopying. These assistants may share their time between a number of classes or be attached to a particular class for a period of time. Some TAs have dedicated support roles with respect to literacy or mathematics across a number of classes or take on responsibility for leadership in certain areas of the curriculum, e.g. ICT or art. A number of these assistants have achieved the status of Higher Level Teaching Assistant (HLTA) which enables them to teach full classes under the supervision of a teacher.

TAs are also found in early years settings but there are also usually a range of other practitioners including nursery nurses and, increasingly, practitioners who have achieved Early Years Professional Status (EYPS). In addition to paid staff, there are many volunteers who work in schools – to hear children read, to carry out art, craft and music activities or to share their expertise in specific areas of the curriculum. Many volunteers are parents or members of the local community, members of faith groups or service providers such as shopkeepers, dentists or the police who provide important links for children with the world outside the school or setting.

While teachers are members of these often large and diverse learning and teaching teams, they also need to be able to lead and manage the team working in their classroom. So a key skill needed is the ability to manage situations where there are a number of adults working together. However, this does not necessarily mean managing people in the sense of having line management responsibility for them. In most schools teachers do not line-manage teaching assistants – they are line-managed by a senior member of staff who may be a teaching assistant or a teacher. Another key skill is the ability to be able to lead practice in situations where practitioners may have different values, beliefs and approaches at a point in one's career when one is still developing one's own!

Cameo 2

Megan, a Year 6 class teacher, comments on the qualities she values in the bilingual teaching assistant she works with.

I would say her professionalism and her dealings with the children . . . she demands high standards from the children: they really respect her and she won't let them get away with anything. She demands higher order thinking; she won't just tell them the answer and I think that's the big difference with people I have worked with in other schools. Sometimes TAs feel that they are there just to tell children the equivalent word in the equivalent language, where she will challenge them to think . . . she will repeat what I have said in the questioning and she will get them to work it through and, yes, they will tell her the answer in Polish, let's say, and then she will say, 'Well, what is that in . . .?' but again she will make them work out what the word is in English and I think there is a real skill level in her ability to get the children to think.

I think she is really good about taking on a new initiative – taking it on board – everyone will take it on board and go with it; so I think that's one thing. I think the fact that she knows what happens; she knows the routines . . . You know, just the respect that she has got for the children, using positive reinforcement. Everything that I would see as good practice, she will do it.

As well as taking account of the range of skills and expertise of individuals, a considerable challenge is that people will work for different periods of time and on different days. It is important that everyone knows their roles and responsibilities, both legal and moral, to ensure children's safety, well-being and education in terms of ensuring consensus about the aims and values underpinning provision and practice for learning and teaching. This may seem like a daunting role for a teacher new to teaching and to a school or setting. Many of these practitioners may already have been working in schools for some time; they may already know the children and their parents well and may be more familiar with the school, the community and the local environment and, indeed, be members of the local community and/or parents whose children have attended the school. They may be older and/or more experienced in certain areas of learning and teaching: they may also be used to working in particular ways or working with particular members of staff.

The planning team

Except perhaps in very small schools or settings teachers are also likely to be members of a wider team beyond the classroom. In larger schools, this may be as members of a key stage or year team. These teams usually have responsibility for planning the curriculum and developing long-term (often yearly) plans, medium-term (often termly or half termly) plans and short-term (often weekly or fortnightly) plans (see Chapter 5). While many schools draw on National Curriculum guidance and commercial schemes of work, most teachers plan the detail of what they are going to teach and the learning outcomes they are going to address so that they can draw on children's interests, previous learning and school and community resources. Collective discussions and decisions are informed by teachers' reflections on what has gone well and what hasn't and how children have responded. Teachers, therefore, need to be able to listen to the voices of the children and adults they work with in their classrooms and to other teachers in their team, to ask questions to further their understanding and to make suggestions. Reflection-on-action and the ability to articulate and communicate views based on knowledge and evidence drawn from one's own experience are necessary skills for all teachers.

Roles and responsibilities within these teams vary from school to school and setting to setting and can depend on the approach to the curriculum. In some schools, individual teachers take on responsibility or leadership for different areas of the curriculum which may involve interpreting national guidance and schemes of work, preparing lesson plans and resources and even teaching, e.g. one teacher may teach music to all classes in a year group or Key Stage. Other members of the team will look to these 'experts' for guidance and support even in situations where the teacher may not initially have particular expertise in this area. In some schools, responsibilities are rotated within year or key stage teams to ensure fresh insights and to support professional development. In early years units or classes, and increasingly in some primary schools adopting a more holistic approach to learning, the curriculum may be planned in terms of themes or topics with links being made to areas of learning or curriculum subjects. In these situations individuals may take responsibility for an aspect of learning, e.g. learning outside.

Cameo 3

Melanie talks about a specific leadership role she has taken on in her school.

I run the Forest School with another colleague of mine. We did a year's training about Forest School leadership. It's really about skills development in that it helps teachers to use a different tool to support children's learning.

It's an outside activity and we take the children to another part of the school which is like a woodland so we can learn about the environment. It's also about giving children confidence and developing their self-esteem. We take children down to the woodland. We don't give them anything specific to do but there are set rules, and one rule is that we stay in the Forest School boundary. The other rule is that everything in the Forest School belongs there and it's there for a purpose. And then the children are free to explore the forest and we actually watch to see what they do. The important thing is it is up to them. It's an opportunity to develop their self-esteem, their imagination and creativity and to learn about the environment; about caring for the environment because a lot of children live in flats and they don't go out much or get many opportunities to explore on their own.

Planning is an essential element of learning and teaching and involves liaison with others (see Chapter 5). Meetings may be held after school or during preparation, planning and assessment time (PPA). However, sometimes it is impossible for all members of staff to attend these meetings because they do not work at the time of the meetings or because they are not paid to work at these times. This means that teachers need to take responsibility for communicating decisions to other members of the class or team.

The team around the child

Increasingly, and as a direct result of the *Every Child Matters* agenda (DfES 2003), teachers also work with practitioners from outside the school or setting particularly in situations where there are concerns about the child (see Chapters 4 and 23). This involves the ability to relate to a diverse range of people with different backgrounds, roles, responsibilities, expertise and expectations. It also involves acceptance of being a learner and the ability to relate to the views and perspectives of others (relational agency). Teachers may be working with numerous other adults including bilingual teachers, interpreters and translators, advisors from the local authority, members of support services for travellers or ethnic minority achievement (EMAG), speech and language therapists, teachers for deaf or blind children or children with other disabilities, portage services, educational psychologists, health practitioners, social care practitioners or social workers. Some contacts with external practitioners will be facilitated or mediated by senior members of staff in the school or setting and, in some schools, teachers may not be involved in case meetings. Teachers will often be expected to prepare formal reports for meetings even if they do not attend in person: this involves the development of clear and accurate recording and writing skills. Teachers also need to liaise with other staff working directly with children in their classes when using specific approaches or resources to support children's learning. This means being prepared to learn enough about another area of professional expertise, to engage in a dialogue with others supporting children in their classroom. Teachers need to be able to clarify exactly the approach to be taken and, perhaps, work with an assistant to support the child's learning. They will also need to plan how they will integrate any special requirements into their overall approach to children's learning.

Working with parents

The importance of parents as the child's first and ongoing educator is now widely recognized. Developing respectful and positive relationships with parents is also a key professional attribute that requires teachers to be effective communicators with good listening skills (see Chapter 20). Too often parents perceive the home–school relationship as one-sided; one where they are told things rather than consulted, where their knowledge and views are disregarded or given little consideration and one where they are only contacted when something is wrong. Those working in the early years tend to have more positive, stronger and richer relationships because they are more accessible to parents and engage in more frequent and less formal contact, for example, at the beginning and end of sessions. Home visits, key workers plus workshop and drop-in sessions all support the sharing of knowledge and understanding and the development of partnership working and reciprocal relations. Schools are not the forbidding places that many were in the past but, for some parents who may have unhappy memories of their own schooling or who are unfamiliar with the educational system, they can still be intimidating. Other parents may have strong views and expectations about schooling which may not accord with the ethos or practices in the school or setting. Learning to listen to and respect the views of parents while confidently being able to communicate the values and learning aims of the school or setting requires teachers to develop their own knowledge, understanding and communication skills.

A member of the school community

Schools as organizations need to be led and managed. The style of leadership and management will depend to a great extent on the head teacher and senior members of staff. These people have roles and responsibilities that go beyond those of a class teacher including legal and statutory obligations. As members of an organization, there are certain things that all staff need to accept and certain procedures that need to be adhered to, for example, those who safeguard the well-being of children (see Chapter 4). However, most primary schools, children's centres and early years units are not run on hierarchical lines. Policies and new initiatives are usually developed through collaboration, often by working in groups which may involve children and parents as well as staff members. One or two teachers may lead these developments and share findings or suggestions with other staff at a staff or parents' meeting. This is a form of devolved or distributed leadership which can draw on and enable the development of collaboration and teamwork.

Working in teams

> **Cameo 4**
>
> Louise, an experienced teacher, talks about the positive learning experience team working has been for her.
>
> I've found that by working in a team you can just do so much more because there's not just one of you . . . and you can draw on other people's expertise, other people's strength. And I've found that really, really rewarding. I've worked in three different classes and I've worked with different adults and, in doing so, I've got to know those adults; I've got to know what are their strengths and really learnt from them in a way that we've been able to plan and enrich children's lives and not just children's lives but our own. For example, I have some colleagues that have tremendous strength creatively and yesterday I was thinking, 'Oh, I want to do a display' and how was I going to do a display? And then I just mentioned it to a colleague, and then he says, 'Oh yes, I can do this, this and this' and I said 'Oh, you know, why don't you go ahead and do it?' And he went ahead and did it and I just thought, 'Wow, I would never have implemented it in the way that you've implemented it.' So each time, you know, it's giving people opportunities . . . to express themselves and, in expressing themselves, I've learnt something from it.

Importantly, at any one point in time, a teacher might be assuming different roles in different groups and teams. A possible list could include: leader, learner, listener, contributor, actor, collaborator, note taker, report writer, raconteur, discussant, designer, planner, and you can probably think of many more. These roles will also change as teachers work with different people, teach different classes, undertake professional development and assume specific roles or responsibilities. Importantly, they all involve leadership qualities and skills that can be developed over time and lead to the ability to engage in what have been termed 'leaderful' teams (Raelin 2003).

Characteristics of leaders

Pound (2008), drawing on the work of Rodd (2006), identifies seven essential characteristics of effective leaders. However, I would suggest that these characteristics apply equally to all teachers who are working within schools and settings and who are engaged in supporting the work of others, working within teams and engaging in their own professional development:

- *Curiosity* – an openness and a desire to know and learn including the ability to engage in a reflective learning community.
- *Candour* – an honest search for understanding and an acceptance that there are different ways of seeing and believing.

- *Courtesy* – recognizing the contributions of others and understanding the importance of the way we communicate with and acknowledge other people and their contributions.

- *Courage* – taking risks, admitting when things go wrong, building on mistakes and seeing this as part of a creative endeavour.

- *Compassion* – concern for others, the ability to listen and learn, empathy and sincerity.

- *Confidence* – in one's own values, beliefs and understandings gained through reading, discussion and reflection.

- *Communication* – with other adults as well as with children and parents.

Learning about leadership

Working with others entails seeing oneself as part of a team and also recognizing that membership involves leadership. Many people have an idea of a leader as someone who is charismatic, inspiring and frequently forceful – the hero leader who drives change through a belief in themselves. This tends to be reinforced by the importance given to organizational leadership and management in inspection reports (OfSTED 2003, 2008, 2010) and guidance provided by bodies such as the National College and the Department for Education's White Paper, *The Importance of Teaching* (DfE 2010).

The ways in which leadership has been conceptualized in the past and in areas outside primary schools and early years settings can tend to suggest that the ability to be a leader is something that people are born with – a set of inherent abilities. More contemporary views of leadership tend to view it as a set of skills and abilities that can be learnt and developed over time. The importance of context or situation is also acknowledged – different types of leadership may be more appropriate at different times depending on the goals of a school or setting and the stage of its development. Some commentators also argue that views of leadership largely developed in North America and in the world of business tend to foreground types of leadership which are often, though not exclusively, associated with white males. These emphasize rational behaviours including being in control, exercising power and encouraging competition. However, most people would also say that this type of leadership doesn't sit well with holistic, enabling approaches to learning and teaching in the early and primary years. Collaboration and cooperation are usually considered more important qualities for leaders in these organizations. This does not of course, mean that charismatic, inspiring or forceful people cannot contribute to the development of schools and settings. It does means they need to see themselves, their ideas and energy as contributing to overall developments and learning, positioning themselves as members of a team and valuing the contributions of others.

There are ongoing debates about the difference between leadership and management. Definitions of management tend to focus on organization, planning, decision-making and monitoring and evaluation, while definitions of leadership tend to foreground providing vision and inspiration, modelling behaviours and facilitating teamwork. However, it can be difficult to separate out these functions in schools and early years settings. A study on the role of head teachers by Hall (1996) found that they undertook both roles simultaneously and led her to conclude that 'management without leadership was unethical . . . leadership without management was irresponsible' (Hall, quoted in Whalley 2011: 14). There is also currently a growing emphasis on the role of head teachers and senior managers in promoting positive outcomes for children, ensuring they progress well (OfSTED 2008) and leading practice and outcomes for children.

> The best leadership in schools focuses on improving teaching and learning with head teachers seeing this as their core business. Common characteristics of the best leadership include honest self-evaluation and leadership shared across the school.
>
> (OfSTED 2010; website summary)

This accords with the emphasis on leadership of learning outlined in the National College publication *Everyone a Leader* (NCSL 2008) which outlines four areas for development of all staff in schools:

- Leadership of learning
- Reflective leadership
- Leadership learning
- Systemic leadership.

> (NCSL 2008: 6)

Leadership of learning covers 'leading outside the classroom' with possible examples being taking assemblies and organizing trips and events, 'leading other staff' which might include preparing a unit of work or contributing to a working group, and 'having experiences beyond the familiar' which might include making presentations to parents or leading and coordinating an area of the curriculum across the school.

The suggestions relating to reflective leadership include monitoring and evaluation and mentoring and coaching; those for leadership learning include assuming responsibility for performance management and engaging in apprenticeship learning; and finally those for systemic leadership include stepping up and participation in whole school and community development. It is significant and interesting that leading and managing the work of others is not suggested as an example although it has clear resonance with each of the four areas. However, it is also noticeable that most of the suggestions are roles that, as we saw above, teachers will need to begin to develop from when they start teaching.

Leadership *for* learning (in contrast to leadership *of* learning) is also of importance to teachers. In a study examining leadership in the early years and drawing on wider leadership theory, Siraj-Blatchford and Manni (2007) highlight this as the key role. They suggest that one of the requirements in providing leadership for learning is the development of 'contextual literacy' – developing the ability to take account of specific situations and circumstances. They conclude that this involves engaging with the specific school or setting and the people (other adults, children and parents) and the specific place they are at in terms of their learning and development rather than bringing in or trying to impose ideas or procedures or ways of working from other contexts. Leadership is thus seen very much as engagement in a process of learning which takes account of community, environment, local constraints and opportunities and diversity. Leadership can then seek to combine the ability to lead and manage change and take account of external orientation and internal orientation for the benefit of all staff, children and parents.

Learning to lead

It is challenging for a new teacher to take on the overall responsibility for the learning of a large group of children and at the same time learn to work with a range of other adults in a range of different teams. Resistance to change is not uncommon, whether it involves working with new people, working in different ways or responding to new initiatives and managing conflict can be time consuming and exhausting. The ethos of the school or setting and how it views leadership, collaboration, team working, professional development and support is, of course, critical. McCall and Lawlor suggest that effective teams do the following:

- accept a team culture which implies working honestly and fairly for the team, rather than for oneself;
- develop the capacity to work together and be prepared to learn as a team;
- work towards consensus decision-making, as opposed to citing individual preferences;
- are open-minded about tasks and obstacles, including facing change and trying out new ideas and methods;
- act responsibly together; without the need for head teacher or lead manager supervision;
- are able to explain and justify the team's manner and modes of working, and modify these as necessary;
- accept that teams, like individuals are accountable for results.

(McCall and Lawlor 2000, cited in Jones and Pound 2008: 35/36)

Conclusion

Developing the attitudes, skills and abilities to work effectively with others and to lead practice needs to be seen as an ongoing process involving learning from and with others. As teachers, we learn from the children we teach, their parents and the staff we work with and we need to recognize their expertise and the insights they can provide us with on our learning journeys. We also need to recognize that there are different ways of seeing and doing and to learn to reflect thoughtfully and critically on our own assumptions, values and beliefs. Defining clear roles and expectations also involves seeing our work in relation to others and valuing what others can do. Learning to communicate our views to others in non-challenging and supportive ways and to work collaboratively takes time but being members of a learning community is what makes being a teacher such a rewarding career.

> ### Questions to Promote Thinking
>
> 1 Think about the adults you work with regularly. What do you know about their backgrounds and experiences? How could you find out more?
> 2 What do you value about the other staff who work in your classroom? What do the children value? How could you build on their skills and expertise to enhance children's learning?
> 3 Consider the different teams you work in. What is your current role in each team? How could you develop your role to enhance your contribution?
> 4 Which of the leadership skills and abilities referred to in this chapter do you feel you already possess? How could you develop these and other leadership skills?

Useful websites

http://www.nationalcollege.org.uk
http://www.naldic.org.uk/ITTSEAL2/ite/Workingwithothers-Professionalmodule.cfm

References and suggested further reading

Coleman, M. and Glover, D. (eds) (2010) *Educational Leadership and Management: Developing Insights and Skills*. Maidenhead: Open University Press.

Day, W., Hall, C. and Whittaker P. (1998) *Developing Leadership in Primary Schools*. London: Sage.

DfE (Department for Education) (2010) *The Importance of Teaching: The Schools White Paper 2010*. Available online at: http://publications.education.gov.uk/ (accessed 15 December 2010).

DfES (Department for Education and Skills) (2003) *Every Child Matters, Green Paper*. Nottingham: DfES.

Hall, V. (1996) *Dancing on the Ceiling*. London: Paul Chapman.

Jones, C. and Pound, L. (2008) *Leadership and Management in the Early Years*. Maidenhead: Open University Press.

NCSL (National Council for School Leadership) (2008) *Everyone a Leader*. Available online at: http://www.nationalcollege.org.uk/docinfo?id=21820&filename=everyone-a-leader.pdf (accessed 15 December 2010).

OfSTED (Office for Standards in Education) (2003) *Leadership and Management: Managing the School Workforce*. London: OfSTED.

OfSTED (2008) *Early Years Leading to Excellence*. Available online at: http://www.ofsted.gov.uk/Ofsted-home/Leading-to-excellence (accessed 15 December 2010).

OfSTED (2010) *Developing leadership: National Support Schools Summary*. Available online at: www.ofsted.gov.uk/publications/090232 (accessed 15 December 2010).

Pound, L. (2008) Leadership in the early years, in L. Miller and C. Cable (eds) *Professionalism in the Early Years*. London: Hodder Arnold.

Raelin, J. (2003) *Creating Leaderful Organizations*. San Francisco: Berrerr-Koehler Publishers.

Rodd, J. (2006) *Leadership in Early Childhood*, 3rd edn. Maidenhead: Open University Press.

Siraj-Blatchford, I. and Manni, L. (2007) *Effective Leadership in the Early Years Sector: The ELEYS Study.* London: Institute of Education, University of London.

Whalley, M. (2011) Leading and managing in the early years, in L. Miller and C. Cable (eds) *Professionalization, Leadership and Management in the Early Years*. London: Sage.

23

GARY WALKER
Beginning to work with other agencies

Summary

This chapter examines the role of the teacher in fulfilling the requirements developed under the *Every Child Matters* agenda for all professionals involved with children to work closely together to maximize the potential of every child. The frameworks and systems in place to support children across four categories – those with 'additional needs', 'in need', 'in need of protection' and 'looked after children' are explored. Using two cameos, the chapter goes on to analyse both the benefits and possible barriers to a multi-agency approach, emphasizing the unique role of the teacher in this complex process.

Introduction

Teachers have long worked collaboratively with other agencies for the benefit of children in their care, so the idea and practice of multi-agency working are certainly not new. What is more recent, however, is the notion that placing the child at the centre of a strong and committed team of professionals from a variety of backgrounds is essential to achieve good outcomes for children. In 2003, the then Labour government published the seminal document *Every Child Matters*, which set out their vision for a planned programme of change which, they argued, would help ensure that all children would not only be kept safe and healthy, but would also maximize life chances in terms of their longer-term prospects. Central to this was the idea of close cooperation between the many agencies involved in supporting children and meeting their needs.

Who might be involved in multi-agency work?

It is not possible to list every agency that might be involved in the life of a child. However, it is useful to think about the key agencies that are likely to have an interest in children's development. These can be divided into two types as follows:

- *Universal services*, to which all children are entitled. These include early years settings, schools, general practitioner (GP), health visitor, school nurse.

- *Targeted services,* to which only children who meet certain criteria are entitled. These include children's social care (social worker), child mental health services, youth offending teams.

The impact of *Every Child Matters* on teachers

The integrated approach integral to the *Every Child Matters* programme has had, and will continue to have, important implications for teachers working in primary schools. Indeed, schools were seized upon as offering the ideal location for the delivery of key elements of the programme. Schools were seen as the hub of the community, the place where not only most children spent a large portion of their waking hours, but also, at least at primary level, where many parents visited every day, and where various professionals could congregate to offer advice and support to children and parents on a range of issues. Thus the notion of the school at the centre of a new, integrated service was born. Schools now were expected not only to educate children in the traditional sense, but also to house child-care facilities from 8.00 a.m. to 6.00 p.m. in order to support working parents and to provide children with stimulating experiences. Schools were also expected to offer (or coordinate the provision of) a range of other extended services, including:

- study support, sport and music clubs for children;
- parenting and family support groups;
- access for facilities for parents including adult and family learning, ICT and sports grounds;
- swift and easy access to targeted and specialist services, where schools are involved in planning and delivering support services for children and families, with other agencies.

This final commitment means that a range of professionals including, for example, social workers, health professionals, housing or benefits officers are located, at least for set times during the week, within the school.

One of the key implications of this for classroom-based teachers, then, is that they need to be aware not only of the range of services on offer through the school, but also of the range of professionals available for consultation, and of what the roles are of these other professionals. Teachers need to see themselves much more clearly now as being part of an ongoing multi-agency team working for the benefit of the children, rather than as an essentially isolated professional based in a classroom and occasionally liaising with other agencies in the event of a crisis. Now, in order to enable children to reach their full potential, teachers are expected to respond and intervene early if they have the slightest concern about a child's welfare, development or learning, and then work closely with other professionals to meet the child's identified needs.

The categorization of children's needs

This change of emphasis, from an essentially 'silo-based' way of working to integration of services and approaches, presents many challenges. Teachers need to understand and be able to implement a complex range of legislation and guidance that governs multi-agency working, and have clarity about their specific role as a class-based teacher, and the role of the school within this network of professionals. This guidance and legislation cover how professionals should respond to the range of children's needs as prescribed by the government, who have conceptualized these needs in terms of an ever-increasing depth of seriousness, as follows (the approximate numbers of children in each category relate to England):

- All children aged birth-to-17-years (11 million).
- Children with 'additional needs' (up to 4 million). These are children who, in the professional's view, may not meet the five *Every Child Matters* outcomes which are that all children should Stay safe, Be healthy, Achieve at school and enjoy leisure activities, Make a positive contribution of their communities, and Achieve economic well-being. In other words, these are children with a relatively low level of need who may not reach their full potential without support.
- Children 'in need' as defined in Section 17 of the Children Act 1989 (400,000). These are children whose are unlikely to maintain a reasonable standard of health or development, or whose health or development is likely to be impaired without the provision of support services. Disabled children (including those with a sensory impairment and learning disability) are automatically classed as being 'in need'. These children have a greater level of need than those with 'additional needs' as they are likely to be harmed in some way unless they receive support.
- Children 'in need of protection' as defined in Section 47 of the Children Act 1989 (34,000). These are children at continued risk of significant harm and for whom there is a formal multi-agency child protection plan in place. Most of these children live at home. These children are at risk of serious harm, usually as a result of abuse or neglect by their parents or carers, and need to be protected from this harm.
- Looked after children, also called children in care (60,000). These are children in the care of the local authority, usually as a result of abuse or neglect, but including those children in care as a result of a voluntary agreement between their parents and the local authority.

Cameo 1

Katie is a 6-year-old child in Year 1 of primary school. She is white British, an only child, and lives with both her parents in local authority housing within walking distance of the school. She is of average ability and is settled and sociable at school, having three or four close friends in her class. Recently, however, the teacher has noticed that she seems somewhat 'distant' in class. Her concentration has waned, and the standard of her work has started to slip. Unusually for Katie, she has started to arrive late for school and in a dishevelled state – her uniform is dirty, and her hair unwashed and uncombed.

Reflect for a moment:

1 To which group of children as classified above do you think Katie belongs?
2 What, if anything, do you think the teacher should do about what she has observed?

This cameo illustrates one of the first potential difficulties which class teachers may face: how to decide whether a child has 'additional needs' or indeed a greater level of need. Here, the teacher has noticed a change in Katie that appears to be linked to her home life. Some teachers may decide that Katie has 'additional needs' and that she may not reach the *Every Child Matters* outcomes as a result (particularly 'Be healthy, Achieve at school, and Make a positive contribution). Other teachers may think she has a greater level of need, and would consequently classify her as a 'child in need' as they believe her health or development is likely to be impaired without some help. Both would call for a response from the school as discussed in the section that now follows.

Multi-agency responses to children's needs

For children with 'additional needs', the role of front-line staff such as teachers is vital in the early identification and further assessment of these needs. The clear expectation now, under the relevant guidance (CWDC 2010) is that all practitioners working with children in any capacity are aware of the Common Assessment Framework (CAF), which is a nationally standardized form and process which is completed with the consent of parents and/or the children concerned. The aim is to identify further support from other agencies that ensures the child is appropriately supported and that their needs are subsequently met. Each setting should have at least one member of staff who is trained to conduct CAF assessments.

If the teacher classed Katie as having 'additional needs', she would therefore have a responsibility to share these concerns with a more senior member of staff within the school. If they agree, then a school staff member (or perhaps two staff – the class teacher and a more senior staff member) would be expected to share their concerns with Katie's parents. The school staff should offer to undertake a CAF as part of this discussion, although it is entirely voluntary and the parents can decline to take part. If a CAF is completed, the school staff should seek consent from Katie's parents to share the contents with any other agencies offering universal services that may need to be approached about contributing to a package of support for Katie.

If the completion of a CAF does lead to a multi-agency support package being put in place for any child, a key role within this process is that of the 'lead professional'. They can be chosen from any of the practitioners engaged in the work, including those based in schools. While it is unlikely that class teachers will act as lead professionals (learning mentors or educational welfare officers are more likely to take on the role), it is possible that they will do. At the very least, however, class teachers need to be aware of the CAF process, as they will be responsible for noting early concerns about children in their classrooms, and passing these concerns on appropriately within the school, as described above in relation to Katie. Furthermore, teachers should have knowledge of the role of the lead professional, who is responsible for co-ordinating the work of the various other professionals to ensure the child's identified needs are met. For these children with 'additional needs', teachers will remain closely involved, as a minimum, in providing and receiving ongoing information about the child's progress and liaising with the lead professional, who could be based within the school, or within an external agency such as health.

Where a teacher identifies that a child may be 'in need' or 'in need of protection' (in other words, where the perceived need is greater than 'additional needs'), a different set of legislation and guidance applies. The key relevant national guidance here (which applies to England) is entitled *Safeguarding Children and Safer Recruitment in Education* (DCSF 2010) which applies to the whole school sector (see also Chapter 4).

This guidance explains that for schools, it is technically the responsibility of governing bodies to ensure that each establishment has effective safeguarding children procedures, and that it adheres to them. Governing bodies should have no involvement with, or oversight of, individual cases; rather they take a strategic lead in ensuring compliance with the guidance. The governing body should ensure that the school:

- has a child protection policy in place;
- operates safe recruitment procedures;
- has proper procedures for dealing with allegations against members of staff and volunteers;
- has in place a senior member of the school's leadership team to take lead responsibility for child protection (called the senior designated person). This role includes dealing with child protection issues as they arise, providing advice and support to other staff, liaising with the local authority, and working with other agencies.
- ensures all staff receive appropriate training regarding child protection;
- reviews the policies and procedures at least once a year.

This national guidance is not designed to provide guidance to individual staff members such as class teachers – for this they have to consult a different booklet entitled *What to Do if You're Worried a Child is Being Abused* (DfES 2006). This guidance, which mainly focuses on children who may be 'in need of protection' sets out in some detail the importance of workers being familiar with their own organization's procedures for safeguarding children, including knowing who to approach with a concern about a child, knowing how to speak to and support children in the short term, knowing how to record their concerns, and understanding the procedures once other agencies such as Children's Social Care, become involved.

Once a child is referred to Children's Social Care, either because they might be 'in need' or 'in need of protection', a social worker will, if the referral is confirmed, take the lead in coordinating further enquiries and an assessment under guidance entitled *Framework for the Assessment of Children in Need and their Families* (DoH/DfEE/HO 2000) which covers both groups of children. In these instances, the social worker will always act as the 'lead professional' and the teacher will remain a crucial member of the multi-agency network, providing further information and support, and engaging in decision-making where required, including attendance at formal multi-agency planning meetings such as 'family support meetings' for children in need, Initial Child Protection Conferences for children who may be in need of protection, or Child Protection Review Conferences for children who are subject of a formal child protection plan.

Teachers also have a vital role to play within a multi-agency network for looked after children. These children will also have a social worker taking the lead in ensuring that their care plans remain relevant and focused on meeting their needs. Teachers here are responsible for keeping the social worker (and the carer with whom the child lives on a day-to-day basis) informed of the child's progress, for helping to complete a multi-agency Personal Education Plan which is required for every child in care, and for attending the care planning review meetings, at which the efficacy of the care plan is discussed, and any required changes are made.

Information sharing

In addition to the plethora of guidance and legislation relating to a multi-agency response to the full range of children's needs, there exists complex legislation governing the sharing of information which of course is an inherent part of multi-agency working. The key relevant legislation here is:

- The Data Protection Act 1998;
- The Human Rights Act 1998;
- The Common Law Duty of Confidence.

The government has produced guidance for workers on these in an effort to facilitate understanding of when and how to share personal information (DCSF 2009). Teachers, along with all practitioners working with children, are expected to be familiar with the contents of this guidance.

Cameo 2

Jacob is 10-years-old and in year 5 of primary school. He is white British and lives with both parents and his younger sisters aged 7 (who attends the same school) in privately owned housing in a well-to-do part of town. Both his parents work long hours in professional jobs, and Jacob attends the 'before and after-school club' each day. One day, he comes into school in a very quiet mood. When the teacher comments on this to him, he tells her that last night he woke up hungry in the middle of the night, crept downstairs and helped himself to some biscuits. His father came downstairs and caught him, and hit him across the back several times with a belt he was carrying. He says he has red marks on his back which are very sore.

Reflect for a moment:

1   To which group of children do you think Jacob belongs?
2   What do you think the teacher should do about what Jacob has told her?
3   What are the responsibilities of the school both immediately and in the longer term?

This situation differs markedly from that described for Katie in several ways. First, the teacher has been directly told by Jacob that he has been harmed, rather than the teacher observing something about which she is concerned. Second, the harm described by Jacob appears to amount to 'significant' harm, thus placing him in the category of child in need of protection. The teacher should therefore invoke the school's child protection policy and procedures. The school should then make a referral to Children's Social Care and they have a duty to inform them of what Jacob has told them, and of any relevant background information they have about him and the family (including his sister). They have to support Jacob through the immediate period of the enquiries led by the social worker, and subsequently have a responsibility to be directly involved in providing information for the social work assessment, and in attending any multi-agency meetings which are called to make decisions about Jacob's future welfare.

Benefits of multi-agency working

Multi-agency work has been defined as 'a range of different services which have some overlapping or shared interests and objectives, brought together to work collaboratively towards some common purposes' (Wigfall and Moss 2001: 71). This definition demonstrates the clear benefits of multi-agency working, which include:

•   coordination of the work of those involved to ensure a coherent service;
•   a possible sharing of resources;
•   possible joint funding of projects;
•   better outcomes for children, as their holistic needs are addressed.

(Walker 2008: 15)

Thus, multi-agency working is in essence the idea and practice of different workers from different agencies joining together with a shared aim of understanding, and then trying to solve or alleviate a problem. Relating this to Katie, a multi-agency approach would try to ensure that the deterioration in her overall situation is addressed promptly and 'in the round' by harnessing the existing knowledge, skills and resources of staff within such universal services as the school and health. Her parents would also have a key role to play in determining the direction of the work. The benefits of multi-agency work for Jacob would be, first, that his immediate safety would be assessed, and second, that a full assessment would be made of his circumstances, led by a social worker but involving all the agencies with an interest in his welfare. This in turn would lead to a multi-agency plan of protection for Jacob, which would aim to address his (and his parents') holistic needs.

Barriers to multi-agency working

The complexities of multi-agency working have long been the subject of research. Some of the key publications here are Stainton Rogers (1989), Frost (2005), Fitzgerald and Kay (2008), Foley and Rixon (2008), and Anning et al. (2010). This work has thrown light on the attendant and inherent tensions and difficulties involved in multi-agency working, in spite of the compelling positive consequences of such an approach. The key barriers to multi-agency working can be summarized as follows:

- Agencies have different core functions which may clash with one another. With Jacob, for instance, the teacher's core role of educating children might be compromised if her attendance at a meeting concerning him means the rest of the class has to join a much larger group for an afternoon, thus potentially having a deleterious impact on the education of these other children.

- Agencies have different values, cultures and practices. With Katie, for example, we have seen above that the teacher may decide she is 'in need' rather than that she has 'additional needs'. Consequently, the teacher may believe Katie is entitled to receive a full assessment led by a social worker. However, when the referral is made, the social worker may decide the circumstances indicate the child has 'additional needs' and therefore suggests the teacher carries out a Common Assessment Framework (CAF) assessment to determine what support is needed. This may leave the teacher feeling irked that their judgement has been ignored and that they are being asked to take on extra work, based on the decision of a worker who does not know the child.

- Legislation governing the work of different agencies may conflict with each other. Laws affecting families and children are plentiful and complex. Where these clash, this could lead to confusion, or the inability to fulfil multi-agency plans as some agencies feel unable to contribute.

- Agencies may interpret legislation differently, as it may be open to interpretation. Before sharing personal information about Jacob with another agency, for example, the teacher would have to decide whether his welfare interests justify this, and if they do, whether or not to then gain the consent of the parent (or child if mature enough) to share this information. Clearly, these decisions involve judgements which may clash with those of different workers, potentially leading to conflict between them.

- Boundaries between agencies may be unclear. Workers need to be clear about their own role, and that of others. If they are not, this could lead to them duplicating the work of others, or giving advice that might conflict with that given from a different worker.

- The structure of authority and decision-making may be unclear. Where several agencies are involved in supporting a child, if it is not clear who has the final 'say', or how major planning decisions are arrived at, this can lead to confusion and conflict between agencies. Particularly in the support of children with 'additional needs' such as Katie, the various services would need to agree who the 'lead professional' is and what authority they have.

- Agencies may have a history of jealousy or rivalry between themselves. This antagonism may be caused by a difference in outlook on a particular issue or a clash of personality between individuals. Resentment can build up, potentially leading to efforts to outwit or outperform the other agency instead of focusing on the needs of the child.

- Agencies may be unclear why other agencies are involved. If anyone in the multi-agency network is not clear why the others are involved, this could lead to confusion, or false assumptions being made as to what their work involves.

- Workers within particular agencies may lack confidence in carrying out multi-agency roles. An early evaluation of the implementation of the Common Assessment Framework (Brandon et al. 2006) demonstrated that the role of the 'lead professional' creates real challenges such as workers lacking confidence and clarity in what a holistic assessment entails, experiencing a lack of support for their role, and having concerns about the amount of additional work generated by the role. Furthermore, they found the unfamiliar high level of responsibility and the chairing of meetings daunting. There was uncertainty about what to do if disagreements arose, and a reluctance to share equally the responsibility for taking on the lead professional role, such that those who appeared confident in the role were left to take it on.

In addition, the work of Morrison (1991) shows that different agencies are likely to hold different attitudes towards the very idea of collaboration with others. These are:

- *Paternalism:* Agencies with a paternalistic approach only collaborate if they approve of it, and do so on their terms. Agencies see themselves as the 'experts' where others should be grateful for receiving their advice. The paternalistic agency may find it hard to see that other agencies having equal expertise or valid skills.

- *Strategic adversarial:* Agencies with this approach view collaboration warily, as they see it involving more losses than gains. This could lead to a siege mentality, with time spent negotiating the terms of engagement or checking up on what others are doing. The collaboration is based on mistrust.

- *Play fair:* Agencies who take this approach believe that clients have the right to an effective multi-agency service. The agency tries to ensure that everyone is clear about their role and responsibilities. They appreciate and respect the roles of other agencies.

- *Developmental:* Here, collaboration is seen by the agency who takes this approach as a dynamic process to motivate staff and clients to change. Multi-agency work is seen as organic, alive and changing, including such things as taking risks, learning from mistakes or pooling resources.

If, within one piece of multi-agency work, these differences in attitudes and approaches are present within the agencies, this could well lead to tensions where the different agencies try to negotiate their way through these conflicting positions.

These structural barriers to multi-agency work are inherent in the very fabric and nature of the work. In addition, there exists what might be called a range of operational issues within and between agencies. Some of these are:

- Individuals in the network having or using power or status, and trying to impose their will upon others.

- Problems within another agency, for example, staff shortages or delays which are impacting on the work.

- Workers not delivering promises which they have made to support a child.

- Professionals acting in a way others believe is against the child's interests.

- An agency making unreasonable demands upon another agency, such as asking them to perform duties which are outside their remit (Walker 2008: 44).

Strong emotions can be elicited in the circumstances described above, especially if they resonate with the teacher's own value base. They can easily become flash points which deepen divisions between agencies. If teachers decide to challenge the other agency, they will need to do so in a way that maintains a positive relationship with them.

Conclusion

Multi-agency working has a long history, although the impetus for closer inter-professional working has intensified significantly recently. While there are clear benefits to be gained for children and families with this approach, the issues involved are complex. This complexity arises chiefly out of structural and inherent factors associated with multi-agency work rather than the acts of individuals within the network, although the latter can exacerbate the former. Within this milieu, teachers should remember that of all the agencies involved, they have the most contact time with children, and are therefore likely to have the most in-depth knowledge of the child. During multi-agency working, therefore, teachers can and should be confident in using this knowledge to contribute to joint planning and decision-making, thus ensuring they place themselves at the heart of the processes that support the many and complex needs of children within their care.

Questions to Promote Thinking

1   As a teacher, what skills do you think you would possess that would enable you to conduct a CAF assessment and act as a lead professional if you were called upon to do so?
2   How might you react if you were part of a multi-agency team supporting a child, and you found out that a professional in a different service had not been fulfilling their pledge to visit the family every fortnight?
3   If you were in a meeting, and a psychiatrist who has met the parents and child only once tries to impose their view of the family (which you believe is incorrect) onto you and the other professionals at the meeting, how would you respond?

Useful websites

The Teacher Training Resource Bank has a webpage entitled 'Multi-professional/Multi-agency working'. Available online at: http://www.ttrb.ac.uk/viewarticle2.aspx?contentId=10633 (accessed 20 January 2011).
The *Early Years Foundation Stage* contains a section on 'Effective Practice: Multi-agency working'. Available online at: http://eyfs.keymedia.info/resources/downloads/3.4b_ep.pdf.

References and suggested further reading

Allen, C. (2003) **Desperately seeking fusion: on 'joined-up thinking', 'holistic practice' and the new economy of welfare professional power,** *British Journal of Sociology*, 54(2): 287–306.
Anning, A., Cottrell, D., Frost, N. and Green, J. (2010) *Developing Multi-professional Teamwork for Integrated Children's Services: Research, Policy and Practice.* Maidenhead: Open University Press.
Barker, R. (ed.) (2008) *Making Sense of Every Child Matters: Multi-Professional Practice Guidance.* Bristol: The Policy Press.
Brandon, M., Howe, A., Dagley, V., Salter, C., Warren, C. and Black, J. (2006) *Evaluating the Common Assessment Framework and Lead Professional Guidance and Implementation in 2005–6.* London: DfES.
Broadhurst, K., Grover, C. and Jamieson, J. (eds) (2009) *Critical Perspectives on Safeguarding Children.* Chichester: John Wiley and Sons.
Cheminais, R. (2009) *Effective Multi-Agency Partnership: Putting Every Child Matters into Practice.* London: Sage.
CWDC (Children's Workforce Development Council) (2010) *Early Identification, Assessment of Needs and Intervention. The Common Assessment Framework for Children and Young People: A Guide for Practitioners.* Leeds: CWDC.
DCSF (Department for Children, Schools and Families) (2009) *Information Sharing: Guidance for Practitioners and Managers.* Nottingham: DCSF.
DCSF (2010) *Safeguarding Children and Safer Recruitment in Education.* London: DCSF.
DfES (Department for Education and Skills) (2006) *What to Do if You're Worried a Child is Being Abused.* Nottingham: DfES.

DoH/DfEE/HO (Department of Health, Department of Education and Employment and Home Office) (2000) *Framework for the Assessment of Children in Need and their Families*. London: The Stationery Office.

Fitzgerald, D. and Kay, J. (2008) *Working Together in Children's Services*. London: Routledge.

Foley, P. and Rixon, A. (eds) (2008) *Changing Children's Services: Working and Learning Together*. Bristol: The Policy Press in association with the Open University.

Frost, N. (2005) *Professionalism, Partnership and Joined-up Thinking*. Dartington: Research into Practice.

Morrison, T. (1991) Partnership, collaboration and change under the Children Act, in M. Adcock and R. White (eds) *Significant Harm: Its Management and Outcome*. Croydon: Significant Publications.

Stainton Rogers, W. (1989) Effective co-operation in child protection work, in S. Morgan and P. Righton (eds) *Child Care: Concerns and Conflicts*. London: Hodder and Stoughton.

Walker, G. (2008) *Working Together for Children: A Critical Introduction of Multi-Agency Working*. London: Continuum.

Whitney, B. (2004) *Protecting Children: A Handbook for Teachers and School Managers*. London: RoutledgeFalmer.

Wigfall, V. and Moss, P. (2001) *More Than the Sum of its Parts? A Study of a Multi-agency Child Care Network*. London: National Children's Bureau.

JANE PAYLER, JAN GEORGESON AND JANET MOYLES
Afterword

For all our contributors, this has proved to be a rather tricky time to be writing about the UK education system. Although much of the past 30 years could be described as 'a time of change', the arrival of a new government with new ideas at a time of great economic difficulty has led to further changes already but more unsettling has been the atmosphere of uncertainty. Many of the buzzwords and mantra of the previous regime have been outlawed and we have found ourselves questioning many of the phrases we have become accustomed to using (does Every Child still Matter? – of course!) This questioning is of itself no bad thing: Revell argues that teachers have stopped questioning, lulled into compliance by the constant changes and checking regimes since 1976 and are missing opportunities to challenge proposed changes in the way which we might expect professionals to do (2005: 103).

But starting a career in teaching now, we would like to argue, has its advantages. Whether you agree with the initiatives of the old regime or the reshaping zeal of the new coalition, it is a time for a new start and for everyone to be thinking clearly about what is really important to them in teaching. Some of the proposed changes that you will need to consider are about greater professional and parental freedom (to set up own schools), while others are concerned with a stronger focus on traditional subjects, with plenty more opportunities to engage in stimulating debate about teaching phonics as a route to learning to read. The new Standards set out by the English government to ensure higher quality teaching and teachers will also be working their way into the system as this book is published.

What do beginning teachers need to know as they walk through the door on their first day in a new school or early years setting? For the first few weeks perhaps survival techniques have the most appeal; the hints and tips passed on by experienced colleagues about how to maintain some sense of order. Then there comes a point when the panic has subsided and things are settling down into a routine and you think, 'I can do this!' Until one day something out of the ordinary happens; maybe a child arrives in the class with a completely different way of behaving or talking and your routine ways of responding, perhaps learnt through trial and error, perhaps from watching colleagues – none of them work! It's then that theory and research come into their own as you benefit from those who have already thought long and hard about the pedagogical, social or cultural issues that underlie the problem you have encountered. That's when you are really beginning to learn about teaching, instead of just surviving.

Several themes emerge from the chapters, sometimes explicitly, sometimes implicitly, which can serve as beacons to guide beginning teachers (as well as experienced colleagues) through their own darker days, and the current fog of confusion that surrounds us all, lighting up what is important in helping babies, toddlers and children up to 11 years learn. These include:

- 'funds of knowledge'(Moll et al. 2001); valuing and using as learning resources children's and families' ways of being, doing, saying. This is made possible by genuine participation by children and families in all aspects of education.
- 'distributed expertise'; thinking about your role as teacher/EYP as one member of the team – or many teams – drawing on and contributing to the expertise around you to ensure that children's learning and development is as strong as possible.
- being creative throughout the curriculum; in devising pedagogy, tapping different sources of knowledge, mining others' expertise, problem-solving, constructing, using your imagination.

Frameworks and contexts will change around you during your career: you will need to discover what it is that you hold dear as unchanging principles and ideals. We hope in this book we have offered you some insight into what these principles might be and would like to leave you with some words of advice offered by our colleagues and successful graduates.

> Don't lose sight of the bigger picture. Curricula and frameworks come and go but the memories you create now for children last a lifetime. Make them fun!
> (Headteacher of an Outstanding primary school)

> Use your NQT time wisely, not catching up on paperwork but use for networking opportunities. For example, visit other schools in your year group and feeder settings. You will come back with ideas and will have had meaningful discussions to reflect on.
> (Early Years Advisory Teacher)

> Don't wear white – especially if you've planned to do finger painting. Make sure you're wearing something that you can crawl around the floor in – without losing your dignity!
> (EYPS candidate)

> Talk *with* the children, not at them. Get into the habit of adding 'Do you think . . .?' to your questions (What do you think will happen if we put this ice on the radiator. . .?)
> (Early Childhood Studies Tutor)

Always consider your work–life balance. Always have a midday break; you will be nicer in the afternoon so both you and the children will benefit.

(Experienced headteacher)

If you wear glasses, make sure you have a spare pair at school so when you break them playing basketball you can still see to drive home!

(Senior Lecturer in Education)

And one final cameo

Gina, on her first placement, had been told all about Tim, who just wouldn't talk to staff. He talked to a few of the other boys; he talked to adults outside of nursery, including staff acting as babysitters. It was clear from his conversations with his friends and family that his speech was not delayed or impaired in any way. Staff were mystified but Gina began to notice that Tim followed her around the nursery and watched while she was involved in activities with other children; she tried to engage him in conversation but received no response. Then one afternoon, all the children were getting their wellington boots on to go in the garden, and Tim could not find his boots. He just stood by the door as all the other children went out. Gina went up to him and asked him where his boots were. He didn't respond, just shrugged. Gina asked him if he could use his voice to tell her where his boots were and explained that sometimes it can be a bit rude not to talk to people if they ask you a question; it makes them sad. After a moment's pause Tim said 'I don't know where they are.' A breakthrough!! Tim was awarded a sticker for using his voice, which he was very pleased about and even told his mother. As the weeks progressed, his conversation with other children improved, so he began to make more friends in nursery and is now chatting happily (and cheekily!) to everyone. Gina was delighted; this was only her first placement but she had already made a difference.

May you always make the difference for the children you teach! We certainly hope this book will help in some way.

References

Moll, L., Amanti, C., Neff, D. and Gonzalez, N. (2001) Funds of knowledge for teaching: using a qualitative approach to connect homes and classrooms, *Theory into Practice*, XXXI(2): 132–41.

Revell, P. (2005) *The Professionals: Better Teachers, Better Schools*. Stoke-on-Trent: Trentham Books.

Author Index

Subject Index